PIONEERS OF THE BLACK ATLANTIC

OTHER BOOKS FROM CIVITAS

The Civitas Anthology of
African American Slave Narratives
edited by William L. Andrews
and Henry Louis Gates Jr.

Black Saga: The African American
Experience: A Chronology
by Charles M. Christian

The Ordeal of Integration:
Progress and Resentment in
America's "Racial" Crisis
by Orlando Patterson

Rituals of Blood
by Orlando Patterson

PIONEERS OF THE BLACK ATLANTIC

FIVE SLAVE NARRATIVES FROM
THE ENLIGHTENMENT, 1772–1815

Edited by
Henry Louis Gates Jr.
William L. Andrews

CIVITAS
COUNTERPOINT
Washington, D.C.

Library of Congress Cataloging-in-Publication Data

Pioneers of the Black Atlantic : five slave narratives from the Enlightenment, 1772–1815 / edited by Henry Louis Gates, Jr., William L. Andrews.
p. cm.
1. Slaves—United States—Biography. 2. Slaves—Caribbean Area—Biography. 3. Afro-Americans—History—To 1863—Sources. 4. Slaves' writings, American. 5. American prose literature—Afro-American authors. 6. Autobiography—Afro-American authors. 7. Slavery in literature. I. Gates, Henry Louis. II. Andrews, William L., 1946– .
E444.P56 1998
973'.0496073—dc21 98-34796
CIP

ISBN 1-887178-98-8 (alk. paper)

Book design by David Bullen
Composition by Wilsted & Taylor Publishing Services

Printed in the United States of America on acid-free paper that meets the American National Standards Institute Z39-48 Standard.

COUNTERPOINT
P.O. Box 65793
Washington, D.C. 20035-5793

Counterpoint is a member of the Perseus Books Group.

10 9 8 7 6 5 4 3 2 1

FIRST PRINTING

CONTENTS

PREFACE

William L. Andrews

THIS BOOK CONTAINS the best work of the pioneers of the Black Atlantic literary and cultural tradition, now more than two centuries old. Instead of defining the African-descended peoples of the Atlantic world—triangulated by England, Africa, and the Americas—simply according to race, ethnicity, or nationality, Paul Gilroy, author of the widely influential *The Black Atlantic: Modernity and Double Consciousness* (1993), has argued that the Black Atlantic ought to be seen as "one single, complex unit" in which cultural, racial, economic, and political intermixing and exchange have been going on for four centuries. What if we seek the intellectual and expressive roots of English-speaking African-descended peoples of the Atlantic world in a transnational culture that, going back to the sixteenth, seventeenth, and eighteenth centuries, has always been malleable, multiple, and hybrid? What if we try to re-envision black writers of the past as sharing a common creolized cultural heritage that crossed national and ethnic boundaries and defied conventional political categories, social norms, and even literary genres? If such a creole heritage exists now, when did it begin? When eighteenth-century writers of the Black Atlantic confronted European Enlightenment notions of selfhood, race, and literacy, did their critique of these notions stem from simply a personal standpoint? Or did these early Black Atlantic writers also represent through their personal experience a cultural point of view, a set of beliefs and values embraced by African-descended peoples in the Atlantic world and articulated into a nascent literary tradition for successive generations of Black Atlantic writers to follow? The personal writings of the pioneering Black Atlantic writers in English—James Albert Ukawsaw Gronniosaw, Ottobah Cugoano, John Marrant, Olaudah Equiano, and John Jea—address these questions, revealing the bedrock experience and cultural commonalities on which many Black Atlantic literary traditions rest.

The idea of a Black Atlantic community of English-speaking writers, intellectuals, and activists visibly at work in the late eighteenth century, and transnational in their experience and point of view, is still relatively new. But the research of historians and critics such as

Henry Louis Gates Jr., Vincent Carretta, and Paul Edwards has provided considerable convincing evidence of a vibrant community of eighteenth-century black writers who knew and read each other and who shared common themes and aims. As we come to understand the so-called Age of Enlightenment in the West also as an age of unprecedented slave trading among Europe, Africa, and the Western Hemisphere, we realize that the struggle of African-descended people in that era to speak truth to white power and privilege originated in a community of unusually cosmopolitan and sophisticated people of color. *Pioneers of the Black Atlantic* attests to the key role that autobiography played in launching a cosmopolitan, transnational literary tradition by African-descended writers of the eighteenth and early nineteenth centuries.

At home in a fluid and dynamic Atlantic world defined by multiple identifications with Africa, England, and America, the writers represented in *Pioneers of the Black Atlantic* cannot be easily categorized as African, African-American, or Afro-British. They were all truly men of the world. They were social and cultural creoles—incontestably and unashamedly black but with affinities, either by birth or experience, to various nations, colonies, and peoples. Hardy and adaptable by virtue of their wide travels in the Atlantic world, these writers seem to be at home everywhere and nowhere. Their unwavering commitment to Christianity, a bedrock of faith in their stormy, often perilous lives, reminds us of the spiritual foundation on which the antislavery movement in England and North America was built in the eighteenth century. The literary efforts of these pioneering writers to fashion a distinctly multicultural identity for themselves in their autobiographies resonate powerfully with our contemporary world.

Beginning in the 1770s, a handful of African-born men and women who had grown up in England or the Americas began to contribute in signal ways to the literature of the English-speaking world. In 1772, James Albert Ukawsaw Gronniosaw, a sixty-year-old former slave born in what is now Nigeria, interposed his African voice into English autobiography, dictating the harrowing story of his life to a white woman in the English midland town of Leominster. *A Narrative of the Most Remarkable Particulars in the Life of James Albert Ukawsaw Gronniosaw, an African Prince, As Related by Himself* was published in Bath in 1772; in Newport, Rhode Island, in 1774; in Dublin in 1790; and in Salem, New York, in 1809. A year after Gronniosaw's notable beginning, Phillis Wheatley, stolen from West Africa and enslaved in Boston, seized international celebrity through the publication in England of her *Poems on Various Subjects, Religious and Moral* (1773). In a letter to her patron, Selina Hastings, countess of Huntington, to whom Wheatley had dedicated her book, the poet praised the countess for her financial support of and friendship toward Gronniosaw, who had also dedicated his narrative to the countess. In 1785 a third black writer who benefitted from the countess's patronage, John Marrant, gave the Atlantic world his story under the title *A Narrative of the Lord's Wonderful Dealings with John Marrant, a Black, (Now Going to Preach the Gospel in Nova Scotia) Born in New York, in North America.* Unlike Gronniosaw and Wheatley, Marrant was born in North America, not Africa. Since his parents were free, Marrant had no direct experience as a slave, although he witnessed the sufferings of slaves in South Carolina, where he spent much of his teenage years. What impressed William Aldridge, the Methodist minister who wrote Marrant's story and got it published in London, was the black man's gripping account of his captivity, deliverance, and successful preaching among the Cherokee Indians of South Carolina. Within three years of its appearance in 1785, Marrant's narrative had gone through six editions in England. As a story of the triumph of Christian faith over the trials of Indian captivity, Marrant's compact autobiography remained in print in multiple editions in England throughout the first three decades of the nineteenth century.

In 1787, a new tone of antislavery militance arose among Black Atlantic writers. Gronniosaw and Marrant said comparatively little about the injustices of slavery, stressing instead their deliverance from the bondage of sin and their dedication to serve as witnesses to God's redemptive work in their lives. In bold contrast, when Quobna Ottobah Cugoano, a native of the coastal regions of Ghana who had been sold into slavery in Grenada as a child, took up his pen, he used his autobiography as a pretext for an uncompromising critique of slavery and the slave trade. Published in London in 1787, *Thoughts and Sentiments on the Evil and Wicked Traffic of the Slavery and Commerce of the Human Species, Humbly Submitted to the Inhabitants of Great Britain, by Ottobah Cugoano, a Native of Africa* recounts enough of the author's past to establish his credentials as a knowledgeable commentator on the slave trade and slavery. The narrative then evolves into a treatise detailing Cugoano's case for the universal abolition of slavery. Translated into French, *Thoughts and Sentiments* appeared in Paris in 1788; in 1791 a short version of the text was published again in London. By this time Cugoano, a seasoned antislavery agitator in a London-based black civil rights group known as the Sons of Africa, had witnessed the literary success of one of his fellow Sons of Africa activists, Olaudah Equiano, whose two-volume autobiography had created a sensation when it appeared in London in 1789. Authored by probably the most prominent black abolitionist of the Atlantic world, *The Interesting Narrative of the Life of Olaudah Equiano, or Gustavus Vassa, the African, Written by Himself* knit together the personal and the political so memorably that for the next fifty years it was Equiano's text, not those of Gronniosaw, Marrant, or even Cugoano, that would be cited as the founding narrative of slavery and freedom in English and American letters. More movingly than Gronniosaw or Cugoano, Equiano cast the Africa of his childhood as a pastoral idyll, far removed from the benighted and savage Africa of popular European myth. Equiano's was also a narrative of Christian conversion like that of Gronniosaw and Marrant, but unlike the other-worldliness of his predecessors' perspectives, in the early chapters of Equiano's *Life* the narrator's spiritual and secular aspirations emerge interdependently, leaving the reader with a sense that conversion and freedom are mutual and naturally linked. Written in an engaging plain style, Equiano's book received a number of favorable reviews in the British press, went through eight printings in its first five years, and had a substantial readership in the nineteenth-century United States as well as Great Britain.

As an all-purpose antislavery document and narrative of slavery overcome and Christian salvation attained, Equiano's narrative became, in effect, the canonical text, the measuring standard by which most slave narratives for the next quarter-century were read. During this time only a few slave narratives were published in English, and none had the backing of well-established whites or the reviews and international exposure of the *Life*. Still, John Jea's *Life, History, and Unparalleled Sufferings of John Jea, the African Preacher, Compiled and Written by Himself* (1815) belongs to the literary fraternity of Gronniosaw, Marrant, Cugoano, and Equiano. One of the last of the Black Atlantic slave narrators, Jea could claim actual African birth and a truly international purview. He had experienced the harsh lot of a slave in New York. After gaining his freedom he had pursued an itinerant preaching career that crisscrossed the Atlantic from the late 1790s to the time of the publication of his autobiography by an unknown English printer. Jea's outrage over slavery was as deep as Cugoano's. His

Christian faith was as firm as Gronniosaw's or Marrant's. His adventures at sea, had he portrayed them as fully as Equiano, had much potential appeal, especially among the English in the wake of the lost War of 1812. But John Jea was primarily a preacher, and his conviction that this part of his life, not his experience as a slave or his travels in the Atlantic world, was what most needed to be recorded suggests one reason why Jea's autobiography was the least read and, until recently, hardly known in comparison to the other four texts reprinted in *Pioneers of the Black Atlantic*.

Still, like his predecessors in the invocation of the "trope of the talking book" (discussed in detail in the introduction to this volume), John Jea was a Black Atlantic writer who featured in a dramatic and highly individualized way his coming to self-consciousness and to a sense of his destiny as a free man through the attainment of literacy. Making literacy the key to both secular and spiritual salvation for black people throughout the Atlantic world, and demonstrating the liberating effect of the power of the word in their own lives, Gronniosaw, Marrant, Cugoano, Equiano, and Jea laid the literary and sociopolitical groundwork for the great slave narratives of Frederick Douglass, Harriet Jacobs, and the North American antislavery crusade of the nineteenth century.

EDITOR'S NOTE

THE TEXTS IN THIS VOLUME have been edited, but not abridged, to facilitate contemporary reading. The long *s* [f], which was used routinely in eighteenth-century English printing, but which looks like an *f* to today's reader, has been printed as an *s* in the texts of this edition. We have modernized and/or emended the spelling of words in these texts to conform to contemporary American English usage. Thus words such as "honour," "defence," "chequered," "staid," "shew," "ancles," and "merchandize" in the original texts are emended to read "honor," "defense," "checkered," "stayed," "show," "ankles," and "merchandise," respectively. Whenever the spelling of a proper name differs significantly from today's spelling, we have emended the spelling of that proper name. Thus "Martinico," "Charles-town," and "Musquito," for instance, have been emended to Martinique, Charleston, and Miskito. Italicized words and passages in the original texts have been preserved in italics in this edition, but some unitalicized terms that are normally italicized in today's usage—such as the names of ships or the titles of books—have been italicized in this edition as an aid to the reader. Single words such as "anything," "everyone," "forever," and "today" that in the eighteenth century usually appeared as two words—"any thing," "every one," "for ever," and "to-day"—are printed in accordance with twentieth-century usage. The archaic term "viz." (an abbreviation of the Latin *videlicet*) has been translated into "namely" in this edition. Obvious inconsistencies in spelling within a given text have been silently corrected, but when a text employs variant spellings of a word, such as "intreat" and "entreat," and there is no clear indication of which spelling would have been the author's preference or in established usage at the time, we have not emended or attempted to regularize the variants. The inconsistent use of "an" and "a" in these texts, yielding constructions such as "an universal good" or "an history," has been regularized in accordance with twentieth-century practices.

We have generally not attempted to regularize inconsistencies in capitalization within or among the texts, nor have we imposed contemporary capitalization style. Terms normally capitalized today, such as Negro or the Bible, often appear in lower case. Punctuation practices in these texts often diverge markedly from contemporary practices, for example, in the use of commas and the use of dashes. To preserve the flavor of eighteenth-century punctuation, we have generally left punctuation unaltered, substituting contemporary practices only in certain instances for clarity's sake, such as in the treatment of block quotations. Quotations from the Bible in these texts have not been emended or corrected, nor have their accompanying biblical citations been corrected. However, the style of biblical citations has been regularized throughout.

William L. Andrews

PIONEERS OF THE BLACK ATLANTIC

FIVE SLAVE NARRATIVES FROM
THE ENLIGHTENMENT, 1772–1815

Introduction: The Talking Book

Henry Louis Gates Jr.

Let us to the Press Devoted Be,
Its Light *will* Shine *and* Speak Us Free.
—DAVID RUGGLES, 1835

THE AFRO-AMERICAN LITERARY TRADITION begins, tellingly, with the writings of African slaves in the New World. But "the literature of the slave" is an ironic phrase, at the very least. "Literature," as Samuel Johnson used the term, denoted an "acquaintance with 'letters' or books"; it also connoted "polite or humane learning" and "literary culture." While it is clearly true that the slaves who had managed to "steal" some learning (in Frederick Douglass's phrase) were keen to demonstrate an acquaintance with letters or books to a skeptical public, it is difficult to claim that slave literature was meant to exemplify polite or humane learning, or to serve as evidence of a black literary culture. Indeed, it is more accurate to say that these texts represent *impolite* learning, and that they rail against the *arbitrary* and *inhumane* learning that masters foisted on slaves in order to reinforce a perverse fiction of the "natural" order of things. The slave wrote not only to demonstrate humane letters, but also to demonstrate his or her own membership in the human community.

To a remarkable extent, black writers have created works that express a broad "concord of sensibilities"[1] shared by persons of African descent in the Western Hemisphere, works that continue to be strangely resonant, and relevant, as the twenty-first century draws near. Indeed, the texts of the Afro-American literary tradition share patterns and details of striking similarity. But why? Has a common experience—or, more accurately, a shared perception of a common experience—been responsible for the sharing of this text of blackness? It would be foolish to say no. But shared modes of figuration only result when writers read each other's texts and seize upon themes and

1. The phrase, used to brilliant effect by Ralph Ellison, belongs to Kenneth Burke.

I

figures to revise in their own texts. This form of revision grounds each
individual work in a larger context, and creates formal lines of conti-
nuity between the texts that together constitute the shared text of
blackness.

What seems clear upon reading the earliest texts by black writers in
English—and the critical texts that respond to these black writings—
is that the production of literature was taken to be the central arena in
which persons of African descent could establish and redefine their
status within the human community. Black people, the evidence suggests, had to represent themselves as "speaking subjects" before they
could begin to destroy their status as objects, as commodities, within
Western culture. For centuries, Europeans had questioned whether
the African "species of men" could ever master the arts and sciences;
that is, whether they could create literature. If they could, the argument ran, then the African variety of humanity and the European
variety were fundamentally related. If not, then it seemed that the African was predestined by nature to be a slave.

To answer that question, several whites in Europe and America undertook experiments in which young African slaves were tutored
alongside white children. Phillis Wheatley was the result of one such
experiment; other notables include Francis Williams, a Jamaican who
took the B.A. at Cambridge before 1750; Jacobus Capitein, who
earned several degrees in Holland; Anton Wilhelm Amo, who took the
doctorate in philosophy at Halle, Germany; and Ignatius Sancho, who
published a volume of letters in 1782. Their published writings, in
Latin, Dutch, German, and English, were scrutinized and employed
by both sides in the slavery debates.

So widespread was the debate over "the nature of the African" in
the eighteenth and early nineteenth centuries that writing by blacks
found a large audience, and was often subject to review by the most
eminent authorities. (Not until the Harlem Renaissance would black
literature again be taken so seriously.) Phillis Wheatley's reviewers
included Voltaire, Thomas Jefferson, George Washington, Samuel
Rush, and James Beatty, to name only a few. Francis Williams's work
was analyzed by David Hume and Immanuel Kant. (Hegel, writing in
the *Philosophy of History* in 1813, took the absence of writing among
Africans as the sign of their innate inferiority.) The list of commenta-
tors is extensive, amounting to a veritable "Who's Who" of the
French, Scottish, and American Enlightenments.

Why was the writing of the African of such importance to the eighteenth century's debate over slavery? I can briefly outline one thesis: after Descartes, reason was privileged over all other human characteristics, and writing was taken to be the visible sign of reason. Blacks were reasonable, and hence "men," only if they could demonstrate mastery of "the arts and sciences"—that is, writing. Although the Enlightenment was predicated on man's ability to reason, it also made the "absence" of reason the criterion by which to circumscribe the humanity of the people and cultures of color that Europeans had been "discovering" since the Renaissance. The concomitant urge to systematize all human knowledge resulted in the relegation of black people to a lower rung on the "Great Chain of Being," a way of ordering the universe and a metaphor that arrayed all of creation on a vertical scale from animals, plants, and insects, to humans, and on to the angels and to God himself. By 1750, "man" had been further subdivided, on a human scale that ascended from "the lowliest Hottentot" to "glorious Milton and Newton."

The stakes were high: if blacks could be shown to be capable of imaginative literature, they might jump a few links of the Chain of Being, in a pernicious game of "Mother, May I?" The Reverend James W. C. Pennington, a former slave and prominent black abolitionist—and also, incidentally, the author of a slave narrative—appealed to this faintly perverse notion in his prefatory note to Ann Plato's 1841 collected writings: "The history of the arts and sciences is the history of individuals, of individual nations." Only by publishing these kinds of books, he argues, can blacks demonstrate "the fallacy of that stupid theory, that nature has done nothing but fit us for slaves, and that art cannot unfit us for slavery!"

If writing, then, was a crucial terrain of black struggles in the Age of Enlightenment, the concern to make themselves heard—that is, to inscribe their voices in the written word—was a primary motivation for those former slaves who chose to narrate the stories of their enslavement and redemption. Among the most compelling documents of this effort to record an authentic black voice in the text of Western letters is the trope of the Talking Book, a strangely insistent metaphor, a curious image that appears in many of the eighteenth-century black texts published in English. The repetition of this figure—and, more importantly, the revision of it—is also our best evidence that the earliest writers of the Anglo-African tradition were self-conscious readers of each other's texts.

While the explication of the trope of the Talking Book enables us to listen in on the literary conversation that inaugurated Afro-American letters, it also reveals the abiding tension between the spoken and the written word, between the black vernacular and the literate white text, between the oral and the printed forms of literary discourse. This tension (a creative vexation still very much alive in the present day, in the literary debates about hip hop) has been represented in black letters at least since slaves and ex-slaves met the challenge of the Enlightenment by writing themselves into being.

Literacy stood as the ultimate measure of humanity for those struggling to define an African self in Western letters; their project was to establish a collective black voice through the sublime example of an individual text, and thereby to register a black presence in letters. The paradox of somehow containing the oral within the written, precisely when oral black culture was transforming itself into a written culture, proved to be of sufficient concern for five of the earliest black autobiographers to repeat the figure of a Talking Book that fails to speak. In the slave narratives of James Gronniosaw, John Marrant, Olaudah Equiano, and John Jea, and in the anti-slavery broadside of Ottobah Cugoano, the Talking Book appears as the preeminent instance of disjunction between the oral and the written.

This question of voice is significant for Afro-American literature as a whole, where the oral and the written appear as separate and distinct discursive universes which only occasionally overlap. Precisely because successive Western cultures have privileged written art over oral and musical forms, the writing of black people in Western languages has remained political, implicitly or explicitly, regardless of its intent or its subject. The very proliferation of black written voices, and the concomitant political import of them, led fairly rapidly in our literary history to demands both for the coming of a "black Shakespeare or Dante," as one critic put it in 1925, and for an authentic black printed voice of deliverance, whose presence would, by definition, put an end to all claims of the black person's subhumanity. In the black tradition, *writing* became the visible sign, the commodity of exchange, the text and technology of reason.

THE FIRST TEXT in which the trope of the Talking Book appears is James Albert Ukawsaw Gronniosaw's *A Narrative of the Most Remarkable Particulars in the Life of James Albert Ukawsaw Gronniosaw, An African Prince, As Related by Himself,* first published in 1770. (The first American edition was published in 1774.) By 1811, there were already seven editions of the text, which differ mildly in particulars from pagination to title.[2]

Gronniosaw's text has not engendered much in the way of criticism, literary or historical. What we know of him comes directly from his narrative. He tells us that he was born "in the city of Bournou," which is the "chief city" of the Kingdom of Zaara, that his mother was the oldest daughter of "the reigning King of Zaara," and that he was the youngest of six children. Gronniosaw stresses his relationships with his mother and maternal grandfather, but rarely mentions his father, who seems to have been a commoner. Gronniosaw's identification of himself in his narrative's title helps to explain the significance of this rhetorical gesture: by representing himself as "an African Prince," Gronniosaw implicitly ties his narrative to the literary tradition of the "Noble Savage."

One of the ironies that attend that subgenre of the Noble Savage, the "Noble Negro," is that he or she is rendered noble through a series of contrasts with other blacks. Oroonoko, the protagonist of Aphra Behn's famed 1688 novel *Oroonoko, or the Royal Slave,* bears aquiline features, has managed through some miraculous process to straighten his kinky hair, and speaks fluent French, among other languages. Oroonoko, in other words, looks like a European, speaks like a European, and thinks and acts like a European—or, more properly, like a European king. Unlike the conventions of representing most other Noble Savage protagonists, then, Oroonoko and his fellow black princes-in-bondage are made noble by a dissimilarity with their native countrymen. He is the exception, and not in any way the rule. (Several Africans gained notoriety in eighteenth-century England and France by claiming royal lineage, going so far as to make elaborate scenes at stage performances of Oroonoko, weeping loudly as they were carried from the theater.) Faced with what must have seemed a void of black literary ancestors, Gronniosaw turned to the fictions of the Noble Savage to ground his text within a tradition.

He also turned to the literature of Christian confession. Like the hero of John Bunyan's *Pilgrim's Progress,* Gronniosaw is on a quest—a search to learn the identity of "some great Man of Power." Gronnio-

2. The version included in this collection is the 1840 edition, published simultaneously in London, Manchester, and Glasgow. The question of literacy figures even in Gronniosaw's title: while the 1770 edition proclaims that Gronniosaw "related" his tale "himself," the 1774 edition (Newport, Rhode Island) avers that his narrative was "written by himself." In editions published after 1840, "related" or "dictated" are preferred to "written by himself."

saw presents himself as the only person in his grandfather's kingdom aware that "some great Man of Power . . . resided above the sun, moon, and stars, the objects of our [African] worship." The sign of Gronniosaw's difference is his intimation that there is but one God, rather than the many worshipped in the Kingdom of Zaara; he will become, for us, an ebony admixture of Oroonoko and the Lord's questing Pilgrim.

The little prince's noble beliefs lead, as we might suspect, to an estrangement from his brothers and sisters and even, eventually, from his father, his grandfather, and his devoted mother. Gronniosaw represents his discourse with his mother as follows:

> My dear mother says I, pray tell me who is the Great Man of Power that makes the thunder? She said, there was no power but the sun, moon and stars; that they made all our country. I then enquired how all our people came? She answered me, from one another; and so carried me to many generations back. Then says I, who made the First Man? and who made the first cow, and the first lion, and where does the fly come from, as no one can make him? My mother seemed in great trouble; she was apprehensive that my senses were impaired, or that I was foolish. . . . I resolved never to say anything more to him [my father]. But I grew very unhappy in myself.
> (pp. 36–37)

Gronniosaw's alienation increased to such an uncomfortable extent that when "a merchant from the Gold Coast" offered to take the young man to a land where he "should see houses . . . walk upon the water" and "see the white folks," he beseeched of his parents the freedom to leave. The only family tie that he regretted severing was with his sister Logwy, who was "quite white and fair, with fine light hair, though my father and mother were black."[3]

The young prince was, of course, traded into slavery and sailed to "Barbadoes," where he was purchased by a Mr. Vanhorn of New York. Upon achieving his freedom, Gronniosaw—motivated by a desire to live among the "holy" inhabitants of England ("because the authors of the books that had been given me were Englishmen")—traveled from "St. Domingo," "Martinco," and "Havannah," to London and Holland, before he returned to marry and raise a family in England. The

3. Gronniosaw's affection for his "white" sister is one of the curious figures that he uses to represent his inherent difference from other black people. On one occasion, he describes "the devil" as "a black man" who "lives in hell," while he by contrast seeks to be washed clean of the blackness of sin. Moreover, the woman ordained by God for him to marry turns out to be white, echoing his bond with his "white" sister.

remainder of the narrative depicts the economic hardships he suffers from racism and from evil people generally, and his fervent devotion to the principles of Christian dogma.

Indeed, from his earliest days in captivity, Gronniosaw seems to have been determined to allow nothing to come between his desire to know the name of the Christian God and its fulfillment. His conversion to European culture—and the first appearance of the trope of the Talking Book—occurs in this extended account of one incident from his Middle Passage, involving the principal material sign of his African heritage:

> When I left my dear mother I had a large quantity of gold about me, as is the custom of our country, it was made into rings, and they were linked into one another, and formed into a kind of chain, and so put round my neck, and arms and legs, and a large piece hanging at one ear almost in the shape of a pear. I found all this troublesome, and was glad when my new Master [a Dutch ship captain] took it from me—I was now washed, and clothed in the Dutch or English manner. (p. 40)

This scene is a kind of secular baptism, in which Gronniosaw is reborn a European. Gronniosaw eagerly abandons the visible sign of his African past—a signifying chain—just as he longs to abandon the language that his European captors "did not understand."

> [My master] used to read prayers in public to the ship's crew every Sabbath day; and when first I saw him read, I was never so surprised in my whole life as when I saw the book talk to my master; for I thought it did, as I observed him to look upon it, and move his lips.— I wished it would do so to me.—As soon as my master had done reading I followed him to the place where he put the book, being mightily delighted with it, and when nobody saw me, I opened it and put my ear down close upon it, in great hope that it would say something to me; but [I] was very sorry and greatly disappointed when I found it would not speak; this thought immediately presented itself to me, that everybody and everything despised me because I was black. (pp. 40–41)

The book had no voice for Gronniosaw; it simply refused to speak to him.

Gronniosaw can speak to the text only if the text first speaks to him, which it will not—not even in the faintest whisper. The text does not recognize him, and so refuses to share its secrets or decipher its coded message. Gronniosaw and the text are silent; the "dialogue" that he observed between the book and his master eludes him. Gronniosaw explains the text's silence by resorting to an oxymoronic figure in which an oral figure (voice) and a visual figure (his black face) are conflated. Gronniosaw's explanation of the silence of the text allows for but one possibility, which suggested itself on the spot: "This thought immediately presented itself to me, that everybody and everything despised me because I was black."

What is interesting here is the conflation of the senses, of the oral and the visual—"the book refused to speak to me because my face was black." The text's voice, for Gronniosaw, presupposed a face; and a black face, in turn, presupposed the text's silence, since blackness was a sign of absence, the ultimate absence of face *and* voice. Gronniosaw could achieve no recognition from this canonical text of Western letters—either the Bible or a prayer book—because the text could neither see nor hear him.

This desire for recognition in the text of Western letters motivates Gronniosaw's creation of a text, in both literal and figurative ways. Literally, this trope of the (non-) Talking Book becomes the central scene of instruction against which this black African's entire autobiography must be read. The text refuses to speak to young Gronniosaw, so some forty-five years later, Gronniosaw writes a text that speaks his face into existence among the authors and texts of the Western tradition. Gronniosaw presents his sixty years in a brief text that depends on tropes of reading and writing. In other words, he narrates a text that simultaneously voices, contains, and reflects the peculiar contours of his (black) face. Given the fact that by 1770 only four black people are thought to have published books in European languages, Gronniosaw's gesture is a major one, even if its motivation as inscribed in his central trope is ironic.[4]

But is his a black face? When I wrote that the ship captain's book—and its refusal to speak to the slave—motivated the slave to seek recognition in other Western texts, I argued that this motivation was both literal and figurative. By figurative, I mean that the face of the author at sixty is fundamentally altered from that black African face that the adolescent Gronniosaw first presented in his encounter with his first

4. Three of them, Juan Latino, Jacobus Capitein, and Anton Wilhelm Amo, wrote in Latin. Briton Hammon wrote in English, and is the author of what is generally considered the first English slave narrative, the 1760 *Narrative of the Uncommon Sufferings and Surprising Deliverance of Briton Hammon, A Negro Man.*

Western text. The elder Gronniosaw was fluent in two European languages, Dutch and English; he was a freed man; he was a master of the "Calvinist" interpretation of Christianity, and could discourse about religion "before thirty-eight [Dutch] ministers every Tuesday, for seven weeks together, and they were all very well satisfied"; and he was the husband of an English wife and the father of both her child by an English first marriage and their "mulatto" children. The Christian text that had once refused to acknowledge him had been mastered—indeed, not only could he "persuade" others by his eloquence "that I was what I pretended to be," but his autobiographical text is shot through with references from Protestant Christianity. What is absent from his account is the African's black mask of humanity, a priceless heritage discarded as readily as was a priceless gold chain.

The figure of the Talking Book draws upon several textual sources in the Western tradition. One of them, Willem Bosman's 1704 *New and Accurate Description of the Coast Guinea,* was particularly influential for its discussion of West African religions. Bosman was a Dutch official at the Fort of Elmira on the coast of West Africa, in the territory then known as "Guinea" or "Gold Coast," what is now Ghana. There is an intriguing possibility that Gronniosaw may have encountered Bosman at the Fort of Elmira: it is likely that the Dutch slave ship that brought Gronniosaw west set sail from there. What is more probable is that Gronniosaw knew Bosman's work in the Dutch language.

Bosman recounts the Ashanti people's myth of creation in terms reminiscent of Gronniosaw's text:

> [A] great part of the *Negroes* believe that man was made by Anansie, that is, a great Spider: the rest attribute the Creation of Man to God which they assert to have happened in the following manner: They tell us, that in the beginning God created Black as well as White Men; thereby not only hinting but endeavouring to prove that their race was as soon in the World as ours; and to bestow a yet greater Honour on themselves, they tell us that God, having created these two sorts of Men, offered two sorts of Gifts, *viz,* Gold, and the Knowledge of Arts of Reading and Writing, giving the Blacks, the first Election, who chose Gold and left the Knowledge of Letters to the White. God granted their Request, but being incensed at their Avarice, resolved that the Whites should for ever be their Masters, and they obliged to wait on them as their Slaves.

"Gold," spake God to the African, "or the arts of Western letters"—*choose!* And if the African at the Creation was foolish enough to select gold over reading and writing, Gronniosaw, an African man but a European-in-the-making, would not repeat that primal mistake. He eschewed the temptation of his gold chain and all that it signified, and sought a fluency in Western languages through which he could remake the features and color of his face.

If Gronniosaw's evocation of Bosman is, in all likelihood, self-conscious, his evocation of Immanuel Kant is probably not. Kant's 1764 German text, *Observations on the Feelings of the Beautiful and the Sublime,* prefigures Gronniosaw's equation of his black skin with the text's refusal to speak to him. Drawing upon Hume's note on blacks in "Of National Characters," Kant argues that "So fundamental is the difference between these two races of man, [that] it appears to be as great in regard to mental capacities as in color." At another point, glossing a black man's seemingly thoughtful commentary about male-female relations in Europe, Kant minces no words in valorizing the visual over the oral: "And it might be that there was something in this which perhaps deserved to be considered; but in short, this fellow was quite black from head to foot, a clear proof that what he said was stupid." Gronniosaw devoted his next forty-five years to acquiring the skills to make a clear proof to the contrary, until he was fully able to structure the events of his life into a pattern that speaks quite eloquently, if ironically, to readers today.

The Narrative of the Lord's Wonderful Dealings with John Marrant, A Black (1785)[5] is not, properly speaking, a slave narrative. Rather, it is an Indian captivity tale—an extraordinarily popular genre in the eighteenth century—and an unusual one, given its black protagonist. In his study of the genre, *Held Captive by Indians* (1973), Richard Van Der Beets found that Marrant's narrative was "one of the three most popular stories of Indian captivity, surpassed in number of editions only by those of Peter Williamson (1757) and Mary Jemison (1784)."[6]

5. Four more editions were published that same year. By 1835, Marrant's book had been printed no less than twenty times, in locations from Caerdydd, Wales, to Dublin, Ireland, and in the colonies from Halifax to Middletown, Connecticut.
6. Williamson's *French and Indian Cruelty* was republished several times, including the 1807 *Authentic Narrative of the Life and Surprising Adventures of Peter Williamson: Who was Kidnapped When an Infant, from His Native Place, Aberdeen, and Sold for a Slave in America: His Marriage, Perils, Hardships, and Escapes, and His Great Services to the English Interest, by His Intimate Acquaintance with the Indian Language and Manners, Written by Himself at Intervals, and Published at his Coffee-room, in Edinburgh*; Jemison's was titled *The Life Story of Mary Jemison*.

Marrant's text was "related" to the Reverend William Aldridge, who notes in his preface that he has "always preserved Mr. Marrant's ideas, tho' I could not his language," assuring Marrant's readers, however, that "no more alterations . . . have been made, than were thought necessary," whatever that means. The opening lines of Marrant's narrative state that he was "born June 15th, 1755, in New York," to free black parents. Marrant was never a slave, and his story contains scant references to black people outside of his immediate family. Like Gronniosaw, Marrant found that his religious convictions alienated him from his African kin. One day, the unhappy Marrant "went over the fence, about half a mile from our house, which divided the inhabited and cultivated parts of the country from the wilderness." It is in this South Carolina "wilderness" (which he calls "the desert") that the recently converted Christian is captured by Cherokee Indians.

Marrant, like Gronniosaw, was fifteen years old at his capture. Wandering through the wilderness, Marrant encounters an Indian fortification, protected by strategically placed guards. The Cherokee guard politely informs him that he must be put to death for venturing onto Cherokee land. A resident judge next sentences Marrant to death by fire. At his execution, Marrant begins to pray, politely if enthusiastically reminding the Lord that he had delivered "the three children in the fiery furnace" and "Daniel in the lion's den," and asking if perhaps his servant John might be delivered in such fashion. At "about the middle of my prayer," Marrant states, "the Lord impressed a strong desire upon my mind to turn into their language, and pray in their tongue." This sudden display of fluent Cherokee "wonderfully affected the people" who had gathered to watch him slowly roast. The executioner, "savingly converted to God," interrupts the proceedings to take the black captive off for an audience with the king.

In his audience with the king, however, Marrant's gift of tongues backfires, and he is sentenced to die once again, this time for being a "witch." Marrant's account of these events contains his curious inversion of the trope of the Talking Book:

> At this instant the king's eldest daughter came into the chamber, a person about nineteen years of age, and stood at my right-hand. I had a Bible in my hand, which she took out of it, and having opened it, she kissed it, and seemed much delighted with it. When she had put it into my hand again, the king asked me what it was? and I told him, the name of my God was recorded there; and, after several

questions, he bid me read it, which I did, particularly the fifty-third
chapter of Isaiah, in the most solemn manner I was able; and also the
twenty-sixth chapter of Matthew's Gospel; and when I pronounced
the name of Jesus, the particular effect it had upon me was observed
by the king. When I had finished reading, he asked me why I read
those names with so much reverence? I told him, because the Being
to whom those names belonged made heaven and earth, and I and
he; this he denied. I then pointed to the sun, and asked him who
made the sun, and moon, and stars, and preserved them in their regular order? He said there was a man in their town that did it. I labored
as much as I could to convince him to the contrary. His daughter
took the book out of my hand a second time; she opened it, and
kissed it again; her father bid her give it to me, which she did; but
said, with much sorrow, the book would not speak to her. The executioner then fell upon his knees, and begged the king to let me go to
prayer, which being granted, we all went upon our knees, and now
the Lord displayed his glorious power. (pp. 74–75)

The king's daughter and several of his retainers are struck down, and
the king proceeds to sentence Marrant to death for a second time.
His death is narrowly averted, again, when the daughter's affliction
is cured through Marrant's prayer. Shortly thereafter, "the Lord
appeared most lovely and glorious," and Marrant's freedom was
achieved.

What is most interesting in Marrant's handling of Gronniosaw's
trope is the place accorded to blackness: in the Kingdom of the Cherokee, only the black man can make the text speak. The book will not
speak to the king's daughter, who stands for the whole Cherokee
people. If in Gronniosaw the voice can only be heard by a white (or
whitened) face, in Marrant the voice is heard (and spoken) by a black
face, in the luminous presence of God himself. Where blackness in
Gronniosaw had underwritten a series of invidious comparisons, in
Marrant the Cherokee assume the perilous burden of negation.

If Marrant substitutes the oppositions of black/Cherokee and
Christian/non-Christian for Gronniosaw's black illiterate African/
white literate European, what has become of Gronniosaw's "signifying chain"? Marrant does not disappoint us; the chain is inverted as
well, although it is still made of gold. Marrant associates the golden
chain with his own mastery of language, the Cherokee language. The
Cherokee king possesses an item fashioned from gold, a set of "chain

and bracelets," and it is John Marrant, the literate black man from another world, who (for reasons never explained) has the power over the
king to command him to put them on, or take them off, "like a child."
But Marrant is not only the king's master because of his mastery of the
English text of the Bible; he soon becomes master of the king's language as well. At the end of this section, Marrant announces: "Here I
learnt to speak their tongue in the highest style." He can now live with
the Cherokee in "perfect liberty," "treated like a prince." Marrant, in
other words, has turned Gronniosaw's trope of the Talking Book inside out, reversing Gronniosaw's figures—the text that refuses to
speak, the golden chain, and the movement from prince to commoner—detail by detail. Marrant wrestles from Gronniosaw a space
for his own representation of a pious black life, by revising his only antecedent text and its central trope.

JOHN STUART WAS A BLACK MAN who wrote letters. He was concerned to influence certain powerful members of English society
about "the evil and wicked traffic of the slavery and commerce of the
human species." His correspondents included the Prince of Wales,
Edmund Burke, King George III, and Granville Sharp. Stuart aimed
to convince these gentlemen that human bondage was a form of oppression that militated against "the natural liberties of Men," as he
wrote to King George; an "abandoned wickedness" that struck at the
moral fabric of a kingdom dedicated to the rights of man. Some of his
correspondents were provided with a copy of a 148-page book, and
they were advised, lest they suffer any momentary confusion, that
their correspondent was indeed "He whose African Name is the title
of the book": Quobna Ottobah Cugoano.

Cugoano published his *Thoughts and Sentiments on the Evil and
Wicked Traffic of the Slavery and Commerce of the Human Species, Humbly Submitted to the Inhabitants of Great Britain, by Ottobah Cugoano, a
Native of Africa* in 1787. Cugoano was born a member of the "Fantee"
(Fanti) people in about 1757, near Ajumako, in what is now Ghana. If
not quite born to royalty like Gronniosaw, Cugoano's family nevertheless enjoyed the intimate acquaintance of royals; his father "was a
companion to the chief," and Cugoano was a friend of the chief's
nephew. In 1770, at about the age of thirteen, Cugoano was captured,
sold into slavery, and taken to Grenada.

At Grenada, the young slave was purchased by "a gentleman coming to England," who "took me for his servant." Thus was he "deliv-

ered from Grenada, and that horrid brutal slavery" in 1772. Cugoano became a freedman, and by 1786 emerged as a leader of the "black poor" of London. Cugoano was also a friend of Olaudah Equiano, and of Scipione Piattoli, a member of the Polish patriotic movement led by King Stanislaw II. Cugoano, then, was for several years a major black public figure in England.

It was at the height of his authority that he published his *Thoughts and Sentiments*, a book that is not primarily an autobiography. While the genre of the slave narrative is characterized by both polemics and autobiography ("my bondage and my freedom," as Frederick Douglass put it in 1855), Cugoano tends toward the polemic. His text wrestles with several other eighteenth-century works on slavery, some named and some unnamed, including David Hume's 1754 version of his well-known essay "Of National Characters," Patrick Gordon's *Geography Anatomized* (London, 1693) and *The Geography of England* (London, 1744), Anthony Benezet's *Some Historical Account of Guinea* (London, 1771), James Ramsay's *Essay on the Treatment and Conversion of the African Slaves in the British Sugar Colonies* (London, 1784), James Tobin's *Cursory Remarks upon the Reverend Mr. Ramsay's Essay* (London, 1785), and Gordon Tumbult's *Apology for Slavery* (London, 1786), among other texts. Thus, Cugoano's book is offered as an African response to the eighteenth century's major treatises on African enslavement.

Early in his text, Cugoano accounts for his literacy and for his familiarity with the works of Europeans on slavery:

> After coming to England, and seeing others write and read, I had a strong desire to learn, and getting what assistance I could, I applied myself to learn reading and writing, which soon became my recreation, pleasure, and delight; and when my master perceived that I could write some, he sent me to a proper school for that purpose to learn. Since, I have endeavored to improve my mind in reading, and have sought to get all the intelligence I could, in my situation of life, towards the state of my brethren and countrymen in complexion, and of the miserable situation of those who are barbarously sold into captivity, and unlawfully held in slavery. (p. 96)

The representation of this scene of instruction became, after Cugoano, a necessary moment in virtually every subsequent slave narrative. Like Job Ben Solomon in 1731, Cugoano suggests that he virtually "wrote" his way from bondage to freedom. Cugoano acknowledges that despite the brutality of his enslavement, it has not been without reward:

> [O]ne great duty I owe to Almighty God, . . . that, although I have been brought away from my native country, . . . I have both obtained liberty, and acquired the great advantages of some little learning, in being able to read and write, and, what is still infinitely of greater advantage, I trust, to know something of HIM who is that God whose providence rules over all. . . . In this respect, I am highly indebted to many of the good people of England for learning and principles unknown to the people of my native country. (pp. 96–97)

Despite this appreciation, however, Cugoano is no pious pilgrim; he is determined to show that slavery is both a defilement of sacred writ and contrary to the secular notion of liberty to which all Englishmen are heir.

If Cugoano claims to have read the major texts on slavery, he also intimates that he has read the works of Gronniosaw and Marrant, making both of his literary antecedents actual characters in his text. Both appear as examples of blacks who managed to "get their liberty" and who were able "eventually [to] arrive at some knowledge of the Christian religion, and the great advantages to it." Of Gronniosaw, Cugoano writes:

> Such was the case of Ukawsaw Gronniosaw, an African prince, who lived in England. He was a long time in a state of great poverty and distress, and must have died at one time for want, if a good and charitable Attorney had not supported him. He was long after in a very poor state, but he would not have given his faith in the Christian religion, in exchange for all the kingdoms of Africa, if they could have been given to him, in place of his poverty, for it. (p. 102)

Cugoano knew his Gronniosaw, as his final sentence ironically suggests, for Gronniosaw, seeking to become a "man of parts and learning," wanted no parts of Africa, not even its gold.

And what of John Marrant? Cugoano compares him favorably with Gronniosaw:

> And such was A. Marrant in America. When a boy, he could stroll away into a desert, and prefer the society of wild beasts to the absurd

Christianity of his mother's house. He was conducted to the king of
the Cherokees, who, in a miraculous manner, was induced by him to
embrace the Christian faith. This Marrant was in the British service
last war, and his royal convert, the king of the Cherokee Indians, accompanied General Clinton at the siege of Charleston. (p. 102)

Cugoano recapitulates the import of Marrant's text by focusing on the
miracle of the Talking Book and of God emerging from the text. He
does so as a delayed preface to his own revision of the trope of the Talking Book.

Fifty-odd pages after introducing Gronniosaw and Marrant, Cugoano gives his own account of a text that speaks. He does so in a most
enterprising manner, as the climax of a narrative of "the base perfidy
and bloody treachery of the Spaniards" in their treatment of the Native Americans. It is buried in an aside, an embedded narrative inside
his larger narrative of those actions "so very disgraceful to human nature," occasioned by the "barbarous inhuman Europeans" as they enslaved the peoples of Africa, Mexico, and Peru.

Cugoano is recounting his version of "the base treacherous bastard" Pizarro, who stood "at the head of the Spanish banditti of miscreant depredators," and his brutal slaughter of "the Peruvian empire"
and of "the noble Atahualpa, the great Inca or Lord of that empire." At
this point in the story, Pizarro has deceived Atahualpa into believing
that his was "an embassy of peace from a great monarch." Atahualpa,
distrustful of the Spaniards but fearful of their overwhelming military
superiority, and "thinking to appease them by complying with their
request, relied on [Pizarro's] feigned pretensions of friendship." Cugoano narrates the subsequent events:

As [Atahualpa] approached near the Spanish quarters the arch fanatic Father Vincente Valverde, chaplain to the expedition, advanced with a crucifix in one hand and a breviary in the other, and
began with a long discourse, pretending to explain . . . that the then
Pope, Alexander, by donation, had invested their master as the sole
Monarch of all the New World. . . . [Atahualpa] observed [in re-
sponse] that he was lord of the dominions over which he reigned by
hereditary succession; and said, that he could not conceive how a
foreign priest should pretend to dispose of territories which did not
belong to him, and that if such a preposterous grant had been made,
he, who was the rightful possessor, refused to confirm it; that he had
no inclination to renounce the religious institutions established by

his ancestors; nor would he forsake the service of the Sun, the immortal divinity whom he and his people revered, in order to worship the God of the Spaniards, who was subject to death; and that with respect to other matters, he had never heard of them before, and did not then understand their meaning. And he desired to know where Valverde had learned things so extraordinary. In this book, replied the fanatic Monk, reaching out his breviary. The Inca opened it eagerly, and turning over the leaves, lifted it to his ear: This, says he, is silent; it tells me nothing; and threw it with disdain to the ground. The enraged father of ruffians, turning toward his countrymen, the assassinators, cried out, To arms, Christians, to arms; the word of God is insulted; avenge this profanation on these impious dogs. (pp. 137–38)

The Spaniards, we know, slaughtered the Incas and captured Atahualpa, deceiving him a second time before murdering him.

If Cugoano's narrative of Atahualpa and the Talking Book retains Marrant's substitution of the Indian supplicant before the text, he, too, inverts its meaning by having the noble Indian disdainfully throw the silent book to the ground. A text that contained no voice had no significance for Atahualpa; its silent letters were dead. Unlike Marrant's Cherokee king, the king of the Incas was not awed by Friar Vincento's silent text. Cugoano has revised Marrant's trope by transforming it into an allegory of evil—the evils of colonization, to be sure, but also the evils of the abuses of biblical exegesis. Our sympathies remain with Atahualpa, just as Cugoano intended. Cugoano writes primarily to indict a perverted economic and moral order, rather than to exemplify the living wonders of Protestant Christianity or to fashion a public persona. By turning the trope of The Talking Book back upon itself, he underscores the nobility of the Inca, simultaneously showing the perversity of a "civilization" that justifies murder and pillage through the most sacred of written words. Cugoano, like Caliban, masters the master's tongue only to curse him more satisfactorily.

But what of the gold chain, which seems to be so intimately associated with the trope of the Talking Book? There is, it turns out, no chain, but there is gold aplenty. The Inca king, hoping to escape execution, offers to his captors to fill his extensive prison "apartment" with "vessels of gold as high as he could reach." The Spaniards accept this proposal eagerly, and dutifully the Incas fill the apartment; at which point "poor Atahualpa was cruelly murdered, and his body burnt by a military inquisition and his extensive and rich dominions devoted to destruction and ruin by these merciless depredators." The power of the speaking text that allows Marrant to "unchain" the king of the Cherokee does not figure in this story because the Spaniards' breviary has no power over the Inca king. Only the guns of the Spaniards have power, a power of negation that is the objective counterpart of the Spaniards' deceitful words: only their word is necessary to extract Inca riches from Atahualpa. The Spaniards exchange their sacred oath, sworn no doubt on their sacred breviary, for the Inca's gold. Cugoano's account transforms the gold chains that appear in Gronniosaw and Marrant into a perverted booty, a sign of the duplicity of European words.

Cugoano's use of the tale-within-a-tale serves to emphasize that the Talking Book is a literary device. By calling attention to the figurative nature of the trope itself instead of drawing upon it as a primary element in his narrative line, Cugoano highlights his own rhetorical strategies, and displays control over his materials. It is useful to recall that Cugoano is a writer, whereas both Gronniosaw and Marrant dictated their tales to others, who then edited them for publication. As it happens, Cugoano's tale of Atahualpa is drawn from other sources. Cugoano does not cite the original, but his detailed portrait of this encounter clearly points to some other source.

It turns out that the story of Atahualpa and Friar Vincente de Valverde was published by Gracilasso de la Vega, the Inca, in 1617. Gracilasso published the story in his *Historia General del Perú*, which is Part II of his *Comentarios reales del Perú*, a work translated by Sir Paul Rycaut into English and published in 1638 as *The Royal Commentaries of Peru*. Gracilasso's presentation is intriguing not only for the vividness of its depiction of their encounter, but also for its assertion that the encounter never took place. According to Gracilasso's "true account," the conversation between Spaniard and Inca was extremely difficult, owing to problems of translation. (At one point, frustrated by words, they attempted to use *quipus,* a kind of writing that used knots as signs.) Gracilasso goes on to refute the story that Cugoano uses to such effect:

> And here It is to be noted, that it is not true that some Historians report of Atahualpa, that he should say, "You believe that Christ is God and that he died: I adore the Sun and the Moon, which are immortal: And who taught you, that your God created the Heaven

and the Earth?" to which Valverde made answer, "This book hath taught it to us": Then the King took it in his hand, and opening the Leaves, laid it to his Ear: and not hearing it speak to him, he threw it upon the ground. Upon which, they say, that the Friar starting up, ran to his Companions, crying out that the Gospel was despised and trampled under foot; "Justice and Revenge upon those who contemn our Law and refuse our Friendship."

Regardless of what Atahualpa actually said, Rycaut's 1688 translation may well have been Cugoano's source; it is certainly an arresting description, and a text ripe with possibilities. It is possible that Gracilasso's text may have been Marrant's source, as well. At the very least, it is clear from all this that, as early in the Anglo-African tradition as 1787, black texts were already "mulatto" texts, with complex literary heritages.

IN 1789, CUGOANO'S FRIEND Olaudah Equiano published his slave narrative, *The Interesting Narrative of the Life of Olaudah Equiano, or Gustavus Vassa, the African, Written by Himself.* Equiano's narrative was so powerfully structured that it became the prototype of the nineteenth-century slave narrative. From his subtitle, "Written by Himself," to the signed engraving of the black author holding an open text (the Bible) in his lap, to more subtle rhetorical strategies such as the overlapping of the slave's arduous journey to freedom and his simultaneous journey from orality to literacy, Equiano's strategies of self-presentation and rhetorical representation heavily informed the shape of black narrative before Emancipation, including the works of Frederick Douglass, William Wells Brown, and Harriet Jacobs.[7]

Equiano told a good story, and he even gives a believable account of cultural life among the Ibo peoples of what is now Nigeria. His plot is structured by the movement from African freedom through European enslavement to Anglican freedom. Both his remarkable command of narrative devices and his detailed accounts of his stirring adventures no doubt combined to create a readership broader than that enjoyed by any previous black writer. When we recall that his adventures include service in the Seven Years War with General Wolfe in

7. Equiano's two-volume work was exceptionally popular. Eight editions were printed in Great Britain during the author's lifetime, and a first American edition appeared in New York in 1791. By 1837, another eight editions had appeared, including an abridgment in 1829. Three of these editions were published together with Phillis Wheatley's *Poems.* Dutch and German translations were published in 1790 and 1791.

Canada and Admiral Boscawen in the Mediterranean, voyages to the Arctic with the 1772–73 Phipps expedition, six months among the Miskito Indians in Central America, and "a grand tour of the Mediterranean as personal servant to an English gentleman," it is clear that this ex-slave was one of the best-traveled people in the world when he decided to write a story of his life.

Like his friend Cugoano, Equiano was extraordinarily well read, and, like Cugoano, he borrowed freely from other texts, including Constantine Phipps's *A Journal of a Voyage Towards the North Pole* (London, 1774), Anthony Benezet's *Some Historical Account of Guinea* (London, 1771), and Thomas Clarkson's *Essay on the Slavery and Commerce of the Human Species* (London, 1785). He also paraphrased frequently, sometimes by inventing "direct" quotations from Milton, Pope, and Thomas Day. Nevertheless, Equiano was an impressively self-conscious writer and developed highly influential rhetorical strategies, especially his use of two distinct voices to distinguish the simple wonder with which the young Equiano approaches the New World of his captors, and a more eloquent voice to describe the author's narrative present. The frequent reversals of plot, too, serve to highlight the sense of becoming, of a development of a self that not only has a past and a present but multiple languages, all of which serve to enliven the narrative present. Rarely would a slave narrator match Equiano's mastery of self-representation.[8]

Equiano uses the trope of the Talking Book in his third chapter, in which he describes his voyages from Barbados to Virginia and on to England—a portentous voyage, on which he begins to learn the English language. Exploring a shipboard cabin, a wide-eyed Equiano confronts the sublime artifacts of Western Culture:

> The first object that engaged my attention was a watch which hung on the chimney, and was going. I was quite surprised at the noise it made, and was afraid it would tell the gentleman anything I might do amiss: and when I immediately after observed a picture hanging in the room, which appeared constantly to look at me, I was still more affrighted, having never seen such things as these before. At one time I thought it was something relative to magic; and not seeing it move, I thought it might be some way the whites had to keep their

8. Equiano's self-confident writing led one *Monthly Review* critic to ask whether "some English writer" had participated in the writing of his narrative. Equiano's text seems to anticipate such a response by making repeated references to his various lessons in literacy.

great men when they died, and offer them libations as we used to do our friendly spirits. . . .

. . . I was astonished at the wisdom of the white people in all things I saw. (pp. 224, 228)

From these wonderments, Equiano proceeds to describe another marvelous sight:

I had often seen my master . . . employed in reading; and I had great curiosity to talk to the books, as I thought [he] did; and so to learn how all things had a beginning: for that purpose I have often taken up a book, and have talked to it, and then put my ears to it, when alone, in hopes it would answer me; and I have been very much concerned when I found it remained silent. (p. 228)

A watch, a portrait, a book that speaks: these are signs through which Equiano represents the difference in subjectivity that separates his now lost African world from the New World of "white folks" that has been thrust upon him.

Significantly, Equiano endows each of these objects with his master's subjectivity. The portrait seems to be watching him as he moves through the room; the watch, he fears, can see, hear, and speak. The watch is his master's surrogate overseer, standing in for the master as an authority figure, even while he sleeps. The Talking Book talks only to "my master." By presenting these objects in this manner, Equiano dramatizes the sensitive child's naiveté and curiosity, as well as his ability to interpret the culture of the Europeans from a distinctly African point of reference. But he also, implicitly, contrasts this earlier self with the self that narrates his text. His ability to show his readers his own naiveté, rather than merely to tell us about it or to claim it, and to make this earlier self the focus of his readers' sympathy and amusement, are extraordinarily effective rhetorical strategies that serve to heighten our identification with the openly honest subject.

There is another purpose to this bestowal of subjectivity on the master's things. The young Equiano, as a slave, is a thing: the master's object, to be used and enjoyed, purchased, sold, or discarded, just like a watch, a portrait, or a book. By law, the slave has no more and no less rights than the other objects that the master endows with his subjectivity. When Equiano, the object, attempts to speak to the book, there follows only the deafening silence that obtains between two lifeless objects. When the master's book looks to see whose face is behind the voice that Equiano speaks, it can only see an absence, the invisibility that dwells in an unattended looking glass. Only through the act of writing can Equiano announce and preserve his newfound status as a subject. It is he who is the master of his text, a text that speaks volumes of experience and subjectivity. Equiano the author has changed, from African to Anglo-African, from slave to potential freedman, from an absence to a presence, and from an object to a subject.

What does this complex mode of representation suggest about Equiano's textual relationship to Cugoano, his friend and companion? Cugoano's take on the Talking Book had left Equiano very little room to maneuver; Cugoano's bracketed narrative of Atahualpa calls attention to itself by its removal from the linear flow of the rest of his narrative, in a manner foreign to both Gronniosaw and Marrant. By Cugoano's day, the figure could not be utilized without a remarkable degree of self-consciousness. So he proceeded to use the Talking Book as an allegory of storytelling—allowing the characters even to speak in direct discourse—and went so far as to name his antecedents: Gronniosaw and Marrant in one line of descent, and an Inca historian on the other. Like Cugoano, Equiano could not simply make the trope a part of a linear narrative. So he subordinates it to a list of latent readings of the "true" nature of Western culture, and simultaneously allows it to function as an allegory of his own act of fashioning an Anglo-African self through language.

JOHN JEA ENJOYS A RARE DISTINCTION in the Anglo-African tradition: he is one of the few black writers—perhaps the only black writer—to publish both an autobiography and a work of imaginative literature prior to the twentieth century. But he is also among the least known, in large part because both of Jea's works were lost for centuries, until 1983.

We do not yet know very many of the particulars of Jea's life, beyond those narrated in his autobiography, *The Life, History, and Unparalleled Sufferings of John Jea, the African Preacher, Compiled and Written by Himself.* He tells us that he was born in "Old Callabar, in Africa, in the year 1773." Jea tells his readers that he, his parents, and his brothers and sisters "were stolen" from Africa and taken to New York. His master and mistress, Oliver and Angelika Triehuen, were Dutch. Jea's narrative is an account of the arduous labors forced upon the Triehuen slaves, and of Jea's rescue by God and Christianity, despite Jea's receiving severe beatings from his master any time he attended a religious gathering. Jea eventually wins his freedom and becomes an itinerant preacher, traveling to Boston, New Orleans, the "East Indies," South America, Holland, France, Germany, Ireland, and England. Jea's travels, replete with "surprising deliverances" effected by Divine Providence, make for fascinating reading, but his text is also remarkable for its rhetorical strategies.

The discovery of Jea's narrative enables us to gain a much better understanding of the formal development of the slave narrative. Jea's text is one of the few black autobiographies published between 1800 and 1830; it represents a missing link of sorts, retaining the conventions of the earliest slave narratives but previewing, as it were, the conceits of the narratives of the Abolitionist period. Jea's text is replete with animal metaphors drawn upon to describe the life of the slave. These metaphors are much less common in the narratives published in the eighteenth century than they are in those published after 1830. Jea's text, moreover, is explicitly concerned with literacy as the element that enables the slave to reverse his or her status, from a condition of slave/animal to that of articulate subject. Jea wants to be a voice for the abolition of slavery, an institution that he repeatedly claims is at odds with the divine order. Jea's narrative also is the last of the great black "sacred" slave autobiographies. After his text, slave narrators generally relegate the sacred to a tacit presence, while the secular concern with abolition becomes predominant.

Jea introduces two major revisions of the slave narrative structure that he received from the eighteenth century. These include the visual representation of the text's subject, which prefaces his text, and the trope of the Talking Book. As Equiano had done twenty-six years before him, Jea prefaces his text with his own image, but an image represented both in profile and in silhouette. Jea's representation of himself in shadow draws attention primarily to his "African" features, especially to his "Bantu" nose, his thick lips, and his "Ibo" forehead, unlike the engravings of Phillis Wheatley and Equiano, which call attention to the assimilated presence of a subject who is Anglo-African, a hybrid third term meant to mediate between the opposites signified by "African" and "Anglo-Saxon." Jea's choice of representation of himself, while common among other Protestant ministers who published autobiographies contemporaneous with Jea's, is the negative of the positive image selected by Wheatley and Equiano. Jea reverses the convention of self-presentation by employing the silhouette to underscore a literal blackness of the subject, represented as black upon black.

But even more curious is Jea's revision of the trope of the Talking Book, which he also seeks to literalize. By this I mean that Jea—like Gronniosaw and Marrant before him—uses the trope of the Talking Book as an element in a larger linear narrative, unlike Cugoano, who brackets the trope by making it a narrative-within-a-narrative, and Equiano, who utilizes it as a signal element in his "list of differences" that separated the African from the European. Jea also makes this scene a part of his linear plot development, but with one major difference: he reads the trope literally as "the word made flesh."

Jea's account of the Talking Book unfolds over five pages of his text. It occurs in Jea's narrative immediately after he tells us that he "ran from" his last human master's house "to the house of God, [and] was baptized unknown to him." (Jea tells us later that "It was a law of the state of the city of New York, that if any slave could give a satisfactory account of what he knew of the word of the Lord on his soul, he was free from slavery." This process was responsible for "releasing some thousands of us poor black slaves from the galling chains of slavery.") Jea's master, upon discovering that his slave was now legally free, attempted to convince him that the Bible itself demanded that Jea remain with him and continue to serve as his slave:

> [M]y master strove to baffle me, and to prevent me from understanding the Scriptures: so he used to tell me that there was a time to every purpose under the sun, to do all manner of work, that slaves were in duty bound to do whatever their masters commanded them, whether it was right or wrong; so that they must be obedient to a hard spiteful master as to a good one. He then took the Bible and showed it to me, and said that the book talked with him. Thus he talked with me endeavoring to convince me that I ought not to leave him, although I had received my full liberty from the magistrates, and was fully determined by the grace of God, to leave him. . . .
>
> My master's sons also endeavored to convince me, by their reading in the behalf of their father; . . . for it surprised me much, how they could take that blessed book into their hands, and to be so superstitious as to want to make me believe that the book did talk with them; so that every opportunity when they were out of the way, I took the book, and held it up to my ears, to try whether the book would talk with me or not, but it proved to be all in vain, for I could not hear it speak one word, which caused me to grieve and lament, that after God had done so much for me as he had, in pardoning my

sins, and blotting out my iniquities and transgressions, and making me a new creature, the book would not talk with me. . . . Then I began to ask God in faithful and fervent prayer, as the Spirit of the Lord gave me utterance, begging earnestly of the Lord to give me the knowledge of his word, that I might be enabled to understand it in its pure light, and be able to speak it in the Dutch and English languages, that I might convince my master that he and his sons had not spoken to me as they ought, when I was their slave. (pp. 391–92)

Jea kept on at his master's work for six weeks, praying all the while, despite the scorn of the master and mistress, until:

[M]y eyes were opened . . . while I was praying, in the place where I slept; although the place was as dark as a dungeon, I awoke, as the Scripture saith, and found it illuminated with the light of the glory of God, and the angel standing by me, with the large book open, which was the Holy Bible, and said unto me, *"Thou has desired to read and understand this book, and to speak the language of it both in English and in Dutch; I will therefore teach thee, and now read."* . . .

This caused them to spread a rumor all over the city of New York, saying, that the Lord had worked great miracles on a poor black man. The people flocked from all parts to know whether it was true or not; and some of them took me before the magistrates, and had me examined concerning the rumor that was spread abroad, to prevent me, if possible, from saying the Lord had taught me to read in one night, in about fifteen minutes; for they were afraid that I should teach the other slaves to call upon the name of the Lord, as I did aforetime, and that they should come to the knowledge of the truth. . . .

From that hour, in which the Lord taught me to read, until the present, I have not been able to read in any book, nor any reading whatever, but such as contain the word of God. (pp. 392–95)

What are we to make of Jea's fantastic revision of the trope of the Talking Book? And where is the gold chain, chains that appear in Gronniosaw, Marrant, and Cugoano? Jea's chains are the "chains of sin," which he has carefully elaborated upon before he tells us of the Talking Book:

[U]nless you improve your advantages, you had better be a slave in any dark part of the world, than a neglecter of the gospel in this highly favored land; recollect also that even here you might be a slave

of the most awful description: a slave to your passions, a slave to the
world, a slave to sin, a slave to Satan, a slave to hell, and, unless you
are made free by Christ, through the means of the gospel, you will
remain in captivity, tied and bound in the chains of your sin, till at
last you will be bound hand and foot, and cast into outer darkness,
there shall be weeping and gnashing of teeth forever. (p. 373)

Jea reverses the semantic associations of "slave" and "chains," making
his condition a metaphor for the human condition. It is clear early on
in his text, then, that this Christian life of a slave bears a relationship to
other lives as the part stands for the whole.

But let us be clear about Jea's chain: while nominally freed by the
laws of New York it was not until he demonstrated his ability to "read"
the first chapter of the Gospel of John, "very well and distinct," that his
rights to "liberty" were confirmed by the magistrates of New York after he had been "taught by God." Jea, in other words, literally reads his
way out of slavery by literalizing the metaphor of the Talking Book. Jea
sets the scene of instruction in great detail: he names the text that the
angel teaches him to read; he adds that the event occurs just before
dawn, "being about four o'clock in the morning," and that the entire
reading lesson unfolded "in about fifteen minutes." Jea also gives his
readers a fairly precise account of events that led to the angel's appearance, and of his actions immediately before and after this supernatural
visitation. Finally, he tells us three times that his request of God and
God's gift in return was to "read," "understand," and "speak the language" of this chapter of the Bible in both "the English and Dutch languages."

It is not an arbitrary text that the divinity selects for the black slave's
mastery, either. It is the Gospel of John, which opens: "In the beginning was the Word, and the Word was with God, and the Word was
God." Jea's "mastery" of reading is centered upon the curious sentence of the New Testament that explicitly concerns the nature of "the
Word"—the logos, speech or the word as reason. And let us recall the
first chapter's final verse: "And he saith unto him, Verily, verily, I say
unto you, Hereafter ye shall see heaven open, and the angels of God as-
cending and descending upon the Son of man." Jea takes this major
text and represents its wonders in the most literal manner possible, by
having "heaven open" and an angel both descend and then ascend,
and also by literally dramatizing the text's first verse, that "the word"
is the beginning, and is with God in the beginning, and indeed "was

God." Only God, epitome and keeper of the Word, can satisfy the illiterate slave's desire to know this Word, "in the English and Dutch languages," because all human agencies are closed off to him by slavery. The Lord emerges from the text, rewarding his servant's unusual plea by fulfilling it at its most literal level. While we, his readers, find Jea's account of his literacy training to be allegorical at best, he does not seek to emphasize the event as figurative; on the contrary, by making it one more element in his linear narration, and by representing it as the event that leads directly to his attainment of legal liberty, Jea attempts to represent the several literal and figurative elements of the received trope as if they all happened.

But Jea's revision does more than make the trope literal. His revision names the trope and all of the transferences that we have seen in his antecedent narrators' revisions. His naming of the trope, moreover, is the event that, at last, enables him to tell *his* name, a name that he places in his title and that the text of his life elaborates upon in some detail. Jea's concern with naming is explicitly stated in the John Wesley hymn that appears as a coda on the last page of his narrative. In one of the hymn's five stanzas, Wesley addresses the significance of naming explicitly and provocatively:

> *Wilt thou not yet to me reveal*
> *Thy new, unutterable Name?*
> *Tell me, I still beseech thee, tell;*
> *To know it now, resolv'd I am:*
> *Wrestling I will not let thee go,*
> *Till I thy name, thy Nature know.*

Through a long dark night of the soul, the subject of the hymn wrestles like Jacob with "the God-man" only to learn His name. In one's name is one's "Nature," the hymn says, arguing for an intrinsic relationship between signs and what they signify. Jea inscribes his name in his autobiographical text, so that his readers can also know his name and thereby know his nature—and that of the black slaves for whom he stands.

What are the names he gives to the trope through his revision? Jea shows us that the trope of the Talking Book figures the difference that obtains in Western culture between the slave and the free, between African and European, between pagan and Christian. His revision tells us that true freedom turns upon the mastery of Western letters. He tells us that literacy was the sole sign of difference separating chattel property from human being. And he tells us that this figure, as encoded in the tropes that he received from Gronniosaw, Marrant, Cugoano, and Equiano, was not merely a metaphor for literacy, but for white supremacy as well: literacy had been the central concept underwriting the West's superiority to the peoples of color it had "discovered," colonized, and enslaved since the fifteenth century. Jea's revision also tells us that the trope, all along, has been one of presence, the presence of the human voice necessary for the black slave narrator effectively to transform himself—and to represent this transformation—from silent object to speaking subject.

Jea's revision also addresses the complex matter of the distance that separates the oral from the written. Just as the trope of the Talking Book in fact is more properly the trope of the Silent Book, in which the canceled presence of an opposite term is enunciated by the silence or absence of the text, so too is Jea's literacy a canceled presence because he can only read one chapter of one book, albeit a major chapter of a major book. Indeed it is not clear if Jea could read or write at all; despite the claim of his text's subtitle that the autobiography has been "Compiled and Written by Himself," Jea tells us near the end of his tale, "My dear reader, I would now inform you, that I have stated this in the best manner I am able, for I cannot write, therefore it is not so correct as if I had been able to have written it myself." Jea, in other words, can only make the text speak, as it were, by memorization, rather than by the true mastery of its letters. His is the oral reading and writing of memory, of the sort practiced by the Yoruba *babalawo*. (Jea's birthplace, "Old Callabar," we recall, is in the east of Nigeria, where similar modes of narration would have obtained even in the eighteenth century.) Jea's is at best an ironic mode of reading. Like Gronniosaw and Marrant before him, never is he able to write his life, only to relate it by oral narration. Jea is the third-term resolution between the illiterate slave and the fully literate European.

With Jea's *Life,* the trope of the Talking Book disappears from the slave narrative. This undoubtedly has something to do with the vagaries of the slave trade: Jea is among the last of the slave narrators to be born in Africa, with an African name and speaking an African language; henceforth, the tales of American-born blacks, with American names, will begin to predominate. Furthermore, Jea's miraculous scene of instruction is perhaps *too* literal to be passed on. In the narratives composed after 1830, the "angels" will be human: Frederick Douglass is taught by his master's wife; many other slave narrators will learn to read and write through the intercession of white women or children. This is, indeed, something of a narrative necessity: if the narrator is to be believable in the more secular context of the abolitionist movement, he or she cannot afford to appeal, as Jea does, primarily to the Christian converted. They long for a secular freedom now, and they no longer entertain the idea that books speak when their masters speak to them. The freedom dreamed by Frederick Douglass, represented primarily in metaphors of writing rather than speaking, puts paid to the eighteenth-century trope of the Talking Book.

A

NARRATIVE

OF THE

Most Remarkable Particulars

In the L I F E of

James Albert Ukawsaw Gronniosaw

An African Prince,

As related by H I M S E L F.

I will bring the Blind by a Way that they know not, I will lead them in Paths that they have not known: I will make Darkness Light before them and crooked Things straight. These Things will I do unto them and not forsake them.   Isa. 42: 16

B A T H :

Printed by W. GYE in Westgate Street; and sold by T. MILLS, Bookseller, in King's-Mead-Square. Price Six Pence.

I

A NARRATIVE OF THE

MOST REMARKABLE PARTICULARS

IN THE LIFE OF

JAMES ALBERT

UKAWSAW GRONNIOSAW

AN AFRICAN PRINCE,

AS RELATED BY HIMSELF

To the

Right Honorable

The Countess of Huntingdon,

this Narrative

Of my Life,

And of God's wonderful Dealings

with me, is,

(Through Her Ladyship's Permission)

Most Humbly Dedicated,

By her Ladyship's Most obliged

And obedient Servant,

James Albert

THIS ACCOUNT of the life and spiritual experience of James Albert was taken from his own mouth and committed to paper by the elegant pen of a young lady of the town of Leominster, for her own private satisfaction, and without any intention at first that it should be made public. But she has now been prevailed on to commit it to the press, both with a view to serve Albert and his distressed family, who have the sole profits arising from the sale of it; and likewise as it is apprehended, this little history contains matter well worthy the notice and attention of every Christian reader.

Perhaps we have here in some degree a solution of that question that has perplexed the minds of so many serious persons, namely, in what manner will God deal with those benighted parts of the world where the gospel of Jesus Christ hath never reached? Now it appears from the experience of this remarkable person, that God does not save without the knowledge of the truth; but, with respect to those whom he hath foreknown, though born under every outward disadvantage, and in regions of the grossest darkness and ignorance, he most amazingly acts upon and influences their minds, and in the course of wisely and most wonderfully appointed providences, he brings them to the means of spiritual information, gradually opens to their view the light of his truth, and gives them full possession and enjoyment of the inestimable blessings of his gospel. Who can doubt but that the suggestion so forcibly pressed upon the mind of Albert (when a boy) that there was a being superior to the sun, moon, and stars (the objects of African idolatry) came from the Father of Lights, and was, with respect to him, the first fruit of the display of gospel glory? His long and perilous journey to the coast of Guinea, where he was sold for a slave, and so brought into a Christian land; shall we consider this as the lone effect of a curious and inquisitive disposition? Shall we in accounting for it refer to nothing higher than mere chance and accidental circumstances? Whatever infidels and deists may think; I trust the Christian reader will easily discern an all-wise and omnipotent appointment and direction in these movements. He belonged to the redeemer of lost sinners; he was the purchase of his cross; and therefore the Lord undertook to bring him by a way that he knew not, out of darkness into his marvellous light, that he might lead him to a saving heart acquaintance and union with the triune God in Christ reconciling the world unto himself; and not imputing their trespasses. As his call was very extraordinary, so there are certain particulars exceedingly remarkable in his experience. God has put singular honor upon him in the exercise of his faith and patience, which in the most distressing and pitiable trials and calamities have been found to the praise and glory of God. How deeply must it affect a tender heart, not only to be reduced to the last extremity himself, but to have his wife and children perishing for want before his eyes! Yet his faith did not fail him; he put his trust in the Lord, and he was delivered. And at this instance, though born in an exalted station of life, and now under the pressure of various afflicting providences, I am persuaded (for I know the man) he would rather embrace the dunghill, having Christ in his heart, than give up his spiritual possessions and enjoyment, to fill the throne of princes. It perhaps may not be amiss to observe that James Albert left his native country, (as near as I can guess from certain circumstances) when he was about fifteen years old. He now appears to be turned of sixty; has a good natural understanding; is well acquainted with the Scriptures, and the things of God, has an amiable and tender disposition, and his character can be well attested not only at Kidderminster, the place of his residence, but likewise by many creditable persons in London and other places. Reader, recommending this narrative to your perusal, and him who is the subject of it to your charitable regard,

I am your faithful and obedient servant,
For Christ's sake,
W. Shirley.

An Account of James Albert, etc.

I WAS BORN in the City Bournou; my mother was the eldest daughter of the reigning King there, of which Bournou is the chief city. I was the youngest of six children, and particularly loved by my mother, and my grandfather almost doted on me.

I had, from my infancy, a curious turn of mind; was more grave and reserved in my disposition than either of my brothers and sisters. I often teased them with questions they could not answer: for which reason they disliked me, as they supposed that I was either foolish, or insane. 'Twas certain that I was, at times, very unhappy in myself: it being strongly impressed on my mind that there was some great man of power which resided above the sun, moon and stars, the objects of our worship. My dear indulgent mother would bear more with me than any of my friends beside—I often raised my hand to heaven, and asked her who lived there? was much dissatisfied when she told me the sun, moon and stars, being persuaded, in my own mind, that there must be some Superior Power. I was frequently lost in wonder at the works of the Creation: was afraid and uneasy and restless, but could not tell for what. I wanted to be informed of things that no person could tell me; and was always dissatisfied. These wonderful impressions began in my childhood, and followed me continually till I left my parents, which affords me matter of admiration and thankfulness.

To this moment I grew more and more uneasy every day, in so much that one Saturday, (which is the day on which we keep our sabbath) I labored under anxieties and fears that cannot be expressed; and, what is more extraordinary, I could not give a reason for it. I rose, as our custom is, about three o'clock (as we are obliged to be at our place of worship an hour before the sunrise); we say nothing in our worship, but continue on our knees with our hands held up, observing a strict silence till the sun is at a certain height, which I suppose to be about ten or eleven o'clock in England: when, at a certain sign made by the priest, we get up (our duty being over) and disperse to our different houses. Our place of meeting is under a large palm tree; we divide ourselves into many congregations, as it is impossible for the same tree to cover the inhabitants of the whole City, though they are extremely large, high and majestic; the beauty and usefulness of them are not to be described; they supply the inhabitants of the country with meat, drink and clothes.* The body of the palm tree is very large; at a certain season of the year they tap it, and bring vessels to receive the wine, of which they draw great quantities, the quality of which is very delicious; the leaves of this tree are of a silky nature, they are large and soft; when they are dried and pulled to pieces it has much the same appearance as the English flax, and the inhabitants of Bournou manufacture it for clothing, etc. This tree likewise produces a plant or substance which has the appearance of a cabbage, and very like it, in taste almost the same: it grows between the branches. Also the palm tree produces a nut, something like a cocoa, which contains a kernel, in which is a large quantity of milk, very pleasant to the taste: the shell is of a hard substance, and of a very beautiful appearance, and serves for basins, bowls, etc.

I hope this digression will be forgiven.—I was going to observe that after the duty of our sabbath was over (on the day in which I was more distressed and afflicted than ever) we were all on our way home as usual, when a remarkable black cloud arose and covered the sun; then followed very heavy rain and thunder more dreadful than ever I had heard. The heavens roared, and the earth trembled at it: I was highly affected and cast down; insomuch that I wept sadly, and could not follow my relations and friends home.—I was obliged to stop and felt as if my legs were tied, they seemed to shake under me: so I stood still, being in great fear of the Man of Power that I was persuaded in myself lived above. One of my young companions (who entertained a particular friendship for me and I for him) came back to see for me: he asked me why I stood still in such very hard rain? I only said to him that my legs were weak, and I could not come faster: he was much affected to see me cry, and took me by the hand, and said he would lead me home, which he did. My mother was greatly alarmed at my tarrying out in such terrible weather; she asked me many questions, such as what I did so for, and if I was well? My dear mother says I, pray tell me who is the Great Man of Power that makes the thunder? She said, there was no power but the sun, moon and stars; that they made all our country. I then inquired how all our people came? She answered me, from one another; and so carried me to many generations back. Then says I, who made the First Man? and who made the first cow, and the first lion, and

*It is a generally received opinion, in *England,* that the natives of *Africa* go entirely unclothed; but this supposition is very unjust: they have a kind of dress so as to appear decent, though it is very slight and thin.

where does the fly come from, as no one can make him? My mother seemed in great trouble; she was apprehensive that my senses were impaired, or that I was foolish. My father came in, and seeing her in grief asked the cause, but when she related our conversation to him, he was exceedingly angry with me, and told me he would punish me severely if ever I was so troublesome again; so that I resolved never to say anything more to him. But I grew very unhappy in myself; my relations and acquaintance endeavored by all the means they could think on to divert me, by taking me to ride upon goats (which is much the custom of our country), and to shoot with a bow and arrow; but I experienced no satisfaction at all in any of these things; nor could I be easy by any means whatever. My parents were very unhappy to see me so dejected and melancholy.

About this time there came a merchant from the Gold Coast (the third city in Guinea); he traded with the inhabitants of our country in ivory. He took great notice of my unhappy situation, and inquired into the cause; he expressed vast concern for me, and said, if my parents would part with me for a little while, and let him take me home with him, it would be of more service to me than anything they could do for me. He told me that if I would go with him I should see houses with wings to them walk upon the water, and should also see the white folks; and that he had many sons of my age, which should be my companions; and he added to all this that he would bring me safe back again soon. I was highly pleased with the account of this strange place, and was very desirous of going. I seemed sensible of a secret impulse upon my mind which I could not resist that seemed to tell me I must go. When my dear mother saw that I was willing to leave them, she spoke to my father and grandfather and the rest of my relations, who all agreed that I should accompany the merchant to the Gold Coast. I was the more willing as my brothers and sisters despised me, and looked on me with contempt on the account of my unhappy disposition; and even my servants slighted me, and disregarded all I said to them. I had one sister who was always exceeding fond of me, and I loved her entirely; her name was Logwy, she was quite white, and fair, with fine light hair though my father and mother were black.—I was truly concerned to leave my beloved sister, and she cried most sadly to part with me, wringing her hands, and discovered every sign of grief that can be imagined. Indeed if I could have known when I left my friends and country that I should never return to them again my misery on that occasion would have been inexpressible. All my relations were sorry to part with me; my dear mother came with me upon a camel more than three hundred miles, the first of our journey lay chiefly through woods; at night we secured ourselves from the wild beasts by making fires all around us; we and our camels kept within the circle, or we must have been torn to pieces by the lions, and other wild creatures, that roared terribly as soon as night came on, and continued to do so till morning. There can be little said in favor of the country through which we passed; only a valley of marble that we came through which is unspeakably beautiful. On each side of this valley are exceedingly high and almost inaccessible mountains—some of these pieces of marble are of prodigious length and breadth but of different sizes and color, and shaped in a variety of forms, in a wonderful manner. Most of it [is] veined with gold mixed with striking and beautiful colors; so that when the sun darts upon it, it is as pleasing a sight as can be imagined. The merchant that brought me from Bournou, was in partnership with another gentleman who accompanied us; he was very unwilling that he should take me from home, as, he said, he foresaw many difficulties that would attend my going with them. He endeavored to prevail on the merchant to throw me into a very deep pit that was in the valley, but he refused to listen to him, and said, he was resolved to take care of me: but the other was greatly dissatisfied, and when we came to a river, which we were obliged to pass through, he purposed throwing me in and drowning me; but the Merchant would not consent to it, so that I was preserved.

We traveled till about four o'clock every day, and then began to make preparations for night, by cutting down large quantities of wood, to make fires to preserve us from the wild beasts.—I had a very unhappy and discontented journey, being in continual fear that the people I was with would murder me. I often reflected with extreme regret on the kind friends I had left, and the idea of my dear mother frequently drew tears from my eyes.—I cannot recollect how long we were in going from Bournou to the Gold Coast; but as there is no shipping nearer to Bournou than that city, it was tedious in traveling so far by land, being upwards of a thousand miles. I was heartily rejoiced when we arrived at the end of our journey: I now vainly imagined that all my troubles and inquietudes would terminate here, but could I have looked into futurity, I should have perceived that I had much more to suffer than I had before experienced, and that they had as yet but barely commenced.

I was now more than a thousand miles from home, without a friend or any means to procure one. Soon after I came to the merchant's house I heard the drums beat remarkably loud, and the trumpets blow—the persons accustomed to this employ, are obliged to go upon a very high structure appointed for that purpose, that the sound might be heard at a great distance: They are higher than the steeples are in England. I was mightily pleased with sounds so entirely new to me, and was very inquisitive to know the cause of this rejoicing, and asked many questions concerning it: I was answered that it was meant as a compliment to me, because I was Grandson to the King of Bournou.

This account gave me a secret pleasure; but I was not suffered long to enjoy this satisfaction, for in the evening of the same day two of the merchant's sons (boys about my own age) came running to me, and told me, that the next day I was to die, for the King intended to behead me. I replied that I was sure it could not be true, for that I came there to play with them, and to see houses walk upon the water with wings to them, and the white folks; but I was soon informed that their King imagined that I was sent by my father as a spy, and would make such discoveries at my return home that would enable them to make war with the greater advantage to ourselves; and for these reasons he had resolved I should never return to my native country. When I heard this I suffered misery that cannot be described. I wished a thousand times that I had never left my friends and country—but still the Almighty was pleased to work miracles for me.

The morning I was to die, I was washed and all my gold ornaments made bright and shining, and then carried to the palace, where the King was to behead me himself (as is the custom of the place). He was seated upon a throne at the top of an exceeding large yard, or court, which you must go through to enter the palace; it is as wide and spacious as a large field in England. I had a lane of lifeguards to go through—I guessed it to be about three hundred paces.

I was conducted by my friend, the merchant, about half way up; then he dared proceed no further. I went up to the King alone. I went with an undaunted courage, and it pleased God to melt the heart of the King, who sat with his scimitar in his hand ready to behead me; yet, being himself so affected, he dropped it out of his hand, and took me upon his knee and wept over me. I put my right hand round his neck, and pressed him to my heart. He sat me down and blessed me; and added that he would not kill me, and that I should not go home, but be sold for a slave, so then I was conducted back again to the merchant's house.

The next day he took me on board a French brig; but the Captain did not choose to buy me. He said I was too small; so the merchant took me home with him again.

The partner, whom I have spoken of as my enemy, was very angry to see me return, and again purposed putting an end to my life; for he represented to the other, that I should bring them into troubles and difficulties, and that I was so little that no person would buy me.

The merchant's resolution began to waver, and I was indeed afraid that I should be put to death: but however he said he would try me once more.

A few days after a Dutch ship came into the harbor, and they carried me on board, in hopes that the captain would purchase me. As they went, I heard them agree, that, if they could not sell me *then*, they would throw me overboard. I was in extreme agonies when I heard this; and as soon as ever I saw the Dutch Captain, I ran to him, and put my arms round him, and said, "father, save me" (for I knew that if he did not buy me, I should be treated very ill, or, possibly, murdered). And though he did not understand my language, yet it pleased the Almighty to influence him in my behalf, and he bought me *for two yards of check*, which is of more value *there*, than in England.

When I left my dear mother I had a large quantity of gold about me, as is the custom of our country, it was made into rings, and they were linked into one another, and formed into a kind of chain, and so put round my neck, and arms and legs, and a large piece hanging at one ear almost in the shape of a pear. I found all this troublesome, and was glad when my new Master took it from me—I was now washed, and clothed in the Dutch or English manner. My master grew very fond of me, and I loved him exceedingly. I watched every look, was always ready when he wanted me, and endeavored to convince him, by every action, that my only pleasure was to serve him well. I have since thought that he must have been a serious man. His actions corresponded very well with such a character. He used to read prayers in public to the ship's crew every Sabbath day; and when first I saw him read, I was never so surprised in my whole life as when I saw the book talk to my master; for I thought it did, as I observed him to look upon it, and move his lips.— I wished it would do so to me.—As soon as my master had done reading I followed him to the place where he put the book, being mightily delighted with it, and when nobody saw me, I opened it and put my ear down close upon it, in great hope that it would say something to me; but [I] was very sorry and greatly disappointed when I found it would not speak; this thought immediately presented itself to me, that everybody and everything despised me because I was black.

I was exceedingly seasick at first; but when I became more accustomed to the sea, it wore off. My master's ship was bound for Barbados. When we came there, he thought fit to speak of me to several gentlemen of his acquaintance, and one of them expressed a particular desire to see me. He had a great mind to buy me; but the captain could not immediately be prevailed on to part with me; but however, as the gentleman seemed very solicitous, he at length let me go, and I was sold for fifty dollars (*four and sixpenny-pieces in English*). My new master's name was Vanhorn, a young Gentleman; his home was in New England in the City of New York; to which place he took me with him. He dressed me in his livery, and was very good to me. My chief business was to wait at table, and tea, and clean knives, and I had a very easy place; but the servants used to curse and swear surprisingly; which I learned faster than anything, it was almost the first English I could speak. If any of them affronted me, I was sure to call upon God to damn them immediately; but I was broke of it all at once, occasioned by the correction of an old black servant that lived in the family. One day I had just cleaned the knives for dinner, when one of the maids took one to cut bread and butter with; I was very angry with her, and called upon God to damn her; when this old black man told me I must not say so. I asked him why? He replied there was a wicked man called the Devil, that lived in hell, and would take all that said these words, and put them in the fire and burn them. This terrified me greatly, and I was entirely broke[n] of swearing. Soon after this, as I was placing the china for tea, my mistress came into the room just as the maid had been cleaning it; the girl had unfortunately sprinkled the wainscot with the mop; at which my mistress was angry; the girl very foolishly answered her again, which made her worse, and she called upon God to damn her. I was vastly concerned to hear this, as she was a fine young lady, and very good to me, insomuch that I could not help speaking to her, "Madam," says I, "you must not say so." Why, says she? Because there is a black man called the Devil that lives in hell, and he will put you in the fire and burn you, and I shall be very sorry for that. Who told you this? replied my lady. Old Ned, says I. Very well was all her answer; but she told my master of it, and he ordered that old Ned should be tied up and whipped, and was never suffered to come into the kitchen with the rest of the servants afterwards. My mistress was not angry with me, but rather diverted with my simplicity and, by way of talk, she repeated

what I had said, to many of her acquaintance that visited her; among
the rest, Mr. Freelandhouse, a very gracious, good Minister, heard it,
and he took a great deal of notice of me, and desired my master to part
with me to him. He would not hear of it at first, but, being greatly persuaded, he let me go, and Mr. Freelandhouse gave fifty pounds for me.
He took me home with him, and made me kneel down, and put my two
hands together, and prayed for me, and every night and morning he
did the same. I could not make out what it was for, nor the meaning of
it, nor what they spoke to when they talked—I thought it comical, but
I liked it very well. After I had been a little while with my new master I
grew more familiar, and asked him the meaning of prayer: (I could
hardly speak English to be understood) he took great pains with me,
and made me understand that he prayed to God, who lived in Heaven;
that He was my Father and Best Friend. I told him that this must be a
mistake; that *my* father lived at Bournou, and I wanted very much to
see him, and likewise my dear mother, and sister, and I wished he
would be so good as to send me home to them; and I added, all I could
think of to induce him to convey me back. I appeared in great trouble,
and my good master was so much affected that the tears ran down his
face. He told me that God was a Great and Good Spirit, that He created all the world, and every person and thing in it, in Ethiopia, Africa,
and America, and everywhere. I was delighted when I heard this:
There, says I, I always thought so when I lived at home! Now if I
had wings like an eagle I would fly to tell my dear mother that God is
greater than the sun, moon, and stars; and that they were made by
Him.

I was exceedingly pleased with this information of my master's, because it corresponded so well with my own opinion; I thought now if
I could but get home, I should be wiser than all my countryfolks, my
grandfather, or father, or mother, or any of them. But though I was
somewhat enlightened by this information of my master's, yet, I had no
other knowledge of God but that He was a Good Spirit, and created
everybody, and everything—I never was sensible in myself, nor had
anyone ever told me, that He would punish the wicked, and love the
just. I was only glad that I had been told there was a God because I had
always thought so.

My dear kind master grew very fond of me, as was his Lady; she put
me to school, but I was uneasy at that, and did not like to go; but my
master and mistress requested me to learn in the gentlest terms, and
persuaded me to attend my school without any anger at all; that, at last,

I came to like it better, and learned to read pretty well. My schoolmaster was a good man, his name was Vanosdore, and very indulgent to me.—I was in this state when, one Sunday, I heard my master preach from these words out of Revelations, chapter 1 verse 7. *"Behold, He cometh in the clouds and every eye shall see him and they that pierced Him."* These words affected me excessively; I was in great agonies because I thought my master directed them to me only; and, I fancied, that he observed me with unusual earnestness—I was further confirmed in this belief as I looked round the church, and could see no one person besides myself in such grief and distress as I was; I began to think that my master hated me, and was very desirous to go home, to my own country; for I thought that if God did come (as he said) He would be sure to be most angry with *me,* as I did not know what He was, nor had ever heard of Him before.

I went home in great trouble, but said nothing to anybody.—I was somewhat afraid of my master; I thought he disliked me.—The next text I heard him preach from was, Hebrews 12:14: *"Follow peace with all men, and holiness, without which no man shall see the Lord."* He preached the law so severely, that it made me tremble. He said, that God would judge the whole world; Ethiopia, Asia, and Africa, and everywhere. I was now excessively perplexed, and undetermined what to do; as I had now reason to believe my situation would be equally bad to go, as to stay.—I kept these thoughts to myself, and said nothing to any person whatever.

I should have complained to my good mistress of this great trouble of mind, but she had been a little strange to me for several days before this happened, occasioned by a story told of me by one of the maids. The servants were all jealous, and envied me the regard, and favor shown me by my master and mistress; and the Devil being always ready, and diligent in wickedness, had influenced this girl, to make a lie on me. This happened about hay-harvest, and one day when I was unloading the wagon to put the hay into the barn, she watched an opportunity, in my absence, to take the fork out of the stick, and hide it: when I came again to my work, and could not find it, I was a good deal vexed, but I concluded it was dropped somewhere among the hay; so I went and bought another with my own money; when the girl saw that I had another, she was so malicious that she told my mistress I was very unfaithful, and not the person she took me for; and that she knew, I had, without my master's permission, ordered many things in his name, that he must pay for; and as a proof of my carelessness produced the fork she had taken out of the stick, and said she had found it out of doors. My lady, not knowing the truth of these things, was a little shy to me, till she mentioned it, and then I soon cleared myself, and convinced her that these accusations were false.

I continued in a most unhappy state for many days. My good mistress insisted on knowing what was the matter. When I made known my situation she gave me John Bunyan on the holy war, to read; I found his experience similar to my own, which gave me reason to suppose he must be a bad man; as I was convinced of my own corrupt nature, and the misery of my own heart: and as he acknowledged that he was likewise in the same condition, I experienced no relief at all in reading his work, but rather the reverse. I took the book to my lady, and informed her I did not like it at all, it was concerning a wicked man as bad as myself; and I did not choose to read it, and I desired her to give me another, written by a better man that was holy and without sin. She assured me that John Bunyan was a good man, but she could not convince me; I thought him to be too much like myself to be upright, as his experience seemed to answer with my own.

I am very sensible that nothing but the great power and unspeakable mercies of the Lord could relieve my soul from the heavy burden it labored under at that time. A few days after my master gave me Baxter's *Call to the Unconverted*. This was no relief to me either; on the contrary it occasioned as much distress in me as the other had before done, *as it* invited all to come to *Christ;* and I found myself so wicked and miserable that I could not come. This consideration threw me into agonies that cannot be described; insomuch that I even attempted to put an end to my life—I took one of the large case-knives, and went into the stable with an intent to destroy myself; and as I endeavored with all my strength to force the knife into my side, it bent double. I was instantly struck with horror at the thought of my own rashness, and my conscience told me that had I succeeded in this attempt I should probably have gone to Hell.

I could find no relief, nor the least shadow of comfort; the extreme distress of my mind so affected my health that I continued very ill for three days and nights, and would admit of no means to be taken for my recovery, though my lady was very kind, and sent many things to me; but I rejected every means of relief and wished to die—I would not go into my own bed, but lay in the stable upon straw—I felt all the horrors of a troubled conscience, so hard to be born, and saw all the vengeance of God ready to overtake me—I was sensible that there was no way for me to be saved unless I came to *Christ,* and I could not come to Him: I thought that it was impossible He should receive such a sinner as me.

The last night that I continued in this place, in the midst of my distress these words were brought home upon my mind, *"Behold the Lamb of God."* I was something comforted at this, and began to grow easier and wished for day that I might find these words in my bible—I rose very early the following morning, and went to my schoolmaster, Mr. Vanosdore, and communicated the situation of my mind to him; he was greatly rejoiced to find me inquiring the way to Zion, and blessed the Lord who had worked so wonderfully for me a poor heathen. I was more familiar with this good gentleman than with my master, or any other person; and found myself more at liberty to talk to him: he encouraged me greatly, and prayed with me frequently, and I was always benefitted by his discourse.

About a quarter of a mile from my Master's house stood a large remarkably fine Oak tree, in the midst of a wood. I often used to be employed there in cutting down trees (a work I was very fond of). I seldom failed going to this place everyday; sometimes twice a day if I could be spared. It was the highest pleasure I ever experienced to set under this Oak; for there I used to pour out all my complaints to the Lord: and when I had any particular grievance I used to go there, and talk to the tree, and tell my sorrows, as if it had been to a friend.

Here I often lamented my own wicked heart, and undone state, and found more comfort and consolation than I ever was sensible of before. Whenever I was treated with ridicule or contempt, I used to come here and find peace. I now began to relish the book my Master gave me, Baxter's *Call to the Unconverted,* and took great delight in it. I was always glad to be employed in cutting wood, which was a great part of my business, and I followed it with delight, as I was then quite alone and my heart lifted up to God, and I was enabled to pray continually; and blessed forever be his Holy Name, he faithfully answered my prayers. I can never be thankful enough to Almighty God for the many comfortable opportunities I experienced there.

It is possible the circumstance I am going to relate will not gain credit with many; but this I know, that the joy and comfort it conveyed to me, cannot be expressed and only conceived by those who have experienced the like.

I was one day in a most delightful frame of mind: my heart so overflowed with love and gratitude to the author of all my comforts. I was so drawn out of myself, and so filled and awed by the Presence of God that I saw (or thought I saw) light inexpressible dart down from heaven upon me, and shine around me for the space of a minute. I continued on my knees, and joy unspeakable took possession of my soul. The peace and serenity which filled my mind after this was wonderful, and cannot be told. I would not have changed situations, or been anyone but myself for the whole world. I blessed God for my poverty, that I had no worldly riches or grandeur to draw my heart from Him. I wished at that time, if it had been possible for me, to have continued on that spot forever. I felt an unwillingness in myself to have anything more to do with the world, or to mix with society again. I seemed to possess a full assurance that my sins were forgiven me. I went home all my way rejoicing, and this text of scripture came full upon my mind. *"And I will make an everlasting covenant with them, that I will not turn away from them, to do them good; but I will put my fear in their hearts that they shall not depart from me."* The first opportunity that presented itself, I went to my old schoolmaster, and made known to him the happy state of my soul who joined with me in praise to God for his mercy to me the vilest of sinners. I was now perfectly easy, and had hardly a wish to make beyond what I possessed, when my temporal comforts were all blasted by the death of my dear and worthy Master Mr. Freelandhouse, who was taken from this world rather suddenly: he had but a short illness, and died of a fever. I held his hand in mine when he departed; he told me he had given me my freedom. I was at liberty to go where I would. He added that he had always prayed for me and hoped I should be kept unto the end. My master left me by his will ten pounds, and my freedom.

I found that if he had lived it was his intention to take me with him to Holland, as he had often mentioned me to some friends of his there that were desirous to see me; but I chose to continue with my mistress who was as good to me as if she had been my mother.

The loss of Mr. Freelandhouse distressed me greatly, but I was rendered still more unhappy by the clouded and perplexed situation of my mind; the great enemy of my soul being ready to torment me, would present my own misery to me in such striking light, and distress me with doubts, fears, and such a deep sense of my own unworthiness, that after all the comfort and encouragement I had received, I was often tempted to believe I should be a Castaway at last. The more I saw of the beauty and glory of God, the more I was humbled under a sense of my own vileness. I often repaired to my old place of prayer; I seldom came away without consolation. One day this scripture was wonderfully applied to my mind, *"And ye are complete in Him which is the head of all principalities and power."* The Lord was pleased to comfort me by the application of many gracious promises at times when I was ready to sink under my trouble. *"Wherefore He is able also to save them to the uttermost that come unto God by Him seeing He ever liveth to make intercession for them." "For by one offering He hath perfected forever them that are sanctified."* Hebrews 10:14.

My kind, indulgent Mistress lived but two years after my Master. Her death was a great affliction to me. She left five sons, all gracious young men, and ministers of the gospel. I continued with them all, one after another, until they died; they lived but four years after their parents. When it pleased God to take them to Himself. I was left quite destitute, without a friend in the world. But I who had so often experienced the goodness of God, trusted in Him to do what He pleased with me. In this helpless condition I went in the wood to prayer as usual; and although the snow was a considerable height, I was not sensible of cold, or any other inconvenience. At times indeed when I saw the world frowning around me, I was tempted to think that the Lord had forsaken me. I found great relief from the contemplation of these words in Isaiah 49:16. *"Behold I have graven thee on the palms of my hands; thy walls are continually before me."* And very many comfortable promises were sweetly applied to me. The Eighty-ninth Psalm, verse 34, *"My covenant will I not break nor alter the thing that is gone out of my lips."* (Heb. 16:17 and 18; Phil. 1:6; and several more.)

As I had now lost all my dear and valued friends[,] every place in the world was alike to me. I had for a great while entertained a desire to come to England. I imagined that all the inhabitants of this island were Holy; because all those that had visited my master from thence were good (Mr. Whitefield was his particular friend), and the authors of the books that had been given me were all English. But above all places in the world I wished to see Kidderminster, for I could not but think that on the spot where Mr. Baxter had lived, and preached, the people must be all *Righteous.*

The situation of my affairs required that I should tarry a little longer in New York, as I was something in debt, and was embarrassed how to pay it. About this time a young Gentleman that was a particular acquaintance of one of my young Masters pretended to be a friend to me, and promised to pay my debt, which was three pounds; and he assured me he would never expect the money again. But, in less than a month, he came and demanded it; and when I assured him I had noth-

ing to pay, he threatened to sell me. Though I knew he had no right to
do that, yet as I had no friend in the world to go to, it alarmed me
greatly. At length he purposed my going a privateering, that I might by
these means, be enabled to pay him, to which I agreed. Our Captain's
name was ———— ————; I went in Character of Cook to him. Near St.
Domingo we came up to five French ships, Merchantmen. We had a
very smart engagement that continued from eight in the morning until
three in the afternoon, when victory declared on our side. Soon after
this we were met by three English ships which joined us, and that encouraged us to attack a fleet of thirty-six ships. We boarded the three
first and then followed the others; and had the same success with
twelve, but the rest escaped us. There was a great deal of bloodshed,
and I was near death several times, but the Lord preserved me.

I met with many enemies, and much persecution, among the sailors; one of them was particularly unkind to me, and studied ways to
vex and tease me. I can't help mentioning one circumstance that hurt
me more than all the rest, which was that he snatched a book out of my
hand that I was very fond of, and used frequently to amuse myself
with, and threw it into the sea.—But what is remarkable [is that] he was
the first that was killed in our engagement. I don't pretend to say that
this happened because he was not my friend; but I thought it was a very
awful Providence to see how the enemies of the Lord are cut off.

Our Captain was a cruel hard-hearted man. I was excessively sorry
for the prisoners we took in general; but the pitiable case of one young
Gentleman grieved me to the heart. He appeared very amiable; was
strikingly handsome. Our Captain took four thousand pounds from
him; but that did not satisfy him, as he imagined he was possessed of
more, and had somewhere concealed it, so that the Captain threatened
him with death, at which he appeared in the deepest distress, and took
the buckles out of his shoes, and untied his hair, which was very fine,
and long; and in which several very valuable rings were fastened. He
came into the cabin to me, and in the most obliging terms imaginable
asked for something to eat and drink; which when I gave him, he was
so thankful and pretty in his manner that my heart bled for him; and I
heartily wished that I could have spoken in any language in which the
ship's crew would not have understood me, that I might have let him
know his danger; for I heard the Captain say he was resolved upon his
death; and he put his barbarous design into execution, for he took him
on shore with one of the sailors, and there they shot him.

This circumstance affected me exceedingly; I could not put him out of my mind [for] a long while. When we returned to New York the Captain divided the prize money among us, that we had taken. When I was called upon to receive my part, I waited upon Mr. ——— (the Gentleman that paid my debt and was the occasion of my going abroad), to know if he chose to go with me to receive my money or if I should bring him what I owed. He chose to go with me; and when the Captain laid my money on the table (it was one hundred and thirty-five pounds) I desired Mr. ——— to take what I was indebted to him; and he swept it all into his handkerchief, and would never be prevailed on to give a farthing of money, nor anything at all beside. And he like-wise secured a hogshead of sugar which was my due from the same ship. The Captain was very angry with him for this piece of cruelty to me, as was every other person that heard it. But I have reason to believe (as he was one of the Principal Merchants in the city) that he trans-acted business for him and on that account did not choose to quarrel with him.

At this time a very worthy Gentleman, a Wine Merchant, his name Dunscum, took me under his protection, and would have recovered my money for me if I had chose it; but I told him to let it alone; that I would rather be quiet. I believed that it would not prosper with him, and so it happened, for by a series of losses and misfortunes he became poor, and was soon after drowned, as he was on a party of pleasure. The vessel was driven out to sea, and struck against a rock by which means every soul perished.

I was very much distressed when I heard it, and felt greatly for his family who were reduced to very low circumstances. I never knew how to set a proper value on money. If I had but a little meat and drink to supply the present necessaries of life, I never wished for more; and when I had any I always gave it if ever I saw an object in distress. If it was not for my dear Wife and Children I should pay as little regard to money now as I did at that time. I continued some time with Mr. Dun-scum as his servant; he was very kind to me. But I had a vast inclination to visit England, and wished continually that it would please provi-dence to make a clear way for me to see this Island. I entertained a no-tion that if I could get to England I should never more experience either cruelty or ingratitude, so that I was very desirous to get among Christians. I knew Mr. Whitefield very well. I had heard him preach often at New York. In this disposition I enlisted in the Twenty-eighth Regiment of Foot, who were designed [destined] for Martinique in the late war. We went in Admiral Pocock's fleet from New York to Barbados; from thence to Martinique. When that was taken we proceeded to Havana, and took that place likewise. There I got discharged.

I was then worth about thirty pounds, but I never regarded money in the least, nor would I tarry to receive my prize money least I should lose my chance of going to England. I went with the Spanish prisoners to Spain; and came to Old England with the English prisoners. I cannot describe my joy when we were within sight of Portsmouth. But I was astonished when we landed to hear the inhabitants of that place curse and swear, and otherwise profane. I expected to find nothing but goodness, gentleness and meekness in this Christian Land, I then suffered great perplexities of mind.

I inquired if any serious Christian people resided there, [and] the woman I made this inquiry of, answered me in the affirmative, and added that she was one of them. I was heartily glad to hear her say so. I thought I could give her my whole heart: she kept a Public House. I deposited with her all the money that I had not an immediate occasion for, as I thought it would be safer with her. It was twenty-five guineas but six of them I desired her to lay out to the best advantage, to buy me some shirts, [a] hat and some other necessaries. I made her a present of a very handsome large looking glass that I brought with me from Martinique, in order to recompense her for the trouble I had given her. I must do this woman the justice to acknowledge that she did lay out some little for my use, but the nineteen guineas and part of the six, with my watch, she would not return, but denied that I ever gave it [to] her.

I soon perceived that I was got among bad people, who defrauded me of my money and watch; and that all my promised happiness was blasted; I had no friend but God and I prayed to Him earnestly. I could scarcely believe it possible that the place where so many eminent Christians had lived and preached could abound with so much wickedness and deceit. I thought it worse than *Sodom* (considering the great advantages they have); I cried like a child and that almost continually: at length God heard my prayers and raised me a friend indeed.

This publican [innkeeper] had a brother who lived on Portsmouth common, his wife was a very serious good woman.—When she heard of the treatment I had met with, she came and inquired into my real situation and was greatly troubled at the ill usage I had received, and took me home to her own house. I began now to rejoice, and my prayer was turned into praise. She made use of all the arguments in her power to prevail on her who had wronged me, to return my watch and money, but it was to no purpose, as she had given me no receipt and I had nothing to show for it, I could not demand it. My good friend was excessively angry with her and obliged her to give me back four guineas, which she said she gave me out of charity: though in fact it was my own, and much more. She would have employed some rougher means to oblige her to give up my money, but I would not suffer her. [L]et it go says I, "My God is in heaven." Still I did not mind my loss in the least; all that grieved me was, that I had been disappointed in finding some Christian friends, with whom I hoped to enjoy a little sweet and comfortable society.

I thought the best method that I could take now, was to go to London, and find out Mr. Whitefield, who was the only living soul I knew in England, and get him to direct me to some way or other to procure a living without being troublesome to any person. I took leave of my Christian friend at Portsmouth, and went in the stage to London. A creditable tradesman in the city, who went up with me in the stage, offered to show me the way to Mr. Whitefield's tabernacle. Knowing that I was a perfect stranger, I thought it very kind, and accepted his offer; but he obliged me to give him half a crown for going with me, and likewise insisted on my giving him five shillings more for conducting me to Dr. Gifford's Meeting.

I began now to entertain a very different idea of the inhabitants of England than what I had figured to myself before I came amongst them. Mr. Whitefield received me very friendly, was heartily glad to see me, and directed me to a proper place to board and lodge in Petticoat Lane, till he could think of some way to settle me in, and paid for my lodging, and all my expenses. The morning after I came to my new lodging, as I was at breakfast with the gentlewoman of the house, I heard the noise of some looms over our heads: I inquired what it was; she told me a person was weaving silk. I expressed a great desire to see it, and asked if I might: She told me she would go up with me; she was sure I should be very welcome. She was as good as her word, and as soon as we entered the room, the person that was weaving looked about, and smiled upon us, and I loved her from that moment. She asked me many questions, and I in turn talked a great deal to her. I found she was a member of Mr. Allen's Meeting, and I began to entertain a good opinion of her, though I was almost afraid to indulge this inclination, least she should prove like all the rest I had met with at Portsmouth, and which had almost given me a dislike to all white women. But after a short acquaintance I had the happiness to find she was very different, and quite sincere, and I was not without hope that she entertained some esteem for me. We often went together to hear Dr. Gifford, and as I had always a propensity to relieve every object in distress as far as I was able, I used to give to all that complained to me; sometimes half a guinea at a time, as I did not understand the real value of it.—This gracious, good woman took great pains to correct and advise me in that and many other respects.

After I had been in London about six weeks I was recommended to the notice of some of my late Master Mr. Freelandhouse's acquaintance, who had heard him speak frequently of me. I was much persuaded by them to go to Holland. My Master lived there before he bought me, and used to speak of me so respectfully among his friends there, that it raised in them a curiosity to see me; particularly the gentlemen engaged in the ministry, who expressed a desire to hear my experience and examine me. I found that it was my good old master's design that I should have gone if he had lived; for which reason I resolved upon going to Holland, and informed my dear friend Mr. Whitefield of my intention; he was much averse to my going at first, but after I gave him my reasons appeared very well satisfied. I likewise informed my Betty (the good woman that I have mentioned above) of my determination to go to Holland and I told her that I believed she was to be my wife: that if it was the Lord's will I desired it, but not else. She made me very little answer, but has since told me, she did not think it at that time.

I embarked at Tower wharf at four o'clock in the morning, and arrived at Amsterdam the next day by three o'clock in the afternoon. I had several letters of recommendation to my old master's friends, who received me very graciously. Indeed, one of the chief Ministers was particularly good to me; he kept me at his house a long while, and took great pleasure in asking questions, which I answered with delight, being always ready to say, *"Come unto me all ye that fear God, and I will tell what he hath done for my soul."* I cannot but admire the footsteps of providence; astonished that I should be so wonderfully preserved! Though the Grandson of a King, I have wanted bread, and should have been glad of the hardest crust I ever saw. I who, at home, was surrounded and guarded by slaves, so that no indifferent person might approach me, and clothed with gold, have been inhumanly threatened with death; and frequently wanted clothing to defend me from the inclemency of the weather; yet I never murmured, nor was I discontent. I am willing, and even desirous to be counted as nothing, a stranger in the world, and a pilgrim here; for "*I know that my* Redeemer *liveth*," and I'm thankful for every trial and trouble that I've met with, as I am not without hope that they have been all sanctified to me.

The Calvinist Ministers desired to hear my experience from myself, which proposal I was very well pleased with: So I stood before thirty-eight Ministers every Thursday for seven weeks together, and they were all very well satisfied and persuaded I was what I pretended to be. They wrote down my experience as I spoke it; and the Lord Almighty was with me at that time in a remarkable manner, and gave me words and enabled me to answer them; so great was his mercy to take me in hand a poor blind heathen.

At this time a very rich Merchant at Amsterdam offered to take me into his family in the capacity of his Butler, and I very willingly accepted it. He was a gracious worthy Gentleman and very good to me. He treated me more like a friend than a servant. I tarried there a twelvemonth but was not thoroughly contented, I wanted to see my wife (that is now); and for that reason I wished to return to England. I wrote to her once in my absence, but she did not answer my letter; and I must acknowledge if she had, it would have given me a less opinion of her. My Master and Mistress persuaded me much not to leave them and likewise their two sons who entertained a good opinion of me; and if I had found my Betty married on my arrival in England, I should have returned to them again immediately.

My Lady purposed my marrying her maid; she was an agreeable young woman, had saved a good deal of money, but I could not fancy her, though she was willing to accept of me, but I told her my inclinations were engaged in England, and I could think of no other Person. On my return home, I found my Betty disengaged. She had refused several offers in my absence, and told her sister that, she thought, if ever she married I was to be her husband.

Soon after I came home, I waited on Doctor Gifford who took me into his family and was exceedingly good to me. The character of this pious worthy Gentleman is well known; my praise can be of no use or signification at all. I hope I shall ever gratefully remember the many favors I have received from him. Soon after I came to Doctor Gifford I expressed a desire to be admitted into their Church, and sat down with them; they told me I must first be baptized; so I gave in my experience before the Church, with which they were very well satisfied, and I was baptized by Doctor Gifford with some others. I then made known my intentions of being married; but I found there were many objections against it because the person I had fixed on was poor. She was a widow, her husband had left her in debt, and with a child, so that they persuaded me against it out of real regard to me. But I had promised and was resolved to have her; as I knew her to be a gracious woman, her poverty was no objection to me, as they had nothing else to say against her. When my friends found that they could not alter my opinion respecting her, they wrote to Mr. Allen, the minister she attended, to persuade her to leave me; but he replied that he would not interfere at all, that we might do as we would. I was resolved that all my wife's little debt should be paid before we were married; so that I sold almost everything I had and with all the money I could raise cleared all that she owed, and I never did anything with a better will in all my Life, because I firmly believed that we should be very happy together, and so it proved, for she was given me from the Lord. And I have found her a blessed partner, and we have never repented, although we have gone through many great troubles and difficulties.

My wife got a very good living by weaving, and could do extremely well; but just at that time there was great disturbance among the weavers; so that I was afraid to let my wife work, least they should insist on my joining the rioters which I could not think of, and, possibly, if I had refused to do so they would have knocked me on the head. So that by these means my wife could get no employ, neither had I work enough to maintain my family. We had not yet been married a year before all these misfortunes overtook us.

Just at this time a gentleman, that seemed much concerned for us, advised me to go into Essex with him and promised to get me employed. I accepted his kind proposal, and he spoke to a friend of his, a Quaker, a gentleman of large fortune, who resided a little way out of the town of Colchester; his name was *Handbarar*; he ordered his steward to set me to work.

There were several employed in the same way with myself. I was very thankful and contented though my wages were but small. I was allowed but eight pence a day, and found [took care of] myself; but after I had been in this situation for a fortnight, my master, being told that a Black was at work for him, had an inclination to see me. He was pleased to talk to me for some time, and at last inquired what wages I had; when I told him he declared it was too little, and immediately ordered his steward to let me have eighteen pence a day, which he constantly gave me after; and I then did extremely well.

I did not bring my wife with me: I came first alone and it was my design, if things answered according to our wishes, to send for her. I was now thinking to desire her to come to me when I received a letter to inform me she was just brought to bed and in want of many necessaries. This news was a great trial to me and a fresh affliction; but my God, *faithful and abundant in mercy*, forsook me not in this trouble. As I could not read English, I was obliged to apply to someone to read the letter I received, relative to my wife. I was directed by the good providence of God to a worthy young gentleman, a Quaker, and friend of my Master. I desired he would take the trouble to read my letter for me, which he readily complied with and was greatly moved and affected at the contents; insomuch that he said he would undertake to make a gathering for me, which he did and was the first to contribute to it himself. The money was sent that evening to London by a person who happened to be going there; nor was this all the goodness that I experienced from these kind friends, for, as soon as my wife came about and was fit to travel, they sent for her to me, and were at the whole expense of her coming; so evidently has the love and mercy of God appeared through every trouble that ever I experienced. We went on very comfortably all the summer. We lived in a little cottage near Mr. *Handbarar's* house; but when the winter came on I was discharged, as he had no further occasion for me. And now the prospect began to darken upon us again. We thought it most advisable to move our habitation a little nearer to the town, as the house we lived in was very cold, and wet, and ready to tumble down.

The boundless goodness of God to me has been so very great, that with the most humble gratitude I desire to prostrate myself before Him; for I have been wonderfully supported in every affliction. My God never left me. I perceived light *still* through the thickest darkness.

My dear wife and I were now both unemployed, we could get nothing to do. The winter proved remarkably severe, and we were reduced to the greatest distress imaginable. I was always very shy of asking for anything; I could never beg; neither did I choose to make known our wants to any person, for fear of offending as we were entire strangers; but our last bit of bread was gone, and I was obliged to think of something to do for our support. I did not mind for myself at all; but to see my dear wife and children in want pierced me to the heart. I now blamed myself for bringing her from London, as doubtless had we continued there we might have found friends to keep us from starving. The snow was at this season remarkably deep; so that we could see no prospect of being relieved. In this melancholy situation, not knowing what step to pursue, I resolved to make my case known to a Gentleman's Gardener that lived near us, and entreat him to employ me: but when I came to him, my courage failed me, and I was ashamed to make known our real situation. I endeavored all I could to prevail on him to set me to work, but to no purpose: he assured me it was not in his power: but just as I was about to leave him, he asked me if I would accept of some carrots? I took them with great thankfulness and carried them home: he gave me four, they were very large and fine. We had nothing to make fire with, so consequently could not boil them, but was glad to have them to eat raw. Our youngest child was quite an infant; so that my wife was obliged to chew it, and fed her in that manner for several days. We allowed ourselves but one every day, lest they should not last till we could get some other supply. I was unwilling to eat at all myself; nor would I take any the last day that we continued in this situation, as I could not bear the thought that my dear wife and children would be in want of every means of support. We lived in this manner, till our carrots were all gone: then my wife began to lament because of our poor babies: but I comforted her all I could, still hoping, and believing that *my* God would not let us die but that it would please Him to relieve us, which *He* did by almost a Miracle.

We went to bed, as usual, before it was quite dark (as we had neither fire nor candle), but had not been there long before some person knocked at the door and inquired if *James Albert* lived there? I answered in the affirmative, and rose immediately; as soon as I opened the door I found it was the servant of an eminent Attorney who resided at Colchester. He asked me how it was with me? if I was not almost starved? I burst out crying, and told him I was indeed. He said his master supposed so, and that he wanted to speak with me, and I must return with him. This gentleman's name was Daniel, he was a sincere, good Christian. He used to stand and talk with me frequently when I worked in the road for Mr. *Handbarar,* and would have employed me himself, if I had wanted work. When I came to his house he told me that he had thought a good deal about me of late, and was apprehensive that I must be in want, and could not be satisfied till he sent to inquire after me. I made known my distress to him, at which he was greatly affected, and generously gave me a guinea, and promised to be kind to me in future. I could not help exclaiming, *O the boundless mercies of my God!* I prayed unto Him, and He has heard me; I trusted in Him and He has preserved me: where shall I begin to praise Him, or how shall I love Him enough?

I went immediately and bought some bread and cheese and coal and carried it home. My dear wife was rejoiced to see me return with something to eat. She instantly got up and dressed our babies, while I made a fire, and the first nobility in the land never made a more comfortable meal. We did not forget to thank the Lord for all his goodness to us. Soon after this, as the spring came on, Mr. Peter *Daniel* employed me in helping to pull down a house, and rebuilding it. I had then very good work, and full employ: he sent for my wife and children to *Colchester*, and provided us a house where we lived very comfortably. I hope I shall always gratefully acknowledge his kindness to myself and family. I worked at this house for more than a year, till it was finished; and after that I was employed by several successively, and was never so happy as when I had something to do; but perceiving the winter coming on, and work rather slack, I was apprehensive that we should again be in want or become troublesome to our friends.

I had at this time an offer made me of going to *Norwich* and having constant employ.—My wife seemed pleased with this proposal, as she supposed she might get work there in the weaving manufactory, being the business she was brought up to, and more likely to succeed there than any other place; and we thought as we had an opportunity of moving to a town where we could both be employed[,] it was most advisable to do so; and that probably we might settle there for our lives. When this step was resolved on, I went first alone to see how it would answer; which I very much repented after, for it was not in my power immediately to send my wife any supply, as I fell into the hands of a Master that was neither kind nor considerate; and she was reduced to great distress, so that she was obliged to sell the few goods that we had, and when I sent for her was under the disagreeable necessity of parting with our bed.

When she came to *Norwich* I hired a room ready furnished. I experienced a great deal of difference in the carriage of my master from what I had been accustomed to from some of my other masters. He was very irregular in his payments to me. My wife hired a loom and wove all the leisure time she had and we began to do very well, till we were overtaken by fresh misfortunes. Our three poor children fell ill of the smallpox; this was a great trial to us; but still I was persuaded in myself we should not be forsaken. And I did all in my power to keep my dear partner's spirits from sinking. Her whole attention now was taken up with the children as she could mind nothing else, and all I could get was but little to support a family in such a situation, beside paying for the hire of our room, which I was obliged to omit doing for several weeks: but the woman to whom we were indebted would not excuse us, although I promised she should have the very first money we could get after my children came about; but she would not be satisfied and had the cruelty to threaten us that if we did not pay her immediately she would turn us all into the street.

The apprehension of this plunged me in the deepest distress, considering the situation of my poor babies: if they had been in health I should have been less sensible of this misfortune. But my God, *still faithful to his promise,* raised me a friend. Mr. Henry Gurdney, a Quaker, a gracious gentleman, heard of our distress; he sent a servant of his own to the woman we hired the room of, paid our rent, and bought all the goods with my wife's loom and gave it us all.

Some other gentlemen, hearing of his design, were pleased to assist him in these generous acts, for which we never can be thankful enough; after this my children soon came about; we began to do pretty well again. My dear wife worked hard and constant when she could get work, but it was upon a disagreeable footing as her employ was so uncertain, sometimes she could get nothing to do and at other times when the weavers of *Norwich* had orders from London they were so excessively hurried, that the people they employed were often obliged to work on the *sabbath-day;* but this my wife would never do, and it was [a] matter of uneasiness to us that we could not get our living in a regular manner, although we were both diligent, industrious, and willing to work. I was far from being happy in my master, he did not use me well. I could scarcely ever get my money from him; but I continued patient[ly] till it pleased God to alter my situation.

My worthy friend Mr. Gurdney advised me to follow the employ of chopping chaff, and bought me an instrument for that purpose. There were but few people in the town that made this their business beside myself; so that I did very well indeed and we became easy and happy. But we did not continue long in this comfortable state: Many of the inferior people were envious and ill-natured and set up the same employ and worked under price on purpose to get my business from me, and they succeeded so well that I could hardly get anything to do, and became again unfortunate. Nor did this misfortune come alone, for just at this time we lost one of our little girls who died of a fever; this circumstance occasioned us new troubles, for the Baptist Minister refused to bury her because we were not their members. The Parson of the parish denied us because she had never been baptized. I applied to the Quakers, but met with no success; this was one of the greatest trials I ever met with, as we did not know what to do with our poor baby. At length I resolved to dig a grave in the garden behind the house, and bury her there when the parson of the parish sent for me to tell me he would bury the child, but did not choose to read the burial service over her. I told him I did not mind whether he would or not, as the child could not hear it.

We met with a great deal of ill treatment after this, and found it very difficult to live. We could scarcely get work to do, and were obliged to pawn our clothes. We were ready to sink under our troubles, [w]hen I purposed to my wife to go to *Kidderminster* and try if we could do there. I had always an inclination for that place, and now more than ever as I had heard *Mr. Fawcet* mentioned in the most respectful manner, as a pious worthy gentleman, and I had seen his name in a favorite book of mine, Baxter's *Saints Everlasting Rest*; and as the manufactory of *Kidderminster* seemed to promise my wife some employment, she readily came into my way of thinking.

I left her once more, and set out for *Kidderminster* in order to judge if the situation would suit us. As soon as I came there I waited immediately on *Mr. Fawcet*, who was pleased to receive me very kindly and recommended me to *Mr. Watson* who employed me in twisting silk and worsted together. I continued here about a fortnight, and when I thought it would answer our expectation, I returned to *Norwich* to fetch my wife; she was then near her time, and too much indisposed. So we were obliged to tarry until she was brought to bed, and as soon as she could conveniently travel we came to *Kidderminster*, but we brought nothing with us as we were obliged to sell all we had to pay our debts and the expenses of my wife's illness, etc.

Such is our situation at present. My wife, by hard labor at the loom, does everything that can be expected from her towards the maintenance of our family; and God is pleased to incline the hearts of his people at times to yield us their charitable assistance, being myself through age and infirmity able to contribute but little to their support. As Pilgrims, and very poor Pilgrims, we are traveling through many difficulties towards our Heavenly Home, and waiting patiently for his gracious call, when the Lord shall deliver us out of the evils of this present world and bring us to the Everlasting Glories of the world to come. To Him be Praise for Ever and Ever, Amen.

NARRATIVE

OF THE

LORD's wonderful DEALINGS

WITH

JOHN MARRANT,

A BLACK,

(Now going to Preach the GOSPEL in NOVA-SCOTIA)

Born in NEW-YORK, in NORTH-AMERICA.

Taken down from his own RELATION,

ARRANGED, CORRECTED, and PUBLISHED

By the Rev. Mr. *ALDRIDGE*.

THE SECOND EDITION

THY PEOPLE SHALL BE WILLING IN THE DAY OF
THY POWER, Psa. 110: 3

DECLARE HIS WONDERS AMONG ALL PEOPLE,
Psa. 96: 3

Printed by GILBERT and PLUMMER, No. 13, Cree-Church-Lane, 1785

And sold at the CHAPEL in JEWRY-STREET.–Price 6d.

2

NARRATIVE OF THE LORD'S

WONDERFUL DEALINGS WITH

JOHN MARRANT,

A BLACK

PREFACE

Reader,

THE FOLLOWING NARRATIVE is as plain and artless, as it is surprising and extraordinary. Plausible reasonings may amuse and delight, but facts, and facts like these, strike, are felt, and go home to the heart. Were the power, grace, and providence of God ever more eminently displayed, than in the conversion, success, and deliverances of John Marrant? He and his companion enter the meeting at Charleston together; but the one is taken, and the other is left. He is struck to the ground, shaken over the mouth of hell, snatched as a brand from the burning; he is pardoned and justified; he is washed in the atoning blood, and made happy in his God. You soon have another view of him, drinking into his master's cup; he is tried and perplexed, opposed and despised; the neighbors hoot at him as he goes along; his mother, sisters and brother, hate and persecute him; he is friendless, and forsaken of all. These uneasy circumstances call forth the corruptions of his nature, and create a momentary debate, whether the pursuit of ease and pleasure was not to be preferred to the practice of religion, which he now found so sharp and severe? The stripling is supported and strengthened. He is persuaded to forsake his family and kindred altogether. He crosses the fence, which marked the boundary between the wilderness and the cultivated country; and prefers the habitations of brutal residence, to the less hospitable dwellings of enmity to God and godliness. He wanders, but Christ is his guide and protector. Who can view him among the Indian tribes without wonder? He arrives among the Cherokees, where gross ignorance wore its rudest forms, and savage despotism exercised its most terrifying empire. Here the child, just turned fourteen, without sling or stone, engages, and with the arrow of prayer pointed with faith, wounded *Goliah* [Goliath], and conquers the king.

The untutored monarch feels the truth, and worships the God of the Christians; the seeds of the Gospel are disseminated among the Indians by a youthful hand, and Jesus is received and obeyed.

The subsequent incidents related in this Narrative are great and affecting; but I must not anticipate the reader's pleasure and profit.

The novelty or magnitude of the facts contained in the following pages, may dispose some readers to question the truth of them. My answer to such is,—1. I believe it is clear to great numbers, and to some competent judges, that God is with the subject of them; but if he knowingly permitted an untruth to go abroad in the name of God, whilst it is confessed the Lord is with him, would it not follow, that the Almighty gave his sanction to a falsehood?—2. I have observed him to pay a conscientious regard to his word.—3. He appeared to me to feel most sensibly, when he related those parts of his Narrative, which describe his happiest moments with God, or the most remarkable interpositions of Divine Providence for him; and I have no reason to believe it was counterfeited.

I have always preserved Mr. Marrant's ideas, tho' I could not his language; no more alterations, however, have been made, than were thought necessary.

I now commit the whole to God.—That he may make it generally useful is the prayer of thy ready servant, for Christ's sake,

W. Aldridge.
London,
July 19th, 1785.

A NARRATIVE, ETC.

I JOHN MARRANT, born June 15th, 1755, in New York, in North America, with these gracious dealings of the Lord with me to be published, in hopes they may be useful to others, to encourage the fearful, to confirm the wavering, and to refresh the hearts of true believers. My father died when I was little more than four years of age, and before I was five my mother removed from New York to St. Augustine, about seven hundred miles from that city. Here I was sent to school, and taught to read and spell; after we had resided here about eighteen months, it was found necessary to remove to Georgia, where we remained; and I was kept to school until I had attained my eleventh year. The Lord spoke to me in my early days, by these removes, if I could have understood him, and said, "Here we have no continuing city."

We left Georgia, and went to Charleston, where it was intended I should be put apprentice to some trade. Sometime after I had been in Charleston, as I was walking one day, I passed by a school, and heard music and dancing, which took my fancy very much, and I felt a strong inclination to learn the music. I went home, and informed my sister, that I had rather learn to play upon music than go to a trade. She told me she could do nothing in it, until she had acquainted my mother with my desire. Accordingly she wrote a letter upon it to my mother, which, when she read, the contents were disapproved of by her, and she came to Charleston to prevent it. She persuaded me much against it, but her persuasions were fruitless. Disobedience either to God or man, being one of the fruits of sin, grew out from me in early buds. Finding I was set upon it, and resolved to learn nothing else, she agreed to it, and went with me to speak to the man, and to settle upon the best terms with him she could. He insisted upon twenty pounds down, which was paid, and I was engaged to stay with him eighteen months, and my mother to find me everything during that term. The first day I went to him he put the violin into my hand, which pleased me much, and, applying close, I learned very fast, not only to play, but to dance also; so that in six months I was able to play for the whole school. In the evenings after the scholars were dismissed, I used to resort to the bottom of our garden, where it was customary for some musicians to assemble to blow the French horn. Here my improvement was so rapid, that in a twelvemonth's time I became master both of the violin and of the French horn, and was much respected by the Gentlemen and Ladies whose children attended the school, as also by my master[.] This opened to me a large door of vanity and vice, for I was invited to all the balls and assemblies that were held in the town, and met with the general applause of the inhabitants. I was a stranger to want, being supplied with as much money as I had any occasion for; which my sister observing, said "You have now no need of a trade." I was now in my thirteenth year, devoted to pleasure and drinking in iniquity like water; a slave to every vice suited to my nature and to my years. The time I had engaged to serve my master being expired, he persuaded me to stay with him, and offered me anything, or any money, not to leave him. His intreaties proving ineffectual, I quitted his service, and visited my mother in the country; with her I stayed two months, living without God or hope in the world, fishing and hunting on the sabbath-day.

Unstable as water I returned to town, and wished to go to some trade. My sister's husband being informed of my inclination provided me with a master, on condition that I should serve him one year and a half on trial, and afterwards be bound, if he approved of me. Accordingly I went, but every evening I was sent for to play on music, somewhere or another; and I often continued out very late, sometimes all night, so as to render me incapable of attending my master's business the next day; yet in this manner I served him a year and four months, and was much approved of by him. He wrote a letter to my mother to come and have me bound, and whilst my mother was weighing the matter in her own mind, the gracious purposes of God, respecting a perishing sinner, were now to be disclosed. One evening I was sent for in a very particular manner to go and play for some Gentlemen, which I agreed to do, and was on my way to fulfill my promise; and passing by a large meeting house I saw many lights in it, and crowds of people going in. I inquired what it meant, and was answered by my companion, that a crazy man was hallooing [shouting] there; this raised my curiosity to go in, that I might hear what he was hallooing about. He persuaded me not to go in, but in vain. He then said, "If you will do one thing I will go in with you." I asked him what that was? He replied, "Blow the French horn among them." I liked the proposal well enough, but expressed my fears of being beaten for disturbing them; but upon his promising to stand by and defend me, I agreed. So we went, and with much difficulty got within the doors. I was pushing the people to make room, to get the horn off my shoulder to blow it, just as Mr. Whitefield was naming his text, and looking round, and, as I thought, directly upon me, and pointing with his finger, he uttered these words, "Prepare to meet thy God, O Israel." The Lord accompanied the word with such power, that I was struck to the ground, and lay both speechless and senseless for twenty-four minutes: When I was come a little to, I found two men attending me, and a woman throwing water in my face, and holding a smelling bottle to my nose; and when something more recovered, every word I heard from the minister was like a parcel of swords thrust into me, and what added to my distress, I thought I saw the devil on every side of me. I was constrained in the bitterness of my spirit to halloo out in the midst of the congregation, which disturbing them, they took me away; but finding I could neither walk or stand, they carried me as far as the vestry, and there I remained till the service was over. When the people were dismissed Mr. Whitefield came into the vestry, and being told of my condition he came immediately, and the first word he said to me was, "Jesus Christ has got thee at last." He asked where I lived, intending to come and see me the next day; but recollecting he was to leave the town the next morning, he said he could not come himself, but would send another minister; he desired them to get me home, and then taking his leave of me, I saw him no more. When I reached my sister's house, being carried by two men, she was very uneasy to see me in so distressed a condition. She got me to bed, and sent for a doctor, who came immediately, and after looking at me, he went home, and sent me a bottle of mixture, and desired her to give me a spoonful every two hours; but I could not take anything the doctor sent, nor indeed keep in bed; this distressed my sister very much, and she cried out, "The lad will surely die." She sent for two other doctors, but no medicine they prescribed could I take. No, no; it may be asked, a wounded spirit who can cure? as well as who can bear? In this distress of soul I continued for three days without any food, only a little water now and then. On the fourth day, the minister Mr. Whitefield had desired to visit me [and] came to see me, and being directed upstairs, when he entered the room, I thought he made my distress much worse. He wanted to take hold of my hand, but I durst [dared] not give it to him. He insisted upon taking hold of it, and I then got away from him on the other side of the bed; but being very weak I fell down, and before I could recover he came to me and took me by the hand, and lifted me up, and after a few words desired to go to prayer. So he fell upon his knees, and pulled me down also; after he had

spent some time in prayer he rose up, and asked me now how I did; I
answered, much worse; he then said, "Come, we will have the old
thing over again," and so we kneeled down a second time, and after he
had prayed earnestly we got up, and he said again, "How do you do
now?" I replied worse and worse, and asked him if he intended to kill
me? "No, no," said he, "you are worth a thousand dead men, let us try
the old thing over again," and so falling upon our knees, he continued
in prayer a considerable time, and near the close of his prayer, the Lord
was pleased to set my soul at perfect liberty, and being filled with joy
I began to praise the Lord immediately; my sorrows were turned into
peace, and joy, and love. The minister said, "How is it now?" I answered, all is well, all happy. He then took his leave of me; but called
every day for several days afterwards, and the last time he said, "Hold
fast that thou hast already obtained, till Jesus Christ come." I now read
the Scriptures very much. My master sent often to know how I did,
and at last came himself, and finding me well, asked me if I would not
come to work again? I answered no. He asked me the reason, but receiving no answer he went away. I continued with my sister about three
weeks, during which time she often asked me to play upon the violin
for her, which I refused; then she said I was crazy and mad, and so re-
ported it among the neighbors, which opened the mouths of all around
against me. I then resolved to go to my mother, which was eighty-four
miles from Charleston. I was two days on my journey home, and enjoyed much communion with God on the road, and had occasion to
mark the gracious interpositions of his kind providence as I passed
along. The third day I arrived at my mother's house, and was well received. At supper they sat down to eat without asking the Lord's blessing, which caused me to burst out into tears. My mother asked me
what was the matter? I answered, I wept because they sat down to
supper without asking the Lord's blessing. She bid me, with much surprise, to ask a blessing. I remained with her fourteen days without interruption; the Lord pitied me, being a young soldier. Soon, however,
Satan began to stir up my two sisters and brother, who were then at
home with my mother; they called me every name but that which was
good. The more they persecuted me, the stronger I grew in grace. At
length my mother turned against me also, and the neighbors joined
her, and there was not a friend to assist me, or that I could speak to; this
made me earnest with God. In these circumstances, being the youngest but one of our family, and young in Christian experience, I was
tempted so far as to threaten my life; but reading my Bible one day, and

finding that if I did destroy myself I could not come where God was, I betook myself to the fields, and some days stayed out from morning to night to avoid the persecutors. I stayed one time two days without any food, but seemed to have clearer views into the spiritual things of God. Not long after this I was sharply tried, and reasoned the matter within myself, whether I should turn to my old courses of sin and vice, or serve and cleave to the Lord; after prayer to God, I was fully persuaded in my mind, that if I turned to my old ways I should perish eternally. Upon this I went home, and finding them all as hardened, or worse than before, and everybody saying I was crazy; but a little sister I had, about nine years of age, used to cry when she saw them persecute me, and continuing so about five weeks and three days, I thought it was better for me to die than to live among such people. I rose one morning very early, to get a little quietness and retirement, I went into the woods, and stayed till eight o'clock in the morning; upon my return I found them all at breakfast; I passed by them, and went upstairs without any interruption; I went upon my knees to the Lord, and returned him thanks; then I took up a small pocket Bible and one of Dr. Watts's hymn books, and passing by them went out without one word spoken by any of us. After spending some time in the fields I was persuaded to go from home altogether. Accordingly I went over the fence, about half a mile from our house, which divided the inhabited and cultivated parts of the country from the wilderness. I continued traveling in the desert all day without the least inclination of returning back. About evening I began to be surrounded with wolves; I took refuge from them on a tree, and remained there all night. About eight o'clock next morning I descended from the tree, and returned God thanks for the mercies of the night. I went on all this day without anything to eat or drink. The third day, taking my Bible out of my pocket, I read and walked for some time, and then being wearied and almost spent I sat down, and after resting awhile I rose to go forward; but had not gone above a hundred yards when something tripped me up, and I fell down; I prayed to the Lord upon the ground that he would command the wild beasts to devour me, that I might be with him in glory. I made this request to God the third and part of the fourth day. The fourth day in the morning, descending from my usual lodging, a tree, and having nothing all this time to eat, and but a little water to drink, I was so feeble that I tumbled halfway down the tree, not being able to support myself, and lay upon my back on the ground an hour and a half, praying and crying; after which, getting a little strength, and trying to stand upright to walk, I found myself not able; then I went upon my hands and knees, and so crawled till I reached a tree that was tumbled down, in order to get across it, and there I prayed with my body leaning upon it above an hour, that the Lord would take me to himself. Such nearness to God I then enjoyed, that I willingly resigned myself into his hands. After some time I thought I was strengthened, so I got across the tree without my legs or feet touching the ground; but struggling I fell over on the other side, and then thought the Lord will now answer my prayer, and take me home: but the time was not come. After laying there a little, I rose, and looking about, saw at some distance bunches of grass, called deer grass; I felt a strong desire to get at it; though I rose, yet it was only on my hands and knees, being so feeble, and in this manner I reached the grass. I was three-quarters of an hour going in this form twenty yards. When I reached it I was unable to pull it up, so I bit it off like a horse, and prayed the Lord to bless it to me, and I thought it the best meal I ever had in my life, and I think so still, it was so sweet. I returned my God hearty thanks for it, and then lay down about an hour. Feeling myself very thirsty, I prayed the Lord to provide me with some water. Finding I was something strengthened I got up, and stood on my feet, and staggered from one tree to another, if they were near each other, otherwise the journey was too long for me. I continued moving so for some time, and at length passing between two trees, I happened to fall upon some bushes, among which were a few large hollow leaves, which had caught and contained the dews of the night, and lying low among the bushes, were not exhaled by the solar rays; this water in the leaves fell upon me as I tumbled down and was lost, I was now tempted to think the Lord had given me water from Heaven, and I had wasted it. I then prayed the Lord to forgive me. What poor unbelieving creatures we are! though we are assured the Lord will supply all our needs. I was presently directed to a puddle of water very muddy, which some wild pigs had just left; I kneeled down, and asked the Lord to bless it to me, so I drank both mud and water mixed together, and being satisfied I returned the Lord thanks, and went on my way rejoicing. This day was much checkered with wants and supplies, with dangers and deliverances. I continued traveling on for nine days, feeding upon grass, and not knowing whither I was going; but the Lord Jesus Christ was very present, and that comforted me through all. The next morning, having quitted my customary lodging, and returned thanks to the Lord for my preservation through the night, reading and traveling on, I passed between two bears, about twenty yards distance from each other. Both sat and looked at me, but I felt no fear; and after I had passed them, they both went the same way from me without growling, or the least apparent uneasiness. I went and returned God thanks for my escape, who had tamed the wild beasts of the forest, and made them friendly to me: I rose from my knees and walked on, singing hymns of praise to God, about five o'clock in the afternoon, and about fifty-five miles from home, right through the wilderness. As I was going on, and musing upon the goodness of the Lord, an Indian hunter, who stood at some distance, saw me; he hid himself behind a tree; but as I passed along he bolted out, and put his hands on my breast, which surprised me a few moments. He then asked me where I was going? I answered I did not know, but where the Lord was pleased to guide me. Having heard me praising God before I came up to him, he inquired who I was talking to? I told him I was talking to my Lord Jesus; he seemed surprised, and asked me where he was? for he did not see him there. I told him he could not be seen with bodily eyes. After a little more talk, he insisted upon taking me home; but I refused, and added, that I would die rather than return home. He then asked me if I knew how far I was from home? I answered, I did not know; you are fifty-five miles and a half, says he, from home. He further asked me how I did to live? I said I was supported by the Lord. He asked me how I slept? I answered, the Lord provided me with a bed every night; he further inquired what preserved me from being devoured by the wild beasts? I replied, the Lord Jesus Christ kept me from them. He stood astonished, and said, you say the Lord Jesus Christ do this, and do that, and do everything for you, he must be a very fine man, where is he? I replied, he is here present. To this he made me no answer, only said, I know you, and your mother and sister, and upon a little further conversation I found he did know them. This alarmed me, and I wept for fear he would take me home by force; but when he saw me so affected, he said he would not take me home if I would go with him. I objected against that, for fear he would rob me of my comfort and communion with God: But at last, being much pressed, I consented to go. Our employment for ten weeks and three days, was killing deer, and taking off their skins by day; the means of defense and security against our nocturnal enemies, always took up the evenings: We collected a number of large bushes, and placed them nearly in a circular form, which uniting at the extremity, afforded us both a verdant covering, and a sufficient shelter from the night dews. What moss we could gather was strewed upon the ground, and this composed our bed. A fire was kindled in the front of our temporary lodging room, and fed with fresh fuel all night, as we slept and watched by turns; and this was our defense from the dreadful animals, whose shining eyes and tremendous roar we often saw and heard during the night.

By constant conversation with the hunter, I acquired a fuller knowledge of the Indian tongue: This, together with the sweet communion I enjoyed with God, I have considered as a preparation for the great trial I was soon after to pass through.

The hunting season being now at an end, we left the woods, and directed our course towards a large Indian town, belonging to the Cherokee nation; and having reached it, I said to the hunter, they will not suffer me to enter in. He replied, as I was with him, nobody would interrupt me.

There was an Indian fortification all round the town, and a guard placed at each entrance. The hunter passed one of these without molestation, but I was stopped by the guard and examined. They asked me where I came from, and what was my business there? My companion of the woods attempted to speak for me, but was not permitted; he was taken away, and I saw him no more. I was now surrounded by about fifty men, and carried to one of their chiefs to be examined by him. When I came before him, he asked me what was my business there? I told him I came there with a hunter, whom I met with in the woods. He replied, "Did I not know that whoever came there without giving a better account of themselves than I did, was to be put to death?" I said I did not know it. Observing that I answered him so readily in his own language, he asked me where I learnt it? To this I returned no answer, but burst out into a flood of tears, and calling upon my Lord Jesus. At this he stood astonished, and expressed a concern for me, and said I was young. He asked me who my Lord Jesus was? To this I gave him no answer, but continued praying and weeping. Addressing himself to the officer who stood by him, he said he was sorry; but it was the law, and it must not be broken. I was then ordered to be taken away, and put into a place of confinement. They led me from their court into a low dark place, and thrust me into it, very dreary and dismal; they made fast the door, and set a watch. The judge sent for the executioner, and gave him his warrant for my execution in the afternoon of the next day. The executioner came, and gave me notice of it, which made me very happy, as the near prospect of death made me hope for a speedy deliverance from the body: And truly this dungeon became my chapel, for the Lord Jesus did not leave me in this great trouble, but was very present, so that I continued blessing him, and singing his praises all night without ceasing. The watch hearing the noise, informed the executioner that somebody had been in the dungeon with me all night; upon which he came in to see and to examine, with a great torch lighted in his hand, who it was I had with me; but finding nobody, he turned around, and asked me who it was? and I told him it was the Lord Jesus Christ; but he made no answer, turned away, went out, and locked the door. At the hour appointed for my execution I was taken out, and led to the destined spot, amidst a vast number of people. I praised the Lord all the way we went, and when we arrived at the place I understood the kind of death I was to suffer, yet, blessed be God, none of those things moved me. The executioner showed me a basket of turpentine wood, stuck full of small pieces, like skewers; he told me I was to be stripped naked, and laid down in the basket, and these sharp pegs were to be stuck into me, and then set on fire, and when they had burnt to my body, I was to be turned on the other side, and served in the same manner, and then to be taken by four men and thrown into the flame, which was to finish the execution. I burst into tears, and asked what I had done to deserve so cruel a death! To this he gave me no answer. I cried out, Lord, if it be thy will that it should be so, thy will be done: I then asked the executioner to let me go to prayer; he asked me to whom? I answered, to the Lord my God; he seemed surprised, and asked me where he was? I told him he was present; upon which he gave me leave. I desired them all to do as I did, so I fell down upon my knees, and mentioned to the Lord his delivering of the three children in the fiery furnace, and of Daniel in the lion's den, and had close communion with God. I prayed in English a considerable time, and about the middle of my prayer, the Lord impressed a strong desire upon my mind to turn into their language, and pray in their tongue. I did so, and with remarkable liberty, which wonderfully affected the people. One circumstance was very singular, and strikingly displays the power and grace of God. I believe the executioner was savingly converted to God. He rose from his knees, and embraced me round the middle, and was unable to speak for about five minutes; the first words he expressed, when he had utterance, were, "No man shall hurt thee till thou hast been to the king."

I was taken away immediately, and as we passed along, and I was reflecting upon the deliverance which the Lord had wrought out for me, and hearing the praises which the executioner was singing to the Lord, I must own I was utterly at a loss to find words to praise him. I broke out in these words, what can't the Lord Jesus do! and what power is like unto His! I will thank thee for what is passed, and trust thee for what is to come. I will sing thy praise with my feeble tongue whilst life and breath shall last, and when I fail to sound thy praises here, I hope to sing them round thy throne above: And thus, with unspeakable joy, I sung two verses of Dr. Watts's hymns:

> *My God, the spring of all my joys,*
> *The life of my delights;*
> *The glory of my brightest days,*
> *And comfort of my nights.*
> *In darkest shades, if thou appear,*
> *My dawning is begun;*
> *Thou art my soul's bright morning star;*
> *And thou my rising sun.*

Passing by the judge's door, he stopped us, and asked the executioner why he brought me back? The man fell upon his knees, and begged he would permit me to be carried before the king, which being granted, I went on, guarded by two hundred soldiers with bows and arrows. After many windings I entered the king's outward chamber, and after waiting some time he came to the door, and his first question was, how came I there? I answered, I came with a hunter whom I met with in the woods, and who persuaded me to come there. He then asked me how old I was? I told him not fifteen. He asked me how I was supported before I met with this man? I answered, by the Lord Jesus Christ, which seemed to confound him. He turned round, and asked me if he lived where I came from? I answered, yes, and here also. He looked about the room, and said he did not see him; but I told him I felt him. The executioner fell upon his knees, and intreated the king, and told him what he had felt of the same Lord. At this instant the king's eldest daughter came into the chamber, a person about nineteen years of age, and stood at my right-hand. I had a Bible in my hand, which she took out of it, and having opened it, she kissed it, and seemed much delighted with it. When she had put it into my hand again, the king asked me what it was? and I told him, the name of my God was recorded there; and, after several questions, he bid me read it, which I did, particularly the fifty-third chapter of Isaiah, in the most solemn manner I was able; and also the twenty-sixth chapter of Matthew's Gospel; and when I pronounced the name of Jesus, the particular effect it had upon me was observed by the king. When I had finished reading, he asked me why I read those names with so much reverence? I told him, because the Being to whom those names belonged made heaven and earth, and I and he; this he denied. I then pointed to the sun, and asked him who made the sun, and moon, and stars, and preserved them in their regular order? He said there was a man in their town that did it. I labored as much as I could to convince him to the contrary. His daughter took the book out of my hand a second time; she opened it, and kissed it again; her father bid her give it to me, which she did; but said, with much sorrow, the book would not speak to her. The executioner then fell upon his knees, and begged the king to let me go to prayer, which being granted, we all went upon our knees, and now the Lord displayed his glorious power. In the midst of the prayer some of them cried out, particularly the king's daughter, and the man who ordered me to be executed, and several others seemed under deep conviction of sin: This made the king very angry; he called me a witch, and commanded me to be thrust into the prison, and to be executed the next morning. This was enough to make me think, as old Jacob once did, "All these things are against me"; for I was dragged away, and thrust into the dungeon with much indignation; but God, who never forsakes his people, was with me. Though I was weak in body, yet was I strong in the spirit: The Lord works, and who shall let it? The executioner went to the king, and assured him, that if he put me to death, his daughter would never be well. They used the skill of all their doctors that afternoon and night; but physical prescriptions were useless. In the morning the executioner came to me, and, without opening the prison door, called to me, and hearing me answer, said, "Fear not, thy God who delivered thee yesterday, will deliver thee today." This comforted me very much, especially to find he could trust the Lord. Soon after I was fetched out; I thought it was to be executed; but they led me away to the king's chamber with much bodily weakness, having been without food two days. When I came into the king's presence, he said to me, with much anger, if I did not make his daughter and that man well, I should be laid down and chopped into pieces before him. I was not afraid, but the Lord tried my faith sharply. The king's daughter and the other person were brought out into the outer chamber, and we went to prayer; but the heavens were locked up to my petitions. I besought the Lord again, but received no answer; I cried again, and He was intreated. He said, "Be it to thee as thou wilt"; the Lord appeared most lovely and glorious; the king himself was awakened, and the others set at liberty. A great change took place among the people; the king's house became God's house; the soldiers were ordered away, and the poor condemned prisoner had perfect liberty, and was treated like a prince. Now the Lord made all my enemies to become my great friends. I remained nine weeks in the king's palace, praising God day and night: I was never out but three days all the time. I had assumed the habit of the country, and was dressed much like the king, and nothing was too good for me. The king would take off his golden ornaments, his chain and bracelets, like a child, if I objected to them, and lay them aside. Here I learnt to speak their tongue in the highest style.

I began now to feel an inclination growing upon me to go farther on, but none to return home. The king being acquainted with this, expressed his fears of my being used ill by the next Indian nation, and, to prevent it, sent fifty men, and a recommendation to the king, with me. The next nation was called the Creek Indians, at sixty miles distance. Here I was received with kindness, owing to the king's influence, from whom I had parted; here I stayed five weeks. I next visited the Catawar Indians, at about fifty-five miles distance from the others. Lastly, I went among the Housaw Indians, eighty miles distant from the last mentioned: here I stayed seven weeks. These nations were then at peace with each other, and I passed among them without danger, being recommended from one to the other. When they recollect, that the white people drove them from the American shores, the three first nations have often united, and murdered all the white people in the back settlements which they could lay hold of, man, woman, and child. I had not much reason to believe any of these three nations were savingly wrought upon, and therefore I returned to the Cherokee nation, which took me up eight weeks. I continued with my old friends seven weeks and two days.

I now and then found, that my affections to my family and country were not dead; they were sometimes very sensibly felt, and at last strengthened into an invincible desire of returning home. The king was much against it; but feeling the same strong bias towards my country, after we had asked Divine direction, the king consented, and accompanied me sixty miles with 140 men. I went to prayer three times before we could part, and then he sent forty men with me a hundred miles farther; I went to prayer, and then took my leave of them, and passed on my way. I had seventy miles now to go to the back settlements of the white people. I was surrounded very soon with wolves again, which made my old lodging both necessary and welcome. However it was not long, for in two days I reached the settlements, and on the third I found a house: It was about dinnertime, and as I came up to the door the family saw me, were frightened, and ran away. I sat down to dinner alone, and [ate] very heartily, and, after returning God thanks, I went to see what was become of the family. I found means to lay hold of a girl that stood peeping at me from behind a barn. She fainted away, and it was upwards of an hour before she recovered; it was nine o'clock before I could get them all to venture in, they were so terrified.

My dress was purely in the Indian style; the skins of wild beasts composed my garments, my head was set out in the savage manner, with a long pendant down my back, a sash round my middle without breeches, and a tomohawk [sic] by my side. In about two days they became sociable. Having visited three or four other families, at the distance of sixteen or twenty miles, I got them altogether to prayer on the Sabbath days, to the number of seventeen persons. I stayed with them six weeks, and they expressed much sorrow when I left them. I was now 112 miles from home. On the road I sometimes met with a house, then I was hospitably entertained; and when I met with none, a tree lent me the use of its friendly shelter and protection from the prowling beasts of the woods during the night. The God of mercy and grace supported me thus for eight days, and on the ninth I reached my uncle's house.

The following particulars, relating to the manner in which I was made known to my family, are less interesting; and yet, perhaps, some readers would not forgive their omission: I shall, however, be as brief as I can. I asked my uncle for a lodging, which he refused. I inquired how far the town was off; three quarters of a mile, said he. Do you know Mrs. Marrant and family, and how the children do? was my next question. He said he did, they were all well, but one was lately lost; at this I turned my head and wept. He did not know me, and upon refusing again to lodge me, I departed. When I reached the town it was dark, and passing by a house where one of my old schoolfellows lived, I knocked at the door; he came out, and asked me what I wanted? I desired a lodging, which was granted: I went in, but was not known. I asked him if he knew Mrs. Marrant, and how the family were? He said, he had just left them, they were all well; but a young lad, with whom he went to school, who, after he had quitted school, went to Charleston to learn some trade; but came home crazy, and rambled in the woods, and was torn in pieces by the wild beasts. How do you know, said I, that he was killed by wild beasts? I, and his brother, and uncle, and others, said he, went three days into the woods in search of him, and found his carcass torn, and brought it home, and buried it, and are now in mourning for him. This affected me very much, and I wept; observing it, he said, what is the matter? I made no answer. At supper they sat down without craving a blessing, for which I reproved them; this so affected the man, that I believe it ended in a sound conversion. Here is a wild man, says he, come out of the woods to be a witness for God, and to reprove our ingratitude and stupefaction! After supper I went to prayer, and then to bed. Rising a little before daylight, and praising the Lord, as my custom was, the family were surprised, and got up: I stayed with them till nine o'clock, and then went to my mother's house in the next street. The singularity of my dress drew everybody's eyes upon me, yet none knew me. I knocked at my mother's door, my sister opened it, and was startled at my appearance. Having expressed a desire to see Mrs. Marrant, I was answered, she was not very well, and that my business with her could be done by the person at the door, who also attempted to shut me out, which I prevented. My mother being called, I went in, and sat down, a mob of people being round the door. My mother asked, "what is your business"; only to see you, said I. She was much obliged to me, but did not know me. I asked, how are your children? how are your two sons? She replied, her daughters were in good health, of her two sons, one was well, and with her, but the other,—unable to contain, she burst into a flood of tears, and retired. I was overcome, and wept much; but nobody knew me. This was an affecting scene! Presently my brother came in: He inquired, who I was, and what I was? My sister did not know; but being uneasy at my presence, they contrived to get me out of the house, which, being overheard by me, I resolved not to stir. My youngest sister, eleven years of age, came in from school, and knew me the moment she saw me: She goes into the kitchen, and tells the woman her brother was come; but her news finding no credit there she returns, passes through the room where I sat, made a running curtsey, and says to my eldest sister in the next room, it is my brother! She was then called a foolish girl, and threatened; the child cried, and insisted upon it. She went crying upstairs to my mother, and told her; but neither would my mother believe her. At last they said to her, if it be your brother, go and kiss him, and ask him how he does? She ran and clasped me round the neck, and, looking me in the face, said, "Are not you my brother John?" I answered yes, and wept. I was then made known to all the family, to my friends, and acquaintances, who received me, and were glad, and rejoiced: Thus the dead was brought to life again; thus the lost was found. I shall now close the Narrative, with only remarking a few incidents in my life, until my connection with my Right Honourable Patroness, the Countess of Huntingdon.

I remained with my relations till the commencement of the American troubles. I used to go and hear the word of God, if any Gospel ministers came into the country, though at a considerable distance; and yet, reader, my soul was got into a declining state. Don't forget our Lord's exhortation, "What I say unto you, I say unto all, Watch."—In those troublesome times, I was pressed on board the Scorpion sloop of war, as their musician, as they were told I could play on music.—I continued in his majesty's service six years and eleven months; and with shame confess, that a lamentable stupor crept over all my spiritual vivacity, life and vigor; I got cold and dead. My gracious God, my dear Father in his dear Son, roused me every now and then by dangers and deliverances.—I was at the siege of Charleston, and passed through many dangers. When the town was taken, my old royal benefactor and convert, the king of the Cherokee Indians, riding into the town with General Clinton, saw me, and knew me: He alighted off his horse, and came to me; said he was glad to see me; that his daughter was very happy, and sometimes longed to get out of the body.

Sometime after this I was cruising about in the American seas, and cannot help mentioning a singular deliverance I had from the most imminent danger, and the use the Lord made of it to me. We were overtaken by a violent storm; I was washed overboard, and thrown on again; dashed into the sea a second time, and tossed upon deck again. I now fastened a rope round my middle, as a security against being thrown into the sea again; but, alas! forgot to fasten it to any part of the ship; being carried away the third time by the fury of the waves, when in the sea, I found the rope both useless and an encumbrance. I was in the sea the third time about eight minutes, and the sharks came round me in great numbers; one of an enormous size, that could easily have taken me into his mouth at once, passed and rubbed against my side. I then cried more earnestly to the Lord than I had done for some time; and he who heard Jonah's prayer, did not shut out mine, for I was thrown aboard again; these were the means the Lord used to revive me, and I began now to set out afresh.

I was in the engagement with the Dutch off the Dogger Bank, on board the *Princess Amelia*, of eighty-four guns. We had a great number killed and wounded; the deck was running with blood; six men were killed, and three wounded, stationed at the same gun with me; my head and face were covered with the blood and brains of the slain: I was

wounded, but did not fall, till a quarter of an hour before the engagement ended, and was happy during the whole of it. After being in the
hospital three months and sixteen days, I was sent to the West Indies
on board a ship of war, and, after cruising in those seas, we returned
home as a convoy. Being taken ill of my old wounds, I was put into the
hospital at Plymouth, and had not been there long, when the physician
gave it as his opinion, that I should not be capable of serving the king
again; I was therefore discharged, and came to London, where I lived
with a respectable and pious merchant three years, who was unwilling
to part with me. During this time I saw my call to the ministry fuller
and clearer; had a feeling concern for the salvation of my countrymen:
I carried them constantly in the arms of prayer and faith to the throne
of grace, and had continual sorrow in my heart for my brethren, for my
kinsmen, according to the flesh.—I wrote a letter to my brother, who
returned me an answer, in which he prayed some ministers would
come and preach to them, and desired me to show it to the minister
whom I attended. I used to exercise my gifts on a Monday evening in
prayer and exhortation, and was approved of, and ordained at Bath.
Her Ladyship having seen the letter from my brother in Nova Scotia,
thought Providence called me there: To which place I am now bound,
and expect to sail in a few days.

I have now only to intreat the earnest prayers of all my kind Christian friends, that I may be carried safe there; kept humble, made faithful, and successful; that strangers may hear of and run to Christ; that
Indian tribes may stretch out their hands to God; that the black nations may be made white in the blood of the Lamb; that vast multitudes of hard tongues, and of a strange speech, may learn the language
of Canaan, and sing the song of Moses, and of the Lamb; and, antici-
pating the glorious prospect, may we all with fervent hearts, and willing tongues, sing hallelujah; the kingdoms of the world are become the
kingdoms of our God, and of his Christ. Amen and Amen.

London,
Prescot Street, No. 66,
July 18, 1785.

THOUGHTS

AND

SENTIMENTS

ON THE

Evil and Wicked Traffic

OF THE

Slavery and Commerce

OF THE

HUMAN SPECIES

Humbly Submitted to
The Inhabitants of GREAT-BRITAIN

BY

OTTOBAH CUGOANO,

A Native of Africa.

---

*He that stealeth a man and selleth him, or maketh merchandise
of him, or if he be found in his hand: then that thief shall die.*

Law of God

LONDON:

Printed in the Year MDCCLXXXVII

3

THOUGHTS AND SENTIMENTS

ON THE

EVIL AND WICKED TRAFFIC

OF THE SLAVERY AND COMMERCE

OF THE HUMAN SPECIES,

HUMBLY SUBMITTED TO THE INHABITANTS

OF GREAT BRITAIN, BY

OTTOBAH CUGOANO,

A NATIVE OF AFRICA

---

historical precedents made use of to encourage slavery and extirpation, shown to be unwarrantable and highly absurd.

Page 125

Observation on the brutish stupidity of men in general. Laws of God
considered against slavery, and that the enslavers of men are the servants of the devil. Unlawfulness of slavery, and the European traffic in
it only piracy. Contrary to the law of our Lord Christ. All the dealers of
slaves guilty of death according to the righteous law of God; and if they
do not repent, they must lie under their crimes forever.

Page 130

All the criminal laws of civilization ought to be founded upon the law
of God; and the breakers of that law, in many cases, ought to be enslaved, and those that break the laws of civilization, are the only men
that others have any right to enslave, because they sell themselves to
work iniquity.

Page 134

Every slaveholder is a robber, if he buys a man without his own consent, or by any fraudulent method to obtain his consent unawares; and
it is the duty of every man to deliver himself from rogues and villains if
he can.

Page 134

Historical observations, and the case of the Africans considered.

Page 136

Observations on the cruel invaders and desolaters of the Americans,
and the unchristian barbarities of the Europeans against the heathen
nations. False religion a general cause of it—The symbolical image of
evil and wickedness described.

Page 142

The great wickedness carried on by the British nation, the cause of
leading them into a world of debt—That debt a cause of oppression
and slavery—The various instigators of it profligate and wicked men.

Page 145

The Spanish barbarities imitated by other nations, and the infernal invention of slavery followed after. The sufferings of the Africans described.

Page 148

An estimate of one hundred thousand of the Africans annually murdered by the British instigators and carriers on of slavery, and the
dreadful consequences of it declared.

Page 152

Every man in Great Britain responsible, in some degree, for the shocking and inhuman murders and oppressions of the Africans. Kings and great men considered as more particularly guilty; dead or alive every man must answer before God for all that they do at last.

Page 156

Great Britain considered as more particularly guilty many instances of their barbarity might be added, I have only recited one. What the Africans think and declare of the West India slavery. That the several nations of Europe, who carry on slavery, are become barbarous, and the British nation has joined as the head of that wicked combination.

Page 161

Address to the British inhabitants, why slavery should not be abolished, and why it has not been abolished and prohibited–let the wickedness of the wicked declare their iniquity, because they have not done otherwise. And add to that inquiry, after the interrogation, and why then might not the grand monster and image of iniquity have thundered forth his bulls to prevent all superstition and idolatry, and to prohibit all cruelty, slavery and persecution whatever, and to have caused the genuine word of truth to be read and made known in all languages throughout the world?

Page 165

Address to the saints of God—to the devout among men—to the inhabitants of the land, to plead that slavery ought to be abolished.

Page 167

Supplication of the enslaved Africans. Our case considered before God. Consideration of what ought to be done, three things proposed. Some observations on the three preceding considerations, as only proposed that some wise and righteous plan might be adopted.

Page 174

Particular thanks to the promoters of that laudable and charitable undertaking of sending a company of the black poor to Sierra Leone; but some contrary effects to be feared from the bad conducting of it.

Page 176

Observations for instructing the heathen nations in the knowledge of christianity, etc.

N.B. Since these Thoughts and Sentiments have been read by some, I find a general Approbation has been given, and that the things pointed out thereby might be more effectually taken into consideration, I was requested by some friends to add this information concerning myself:—When I was kidnapped and brought away from Africa, I was then about thirteen years of age, in the year of the Christian era 1770; and after being about nine or ten months in the slave gang at Grenada, and about one year at different places in the West Indies, with Alexander Campbell, Esq.; who brought me to England in the end of the year 1772, I was advised by some good people to get myself baptized, that I might not be carried away and sold again.—I was called *Steuart* by my master, but in order that I might embrace this ordinance, I was called *John Steuart*, and I went several times to Dr. Skinner, who instructed me, and I was baptized by him, and registered at St. James's Church in the year 1773. Some of my fellow servants, who assisted me in this, got themselves turned away for it; I have only put my African name to the title of the book.—When I was brought away from Africa, my father and relations were then chief men in the kingdom of Agimaque and Assinee; but what they may be now, or whether dead or alive, I know not. I wish to go back as soon as I can hear any proper security and safe conveyance can be found and I wait to hear how it fares with the Black People sent to Sierra Leone. But it is my highest wish and earnest prayer to God, that some encouragement could be given to send able schoolmasters, and intelligent ministers, who would be faithful and able to teach the Christian religion. This would be doing great good to the Africans, and be a kind restitution for the great injuries that they have suffered. But still I fear no good can be done near any of the European settlements, while such a horrible and infernal traffic of slavery is carried on by them. Wherever the foot of man can go, at the forts and garrisons it would seem to be wrote with these words:

O earth! O sea! Cover not thou the blood of the poor negro slaves.

Thoughts and Sentiments

on the

Evil of Slavery

---

*One law, and one manner shall be for you, and for the stranger
that sojourneth with you; and therefore, all things whatsoever ye
would that men should do to you, do ye even so to them.*
NUMB. 15:16.—MATH. 7:12.

As several learned gentlemen of distinguished abilities, as
well as eminent for their great humanity, liberality, and candor, have
written various essays against that infamous traffic of the African slave
trade, carried on with the West India planters and merchants, to the
great shame and disgrace of all Christian nations wherever it is admitted in any of their territories, or in any place or situation amongst
them; it cannot be amiss that I should thankfully acknowledge these
truly worthy and humane gentlemen with the warmest sense of gratitude, for their beneficent and laudable endeavors towards a total
suppression of that infamous and iniquitous traffic of stealing, kidnapping, buying, selling, and cruelly enslaving men!

Those who have endeavored to restore to their fellow creatures the
common rights of nature, of which especially the poor unfortunate
Black People have been so unjustly deprived, cannot fail in meeting
with the applause of all good men, and the approbation of that which
will forever redound to their honor; they have the warrant of that
which is divine: *Open thy mouth, judge righteously, plead the cause of the
poor and needy; for the liberal deviseth liberal things, and by liberal thing[s]
shall stand.* And they can say with the pious Job, *Did not I weep for him
that was in trouble; was not my soul grieved for the poor?*

The kind exertions of many benevolent and humane gentlemen,
against the iniquitous traffic of slavery and oppression, has been attended with much good to many, and must redound with great honor
to themselves, to humanity and their country; their laudable endeavors have been productive of the most beneficent effects in prevent-

ing that savage barbarity from taking place in free countries at home. In this, as well as in many other respects, there is one class of people (whose virtues of probity and humanity are well known) who are worthy of universal approbation and imitation, because, like men of honor and humanity, they have jointly agreed to carry on no slavery and savage barbarity among them; and, since the last war, some mitigation of slavery has been obtained in some respective districts of America, though not in proportion to their own vaunted claims of freedom; but it is to be hoped, that they will yet go on to make a further and greater reformation. However, notwithstanding all that has been done and written against it, that brutish barbarity, and unparalleled injustice, is still carried on to a very great extent in the colonies, and with an avidity as insidious, cruel and oppressive as ever. The longer that men continue in the practice of evil and wickedness, they grow the more abandoned; for nothing in history can equal the barbarity and cruelty of the tortures and murders committed under various pretenses in modern slavery, except the annals of the Inquisition and the bloody edicts of Popish massacres.

It is therefore manifest, that something else ought yet to be done; and what is required, is evidently the incumbent duty of all men of enlightened understanding, and of every man that has any claim of affinity to the name of Christian, that the base treatment which the African Slaves undergo, ought to be abolished; and it is moreover evident, that the whole, or any part of that iniquitous traffic of slavery, can nowhere, or in any degree, be admitted, but among those who must eventually resign their own claim to any degree of sensibility and humanity, for that of barbarians and ruffians.

But it would be needless to arrange a history of all the base treatment which the African Slaves are subjected to, in order to show the exceeding wickedness and evil of that insidious traffic, as the whole may easily appear in every part, and at every view, to be wholly and totally inimical to every idea of justice, equity, reason and humanity. What I intend to advance against that evil, criminal and wicked traffic of enslaving men, are only some Thoughts and Sentiments which occur to me, as being obvious from the Scriptures of Divine Truth, or such arguments as are chiefly deduced from thence, with other such observations as I have been able to collect. Some of these observations may lead into a larger field of consideration, than that of the African Slave Trade alone; but those causes from wherever they originate, and become the production of slavery, the evil effects produced by it, must show that its origin and source is of a wicked and criminal nature.

No necessity, or any situation of men, however poor, pitiful and wretched they may be, can warrant them to rob others, or oblige them to become thieves, because they are poor, miserable and wretched: But the robbers of men, the kidnappers, ensnarers and slaveholders, who take away the common rights and privileges of others to support and enrich themselves, are universally those pitiful and detestable wretches; for the ensnaring of others, and taking away their liberty by slavery and oppression, is the worst kind of robbery, as most opposite to every precept and injunction of the Divine Law, and contrary to that command which enjoins that *all men should love their neighbors as themselves,* and *that they should do onto others, as they would that men should do to them.* As to any other laws that slaveholders may make among themselves, as respecting slaves, they can be of no better kind, nor give them any better character, than what is implied in the common report—that there may be some honesty among thieves. This may seem a harsh comparison, but the parallel is so coincident that, I must say, I can find no other way of expressing my Thoughts and Sentiments, without making use of some harsh words and comparisons against the carriers[-]on of such abandoned wickedness. But, in this little undertaking, I must humbly hope the impartial reader will excuse such defects as may arise from want of better education; and as to the resentment of those who can lay their cruel lash upon the backs of thousands, for a thousand times less crimes than writing against their enormous wickedness and brutal avarice, is what I may be sure to meet with.

However, it cannot but be very discouraging to a man of my complexion in such an attempt as this, to meet with the evil aspersions of some men, who say, "That an African is not entitled to any competent degree of knowledge, or capable of imbibing any sentiments of probity; and that nature designed him for some inferior link in the chain, fitted only to be a slave." But when I meet with those who make no scruple to deal with the human species, as with the beasts of the earth, I must think them not only brutish, but wicked and base; and that their aspersions are insidious and false: And if such men can boast of greater degrees of knowledge, than any African is entitled to, I shall let them enjoy all the advantages of it unenvied, as I fear it consists only in a greater share of infidelity, and that of a blacker kind than only skin deep. And if their complexion be not what I may suppose, it is at least the nearest in resemblance to an infernal hue. A good man will neither speak nor do as a bad man will; but if a man is bad, it makes no difference whether he be a black or a white devil.

By some of such complexion, as whether black or white it matters not, I was early snatched away from my native country, with about eighteen or twenty more boys and girls, as we were playing in a field. We lived but a few days journey from the coast where we were kidnapped, and as we were decoyed and drove along, we were soon conducted to a factory, and from thence, in the fashionable way of traffic, consigned to Grenada. Perhaps it may not be amiss to give a few remarks, as some account of myself, in this transposition of capacity.

I was born in the city of Agimaque, on the coast of Fantyn; my father was a companion to the chief in the part of the country of Fanti, and when the old king died I was left in his house with his family; soon after I was sent for by his nephew, Ambro Accasa, who succeeded the old king in the chiefdom of that part of Fanti known by the name of Agimaque and Assinee. I lived with his children, enjoying peace and tranquility, about twenty moons, which, according to their way of reckoning time, is two years. I was sent for to visit an uncle, who lived at a considerable distance from Agimaque. The first day after we set out we arrived at Assinee, and the third day at my uncle's habitation, where I lived about three months, and was then thinking of returning to my father and young companion at Agimaque; but by this time I had got well acquainted with some of the children of my uncle's hundreds of relations, and we were some days too venturesome in going into the woods to gather fruit and catch birds, and such amusements as pleased us. One day I refused to go with the rest, being rather apprehensive that something might happen to us; till one of my playfellows said to me, because you belong to the great men, you are afraid to venture your carcass, or else of the *bounsam,* which is the devil. This enraged me so much, that I set a resolution to join the rest, and we went into the woods as usual; but we had not been above two hours before our troubles began, when several great ruffians came upon us suddenly, and said we had committed a fault against their lord, and we must go and answer for it ourselves before him.

Some of us attempted in vain to run away, but pistols and cutlasses were soon introduced, threatening, that if we offered to stir we should all lie dead on the spot. One of them pretended to be more friendly than the rest, and said, that he would speak to their lord to get us clear, and desired that we should follow him; we were then immediately divided into different parties, and drove after him. We were soon led out of the way which we knew, and towards the evening, as we came in sight of a town, they told us that this great man of theirs lived there, but pretended it was too late to go and see him that night. Next morning there came three other men, whose language differed from ours, and spoke to some of those who watched us all the night, but he that pretended to be our friend with the great man, and some others, were gone away. We asked our keepers what these men had been saying to them, and they answered, that they had been asking them, and us together, to go and feast with them that day, and that we must put off seeing the great man till after; little thinking that our doom was so nigh, or that these villains meant to feast on us as their prey. We went with them again about half a day's journey, and came to a great multitude of people, having different music playing; and all the day after we got there, we were very merry with the music, dancing and singing. Towards the evening, we were again persuaded that we could not get back to where the great man lived till next day; and when bedtime came, we were separated into different houses with different people. When the next morning came, I asked for the men that brought me there, and for the rest of my companions; and I was told that they were gone to the seaside to bring home some rum, guns and powder, and that some of my companions were gone with them, and that some were gone to the fields to do something or other. This gave me strong suspicion that there was some treachery in the cause, and I began to think that my hopes of returning home again were all over. I soon became very uneasy, not knowing what to do, and refused to eat or drink for whole days together, till the man of the house told me that he would do all in his power to get me back to my uncle; then I [ate] a little fruit with him, and had some thoughts that I should be sought after, as I would be then missing at home about five or six days. I inquired every day if the men had come back, and for the rest of my companions, but could get no answer of any satisfaction. I was kept about six days at this man's house, and in the evening there was another man came and talked with him a good while, and I heard the one say to the other he must go, and the other said the sooner the better; that man came out and told me that he knew my relations at Agimaque, and that we must set out tomorrow morning, and he would convey me there. Accordingly we set out next day, and traveled till dark, when we came to a place where we had some supper and slept. He carried a large bag with some gold dust,

which he said he had to buy some goods at the seaside to take with him
to Agimaque. Next day we traveled on, and in the evening came to a
town, where I saw several white people, which made me afraid that
they would eat me, according to our notion as children in the inland
parts of the country. This made me rest very uneasy all the night, and
next morning I had some victuals brought, desiring me to eat and
make haste, as my guide and kidnapper told me that he had to go to the
castle with some company that were going there, as he had told me before, to get some goods. After I was ordered out, the horrors I soon saw
and felt, cannot be well described; I saw many of my miserable countrymen chained two and two, some handcuffed, and some with their
hands tied behind. We were conducted along by a guard, and when we
arrived at the castle, I asked my guide what I was brought there for, he
told me to learn the ways of the *browfow*, that is the white faced people.
I saw him take a gun, a piece of cloth, and some lead for me, and then
he told me that he must now leave me there, and went off. This made
me cry bitterly, but I was soon conducted to a prison, for three days,
where I heard the groans and cries of many, and saw some of my fellow
captives. But when a vessel arrived to conduct us away to the ship, it
was a most horrible scene; there was nothing to be heard but rattling of
chains, smacking of whips, and the groans and cries of our fellow men.
Some would not stir from the ground, when they were lashed and beat
in the most horrible manner. I have forgot the name of this infernal
fort; but we were taken in the ship that came for us, to another that was
ready to sail from Cape Coast. When we were put into the ship, we saw
several black merchants coming on board, but we were all drove into
our holes, and not suffered to speak to any of them. In this situation we
continued several days in sight of our native land; but I could find no
good person to give any information of my situation to Accasa at Agimaque. And when we found ourselves at last taken away, death was
more preferable than life, and a plan was concerted amongst us, that
we might burn and blow up the ship, and to perish all together in the
flames; but we were betrayed by one of our own countrywomen, who
slept with some of the head men of the ship, for it was common for the
dirty filthy sailors to take the African women and lie upon their bodies;
but the men were chained and pent up in holes. It was the women and
boys which were to burn the ship, with the approbation and groans of
the rest; though that was prevented, the discovery was likewise a cruel
bloody scene.

But it would be needless to give a description of all the horrible scenes which we saw, and the base treatment which we met with in this dreadful captive situation, as the similar cases of thousands, which suffer by this infernal traffic, are well known. Let it suffice to say, that I was thus lost to my dear indulgent parents and relations, and they to me. All my help was cries and tears, and these could not avail; nor suffered long, till one succeeding woe, and dread, swelled up together. Brought from a state of innocence and freedom, and, in a barbarous and cruel manner, conveyed to a state of horror and slavery: This abandoned situation may be easier conceived than described. From the time that I was kidnapped and conducted to a factory, and from then in the brutish, base, but fashionable way of traffic, consigned to Grenada, the grievous thoughts which I then felt, still pant in my heart; though my fears and tears have long since subsided. And yet it is still grievous to think that thousands more have suffered in similar and greater distress, under the hands of barbarous robbers, and merciless taskmasters; and that many even now are suffering in all the extreme bitterness of grief and woe, that no language can describe. The cries of some, and the sight of their misery, may be seen and heard afar; but the deep sounding groans of thousands, and the great sadness of their misery and woe, under the heavy load of oppressions and calamities inflicted upon them, are such as can only be distinctly known to the ears of Jehovah Sabaoth.

This Lord of Hosts, in his great Providence, and in great mercy to me, made a way for my deliverance from Grenada. Being in this dreadful captivity and horrible slavery, without any hope of deliverance, for about eight or nine months, beholding the most dreadful scenes of misery and cruelty, and seeing my miserable companions often cruelly lashed, and as it were cut to pieces, for the most trifling faults; this made me often tremble and weep, but I escaped better than many of them. For eating a piece of sugarcane, some were cruelly lashed, or struck over the face to knock their teeth out. Some of the stouter ones, I suppose often reproved, and grown hardened and stupid with many cruel beatings and lashings, or perhaps faint and pressed with hunger and hard labor, were often committing trespasses of this kind, and when detected, they met with exemplary punishment. Some told me they had their teeth pulled out to deter others, and to prevent them from eating any cane in future. Thus seeing my miserable companions and countrymen in this pitiful, distressed and horrible situation, with all the brutish baseness and barbarity attending it, could not but fill my little mind with horror and indignation. But I must own, to the shame of my own countrymen, that I was first kidnapped and betrayed by some of my own complexion, who were the first cause of my exile and slavery; but if there were no buyers there would be no sellers. So far as I can remember, some of the Africans in my country keep slaves, which they take in war, or for debt; but those which they keep are well fed, and good care taken of them, and treated well; and, as to their clothing, they differ according to the custom of the country. But I may safely say, that all the poverty and misery that any of the inhabitants of Africa meet with among themselves, is far inferior to those inhospitable regions of misery which they meet with in the West Indies, where their hard-hearted overseers have neither regard to the laws of God, nor the life of their fellow men.

Thanks be to God, I was delivered from Grenada, and that horrid brutal slavery. A gentleman coming to England, took me for his servant, and brought me away, where I soon found my situation become more agreeable. After coming to England, and seeing others write and read, I had a strong desire to learn, and getting what assistance I could, I applied myself to learn reading and writing, which soon became my recreation, pleasure, and delight; and when my master perceived that I could write some, he sent me to a proper school for that purpose to learn. Since, I have endeavored to improve my mind in reading, and have sought to get all the intelligence I could, in my situation of life, towards the state of my brethren and countrymen in complexion, and of the miserable situation of those who are barbarously sold into captivity, and unlawfully held in slavery.

But among other observations, one great duty I owe to Almighty God, (the thankful acknowledgement I would not omit for any consideration) that, although I have been brought away from my native country, in that torrent of my robbery and wickedness, thanks be to God for his good providence towards me; I have both obtained liberty, and acquired the great advantages of some little learning, in being able to read and write, and, what is still infinitely of greater advantage, I trust, to know something of HIM who is that God whose providence rules over all, and who is the only Potent One that rules in the nations over the children of men. It is unto Him, who is the Prince of the Kings of the earth, that I would give all thanks. And, in some manner, I may say with Joseph, as he did with respect to the evil intention of his brethren, when they sold him into Egypt, that whatever evil intentions and bad motives those insidious robbers had in carrying me away from my native country and friends, I trust, was what the Lord intended for my good. In this respect, I am highly indebted to many of the good people of England for learning and principles unknown to the people of my native country. But, above all, what have I obtained from the Lord God of Hosts, the God of the Christians! in that divine revelation of the only true God, and the Savior of men, what a treasure of wisdom and blessings are involved? How wonderful is the divine goodness displayed in those invaluable books the Old and New Testaments, that inestimable compilation of books, the Bible? And, O what a treasure to have, and one of the greatest advantages to be able to read therein, and a divine blessing to understand!*

But, to return to my subject, I begin with the Cursory Remarker. This man styles himself a friend to the West India colonies and their inhabitants, like Demetrius, the silversmith, a man of some considerable abilities, seeing their craft in danger, a craft, however, not so innocent and justifiable as the making of shrines for Diana, though that was base and wicked enough to enslave the minds of men with superstition and idolatry; but this craft, and the gain of those craftsmen, consists in the enslaving both soul and body to the cruel idolatry, and most abominable service and slavery, to the idol of cursed avarice: And as he finds some discoveries of their wicked traffic held up in a light where truth and facts are so clearly seen, as none but the most desperate villain would dare to obstruct or oppose, he therefore sallies forth with all the desperation of a Utopian assailant, to tell lies by a virulent contradiction of facts, and with false aspersions endeavor to calumniate the worthy and judicious essayist of that discovery, a man, whose character is irreproachable. By thus artfully supposing, if he could bring the reputation of the author, who has discovered so much of their iniquitous

---

*The justly celebrated Dr. Young, in recommending this divine book of heavenly wisdom to the giddy and thoughtless world, in his *Night Thoughts,* has the following elegant lines:

> *Perhaps thou'dst laugh but at thine own expence,*
> *This counsel strange should I presume to give;*
> *Retire and read thy Bible to be gay;*
> *There truths abound of sov'reign aid to peace.*
> *Ah, do not prize it less because inspired.*
> *Read and revere the sacred page; a page,*
> *Where triumphs immortality; a page,*
> *Which not the whole creation could produce;*
> *Which not the conflagration shall destroy;*
> *In nature's ruin not one letter's lost,*
> *'Tis printed in the mind of gods forever,*
> *Angels and men assent to what I sing!*

traffic, into dispute, his work would fall and be less regarded. However, this virulent craftsman has done no great merit to his cause and the credit of that infamous craft; at the appearance of truth, his understanding has got the better of his avarice and infidelity, so far, as to draw the following concession: "I shall not be so far misunderstood, by the candid and judicious part of mankind, as to be ranked among the advocates of slavery, as I must sincerely join Mr. Ramsay,★ and every other man of sensibility, in hoping the blessings of freedom will, in due time, be equally diffused over the whole globe."

By this, it would seem that he was a little ashamed of his craftsmen, and would not like to be ranked or appear amongst them. But as long as there are any hopes of gain to be made by that insidious craft, he can join with them well enough, and endeavor to justify them in that most abandoned traffic of buying, selling, and enslaving men. He finds fault with a plan for punishing robbers, thieves and vagabonds, who distress their neighbors by their thrift, robbery and plunder, without regarding any laws human or divine, except the rules of their own fraternity, and in that case, according to the proverb, there may be some honor among thieves; but these are the only people in the world that ought to suffer some punishment, imprisonment or slavery; their external complexion, whether black or white, should be no excuse for them to do evil. Being aware of this, perhaps he was afraid that some of his friends, the great and opulent banditti of slaveholders in the western part of the world, might be found guilty of more atrocious and complicated crimes, than even those of the highwaymen, the robberies and the petty larcenies committed in England. Therefore, to make the best of this sad dilemma, he brings in a ludicrous invective comparison that it would be "an event which would undoubtedly furnish a new and pleasant compartment to that well known and most delectable print, called, *The world turned upside down,* in which the cook is roasted by the pig, the man saddled by the horse," etc. If he means that the complicated banditties of pirates, thieves, robbers, oppressors and enslavers of men, are those cooks and men that would be roasted saddled, it certainly would be no unpleasant sight to see them well roasted, saddled and bridled too; and no matter by whom, whether he terms them pigs, horses, or asses. But there is not much likelihood of this silly monkeyish comparison as yet being verified, in bringing the opulent pirates and thieves to condign punishment, so that he could very well

★The worthy and judicious author of "An Essay on the Treatment and Conversion of the African Slavers in the British Sugar Colonies."

bring it in to turn it off with a grin. However, to make use of his words, it would be a most delectable sight, when thieves and robbers get the upper side of the world, to see them turned down; and I should not interrupt his mirth, to see him laugh at his own invective monkeyish comparison as long as he pleases.

But again, when he draws a comparison of the many hardships that the poor in Great Britain and Ireland labor under, as well as many of those in other countries; that their various distresses are worse than the West Indian slaves—it may be true, in part, that some of them suffer greater hardships than many of the slaves; but, bad as it is, the poorest in England would not change their situation for that of slaves. And there may be some masters, under various circumstances, worse off than their servants; but they would not change their own situation for theirs: Nor as little would a rich man wish to change his situation of affluence, for that of a beggar: and so, likewise, no freeman, however poor and distressing his situation may be, would resign his liberty for that of a slave, in the situation of a horse or a dog. The case of the poor, whatever their hardships may be, in free countries, is widely different from that of the West India slaves. For the slaves, like animals, are bought and sold, and dealt with as their capricious owners may think fit, even in torturing and tearing them to pieces, and wearing them out with hard labor, hunger and oppression; and should the death of a slave ensue by some other more violent way than that which is commonly the death of thousands, and tens of thousands in the end, the haughty tyrant, in that case, has only to pay a small fine for the murder and death of his slave. The brute creation in general may fare better than man, and some dogs may refuse the crumbs that the distressed poor would be glad of; but the nature and situation of man is far superior to that of beasts; and, in like manner, whatever circumstances poor freemen may be in, their situation is much superior, beyond any proportion, to that of the hardships and cruelty of modern slavery. But where can the situation of any freeman be so bad as that of a slave; or, could such be found, or even worse, as he would have it, what would the comparison amount to? Would it plead for his craft of slavery and oppression? Or, rather, would it not cry aloud for some redress, and what every well regulated society of men ought to hear and consider, that none should suffer want or be oppressed among them? And this seems to be pointed out by the circumstances which he describes; that it is the great duty, and ought to be the highest ambition of all governors, to order and establish such policy, and in such a wise manner, that everything should be so managed, as to be conducive to the moral, temporal and eternal welfare of every individual from the lowest degree to the highest; and the consequence of this would be, the harmony, happiness and good prosperity of the whole community.

But this crafty author has also, in defense of his own or his employer's craft in the British West India slavery, given sundry comparisons and descriptions of the treatment of slaves in the French islands and settlements in the West Indies and America. And, contrary to what is the true case, he would have it supposed that the treatment of the slaves in the former, i[s] milder than the latter; but even in this, unwarily for his own craft of slavery, all that he has advanced, can only add matter for its confutation, and serve to heighten the ardor and wish of every generous mind, that the whole should be abolished. An equal degree of enormity found in one place, cannot justify crimes of as great or greater enormity committed in another. The various depredations committed by robbers and plunderers, on different parts of the globe, may not be all equally alike bad, but their evil and malignancy, in every appearance and shape, can only hold up to view the just observation, that

> *Virtue herself hath such peculiar mien,*
> *Vice, to be hated, needs but to be seen.*

The farther and wider that the discovery and knowledge of such an enormous evil, as the base and villainous treatment and slavery which the poor unfortunate Black People meet with, is spread and made known, the cry for justice, even virtue lifting up her voice, must rise the louder and higher, for the scale of equity and justice to be lifte[d] up in their defense. *And doth not wisdom cry, and understanding put forth her voice?* But who will regard the voice and hearken to the cry? Not the sneaking advocates for slavery, though a little ashamed of their craft; like the monstrous crocodile weeping over their prey with fine concessions (while gorging their own rapacious appetite) to hope for universal freedom taking place over the globe. Not those inebriated with avarice and infidelity, who hold in defiance every regard due to the divine law, and who endeavor all they can to destroy and take away the natural and common rights and privileges of men. Not the insolent and crafty author for slavery and oppression, who would have us to believe, that the benign command of God in appointing the seventh day for a sabbath of rest for the good purposes of our present and eternal welfare, is not to be regarded. He will exclaim against the teachers of obedience to it; and tells us, that the poor, and the oppressed, and the heavy burdened slave, should not lay down his load that day, but appropriate these hours of sacred rest to labor in some bit of useful ground. His own words are, "to dedicate the unappropriated hours of Sunday to the cultivation of this useful spot, he is brought up to believe would be the worst of sins, and that the sabbath is a day of absolute and universal rest is a truth he hears frequently inculcated by the curate of the parish," etc. But after bringing it about in this roundabout way and manner, whatever the curate has to say of it as a truth, he would have us by no means to regard. This may serve as a specimen of his crafty and detestable production, where infidelity, false aspersions, virulent calumnies, and lying contradictions abound throughout. I shall only refer him to that description which he meant for another, most applicable and best suited for himself, and so long as he does not renounce his craft, as well as to be somewhat ashamed of his craftsmen and their insensibility, he may thus stand as described by himself: "A man of warm imagination (but strange infatuated unfeeling sensibility) to paint things not as they really are, but as his rooted prejudices represent them, and even to shut his eyes against the convictions afforded him by his own senses."

But such is the insensibility of men, when their own craft of gain is advanced by the slavery and oppression of others, that after all the laudable exertions of the truly virtuous and humane, towards extending the beneficence of liberty and freedom to the much degraded and unfortunate Africans, which is the common right and privilege of all men, in everything that is just, lawful and consistent, we find the principles of justice and equity, not only opposed, and every duty in religion and humanity left unregarded; but that unlawful traffic of dealing with our fellow creatures, as with the beasts of the earth, still carried on with as great assiduity as ever; and that the insidious piracy of procuring and holding slaves is countenanced and supported by the government of sundry Christian nations. This seems to be the fashionable way of getting riches, but very dishonorable; in doing this, the slaveholders are meaner and baser than the African slaves, for while they subject and reduce them to a degree with brutes, they seduce themselves to a degree with devils.

Some pretend that the Africans, in general, "are a set of poor, ignorant, dispersed, unsociable" people; and that they think it no crime to "sell one another, and even their own wives and children; therefore they bring them away to a situation where many of them may arrive to

a better state than ever they could obtain in their own native country."
This specious pretense is without any shadow of justice and truth,
and, if the argument was even true, it could afford no just and warrant-
able matter for any society of men to hold slaves. But the argument is
false; there can be no ignorance, dispersion, or unsociableness so
found among them, which can be made better by bringing them away
to a state of a degree equal to that of a cow or a horse.

But let their ignorance in some things (in which the Europeans
have greatly the advantage of them) be what it will, it is not the intention of [those] who bring them away to make them better by it; nor is
the design of slaveholders of any other intention, but that they may
serve them as a kind of engines and beasts of burden; that their own
ease and profit may be advanced, by a set of poor helpless men and
women, whom they despise and rank with brutes, and keep them in
perpetual slavery, both themselves and children, and merciful death is
the only release from their toil. By the benevolence of some, a few may
get their liberty, and by their own industry and ingenuity, may acquire
some learning, mechanical trades, or useful business; and some may
be brought away [by] different gentlemen to free countries, where they
get their liberty; but no thanks to slaveholders for it. But amongst those
who get their liberty, like all other ignorant men, are generally more
corrupt in their morals, than they possibly could have been amongst
their own people in Africa; for, being mostly amongst the wicked and
apostate Christians, they sooner learn their oaths and blasphemies,
and their evil ways, than anything else. Some few, indeed, may eventually arrive at some knowledge of the Christian religion, and the great
advantages of it. Such was the case of Ukawsaw Gronniosaw, an African prince, who lived in England. He was a long time in a state of great
poverty and distress, and must have died at one time for want, if a good
and charitable Attorney had not supported him. He was long after in a
very poor state, but he would not have given his faith in the Christian
religion, in exchange for all the kingdoms of Africa, if they could have
been given to him, in place of his poverty, for it. And such was A. Marrant in America. When a boy, he could stroll away into a desert, and
prefer the society of wild beasts to the absurd Christianity of his mother's house. He was conducted to the king of the Cherokees, who, in a
miraculous manner, was induced by him to embrace the Christian
faith. This Marrant was in the British service last war, and his royal
convert, the king of the Cherokee Indians, accompanied General
Clinton at the siege of Charleston.

These, and all such, I hope thousands, as meet with the knowledge and grace of the Divine clemency, are brought forth quite contrary to the end and intention of all slavery, and, in general, of all slaveholders too. And should it please the Divine goodness to visit some of the poor dark Africans, even in the brutal stall of slavery, and from thence to install them among the princes of his grace, and to invest them with a robe of honor that will hang about their necks forever; but who can then suppose, that it will be well pleasing unto him to find them subjected there in that dejected state? Or can the slaveholders think that the Universal Father and Sovereign of Mankind will be pleased with them, for the brutal transgression of his law, in bowing down the necks of those to the yoke of their cruel bondage? Sovereign goodness may eventually visit some men even in a state of slavery, but their slavery is not the cause of that event and benignity; and therefore, should some event of good ever happen to some men subjected to slavery, that can plead nothing for men to do evil that good may come; and should it apparently happen from thence, it is neither fought for nor designed by the enslavers of men. But the whole business of slavery is an evil of the first magnitude, and a most horrible iniquity to traffic with slaves and souls of men; and an evil, sorry I am, that it still subsists, and more astonishing to think, that it is an iniquity committed amongst Christians, and contrary to all the genuine principles of Christianity, and yet carried on by men denominated thereby.

In a Christian era, in a land where Christianity is planted, where everyone might expect to behold the flourishing growth of every virtue, extending their harmonious branches with universal philanthropy wherever they came; but, on the contrary, almost nothing else is to be seen abroad but the bramble of ruffians, barbarians and slaveholders, grown up to a powerful luxuriance in wickedness. I cannot but wish, for the honor of Christianity, that the bramble grown up amongst them, was known to the heathen nations by a different name, for sure the depredators, robbers and ensnarers of men can never be Christians, but ought to be held as the abhorrence of all men, and the abomination of all mankind, whether Christians or heathens. Every man of any sensibility, whether he be a Christian or a heathen, if he has any discernment at all, must think, that for any man, or any class of men, to deal with their fellow creatures as with the beasts of the field; or to account them as such, however ignorant they may be, and in whatever situation, or wherever they may find them, and whatever country or complexion they may be of, that those men, who are the procurers and holders of slaves, are the greatest villains in the world. And surely those men must be lost to all sensibility themselves, who can think that the stealing, robbing, enslaving, and murdering of men can be no crimes; but the holders of men in slavery are at the head of all these oppressions and crimes. And, therefore, however unsensible they may be of it now, and however long they may laugh at the calamity of others, if they do not repent of their evil way, and the wickedness of their doings, by keeping and holding their fellow creatures in slavery, and trafficking with them as with the brute creation, and to give up and surrender that evil traffic, with an awful abhorrence of it, that this may be averred, if they do not, and if they can think, they must and cannot otherwise but expect in one day at last, to meet with the full stroke of the long suspended vengeance of heaven, when death will cut them down to a state as mean as that of the most abjected slave, and to a very eminent danger of a far more dreadful fate hereafter, when they have the just reward of their iniquities to meet with.

   And now, as to the Africans being dispersed and unsociable, if it was so, that could be no warrant for the Europeans to enslave them; and even though they may have many different feuds and bad practices among them, the continent of Africa is of vast extent, and the numerous inhabitants are divided into several kingdoms and principalities, which are governed by their respective kings and princes, and those are absolutely maintained by their free subjects. Very few nations make slaves of any of those under their government; but such as are taken prisoners of war from their neighbors, are generally kept in that state, until they can exchange and dispose of them otherwise; and towards the west coast they are generally procured for the European market, and sold. They have a great aversion to murder, or even in taking away the lives of those which they judge guilty of crimes; and, therefore, they prefer disposing of them otherwise better than killing them.* This gives their merchants and procurers of slaves a power to travel a great way into the interior parts of the country to buy such as are wanted to be disposed of. These slave procurers are a set of as great villains as any in the world. They often steal and kidnap many more than they buy at first if they can meet with them by the way; and they have only their certain boundaries to go to, and sell them from one to

---

*It may be true, that some of the slaves transported from Africa, may have committed crimes in their own country, that require some slavery as a punishment; but, according to the laws of equity and justice, they ought to become free, as soon as their labor has paid for their purchase in the West Indies or elsewhere.

another, so that if they are sought after and detected, the thieves are seldom found, and the others only plead that they bought them so and so. These kidnappers and slave procurers, called merchants, are a species of African villains, which are greatly corrupted, and even vitiated by their intercourse with the Europeans; but, wicked and barbarous as they certainly are, I can hardly think, if they knew what horrible barbarity they were sending their fellow creatures to, that they would do it. But the artful Europeans have so deceived them, that they are bought by their inventions of merchandise, and beguiled into it by their artifice; for the Europeans, at their factories, in some various manner, have always kept some as servants to them, and with gaudy clothes, in a gay manner, as decoy ducks to deceive others, and to tell them that they want many more to go over the sea, and be as they are. So in that respect, wherein it may be said that they will sell one another, they are only ensnared and enlisted to be servants, kept like some of those which they see at the factories, which, for some gewgaws, as presents given to themselves and friends, they are thereby enticed to go; and something after the same manner that East India soldiers are procured in Britain; and the inhabitants here, just as much sell themselves, and one another, as they do; and the kidnappers here, and the slave procurers in Africa, are much alike. But many other barbarous methods are made use of by the vile instigators, procurers and ensnarers of men; and some of the wicked and profligate princes and chiefs of Africa accept of presents, from the Europeans, to procure a certain number of slaves; and thereby they are wickedly instigated to go to war with one another on purpose to get them, which produces many terrible depredations; and sometimes when those engagements are entered into, and they find themselves defeated of their purpose, it has happened that some of their own people have fallen a sacrifice to their avarice and cruelty. And it may be said of the Europeans, that they have made use of every insidious method to procure slaves whenever they can, and in whatever manner they can lay hold of them, and that their forts and factories are the avowed dens of thieves for robbers, plunderers and depredators.

But again, as to the Africans selling their own wives and children, nothing can be more opposite to everything they hold dear and valuable; and nothing can distress them more, than to part with any of their relations and friends. Such are the tender feelings of parents for their children, that, for the loss of a child, they seldom can be rendered happy, even with the intercourse and enjoyment of their friends, for

years. For any man to think that it should be otherwise, when he may
see a thousand instances of a natural instinct, even in the brute creation, where they have a sympathetic feeling for their offspring; it must
be great want of consideration not to think, that much more than
merely what is natural to animals, should in a higher degree be implanted in the breast of every part of the rational creation of man. And
what man of feeling can help lamenting the loss of parents, friends, liberty, and perhaps property and other valuable and dear connections.
Those people annually brought away from Guinea, are born as free,
and are brought up with as great a predilection for their own country,
freedom and liberty, as the sons and daughters of fair Britain. Their
free subjects are trained up to a kind of military service, not so much
by the desire of the chief, as by their own voluntary inclination. It is
looked upon as the greatest respect they can show to their king, to
stand up for his and their own defense in time of need. Their different
chieftains, which bear a reliance on the great chief, or king, exercise a
kind of government something like that feudal institution which prevailed some time in Scotland. In this respect, though the common
people are free, they often suffer by the villainy of their different chieftains, and by the wars and feuds which happen among them. Nevertheless their freedom and rights are as dear to them, as those privileges
are to other people. And it may be said that freedom, and the liberty of
enjoying their own privileges, burns with as much zeal and fervor in
the breast of an Ethiopian as in the breast of any inhabitant on the
globe.

But the supporters and favorers of slavery make other things a pretense and an excuse in their own defense; such as, that they find that it
was admitted under the Divine institution by Moses, as well as the
long continued practice of different nations for ages; and that the Africans are peculiarly marked out by some signal prediction in nature and
complexion for that purpose.

This seems to be greatest bulwark of defense which the advocates
and favorers of slavery can advance, and what is generally talked of in
their favor by those who do not understand it. I shall consider it in that
view, whereby it will appear, that they deceive themselves and mislead
others. Men are never more liable to be drawn into error, than when
truth is made use of in a guileful manner to seduce them. Those who
do not believe the scriptures to be a Divine revelation, cannot, con-
sistently with themselves, make the law of Moses, or any mark or prediction they can find respecting any particular set of men, as found in

the sacred writings, any reason that one class of men should enslave another. In that respect, all that they have to inquire into should be, whether it be right, or wrong, that any part of the human species should enslave another; and when that is the case, the Africans, though not so learned, are just as wise as the Europeans; and when the matter is left to human wisdom, they are both liable to err. But what the light of nature, and the dictates of reason, when rightly considered, teach, is that no man ought to enslave another; and some, who have been rightly guided thereby, have made noble defenses for the universal natural rights and privileges of all men. But in this case, when the learned take neither revelation nor reason for their guide, they fall into as great, and worse errors, than the unlearned; for they only make use of that system of Divine wisdom, which should guide them into truth, when they can find or pick out anything that will suit their purpose, or that they can pervert to such—the very means of leading themselves and others into error. And, in consequence thereof, the pretenses that some men make use of for holding of slaves, must be evidently the grossest perversion of reason, as well as an inconsistent and diabolical use of the sacred writings. For it must be a strange perversion of reason, and a wrong use or disbelief of the sacred writings, when anything found there is so perverted by them, and set up as a precedent and rule for men to commit wickedness. They had better have no reason, and no belief in the scriptures, and make no use of them at all, than only to believe, and make use of that which leads them into the most abominable evil and wickedness of dealing unjustly with their fellow men.

But this will appear evident to all men that believe the scriptures, that every reason necessary is given that they should be believed; and, in this case, that they afford us this information: "That all mankind did spring from one original, and that there are no different species among men. For God who made the world, hath made of one blood all the nations of men that dwell on all the face of the earth." Wherefore we may justly infer, as there are no inferior species, but all of one blood and of one nature, that there does not an inferiority subsist, or depend, on their color, features or form, whereby some men make pretense to enslave others; and consequently, as they have all one creator, one original, made of one blood, and all brethren descended from one father, it never could be lawful and just for any nation, or people, to oppress and enslave another.

And again, as all the present inhabitants of the world sprang from the family of Noah, and were then all of one complexion, there is no doubt, but the difference which we now find, took its rise very rapidly after they became dispersed and settled on the different parts of the globe. There seems to be a tendency to this, in many instances, among children of the same parents, having different color of hair and features from one another. And God alone who established the course of nature, can bring about and establish what variety he pleases; and it is not in the power of man to make one hair white or black. But among the variety which it hath pleased God to establish and caused to take place, we may meet with some analogy in nature, that as the bodies of men are tempered with a different degree to enable them to endure the respective climates of their habitations, so their colors vary, in some degree, in a regular gradation from the equator towards either of the poles. However, there are other incidental causes arising from time and place, which constitute the most distinguishing variety of color, from appearance and features, as peculiar to the inhabitants of one tract of country, and differing in something from those in another, even in the same latitudes, as well as from those in different climates. Long custom and the different way of living among the several inhabitants of the different parts of the earth, has a very great effect in distinguishing them by a difference of features and complexion. These effects are easy to be seen; as to the causes, it is sufficient for us to know, that all is the work of an Almighty hand. Therefore, as we find the distribution of the human species inhabiting the barren, as well as the most fruitful parts of the earth, and the cold as well as the most hot, differing from one another in complexion according to their situation; it may be reasonably, as well as religiously, inferred, that He who placed them in their various situations, hath extended equally his care and protection to all; and from thence, that it becometh unlawful to counteract his benignity, by reducing others of different complexions to undeserved bondage.

According, as we find that the difference of color among men is only incidental, and equally natural to all, and agreeable to the place of their habitation; and that if nothing else be different or contrary among them, but that of features and complexion, in that respect, they are all equally alike entitled to the enjoyment of every mercy and blessing of God. But there are some men of that complexion, because they are not black, whose ignorance and insolence leads them to think, that those who are black, were marked out in that manner by some signal interdiction or curse, as originally descending from their progenitors. To those I must say, that the only mark which we read of, as generally alluded to, and by them applied wrongfully, is that mark or sign which God gave to Cain, to assure him that he should not be destroyed. Cain understood by the nature of the crime he had committed, that the law required death, or cutting off, as the punishment thereof. But God in his providence doth not always punish the wicked in this life according to their enormous crimes (we are told, by a sacred poet, that he saw the wicked flourishing like a green bay tree), though he generally marks them out by some signal token of his vengeance; and that is a sure token of it, when men become long hardened in their wickedness. The denunciation that passed upon Cain was, that he should be a fugitive and a vagabond on the earth, bearing the curse and reproach of his iniquity; and the rest of men were prohibited as much from meddling with him, or defiling their hands by him, as it naturally is, not to pull down the dead carcass of an atrocious criminal, hung up in chains by the laws of his country. But allow the mark set upon Cain to have consisted in a black skin, still no conclusion can be drawn at all, that any of the black people are of that descent, as the whole posterity of Cain were destroyed in the universal deluge.

Only Noah, a righteous and just man, who found grace in the sight of God, and his three sons, Japheth, Shem and Ham, and their wives, eight persons, were preserved from the universal deluge, in the ark which Noah was directed to build. The three sons of Noah had each children born after the flood, from whom all the present world of men descended. But it came to pass, in the days of Noah, that an interdiction, or curse, took place in the family of Ham, and that the descendants of one of his sons should become the servants of servants to their brethren, the descendants of Shem and Japheth. This affords a grand pretense for the supporters of the African slavery to build a false notion upon, as it is found by history that Africa, in general, was peopled by the descendants of Ham; but they forget, that the prediction has already been fulfilled as far as it can go.

There can be no doubt, that there was a shameful misconduct in Ham himself, by what is related of him; but the fault, according to the prediction and curse, descended only to the families of the descendants of his youngest son, Canaan. The occasion was, that Noah, his father, had drank wine, and (perhaps unawares) became inebriated by it, and fell asleep in his tent. It seems that Ham was greatly deficient of that filial virtue as either becoming a father or a son, went into his father's tent, and, it may be supposed, in an undecent manner, had suffered his own son, Canaan, so to meddle with, or uncover, his father, that he saw his nakedness; for which he did not check the audacious rudeness of Canaan, but went and told his brethren without in ridicule of his aged parent. This rude audacious behavior of Canaan, and the obloquy of his father Ham, brought on him the curse of his grandfather, Noah, but he blessed Shem and Japheth for their decent and filial virtues, and denounced, in the spirit of prophecy, that Canaan should be their servant, and should serve them.

It may be observed, that it is a great misfortune for children, when their parents are not endowed with that wisdom and prudence which is necessary for the early initiation of their offspring in the paths of virtue and righteousness. Ham was guilty of the offense as well as his son; he did not pity the weakness of his father, who was overcome with wine in that day wherein, it is likely, he had some solemn work to do. But the prediction and curse rested wholly upon the offspring of Canaan, who settled in the land known by his name, in the west of Asia, as is evident from the sacred writings. The Canaanites became an exceeding wicked people, and were visited with many calamities, according to the prediction of Noah, for their abominable wickedness and idolatry.

Chederluomer, a descendant of Shem, reduced the Canaanitish kingdoms to a tributary subjection; and sometime after, upon their revolt, invaded and pillaged their country. Not long after Sodom, Gomorrah, Admah and Zeboim, four kingdoms of the Canaanites, were overthrown for their great wickedness, and utterly destroyed by fire and brimstone from heaven. The Hebrews, chiefly under Moses, Joshua and Barak, as they were directed by God, cut off most of the other Canaanitish kingdoms, and reduced many of them to subjection and vassalage. Those who settled in the northwest of Canaan, and formed the once flourishing states of Tyre and Sidon, were by the Assyrians, the Chaldeans, and the Persians successively reduced to great misery and bondage; but chiefly by the Greeks, the Romans, and the Saracens, and lastly by the Turks, they were completely and totally ruined, and have no more since been a distinct people among the different nations. Many of the Canaanites who fled away in the Time of Joshua, became mingled with the different nations, and some historians think that some of them came to England, and settled about Cornwall, as far back as that time; so that, for anything that can be known to the contrary, there may be some of the descendants of that wicked generation still subsisting among the slaveholders in the West Indies. For if the curse of God ever rested upon them, or upon any other men, the only visible mark thereof was always upon those who committed the most outrageous acts of violence and oppression. But color and complexion has nothing to do with that mark; every wicked man, and the enslavers of others, bear the stamp of their own iniquity, and that mark which was set upon Cain.

Now, the descendants of the other three sons of Ham, were not included under the curse of his father, and as they dispersed and settled on the different parts of the earth, they became also sundry distinct and very formidable nations. Cush, the oldest, settled in the southwest of Arabia, and his descendants were anciently known to the Hebrews by the name of Cushites, or Cushie; one of his sons, Nimrod, founded the kingdom of Babylon, in Asia; and the others made their descent southward, by the Red Sea, and came over to Abyssinia and Ethiopia, and, likely, dispersed themselves throughout all the southern and interior parts of Africa. And as they lived mostly under the torrid zone, or near the tropics, they became black, as being natural to the inhabitants of these sultry hot climates; and, in that case, their complexion bears the signification of the name of their original progenitor, Cush, as known by the Hebrews by that name, both on the east and on the west, beyond the Red Sea; but the Greeks called them Ethiopians, or black faced people. The Egyptians and Philistines were the descendants of Mizraim, and the country which they inhabited was called the land of Mizraim, and Africa, in general, was anciently called the whole land of Ham. Phut, another of his sons, also settled on the west of Egypt, and as the youngest were obliged to emigrate farthest, afterwards dispersed chiefly up the south of the Mediterranean sea, towards Libya and Mauritania, and might early mingle with some of the Cushites on the more southern, and, chiefly, on the western parts of Africa. But all these might be followed by some other families and tribes from Asia; and some think that Africa got its name from the King of Libya marrying a daughter of Aphra, one of the descendants of Abraham, by Keturah.

But it may be reasonably supposed, that the most part of the black people in Africa, are the descendants of the Cushites, towards the east, the south, and interior parts, and chiefly of the Phutians towards the west; and the various revolutions and changes which have happened among them have rather been local than universal; so that whoever their original progenitors were, as descending from one generation to another, in a long continuance, it becomes natural for the inhabitants of that tract of country to be a dark black, in general. The learned and thinking part of men, who can refer to history, must know, that nothing with respect to color, nor any mark or curse from any original prediction, can in anywise be more particularly ascribed to the Africans than to any other people of the human species, so as to afford any pretense why they should be more evil treated, persecuted and enslaved, than any other. Nothing but ignorance, and the dreams of a vitiated imagination, arising from the general countenance given to the evil practice of wicked men, to strengthen their hands in wickedness, could ever make any person to fancy otherwise or ever to think that the stealing, kidnapping, enslaving, persecuting or killing a black man is in any way and manner less criminal, than the same evil treatment of any other man of another complexion.

But again, in answer to another part of the pretense which the favorers of slavery make use of in their defense, that slavery was an ancient custom, and that it became the prevalent and universal practice of many different barbarous nations for ages: This must be granted; but not because it was right, or anything like right and equity. A lawful servitude was always necessary, and became contingent with the very nature of human society. But when the laws of civilization were broken through, and when the rights and properties of others were invaded, that brought the oppressed into a kind of compulsive servitude, though often not compelled to it by those whom they were obliged to serve. This arose from the different depredations and robberies which were committed upon one another; the helpless were obliged to seek protection from such as could support them, and to give unto them their service, in order to preserve themselves from want, and to deliver them from the injury either of men or beasts. For while civil society continued in a rude state, even among the establishers of kingdoms, when they became powerful and proud, as they wanted to enlarge their territories, they drove and expelled others from their peaceable habitations, who were not so powerful as themselves. This made those who were robbed of their substance, and drove from the place of their abode, make their escape to such as could and would help them; but when such a relief could not be found, they were obliged to submit to the yoke of their oppressors, who, in many cases, would not yield them any protection upon any terms. Wherefore, when their lives were in danger otherwise, and they could not find any help, they were obliged to sell themselves for bond servants to such as would buy them, when they could not get a service that was better. But as soon as buyers could be found, robbers began their traffic to ensnare others, and such as fell into their hands were carried captive by them, and were obliged to submit to their being sold by them into the hands of other robbers, for there are few buyers of men, who intend thereby to make them free, and such as they buy are generally subjected to hard labor and bondage. Therefore at all times, while a man is a slave, he is still in captivity, and under the jurisdiction of robbers; and every man who keeps a slave, is a robber, whenever he compels him to his service without giving him a just reward. The barely supplying his slave with some necessary things, to keep him in life, is no reward at all, that is only for his own sake and benefit; and the very nature of compulsion and taking away the liberty of others, as well as their property, is robbery; and that kind of service which subjects men to a state of slavery, must all times, and in every circumstance, be a barbarous, inhuman and unjust dealing with our fellow men. A voluntary service, and slavery, are quite different things; but in ancient times, in whatever degree slavery was admitted, and whatever hardships they were, in general, subjected to, it was not nearly so bad as the modern barbarous and cruel West India slavery.

Now, in respect to that kind of servitude which was admitted into the law of Moses, that was not contrary to the natural liberties of men, but a state of equity and justice, according as the nature and circumstances of the times required. There was more harm in entering into a covenant with another man as a bond servant, than there is for two men to enter into partnership the one with the other; and sometimes the nature of the case may be, and their business require it, that the one may find money and live at a distance and ease, and the other manage the business for him: So a bond servant was generally the steward in a man's house, and sometimes his heir. There was no harm in buying a man who was in a state of captivity and bondage by others, and keeping him in servitude till such time as his purchase was redeemed by his labor and service. And there could be no harm in paying a man's debts, and keeping him in servitude until such time as an equitable agreement of composition was paid by him. And so, in general, whether they had been bought or sold in order to pay their just debts when they became poor, or were brought from such as held them in an unlawful captivity, the state of bondage which they and their children fell under, among the Israelites, was into that of a vassalage state, which rather might be termed a deliverance from debt and captivity, than a state of slavery. In that vassalage state which they were reduced to, they had a tax of some service to pay, which might only be reckoned equivalent to a poor man in England paying rent for his cottage. In this fair land of liberty, there are many thousands of the inhabitants who have no right to so much land as an inch of ground to set their foot upon, so as to take up their residence upon it, without paying a lawful and reasonable vassalage of rent for it—and yet the whole community is free from slavery. And so, likewise, those who were reduced to a state of servitude, or vassalage, in the land of Israel, were not negotiable like chattels and goods; nor could they be disposed of like cattle and beasts of burden, or ever transferred or disposed of without their own consent; and perhaps not one man in all the land of Israel would buy another man, unless that man was willing to serve him. And when any man had gotten such a servant, as he had entered into a covenant of agreement with, as a bond servant, if the man like his master and his service, he could not oblige him to go away; and it sometimes happened, that they refused to go out free when the year of jubilee came. But even that state of servitude which the Canaanites were reduced to, among those who survived the general overthrow of their country, was nothing worse, in many respects, than that of poor laboring people in any free country. Their being made hewers of wood and drawers of water, were laborious employments; but they were paid for it in such a manner as the nature of their service required, and were supplied with abundance of such necessaries of life as they and their families had need of; and they were at liberty, if they chose, to go away, there was no restriction laid on them. They were not hunted after, and a reward offered for their heads, as it is the case in the West Indies for any that can find a strayed slave; and he who can bring such a head warm reeking with his blood, as a token that he had murdered him—inhuman and shocking to think!—he is paid for it; and, cruel and dreadful as it is, that law is still in force in some of the British colonies.

But the Canaanites, although they were predicted to be reduced to a state of servitude, and bondage to that poor and menial employment, fared better than the West India slaves; for when they were brought into that state of servitude, they were often employed in an honorable service. The Nethenims, and others, were to assist in the sacred solemnities and worship of God at the Temple of Jerusalem. They had the same laws and immunities respecting the solemn days and sabbaths, as their masters the Israelites, and they were to keep and observe them. But they were not suffered, much less required, to labor in their own spots of useful ground on the days of sacred rest from worldly employment; and that, if they did not improve the culture of it, in these times and seasons, they might otherwise perish for hunger and want; as it is the case of the West India slaves, by their inhuman, infidel, hard-hearted master. And, therefore, this may be justly said, that whatever servitude that was, or by whatever name it may be called, that the service which was required by the people of Israel in old time, was of a far milder nature, than that which became the prevalent practice of other different and barbarous nations; and, if compared with modern slavery, it might be called liberty, equity, and felicity, in respect to that abominable, mean, beastly, cruel, bloody slavery carried on by the inhuman, barbarous Europeans, against the poor unfortunate Black Africans.

But again, this may be averred, that the servitude which took place under the sanction of the divine law, in the time of Moses, and what was enjoined as the civil and religious polity of the people of Israel, was in nothing contrary to the natural rights and common liberties of men, though it had an appearance as such for great and wise ends. The Divine Law Giver, in the good providence, for great and wise purposes intended by it, has always admitted into the world riches and poverty, prosperity and adversity, high and low, rich and poor; and in such manner, as in all their variety and difference, mutation and change, there is nothing set forth in the written law by Moses contrary, unbecoming, or inconsistent with that goodness of himself, as the wise and righteous Governor of the Universe. Those things admitted into the law, that had a seeming appearance contrary to the natural liberties of men, were only so admitted for a local time, to point out, and to establish, and to give instruction thereby, in an analogous allusion to other things.

And therefore, so far as I have been able to consult the law written by Moses, concerning that kind of servitude admitted by it, I can find nothing imported thereby, in the least degree, to warrant the modern practice of slavery. But, on the contrary, and what was principally intended thereby, and in the most particular manner, as respecting Christians, that it contains the strongest prohibition against it. And every Christian man, that can read his Bible, may find that which is of the greatest importance for himself to know implied even under the very institution of bond servants; and that the state of bondage which the law denounces and describes, was thereby so intended to point out something necessary, as well as similar to all the other ritual and ceremonial services; and that the whole is set forth in such a manner, as containing the very essence of foundation of the Christian religion.

And, moreover, that it must appear evident to any Christian believer, that it was necessary that all these things should take place, and as the most beautiful fabric of Divine goodness, that in all their variety, and in all their forms, they should stand recorded under the sanction of the Divine law.

And this must be observed, that it hath so pleased the Almighty Creator, to establish all the variety of things in nature, different complexions and other circumstances among men, and to record the various transactions of his own providence, with all the ceremonial economy written in the books of Moses, as more particularly respecting and enjoined to the Israelitish nation and people, for the use of sacred language, in order to convey wisdom to the fallen apostate human race. Wherefore, all the various things established, admitted and recorded, whether natural, moral, typical or ceremonial, with all the various things in nature referred to, were so ordered and admitted, as figures, types and emblems, and other symbolical representations, to bring forward, usher in, hold forth and illustrate that most amazing transaction, and the things concerning it, of all things the most wonderful that ever could take place amongst the universe of intelligent beings; as in that, and the things concerning it, of the salvation of apostate men, and the wonderful benignity of their Almighty Redeemer.

Whoever will give a serious and unprejudiced attention to the various things alluded to in the language of sacred writ, must see reason to believe that they imply a purpose and design far more glorious and important, than what seems generally to be understood by them; and to point to objects and events far more extensive and interesting, than what is generally ascribed to them. But as the grand eligibility and importance of those things, implied and pointed out in sacred writ, and the right understanding thereof, belongs to the sublime science of metaphysics and theology to enforce, illustrate and explain, I shall only select a few instances, which I think have a relation to my subject in hand.

Among other things it may be considered, that the different colors and complexions among men were intended for another purpose and design, than that of being only eligible in the variety of the scale of nature. And, accordingly, had it been otherwise, and if there had never been any black people among the children of men, nor any spotted leopards among the beasts of the earth, such an instructive question, by the prophet, could not have been proposed, as this, *Can the Ethiopian change his skin, or the leopard his spots? Then, may ye also do good, that are accustomed to do evil.* [Jer. 13:23] The instruction intended by this is evident, that it was a convincing and forcible argument to show, that none among the fallen and apostate race of men, can by any effort of their own, change their nature from the blackness and guilt of the sable dye of sin and pollution, or alter their way accustomed to do evil, from the variegated spots of their iniquity; and that such a change is as impossible to be totally and radically effected by them, as it is for a black man to change the color of his skin, or the leopard to alter his spots. But these differences of a natural variety amongst the things themselves, [are] in every respect equally innocent, and what they cannot alter or change, was made to be so, and in the most eligible and primary design, [was] so intended for the very purposes of instructive language to men. And by these extreme differences of color, it was intended to point out and show to the white man, that there is a sinful blackness in his own nature, which he can no more change, than the external blackness which he sees in another can be rendered otherwise; and it likewise holds out to the black man, that the sinful blackness of his own nature is such, that he can no more alter, than the outward appearance of his color can be brought to that of another. And this is imported by it, that there is an inherent evil in every man, contrary to that which is good; and that all men are like Ethiopians (even God's elect) in a state of nature and unregeneracy, they are black with original sin, and spotted with actual transgression, which they cannot reverse. But to this truth, asserted of blackness, I must add another glorious one. All thanks and eternal praise be to God! His infinite wisdom and goodness has found out a way of renovation, and has opened a fountain through the blood of Jesus, for sin and for uncleanness, wherein all the stains and blackest dyes of sin and pollution can be washed away forever, and the darkest sinner be made to shine as the brightest angel in heaven. And for that end and purpose, God alone has appointed all the channels of conveyance of the everlasting Gospel for these healing and purifying streams of the water of life to run in, and to bring life and salvation, with light and gladness to men; but he denounces woe to those who do not receive it themselves, but hinder and debar others who would, from coming to those salutary streams for life. Yet not alone confined to these, nor hindered in his purpose by any opposers, He, who can open the eyes of the blind, and make the deaf hear, can open streams in the desert, and make his benignity to flow, and his salvation to visit even the meanest and most ignorant man, in the darkest shades of nature, as well as the most learned on the earth; and he usually carries on his own gracious work of quickening and redeeming grace, in a secret, sovereign manner. To this I must again observe, and what I chiefly intend by this similitude, that the external blackness of the Ethiopians, is as innocent and natural as spots in the leopards; and that the difference of color and complexion, which it hath pleased God to appoint among men, are no more unbecoming unto either of them, than the different shades of the rainbow are unseemingly to the whole, or unbecoming to any part of that apparent arch. It does not alter the nature and quality of a man, whether he wears a black or a white coat, whether he puts it on or strips it off, he is still the same man. And so likewise, when a man comes to die, it makes no difference whether he was black or white, whether he was male or female, whether he was great or small, or whether he was old or young; none of these differences alter the essentiality of the man, any more than he had wore a black or a white coat and thrown it off forever.

Another form of instruction for the same purpose, may be taken from the slavery and oppression which men have committed upon one another, as well as that kind of bondage and servitude which was admitted under the sanction of the Divine law. But there is nothing set forth in the law as a rule, or anything recorded therein that can stand as a precedent, or make it lawful, for men to practice slavery; nor can any laws in favor of slavery be deduced from thence, for to enslave men, be otherwise, than unwarrantable, as it would be unnecessary and wrong, to order and command the sacrifices of beasts to be still continued. Now the great thing imported by it, and what is chiefly to be deduced from it in this respect, is, that so far as the law concerning bond servants, and that establishment of servitude, as admitted in the Mosaical institution, was set forth, it was thereby intended to prefigure and point out that spiritual subjection and bondage to sin that all mankind, by their original transgression, were fallen into. All men in their fallen depraved state, being under a spirit of bondage, sunk into a nature of brutish carnality, and by the lusts thereof, they are carried captive and enslaved; and the consequence is, that they are sold under sin and in bondage to iniquity, and carried captive by the devil at his will. This being the case, the thing proves itself; for if there had been no evil and sin amongst men, there never would have been any kind of bondage, slavery and oppression found amongst them; and if there was none of these things to be found, the great cause of it could not, in the present situation of men, be pointed out to them in that eligible manner as it is. Wherefore it was necessary that something of that bondage and servitude should be admitted into the ritual law for a figurative use, which, in all other respects and circumstances, was, in itself, contrary to the whole tenure of the law, and naturally in itself unlawful for men to practice.

Nothing but heavenly wisdom, and heavenly grace, can teach men to understand. The most deplorable of all things is, that the dreadful situation of our universal depraved state, which all mankind lieth under, is such that those who are not redeemed in time must forever continue to be the subjects of eternal bondage and misery. Blessed be God! he hath appointed and set up a deliverance, and the Savior of Men is an Almighty Redeemer. When God, the Almighty Redeemer and Savior of his people, brought his Israel out of Egypt and temporal bondage, it was intended and designed thereby, to set up an emblematical representation of their deliverance from the power and captivity of sin, and from the dominion of that evil and malignant spirit, who had with exquisite subtlety and guile at first seduced the original progenitors of mankind. And when they were brought to the promised land, and had gotten deliverance, and subdued their enemies under them, they were to reign over them; and their laws respecting bond servants, and other things of that nature, were to denote that they were to keep under and in subjection the whole body of their evil affections and lusts. This is so declared by the Apostle, that the law is spiritual, and intended for spiritual uses. The general state of slavery which took place in the world, among other enormous crimes of wicked men, might have served for an emblem and similitude of our spiritual bondage and slavery to sin; but, unless it had been admitted into the spiritual and divine law, it could not have stood and become an emblem that there was any spiritual restoration and deliverance afforded to us. By that which is evil in captivity and slavery among men, we are thereby so represented to be under a like subjection to sin; but by what is instituted in the law by Moses, in that respect we are thereby represented as Israel to have dominion over sin, and to rule over and keep in subjection all our spiritual enemies. And, therefore, anything which had a seeming appearance in favor of slavery, so far as it was admitted into the law, was to show that it was not natural and innocent, like that of different colors among men, but as necessary to be made an emblem of what was intended by it, and, consequently, as it stands enjoined among other typical representations, was to show that everything of any evil appearance of it, was to be removed, and to end with the other typical and ceremonial injunctions, when the time of that dispensation was over. This must appear evident to all Christian believers; and since therefore all these things are fulfilled in the establishment of Christianity, there is now nothing remaining in the law for a rule of practice to men, but the ever abiding obligations and ever binding injunctions of moral rectitude, justice, equity and righteousness. All the other things in the Divine law are for spiritual uses and similitudes, for giving instruction to the wise, and understanding to the upright in heart, that the man of God may be perfect, thoroughly furnished unto all good works.

Among other things also, the wars of the Israelites, and the extirpation of the Canaanites, and other circumstances as recorded in sacred history, were intended to give instruction to men, but have often been perverted to the most flagrant abuse, and even inverted to the most notorious purposes, for men to embolden themselves to commit wickedness. Every possession that men enjoy upon earth are the gifts of God, and he who gives them may either take them away again from men, or he may take men away themselves from the earth, as it pleaseth him. But who dare, even with Lucifer, the malignant devourer of the world, think to imitate the most high? The extirpation of the Canaanites out of their land, was so ordered, not only to punish them for their idolatry and abominable wickedness, but also to show forth the honor of his power, and the sovereignty of him who is the only potent one that reigneth over the nations; that all men at that time might learn to fear and know him who is Jehovah; and ever since that it might continue a standing memorial of him, and a standard of honor unto him who doth according to his will among the armies of heaven, and whatever pleaseth him with the inhabitants of the earth. And, in general, these transactions stand recorded for an emblematical use and similitude, in the spiritual warfare of every true Israelite throughout all the ages of time. Every real believer and valiant champion in the knowledge and faith of their Omnipotent Savior and Almighty Deliverer, as the very nature of Christianity requires and enjoins, knoweth the use of these things, *and they know how to endure hardness as good soldiers of Jesus Christ.* They have many battles to fight with their unbelief, the perverseness of their nature, evil tempers and besetting sins, these Canaanites which still dwell in their land. They are so surrounded with adversaries, that they have need always to be upon their guard, and to have all their armor on. They are *commanded to cast off the works of darkness, and to put on the whole armor of righteousness and light; and that they may be strong in the Lord, and in the power of his might.* For it is required *that they should be able to stand against the wiles of the devil, the powers of the rulers of the darkness of this world, against spiritual wickedness in high places.* And as their foes are *mighty and tall like the Anakims, and fenced up to heaven,* they must be mighty warriors, *men of renown, valiant for the truth, strong in the faith, fighting the Lord's battles, and overcoming all their enemies, through the dear might of the Great Captain of their salvation.* In this warfare, should they meet with some mighty *Agag,* some strong corruption, or besetting sin, they are commanded *to cut it down,* and with the sword of Samuel *to hew it to pieces before the Lord.* This, in its literal sense, may seem harsh, as if Samuel had been cruel; and so will our sins, and other sinners insinuate and tell us not to mind such things as the perfect law of God requires. But if we consider that the Lord God who breathed into man the breath of life, can suspend and take it away when he pleaseth, and that there is not a moment we have to exist, wherein that life may not be suspended before the next: it was therefore of an indifferent matter for that man Agag, when the Lord, who hath the breath and life of every man in his hand, had appointed him at that time to die, for his great wickedness and the murders committed by him, whether he was slain by Samuel or any other means. But what Samuel, the servant of the Lord did in that instance, was in obedience to his voice, and in itself a righteous deed, and a just judgment upon Agag. And the matter imported by it, was also intended to show, that all our Amalekite sins, and even the chief and darling of them, the avaricious and covetous Agags, should be cut off forever. But if we spare them, and leave them to remain alive in stubborn disobedience to the law and commandments of God, we should in that case, be like Saul, cut off ourselves from the kingdoms of his grace. According to this view, it may suffice to show (and what infinite wisdom intended, no doubt) that a wise and righteous use may be made of those very things, which otherwise are generally perverted to wrong purposes.

And now, as to these few instances which I have collected from that sacred hypothesis, whereby it is shown, that other things are implied and to be understood by the various incidents as recorded in sacred writ, with a variety of other things in nature, bearing an analogous allusion to things of the greatest importance for every Christian man to know and understand; and that the whole of the ritual law, though these things themselves are not to be again repeated, is of that nature and use as never to be forgotten. And therefore to suppose, or for any Christians to say, that they have nothing to do with those things now in the right use thereof, and what was intended and imported thereby respecting themselves, would be equally as absurd as to hear them speaking in the language of devils; and they might as well say as they did, when speaking out of the demoniac that they have nothing to do with Christ.

Having thus endeavored to show, and what, I think, must appear evident and obvious, that none of all these grand pretensions, as generally made use of by the favorers of slavery, to encourage and embolden them, in that iniquitous traffic, can have any foundation or shadow of truth to support them; and that there is nothing in nature, reason, and scripture can be found, in any manner or way, to warrant the enslaving of black people more than others.

But I am aware that some of these arguments will weigh nothing against such men as do not believe the scriptures themselves, nor care to understand; but let them be aware not to make use of these things against us which they do not believe, or whatever pretense they may have for committing violence against us. Any property taken away from others, whether by stealth, fraud, or violence, must be wrong; but to take away men themselves, and keep them in slavery, must be worse. *Skin for skin, all that a man hath would he give for his life;* and would rather lose his property to any amount whatever, than to have his liberty taken away, and be kept as a slave. It must be an inconceivable fallacy to think otherwise: none but the inconsiderate, most obdurate and stubborn, could ever think that it was right to enslave others. *But the way of the wicked is brutish: his own iniquity shall take the wicked himself, and he shall be holden with the cords of his sins: he shall die without instruction, and in the greatness of his folly he shall go astray.*

Among the various species of men that commit rapine, and violence, and murders, and theft upon their fellow creatures, like the ravenous beasts of the night, prowling for their prey, there are also those that set out their heads in the open day, opposing all the obligations of civilization among men, and breaking through all the laws of justice and equity to them, and making even the very things which are analogous to the obligations, which ought to warn and prohibit them, a pretense for their iniquity and injustice. Such are the insidious merchants and pirates that gladden their ears with the carnage and captivity of men, and the vile negotiators and enslavers of the human species. The prohibitions against them are so strong, that, in order to break through and to commit the most notorious and flagrant crimes with impunity, they are obliged to oil their poisonous pretenses with various perversions of sundry transactions of things even in sacred writ, that the acrimonious points of their arsenic may be swallowed down the better, and the evil effects of their crimes appear the less. In this respect, instead of *the sacred history of the Israelitish nation being made profitable to them, for doctrine, for reproof, for correction, and for instruction in righteousness,* as it was intended, *and given to men* for that purpose; but, instead thereof, the wars of the Israelites, the extirpation and subjection of the Canaanites, and other transactions of that kind, are generally made use of by wicked men as precedents and pretenses to encourage and embolden themselves to commit cruelty and slavery on their fellow creatures: and the merciless depredators, negotiators, and enslavers of men, revert to the very ritual law of Moses as precedent for their barbarity, cruelty, and injustice; which law, though devoid of any iniquity, as bearing a parallel allusion to other things signified thereby, can afford no precedent for their evil way, in any shape or view: what was intended by it is fulfilled, and in no respect, or anything like it, can be repeated again, without transgressing and breaking through every other injunction, precept, and command of the just and tremendous law of God.

The consequence of their apostasy from God, and disobedience to his law, became a snare to those men in times of old, who departed from it; and because of their disobedience and wickedness, the several nations, which went astray after their own abominations, were visited with many dreadful calamities and judgments. But to set up the ways of the wicked for an example, and to make the laws respecting their suppression, and the judgments that were inflicted upon them for their iniquity, and even the written word of God, and the transactions of his providence, to be reversed and become precedents, and pretenses for men to commit depredations and extirpations, and for enslaving and negotiating or merchandising the human species, must be horrible wickedness indeed, and sinning with a high hand. And it cannot be thought otherwise, but that the abandoned aggressors, among the learned nations will, in due time, as the just reward of their aggravated iniquity, be visited with some more dreadful and tremendous judgments of the righteous vengeance of God, than what even befell the Canaanites of old.

And it may be considered further, that to draw any inferences in favor of extirpation, slavery, and negotiation of men from the written word of God, or from anything else in the history and customs of different nations, as a precedent to embolden wicked men in their

wickedness; cannot be more wicked, ridiculous, and absurd to show
any further to these insidious negotiators and enslavers, than it would
be to stand and laugh, and look on with a brutal and savage impunity,
at beholding the following supposition transacted. Suppose two or
three half-witted foolish fellows happened to come past a crowd of
people, gazing at one which they had hung up by the neck on a tree, as
a victim suffering for breaking the laws of his country; and suppose
these foolish fellows went on a little way in a bypath, and found some
innocent person, not suspecting any harm till taken hold of by them,
and could not deliver himself from them, and just because they had
seen among the crowd of people which they came past, that there had
been a man hung by the neck, they took it into their foolish wicked
heads to hang up the poor innocent man on the next tree, and just did
as they had seen others do, to please their own fancy and base foolishness, to see how he would swing. Now if any of the other people happened to come up to them, and saw what they had done, would they
hesitate a moment to determine between themselves and these foolish
rascals which had done wickedness? Surely not; they would immediately take hold of such stupid wicked wretches, if it was in their power,
and for their brutish foolishness, have them chained in a Bedlam, or
hung on a gibbet. But what would these base foolish wretches say for
themselves? That they saw others do so, and they thought there had
been no harm in it, and they only did as they had seen the crowd of
people do before. A poor foolish, base, rascally excuse indeed! But not
a better excuse than this, can the brutish enslavers and negotiators of
men find in all the annals of history. The ensnarers, negotiators, and
oppressors of men, have only to become more abandoned in wickedness than these supposed wretches could be; and to pass on in the
most abominable bypaths of wickedness, and make everything that
they can see an example for their brutal barbarity; and whether it be a
man hanged for his crimes, or an innocent man for the wretched wickedness of others; right or wrong it makes no difference to them, if they
can only satisfy their own wretched and brutal avarice. Whether it be
the Israelites subjecting the Canaanites for their crimes, or the Canaanites subjecting the Israelites to gratify their own wickedness, it
makes no difference to them. When they see some base wretches like
themselves ensnaring, enslaving, oppressing, whipping, starving
with hunger, and cruelly torturing and murdering some of the poor
helpless part of mankind, they would think no harm in it, they would
do the same. Perhaps the Greeks and Romans, and other crowds of

barbarous nations have done so before; they can make that a precedent, and think no harm in it, they would still do the same, and worse
than any barbarous nations ever did before: and if they look backwards
and forwards they can find no better precedent, ancient or modern,
than that which is wicked, mean, brutish, and base. To practice such
abominable parallels of wickedness of ensnaring, negotiating and enslaving men, is the scandal and shame of mankind. And what must we
think of their crimes? Let the groans and cries of the murdered, and
the cruel slavery of the Africans tell!

They that can stand and look on and behold no evil in the infamous
traffic of slavery must be sunk to a wonderful degree of insensibility;
but surely those that can delight in that evil way for their gain, and be
pleased with the wickedness of the wicked, and see no harm in subjecting their fellow creatures to slavery, and keeping them in a state of
bondage and subjection as a brute, must be wretchedly brutish indeed.
But so bewitched are the general part of mankind with some sottish or
selfish principle, that they care nothing about what is right or wrong,
any farther than their own interest leads them to; and when avarice
leads them on they can plead a thousand excuses for doing wrong, or
letting others do wickedly, so as they have any advantage by it, to their
own gratification and use. That sottish and selfish principle, without
concern and discernment among men is such that if they can only
prosper themselves, they care nothing about the miserable situation of
others: and hence it is, that even those who are elevated to high rank of
power and affluence, and as becoming their eminent stations, have opportunity of extending their views afar, yet they can shut their eyes at
this enormous evil of the slavery and commerce of the human species;
and, contrary to all the boasted accomplishments, and fine virtues of
the civilized and enlightened nations, they can sit still and let the torrent of robbery, slavery, and oppression roll on.

*There is a way which seemeth good unto a man, but the end thereof are
the ways of death.* Should the enslavers of men think to justify themselves in their evil way, or that it can in any possible way be right for
them to subject others to slavery; it is but charitable to evince and declare unto them, that they are those who have gone into that evil way of
brutish stupidity as well as wickedness, that they can behold nothing
of moral rectitude and equity among men but in the gloomy darkness
of their own hemisphere, like the owls and nighthawks, who can see
nothing but mist and darkness in the meridian blaze of day. When men
forsake the paths of virtue, righteousness, justice, and mercy, and be-

come vitiated in any evil way, all their pretended virtues, sensibility, and prudence among men, however high they may shine in their own, and of others' estimation, will only appear to be but specious villainy at last. That virtue which will ever do men any good in the end, is as far from that which some men call such, as the gaudy appearance of a glowworm in the dark is to the intrinsic value and lustre of a diamond: for if a man hath not love in his heart to his fellow creatures, with a generous philanthropy diffused throughout his whole soul, all his other virtues are not worth a straw.

The whole law of God is founded upon love, and the two grand branches of it are these: *Thou shalt love the Lord thy God with all thy heart and with all thy soul; and thou shalt love thy neighbor as thyself.* And so it was when man was first created and made: they were created male and female, and pronounced to be in the image of God, and, as his representative, to have dominion over the lower creation; and their Maker, who is love, and the intellectual Father of Spirits, blessed them, and commanded them to arise in a bond of union of nature and of blood, each being a brother and a sister together, and each the lover and the loved of one another. But when they were envied and invaded by the grand enslaver of men, all their jarring incoherency arose, and those who adhered to their pernicious usurper soon became envious, hateful, and hating one another. And those who go on to injure, ensnare, oppress, and enslave their fellow creatures, manifest their hatred to men, and maintain their own infamous dignity and vassalage, as the servants of sin and the devil: but the man that has any honor as a man scorns their ignominious dignity: the noble philanthropist looks up to his God and Father as his only sovereign; and he looks around on his fellow men as his brethren and friends; and in every situation and case, however mean and contemptible they may seem, he endeavors to do them good: and should he meet with one in the desert, whom he never saw before he would hail him my brother! my sister! my friend! how fares it with thee? And if he can do any of them any good it would gladden every nerve of his soul.

But as there is but *one law and one manner* prescribed universally for all mankind, *for you, and for the stranger that sojourneth with you,* and wheresoever they may be scattered throughout the face of the whole earth, the differences of superiority and inferiority which are found subsisting amongst them is no way incompatible with the universal law of love, honor, righteousness, and equity; so that a free, voluntary, and sociable servitude, which is the very basis of human society, either civil or religious, whereby we serve one another that we may be served, or do good that good may be done unto us, is in all things requisite and agreeable to all law and justice. But the taking away the natural liberties of men, and compelling them to any involuntary slavery, or compulsory service, is an injury and robbery contrary to all law, civilization, reason, justice, equity, and humanity: therefore, when men break through the laws of God, and the rules of civilization among men, and go forth to steal, to rob, to plunder, to oppress and to enslave, and to destroy their fellow creatures, the laws of God and man require that they should be suppressed, and deprived of their liberty, or perhaps their lives.

But justice and equity does not always reside among men, even where some considerable degree of civilization is maintained; if it had, that most infamous reservoir of public and abandoned merchandisers and enslavers of men would not have been suffered so long, nor the poor unfortunate Africans, that never would have crossed the Atlantic to rob them, would not have become their prey. But it is just as great and as heinous a transgression of the law of God to steal, kidnap, buy, sell, and enslave any one of the Africans, as it would be to ensnare any other man in the same manner, let him be who he will. And suppose that some of the African pirates had been as dexterous as the Europeans, and that they had made excursions on the coast of Great Britain or elsewhere, and though even assisted by some of your own insidious neighbors, for there may be some men even among you vile enough to do such a thing if they could get money by it; and that they should carry off your sons and your daughters, and your wives and friends, to a perpetual and barbarous slavery, you would certainly think that those African pirates were justly deserving of any punishment that could be put upon them. But the European pirates and merchandisers of the human species, let them belong to what nation they will, are equally as bad; and they have no better right to steal, kidnap, buy, and carry away and sell the Africans, than the Africans would have to carry away any of the Europeans in the same barbarous and unlawful manner.

But again, let us follow the European piracy to the West Indies, or anywhere among Christians, and this law of the *Lord Christ* must stare every infidel slaveholder in the face, *And as ye would that men should do to you, do ye also to them likewise*. But there is no slaveholder would like to have himself enslaved, and to be treated as a dog, and sold like a beast; and therefore the slaveholders, and merchandisers of men, transgress this plain law, and they commit a younger violation against it, and act more contrary unto it, than it would be for a parcel of slaves to assume authority over their masters, and compel them to slavery under them; for, if that was not doing as they would wish to be done to, it would be doing, at least, as others do to them, in a way equally as much and more wrong. But our Divine Lord and *Master Christ* also teacheth men to *forgive one another their trespasses,* and that we are not to do evil because others do so, and to revenge injuries done unto us. Wherefore it is better, and more our duty, to suffer ourselves to be lashed and cruelly treated, than to take up the task of their barbarity. The just law of God requires an equal retaliation and restoration for every injury that men may do to others, to show the greatness of the crime; but the law of forbearance, righteousness and forgiveness, forbids the retaliation to be sought after, when it would be doing as great an injury to them, without any reparation or benefit to ourselves. For what man can restore an eye that he may have deprived another of, and if even a double punishment was to pass upon him, and that he was to lose both his eyes for the crime, that would make no reparation to the other man whom he had deprived of one eye. And so, likewise, when a man is carried captive and enslaved, and maimed and cruelly treated, that would make no adequate reparation and restitution for the injuries he had received, if he was even to get the person who had ensnared him to be taken captive and treated in the same manner. What he is to seek after is a deliverance and protection for himself, and not a revenge upon others. Wherefore the honest and upright, like the just Bethlehem Joseph, cannot think of doing evil, nor require an equal retaliation for such injuries done to them, so as to revenge themselves upon others, for that which would do them no manner of good. Such vengeance belongeth unto the Lord, and he will render vengeance and recompense to his enemies and the violaters of his law.

But thus saith the law of God: *If a man be found stealing any of his neighbors, or he that stealeth a man (let him be who he will) and selleth him, or that maketh merchandise of him, or if he be found in his hand, then that thief shall die.* However, in all modern slavery among Christians, who ought to know this law, they have not had any regard to it. Surely if any law among them admits of death as a punishment for robbing or defrauding others of their money or goods, it ought to be double death, if it was possible, when a man is robbed of himself, and sold into captivity and cruel slavery. But because of his own goodness, and because of the universal depravity of men, the Sovereign Judge of all has introduced a law of forbearance, to spare such transgressors, where in many cases the law denounces death as the punishment for their crimes, unless for those founded upon murder, or such abominations as cannot be forborne within any civilization among men. But this law of forbearance is no alteration of the law itself; it is only a respite in order to spare such as will fly to him for refuge and forgiveness for all their crimes, and for all their iniquities, who is the righteous fulfiller of the law, and the surety and representative of men before God: and if they do not repent of their iniquity, and reform to a life of new obedience, as being under greater obligations to the law, but go on in their evil way, they must at least forever lie under the curse and every penalty of the just and holy law of the Most High. This seems to be determined so by that Great Judge of the law, when the accusers of a woman, taken in adultery, brought her before him, he stooped down as a man and wrote, we may suppose, the crimes of her accusers in the dust, and as the God of all intelligence painted them in their consciences, wherefore they fled away one by one, and the woman was left alone before him; and as there was none of her accusers in that case righteous enough to throw the first stone, and to execute the law upon her, she was, Bid to go and sin no more. But it is manifest that every crime that men may commit, where death is mentioned as the penalty thereof in the righteous law of God, it denotes a very great offense and a heinous transgression; and although, in many cases, it may meet with some mitigation in the punishment, because of the forbearance of God, and the unrighteousness of men, it cannot thereby be thought the less criminal in itself. But it also supposes, where strict severities are made use of in the laws of civilization, that the doers of the law, and the judges of it, ought to be very righteous themselves. And with regard to that law of men stealers, merchandisers, and of slaves found in their hands, that whatever mitigation and forbearance such offenders ought to meet with, their crimes denote a very heinous offense, and a great violation of the law of God; they ought, therefore, to be punished according to their trespasses, which, in some cases, should be death, if the person so robbed and stole[n] should die in consequence thereof, or should not be restored and brought back; and even then to be liable to every damage and penalty that the judges should think proper: for it is annexed to this law and required, *that men should put away evil from among them.* But this cannot now extend to the West India slavery: what should rather be required of them, in their present case of infatuation, is to surrender and give it up, and heal the stripes that they have wounded, and to pour the healing balm of Christianity into the bleeding wounds of Heathen barbarity and cruelty.

All the criminal laws of civilization seem to be founded upon that law of God which was published to Noah and his sons; and, consequently, as it is again and again repeated, it becomes irreversible, and universal to all mankind. *And surely your blood of your lives will I require: at the hand of every beast will I require it; and at the hand of man, at the hand of every man's brother, will I require the life of man. Whoso sheddeth man's blood, by man shall his blood be shed: for in the image of God made he man.* If this law of God had not been given to men, murder itself would not have been any crime; and those who punished it with death would just have been as guilty as the other. But the law of God is just righteous and holy, and ought to be regarded and revered above all the laws of men; and this is added unto it: *What thing soever I command you, observe to do it: thou shalt not add thereto, nor diminish from it.* But it is an exceeding impious thing for men ever to presume, or think, as some will say, that they would make it death as a punishment for such a thing, and such a trespass; or that they can make any criminal laws of civilization as binding with a penalty of death for anything just what they please. No such thing can be supposed; no man upon earth ever had, or ever can have, a right to make laws where a penalty of cutting off by death is required as the punishment for the transgression thereof: what is required of men is to be the doers of the law, and some of them to be judges of it; and if they judge wrongfully in taking away the lives of their fellow creatures contrary to the law of God, they commit murder.

The reason why a man suffers death for breaking the laws of his country is, because he transgresseth the law of God in that community he belongs to: and the laws of civilization are binding to put that law in force, and to point out and show a sufficient warrant wherefore he should suffer, according as the just law of God requires for his trespass; and then it is just and right that he should die for his crime. And as murder is irreversible to be punished with death, sometimes when it is not done, but only implied or eventually intended, it even then requires death; and in this sense it becomes right to face our enemies in the field of battle, and to cut them off. And when spies and incendiaries rise up, or when rebellions break forth, and the lives of the sovereign and others, and the good of the community is not safe while such pretenders and their chief supporters are suffered to live; then it may be lawful, in some cases, that they should die; but in cases of this kind there is generally more cowardice and cruelty than justice and mercy regarded, and more discretionary power left for men to use their authority in, and to establish criminal laws or precedents than in anything else. Hence we may find many of the different chiefs and kings in different parts of the world, in all ages, wading through a sea of blood to their thrones, or supporting themselves upon it, by desolating and destroying others; and we may find good and bad in all ages setting up wretched examples for men to be guided by; and herein we may find a David, a Solomon, a Cromwell, committing murder and death, and Charles the Second committing a greater carnage upon more innocent people than those who suffered in the reign of a bloody Queen Mary; and even in a late rebellion there were many suffered in Britain, which, if they had been preserved to this mild reign, they would have been as good neighbors, and as faithful subjects, as any other. But among all pretenses for taking away the lives of men by any form of law, that for religion is the most unwarrantable: it is the command of God to suppress idolatry, and to break down the images and external pomp of gross superstition, but not to destroy men themselves: that persecution is murder if it takes away the lives of men for their religion, for it has nothing to do with what men may think with respect to their own duty; and if a man is foolish enough to make an image of wood or stone, and to worship it, or even to adore a picture, if he keeps it to himself, persecution has nothing to do with him.

The law of God forbids all manner of covetousness and theft: but when anything is taken away by stealth, it is not like those injuries which cannot be restored, as the cutting off or wounding any of the members of the body; but it admits of a possible restoration, whether the violators can restore it or not as the law requires, so if a man owes a just debt it is not the less due by him if he has got nothing to pay it with; such transgressors ought to be punished according to their trespasses, but not with death: for the law of God is, "If a thief be found breaking up, and he be smitten that he die, if it was in the night there shall be no blood shed for him; but if the sun be risen upon him, there was blood required for him if he was killed; for saith the law it required only he should make full restitution; and if he had nothing, then he should be sold for his theft. And if any manner of theft be found in a man's hand, the law requires a retaliation and restoration; that is, that he should restore double; but if it be sold or made away with, it was then to be four-fold, and, in some cases, five, six or seven times as much."* According to this law, when the property of others is taken away, either by stealth, fraud, or violence, the aggressors should be subjected to such bondage and hard labor (and especially when the trespass is great, and they have nothing to pay) as would be requisite to make restitution to the injured, and to bring about a reformation to themselves. And if they have committed violence either by threats or force, they ought to suffer bodily punishment, and the severity of it according to their crimes, and the stubbornness of their obduracy; and all such punishments as are necessary should be inflicted upon them without pitying or sparing them, though perhaps not to be continued forever in the brutal manner that the West India slaves suffer for almost no crimes.

But whereas the robbing of others in any manner of their property is often attended with such cruelty and violence, and a severe loss to the sufferers, it may, in some cases, be thought that the law of God sufficiently warrants the taking away the lives of the aggressors; for the taking away of a man's property in general may be considered as taking away his life, or at least the means of his support, and then the punishing the transgressors with death can only in that case be reckoned a constructive murder. Wherefore the transgressors ought to be punished severely; but never with any laws of civilization where death is concerned, without a regard to the law of God. And when the law of God admits of a forbearance, and a kind of forgiveness in many things, it ought to be the grand law of civilization to seek out such rules of punishment as are best calculated to prevent injuries of every kind, and to reclaim the transgressors; and it is best, if it can be done, to punish with a less degree of severity than their crimes deserve. But all the laws of civilization must jar greatly when the law of God is screwed up in the greatest severity to punish men for their crimes on the one hand, and on the other to be totally disregarded.† When the Divine law points out a theft, where the thief should make restitution for his trespass, the laws of civilization say, he must die for his crime: and when that law tells us, that he who stealeth or maketh merchandise of men, that such a thief shall surely die, the laws of civilization say, in many cases, that it is no crime. In this the ways of men are not equal; but let the

---

*A great part of this law is strictly observed in Africa, and we make use of sacrifices, and keep a sabbath every seventh day, more strictly than Christians generally do.
†This confessional minstrel may be often repeated, but, I fear, seldom regarded: "We have offended against thy holy laws; we have left undone those things which we ought to have done; and we have done those things which we ought not to have done."

wise and just determine whether the laws of God or the laws of men
are right.

Amongst some of the greatest transgressors of the laws of civilization, those that defraud the public by forgery, or by substituting or
falsifying any of the current specie, ought to have their lives or their
liberties taken away; for although they may not do any personal injury,
they commit the greatest robbery and theft, both to individuals and
the whole community. But even in the suppression of those, men have
no right to add or diminish anything to the law of God, with respect to
taking away their lives. Wherefore, if the law of God does not so clearly
warrant that they should die for their theft, it, at least, fully warrants
that they should be sold into slavery for their crimes; and the laws of
civilization may justly bind them, and hold them in perpetual bondage, because they have sold themselves to work iniquity; but not that
they should be sold to the heathen, or to such as would not instruct
them: for there might be hope, that if good instruction was properly administered unto them, there might be a possible reformation
wrought upon some of them. Some, by their ingenious assiduity, have
tamed the most savage wild beasts; it is certainly more laudable to tame
the most brutish and savage men, and, in time, there might be some
Onesimus found amongst them, that would become useful to reclaim
others. Those that break the laws of civilization, in any flagrant manner, are the only species of men that others have a right to enslave; and
such ought to be sold to the community, with everything that can be
found belonging to them, to make a commutation of restitution as far
as could be; and they should be kept at some useful and laborious employment, and it might be at some embarkation, or recovering of waste
ground, as there might be land recovered on rivers and shores, worth
all the expense, for the benefit of the community they belonged to.
The continuance of that criminal slavery and bondage ought to be according to the nature of their crimes, with a preference to their good
behavior, either to be continued or protracted. Such as were condemned for life, when their crimes were great, and themselves stubborn, might be so marked as to render their getting away impossible
without being discovered, and that the very sight of one of them might
deter others from committing their crimes, as much as hanging perhaps a dozen of them; and it might be made so severe unto them, that
it would render their own society in bondage, almost the only preferable one that they could enjoy among men. The manner of confining
them would not be so impracticable as some may be apt to think; and

all these severities come under the laws of men to punish others for their crimes, but they should not go beyond the just law of God; and neither should his laws be suspended, where greater trespasses are committed.

In this sense every free community might keep slaves, or criminal prisoners in bondage; and should they be sold to any other, it should not be to strangers, nor without their own consent; and if any were sold for a term of years, they would naturally become free as soon as their purchase could be paid. But if any man should buy another man without his own consent, and compel him to his service and slavery without any agreement of that man to serve him, the enslaver is a robber, and a defrauder of that man every day. Wherefore it is as much the duty of a man who is robbed in that manner to get out of the hands of his enslaver, as it is for any honest community of men to get out of the hands of rogues and villains. And however much is required of men to forgive one another their trespasses in one respect, it is also manifest, and what we are commanded, as noble, to resist evil in another, in order to prevent others doing evil, and to keep ourselves from harm. Therefore, if there was no other way to deliver a man from slavery, but by enslaving his master, it would be lawful for him to do so if he was able, for this would be doing justice to himself, and be justice as the law requires, to chastise his master for enslaving of him wrongfully.

Thence this general and grant duty should be observed by every man, not to follow the multitude to do evil, neither to recompense evil for evil; and yet, so that a man may lawfully defend himself, and endeavor to secure himself, and others, as far as he can, from injuries of every kind. Wherefore all along, in the history of mankind, the various depredations committed in the world, by enslaving, extirpating and destroying men, were always contrary to the laws of God, and what he had strictly forbidden and commanded not to be done. But insolent, proud, wicked men, in all ages, and in all places, are alike; they disregard the laws of the Most High, and stop at no evil in their power, that they can contrive with any pretense of consistency in doing mischief to others, so as it may tend to promote their own profit and ambition. Such are all the depredators, kidnappers, merchandisers and enslavers of men; they do not care, nor consider, how much they injure others, if they can make any advantage to themselves by it. But whenever these things were committed by wicked men, a retaliation was sought after, as the only way of deliverance; for he who leadeth into captivity, should be carried captive; and he which destroyeth with the sword, should die with the sword. And as it became necessary to punish those that wronged others, when the punishers went beyond the bounds of a just retaliation, and fell into the same crimes of the oppressors, not to prevent themselves from harm, and to deliver the oppressed and the captive, but to oppress and enslave others, as much as they before them had done, the consequence is plain, that an impending overthrow must still fall upon them likewise. In that respect, so far as conquerors are permitted to become a judgment and a scourge to others, for their enormous transgressions, they are themselves not a bit the more safe, for what they do, they often do wickedly for their own purpose; and when the purpose of Divine Providence, who raised them up, is fulfilled by them, in the punishment of others for their crimes; the next wave thereof will be to visit them also according to their wickedness with some dreadful overthrow, and to swallow them up in the sea of destruction and oblivion.

History affords us many examples of severe retaliations, revolutions and dreadful overthrows; and of many crying under the heavy load of subjection and oppression, seeking for deliverance. And methinks I hear now, many of my countrymen, in complexion, crying and groaning under the heavy yoke of slavery and bondage, and praying to be delivered; and the word of the Lord is thus speaking for them, while they are bemoaning themselves under the grievous bonds of their misery and woe, saying, *Woe is me!* alas Africa! *for I am as the last gleanings of the summer fruit, as the grape gleanings of the vintage, where no cluster is to eat. The good are perished out of the earth, and there is none upright among men; they all lie in wait for blood; they hunt every man his brother with a net. That they may do evil with both hands earnestly, the prince asketh, and the judge asketh for a reward; and the great man he uttereth his mischievous desire; so they wrap it up.* Among *the best* in Africa, we have found them *sharp as briar;* among *the most upright,* we have found them *sharper than a thorn hedge* in the West Indies. Yet, O Africa! yet, poor slave! *The day of thy watchmen cometh, and thy visitation* draweth nigh, *that shall be their perplexity. Therefore I will look unto the Lord; and I will wait for the God of my salvation; my God will hear me. Rejoice not against me, O mine enemy; though I be fallen, I shall yet arise; though I sit in darkness, the Lord shall yet be a light unto me. I will bear the indignation of the Lord, because I have sinned against him, until he plead my cause, and execute judgment for me, and I shall behold his righteousness. Then mine enemies shall see it, and shame shall cover them which said unto me, Where is the Lord thy God,* that regardeth thee: *Mine eyes shall behold them trodden down as the mire of the streets. In that day that thy walls* of deliverance *are to be built, in that day shall the decree* of slavery *be far removed.*

What revolution the end of that predominant evil of slavery and oppression may produce, whether the wise and considerate will surrender and give it up, and make restitution for the injuries that they have already done, as far as they can; or whether the force of their wickedness, and the iniquity of their power, will lead them on until some universal calamity burst forth against the abandoned carriers of it on, and against the criminal nations in confederacy with them, is not for me to determine. But this must appear evident, that for any man to carry on a traffic in the merchandise of slaves, and to keep them in slavery; or for any nation to oppress, extirpate and destroy others; that these are crimes of the greatest magnitude, and a most daring violation of the laws and commandments of the Most High, and which, at last, will be evidenced in the destruction and overthrow of all the transgressors. And nothing else can be expected for such violations of taking away the natural rights and liberties of men, but that those who are the doers of it will meet with some awful visitation of the righteous judgment of God, and in such a manner as it cannot be thought that his just vengeance for their iniquity will be the less tremendous because his judgments are long delayed.

None but men of the most brutish and depraved nature, led on by the invidious influence of infernal wickedness, could have made their settlements in the different parts of the world discovered by them, and have treated the various Indian nations, in the manner that the barbarous inhuman Europeans have done: and their establishing and carrying on that most dishonest, unjust and diabolical traffic of buying and selling, and of enslaving men, is such a monstrous, audacious and unparallelled wickedness, that the very idea of it is shocking, and the whole nature of it is horrible and infernal. It may be said with confidence as a certain general fact, that all their foreign settlements and colonies were founded on murders and devastations, and that they have continued their depredations in cruel slavery and oppression to this day: for where such predominant wickedness as the African slave trade, and the West Indian slavery, is admitted, tolerated and supported by them, as carried on in their colonies, the nations and people who are the supporters and encouragers thereof must be not only guilty themselves of that shameful and abandoned evil and wickedness, so very disgraceful to human nature, but even partakers in those crimes of the most vile combinations of various pirates, kidnappers, robbers and thieves, the ruffians and stealers of men, that ever made their appearance in the world.

Soon after Columbus had discovered America, that great navigator was himself greatly embarrassed and treated unjustly, and his best designs counteracted by the wicked baseness of those whom he led to that discovery. The infernal conduct of his Spanish competitors, whose leading motives were covetousness, avarice and fanaticism, soon made their appearance, and became cruel and dreadful. At Hispaniola the base perfidy and bloody treachery of the Spaniards, led on by the perfidious Ovando, in seizing the peaceable Queen Anacoana and her attendants, burning her palace, putting all to destruction, and the innocent Queen and her people to a cruel death, is truly horrible and lamentable. And led on by the treacherous Cortes, the fate of the great Montezuma was dreadful and shocking; how that American monarch was treated, betrayed and destroyed, and his vast extensive empire of the Mexicans brought to ruin and devastation, no man of sensibility of feeling can read the history without pity and resentment. And looking over another page of that history, sensibility would kindle into horror and indignation, to see the base treacherous bastard Pizarro at the head of the Spanish banditti of miscreant depredators, leading them on, and overturning one of the most extensive empires in the world. To recite a little of this as a specimen of the rest:

It seems Pizarro with his company of depredators, had artfully penetrated into the Peruvian empire, and pretended an embassy of peace from a great monarch, and demanded an audience of the noble Atahualpa, the great Inca or Lord of that empire, that the terms of their embassy might be explained, and the reason of their coming into the territories of that monarch. Atahualpa fearing the menaces of those terrible invaders, and thinking to appease them by complying with their request, relied on Pizarro's feigned pretensions of friendship; accordingly the day was appointed, and Atahualpa made his appearance with the greatest decency and splendor he could, to meet such superior beings as the Americans conceived their invaders to be, with four hundred men in uniform dress, as harbingers to clear the way before him, and himself sitting on a throne or couch, adorned with plumes of various colors and almost covered with plates of gold and silver, enriched with precious stones, and was carried on the shoulders of his principal attendants. As he approached near the Spanish quarters the arch fanatic Father Vincent Valverde, chaplain to the expedition, advanced with a crucifix in one hand and a breviary in the other, and began with a long discourse, pretending to explain some of the general doctrines of Christianity, together with the fabulous notion of Saint Peter's vice-regency, and the transmission of his apostolic power continued in the succession of the Popes; and that the then Pope, Alexander, by dona-tion, had invested their master as the sole Monarch of all the New World. In consequence of this, Atahualpa was instantly required to embrace the Christian religion, acknowledge the jurisdiction of the Pope, and submit to the Great Monarch of Castile; but if he should re-fuse an immediate compliance with these requisitions, they were to declare war against him, and that he might expect the dreadful effects of their vengeance. This strange harangue, unfolding deep mysteries and alluding to such unknown facts, of which no power of eloquence could translate and convey at once, if a distinct idea to an American that its general tenor was altogether incomprehensible to Atahualpa. Some parts in it, as more obvious than the rest, filled him with as-tonishment and indignation. His reply, however, was temperate, and as suitable as could be well expected. He observed that he was lord of the dominions over which he reigned by hereditary succession; and said, that he could not conceive how a foreign priest should pretend to dispose of territories which did not belong to him, and that if such a preposterous grant had been made, he, who was the rightful possessor, refused to confirm it; that he had no inclination to renounce the reli-gious institutions established by his ancestors; nor would he forsake the service of the Sun, the immortal divinity whom he and his people revered, in order to worship the God of the Spaniards, who was subject to death; and that with respect to other matters, he had never heard of them before, and did not then understand their meaning. And he de-sired to know where Valverde had learned things so extraordinary. In this book, replied the fanatic Monk, reaching out his breviary. The Inca opened it eagerly, and turning over the leaves, lifted it to his ear: This, says he, is silent; it tells me nothing; and threw it with disdain to the ground. The enraged father of ruffians, turning towards his coun-trymen, the assassinators, cried out, To arms, Christians, to arms; the word of God is insulted; avenge this profanation on these impious dogs.

At this the Christian desperados impatient in delay, as soon as the signal of assault was given their martial music began to play, and their attack was rapid, rushing suddenly upon the Peruvians, and with their hell-invented enginery of thunder, fire and smoke, they soon put them to flight and destruction. The Inca, though his nobles crowded round him with officious zeal, and fell in numbers at his feet, while they vied one with another in sacrificing their own lives that they might cover the sacred person of their Sovereign, was soon penetrated to by the assassinators, dragged from his throne, and carried to the Spanish quarters. The fate of the Monarch increased the precipitate flight of his followers; the plains being covered with upwards of thirty thousand men, were pursued by the ferocious Spaniards towards every quarter, who, with deliberate and unrelenting barbarity, continued to slaughter the wretched fugitives till the close of the day, that never had once offered at any resistance. Pizarro had contrived this daring and perfidious plan on purpose to get hold of the Inca, notwithstanding his assumed character of an ambassador from a powerful monarch to court an alliance with that prince, and in violation of all the repeated offers of his own friendship. The noble Inca thus found himself betrayed and shut up in the Spanish quarters, though scarce aware at first of the vast carnage and destruction of his people; but soon conceiving the destructive consequences that attended his confinement, and by beholding the vast treasures of spoil that the Spaniards had so eagerly gathered up, he learned something of their covetous disposition; and he offered as a ransom what astonished the Spaniards, even after all they now knew concerning the opulence of his kingdom: the apartment in which he was confined was twenty-two feet in length and sixteen in breadth, he undertook to fill it with vessels of gold as high as he could reach. This tempting proposal was eagerly agreed to by Pizarro, and a line was drawn upon the walls of the chamber to mark the stipulated height to which the treasure was to rise. The gold was accordingly collected from various parts with the greatest expedition by the Inca's obedient and loving subjects, who thought nothing too much for his ransom and life; but, after all, poor Atahualpa was cruelly murdered, and his body burnt by a military inquisition, and his extensive and rich dominions devoted to destruction and ruin by these merciless depredators.

The history of those dreadfully perfidious methods of forming settlements, and acquiring riches and territory, would make humanity tremble, and even recoil, at the enjoyment of such acquisitions and become reverted into rage and indignation at such horrible injustice and barbarous cruelty. "It is said by the Peruvians, that their Incas, or Monarchs, had uniformly extended their power with attention to the good of their subjects, that they might diffuse the blessings of civilization, and the knowledge of the arts which they possessed, among the people that embraced their protection; and during a succession of twelve monarchs, not one had deviated from this beneficent character." Their sensibility of such nobleness of character would give them the most poignant dislike to their new terrible invaders that had desolated and laid waste their country. The character of their monarchs would seem to vie with as great virtues as any King in Europe can boast of. Had the Peruvians been visited by men of honesty, knowledge, and enlightened understanding to teach them, by patient instruction and the blessing of God, they might have been induced to embrace the doctrines and faith of Christianity, and to abandon their errors of superstition and idolatry. Had Christians, that deserve the name thereof, been sent among them, the many useful things that they would have taught them, together with their own pious example, would have captivated their hearts; and the knowledge of the truth would have made it a very desirous thing for the Americans to have those that taught them to settle among them. Had that been the case the Americans, in various parts, would have been as eager to have the Europeans to come there as they would have been to go, so that the Europeans might have found settlements enough, in a friendly alliance with the inhabitants, without destroying and enslaving them. And had that been the case, it might be supposed, that Europe and America, long before now, would both with a growing luxuriancy, have been flourishing with affluence and peace, and their long extended and fruitful branches, laden with benefits to each other, reaching over the ocean, might have been more extensive, and greater advantages have been expected, for the good of both than what has yet appeared. But, alas! at that time there [were] no Christians to send (and very few now), these were obliged to hide themselves in the obscure place of the earth; that was, according to Sir Isaac Newton, to mix in obscurity among the meanest of the people, having no power and authority; and it seems at that time there was no power among Christians on earth to have sent such as would have been useful to the Americans; if there had they would have sent after the depredators, and rescued the innocent.

But as I said before, it is surely to the great shame and scandal of Christianity among all the Heathen nations, that those robbers, plunderers, destroyers and enslavers of men should call themselves Christians, and exercise their power under any Christian government and authority. I would have my African countrymen to know and understand, that the destroyers and enslavers of men can be no Christians;

for Christianity is the system of benignity and love, and all its votaries
are devoted to honesty, justice, humanity, meekness, peace and goodwill to all men. But whatever title or claim some may assume to call
themselves by it, without possessing any of its virtues, can only manifest them to be the more abominable liars, and the greatest enemies unto it, and as belonging to the synagogue of Satan, and not the
adherers to Christ. For the enslavers and oppressors of men, among
those that have obtained the name of Christians, they are still acting
as its greatest enemies, and contrary to all its genuine principles; they
should therefore be called by its opposite, the Antichrist. Such are fitly
belonging to that most dissolute sorceress of all religion and the world:
"With whom the kings of the earth have lived deliciously; and the inhabitants of the earth have been made drunk with the wine of her
abominations; and the merchants of the earth are waxed rich through
the abundance of her delicacies, by their traffic in various things, and
in slaves and souls of men!" It was not enough for the malignant destroyer of the world to set up his hydra-headed kingdom of evil and
wickedness among the kingdom of men; but also to cause an image to
be made unto him, by something imported in the only true religion
that ever was given to men; and that image of iniquity is described as
arising up out of the earth, having two horns like a lamb, which, by its
votaries and adherents, has been long established and supported. One
of its umbrageous horns of apostasy and delusion is founded, in a more
particular respect, on a grand perversion of the Old Testament dispen-
sations, which has extended itself over all the Mohammedan nations
in the East; and the other horn of apostasy, bearing an allusion and
professional respect to that of the new, has extended itself over all the
Christian nations in the West. That grand umbrageous shadow and
image of evil and wickedness, has spread its malignant influence over
all the nations of the earth, and has, by its power of delusion, given
countenance and support to all the power of evil and wickedness done
among men; and all the adherents and supporters of that delusion, and
all the carriers on of wickedness, are fitly called Antichrist. But all the
nations have drunk of the wine of that iniquity and become drunk
with the wine of the wrath of her fornication, whose name, by every
mark and feature, is the Antichrist; and every dealer in slaves, and
those that hold them in slavery, whatever else they may call themselves, or whatever else they may profess. And likewise, those nations
whose governments support that evil and wicked traffic of slavery,
however remote the situation where it is carried on may be, are, in that

respect, as much anti-Christian as anything in the world can be. No man will ever rob another unless he be a villain: nor will any nation or people ever enslave and oppress others, unless themselves be base and wicked men, and who act and do contrary and against every duty in Christianity.

The learned and ingenious author of *Britannia Libera*, as chiefly alluding to Great Britain alone, gives some account of that great evil and wickedness carried on by the Christian nations, respecting the direful effects of the great devastations committed in foreign parts, whereby it would appear that the ancient and native inhabitants have been drenched in blood and oppression by their merciless visitors (which have formed colonies and settlements among them) the avaricious depredators, plunderers and destroyers of nations. As some estimate of it, "to destroy eleven million, and distress many more in America, to starve and oppress twelve million in Asia, and the great number destroyed, is not the way to promote the dignity, strength and safety of empire, but to draw down the Divine vengeance on the offenders, for depriving so many of their fellow creatures of life, or the common blessings of the earth: whereas by observing the humane principles of preservation with felicitation, the proper principles of all rulers, their empire might have received all reasonable benefit, with the increase of future glory." But should it be asked, what advantages Great Britain has gained by all its extensive territories abroad, the devastations committed, and the abominable slavery and oppression carried on in its colonies? It may be answered according to the old proverb,

> *It seldom is the grandchild's lot,*
> *To share of wealth unjustly got.*

This seems to be verified too much in their present situation: for however wide they have extended their territories abroad, they have sunk into a world of debt at home, which must ever remain an impending burden upon the inhabitants. And it is not likely, by any plan as yet adopted, to be ever paid, or any part of it, without a long continued heavy annual load of taxes. Perhaps, great as it is, some other plan, more equitable for the good of the whole community, if it was wanted to be done, and without any additional taxes, might be so made use of to pay it all off in twenty or thirty years time, and in such manner as whatever emergencies might happen, as never to need to borrow any money at interest. The national debt casts a sluggish deadness over the whole realm, greatly stops ingenuity and improvements, promotes idleness and wickedness, clogs all the wheels of commerce, and drains the money out of the nation. If a foreigner buys stock, in the course of years that the interest amounts to the principal, he gets it all back; and in an equitable time the same sum ever after, and in course must take that money to foreign parts. And those who hold stock at home, are a kind of idle drones, as a burden to the rest of the community: whereas if there were no funds, those who have money would be obliged to occupy it in some improvements themselves, or lend it to other manufacturers or merchants, and by that means useful employments, ingenuity and commerce would flourish. But all stock-jobbing, lotteries, and useless business, has a tendency to slavery and oppression; for as the greater any idle part of the community is, there must be the greater labor and hardships resting upon the industrious part who support the rest; as all men are allotted in some degree to eat their bread with the sweat of their brow; *but it is evil with any people when the rich grind the face of the poor.* Lotteries must be nearly as bad a way of getting money for the good of a nation as it is for an individual when he is poor, and obliged to pawn his goods to increase his poverty, already poor. On the reverse, if a nation was to keep a bank to lend money to merchants and others, that nation might flourish, and its support to those in need might be attended with advantage to the whole; but that nation which is obliged to borrow money from others, must be in a poor and wretched situation, and the inhabitants, who have to bear the load of its taxes, must be greatly burdened, and perhaps many of those employed in its service (as soldiers and others) poorly paid. It was otherwise with *the people of Israel of old;* it was the promise and blessing of God to them, *That they should lend unto many nations, but should not borrow.*

But when a nation or people do wickedly, and commit cruelties and devastations upon others, and enslave them, it cannot be expected that they should be attended with the blessings of God, neither to eschew evil. They often become infatuated to do evil unawares; and those employed under their service sometimes lead them into debt, error and wickedness, in order to enrich themselves by their plunder, in committing the most barbarous cruelties, under pretenses of war, wherein they were the first aggressors, and which is generally the case in all unnatural and destructive disputes of war. In this business money is wanted, the national debt becomes increased, and new loans and other sums must be added to the funds. The plunderers abroad send home their cash as fast as they can, and by one means and another the sums wanted to borrow, are soon made up. At last when the wars subside, or other business calls them home, laden with the spoils of the East or elsewhere, they have then the grand part of their business to negotiate, in buying up bank stock, and lodging their plunder and ill-got wealth in the British or other funds. Thus the nation is loaded with more debt, and with an annual addition of more interest to pay, to the further advantage of those who often occasioned it by their villainy; who, if they had their deserts, like the Popish inquisitors, are almost the only people in the world who deserve to be hung on the rack.

But so it happens in general, that men of activity and affluence, by whatever way they are possessed of riches, or have acquired a greatness of such property, they are always preferred to take the lead in matters of government, so that the greatest depredators, warriors, contracting companies of merchants, and rich slaveholders, always endeavor to push themselves on to get power and interest in the favor; that whatever crimes any of them commit they are seldom brought to a just punishment. Unless that something of this kind had been the case, tis impossible to conceive how such an enormous evil as the slave trade could have been established and carried on under any Christian government: and from hence that motley system of government, which hath so sprung up and established itself, may be accounted for, and as being an evident and universal depravity of one of the finest constitutions in the world; and it may be feared if these unconstitutional laws, reaching from Great Britain to her colonies, be long continued in and supported, to the carrying on that horrible and wicked traffic of slavery, must at last mark out the whole of the British constitution with ruin and destruction; and that the most generous and tenacious people in the world for liberty, may also at last be reduced to slaves. And an Ethiopian may venture to assert, that so long as slavery is continued in any part of the British dominions, that more than one-half of the legislature are the virtual supporters and encouragers of a traffic which ought to be abolished, as it cannot be carried on but by some of the most abandoned and profligate men upon earth.

However, the partisans of such a class of men are generally too many and numerous, whose vitiated principles from time to time have led the whole nation into debt, error and disgrace; and by their magnetic influence there is a general support given to despotism, oppression and cruelty. For many have acquired great riches by some insidious traffic or illegal gain; and as these become often leading men in governments, vast multitudes by sea and land pursue the same course, and support the same measures; like adventurers in the lottery, each grasping for the highest prize; or as much enamored with any infamous way of getting riches, as the Spaniards were with the Peruvian vessels of gold. And when ambitious and wicked men are bent upon avarice and covetousness, it leads them on to commit terrible cruelties, and their hearts become hardened in wickedness; so that even their enormous crimes sink in their own estimation, and soften into trivial matters. The housebreakers and highwaymen, petty depredators, think nothing of any mischief or cruelty that they can do, so as they can gain their end and come off safe; and their villainy and crimes appear to other men as they ought to do, and if they can be detected, and taken hold of, they will meet with such punishment as they justly deserve for their crimes. But it is otherwise with the Colonials, the great depredators, pirates, kidnappers, robbers, oppressors and enslavers of men. The laws as reaching from Great Britain to [the] West Indies do not detect them, but protect the opulent slaveholders; though their opulence and protection by any law, or any government whatsoever, cannot make them less criminal than violators of the common rights and liberties of men. They do not take away a man's property like other robbers; but they take a man himself, and subject him to their service and bondage, which is greater robbery, and a greater crime, than taking away any property from men whatsoever. And therefore, with respect to them, there is very much wanted for regulating the natural rights of mankind, and very much wrong in the present forms of government, as well as much abuse of that which is right.

The Spaniards began their settlements in the West Indies and America, by depredations of rapine, injustice, treachery and murder; and they have continued in the barbarous practice of devastation, cruelty, and oppression ever since: and their principles and maxims in planting colonies have been adopted, in some measure, by every other nation in Europe. This guiltful method of colonization must undoubtedly and imperceptibly have hardened men's hearts, and led them on from one degree of barbarity and cruelty to another: for when they had destroyed, wasted and desolated the native inhabitants, and when many of their own people, enriched with plunder, had retired, or returned home to enjoy their ill-gotten wealth, other resources for men to labor and cultivate the ground, and such other laborious employments were wanted. Vast territories and large possessions, without getting inhabitants to labor for them, were of no use. A general part of what remained of the wretched fugitives, who had the best native right to those possessions, were obliged to make their escape to places more remote, and such as could not, were obliged to submit to the hard labor and bondage of their invaders; but as they had not been used to such harsh treatment and laborious employment as they were then subjected to, they were soon wasted away and became few. Their proud invaders found the advantage of having their labor done for nothing, and it became their general practice to pick up the unfortunate strangers that fell in their way, when they thought they could make use of them in their service. That base traffic of kidnapping and stealing men was begun by the Portuguese on the coast of Africa, and as they found the benefit of it for their own wicked purposes, they soon went on to commit greater depredations. The Spaniards followed their infamous example, and the African slave trade was thought most advantageous for them, to enable themselves to live in ease and affluence by the cruel subjection and slavery of others. The French and English, and some other nations in Europe, as they founded settlements and colonies in the West Indies, or in America, went on in the same manner, and joined hand in hand with the Portuguese and Spaniards, to rob and pillage Africa, as well as to waste and desolate the inhabitants of the western continent. But the European depredators and pirates have not only robbed and pillaged the people of Africa themselves; but, by their instigation, they have infested the inhabitants with some of the vilest combinations of fraudulent and treacherous villains, even among their own people; and have set up their forts and factories as a reservoir of public and abandoned thieves, and as a den of desperados, where they may ensnare, entrap and catch men. So that Africa has been robbed of its inhabitants; its freeborn sons and daughters have been stolen, and kidnapped, and violently taken away, and carried into captivity and cruel bondage. And it may be said, in respect to that diabolical traffic which is still carried on by the European depredators, that Africa has suffered as such as more than any other quarter of the globe. O merciful God! when will the wickedness of man have an end?

The Royal African Company (as [it] is called, ought rather to be reversed as unworthy of the name) was incorporated 14th Charles II and empowered to trade from Salle in South Barbary to the Cape of Good Hope, and to erect forts and factories on the western coast of Africa for that purpose. But this trade was laid open by an act of parliament, anno 1697, and every private merchant permitted to trade thither, upon paying the sum of ten pounds towards maintaining the forts and garrisons. This Company, for securing their commerce, created several factories on the coast; the most remarkable are these, namely on the north part of Guinea, James Fort, upon an island in the River Gambia, Sierra Leone, and Sherbro; and on the south part of Guinea, namely on the Gold Coast, Dick's Cove, Succunda, Commenda, Cape Coast Castle, Fort Royal, Queen Anne's Point, Charles Fort, Annamabo, Winebah, Shidoe, Acra, etc. In all these places it is their grand business to traffic in the human species; and dreadful and shocking as it is to think, it has even been established by royal authority, and is still supported and carried under a Christian government; and this must evidently appear thereby, that the learned, the civilized, and even the enlightened nations are become as truly barbarous and brutish as the unlearned.

To give any just conception of the barbarous traffic carried on at those factories, it would be out of my power to describe the miserable situation of the poor exiled Africans, which by the craft of wicked men daily become their prey, though I have seen enough of their misery as well as read; no description can give an adequate idea of the horror of their feelings, and the dreadful calamities they undergo. The treacherous, perfidious and cruel methods made use of in procuring them, are horrible and shocking. The bringing them to the ships and factories, and subjecting them to brutal examinations stripped naked and markings, is barbarous and base. The stowing them in the holds of the ships like goods of burden, with closeness and stench, is deplorable; and, what makes addition to this deplorable situation, they are often treated in the most barbarous and inhuman manner by the unfeeling monsters of Captains. And when they arrive at the destined port in the colonies, they are again stripped naked for the brutal examinations of their purchasers to view them, which, to many, must add shame and grief to their other woe, as may be evidently seen with sorrow, melancholy and despair marked upon their countenances. Here again another scene of grief and lamentation arises; friends and near relations must be parted, never to meet again, nor knowing to whence they go. Here daughters are clinging to their mothers, and mothers to their daughters, bedewing each other's naked breasts with tears; here fathers, mothers, and children, locked in each other's arms, are begging never to be separated; here the husband will be pleading for his wife, and the wife praying for her children, and entreating, enough to melt the most obdurate heart, not to be torn from them, and taken away from her husband, and some will be still weeping for their native shore, and their dear relations and friends, and other endearing connections which they have left behind, and have been barbarously torn away from; and all are bemoaning themselves with grief and lamentation at the prospect of their wretched fate. And when sold and delivered up to their inhuman purchasers, a more heart-piercing scene cannot well take place. The last embrace of the beloved husband and wife may be seen, taking their dear offspring in their arms, and with the most parental fondness, bathing their cheeks with a final parting endearment. But on this occasion they are not permitted to continue long, they are soon torn away by their unfeeling master, entirely destitute of a hope of ever seeing each other again; and no consolation is afforded to them in this sorrowful and truly pitiable situation. Should any of them still linger, and cling together a little longer, and not part as readily as their owners would have them, the flogger is called on, and they are soon driven away with the bloody commiseration of the cutting fangs of the whip lashing their naked bodies. This last exercise of the bloody whip, with many other cruel punishments, generally becomes an appendage of their miserable fate, until their wretched lives be worn out with hunger, nakedness, hard labor, dejection and despair. Alas! alas! poor unhappy mortal! to experience such treatment from men that take upon themselves the sacred name of Christians!

In such a vast extended, hideous and predominant slavery, as the Europeans carry on in their Colonies, some indeed may fall into better hands, and meet with some commiseration and better treatment than others, and few may become free, and get themselves liberated from that cruel and galling yoke of bondage; but what are these to the whole, even hundreds of thousands, held and perpetrated in all the prevalent and intolerable calamities of that state of bondage and exile. The emancipation of a few, while ever that evil and predominant business of slavery is continued, cannot make that horrible traffic one bit the less criminal. For, according to the methods of procuring slaves in Africa, there must be great robberies and murders committed before any emancipation can take place, and before any lenitive favors can be shown to any of them, even by the generous and humane. This must evidence that the whole of that base traffic is an enormous evil and wicked thing, which cries aloud for redress, and that an immediate end and stop should be put to it.

The worthy and judicious author of the *Historical account of Guinea,* and others, have given some very striking estimates of the exceeding evil occasioned by that wicked diabolical traffic of the African slave trade; wherein it seems, of late years, the English have taken the lead, or the greatest part of it, in carrying it on. They have computed that the ships from Liverpool, Bristol and London have exported from the coast of Africa upwards of one hundred thousand slaves annually; and that among other evils attending this barbarous inhuman traffic, it is also computed that the numbers which are killed by the treacherous and barbarous methods of procuring them, together with those that perish in the voyage, and die in the seasoning, amount to at least a hundred thousand, which perish in every yearly attempt to supply the colonies, before any of the wretched survivors, reduced to about sixty thousand, annually required as an additional stock can be made useful. But as the great severities and oppressions loaded upon the wretched survivors are such that they are continually wearing out, and a new annual supply wanted; that the vast carnage, and the great multitude of human souls that are actually deprived of life by carrying on that iniquitous business, may be supposed to be even more than one hundred thousand that perish annually; or supposing that to be greatly less than it is, still it is so great that the very idea is shocking to conceive, at the thought of it sensibility would blush, and feeling nature absolutely turn pale.

"Gracious God! how wicked, how beyond all example impious, must be that servitude which cannot be carried on without the continual murder of so many innocent persons. What punishment is not to be expected from such monstrous and unparalleled barbarity? For if the blood of one man unjustly shed cries with so loud a voice for the Divine vengeance, how shall the cries and groans of a hundred thousand men annually murdered ascend the celestial mansions, and bring down that punishment such enormities deserve?" As this enormous iniquity is not conjecture, but an obvious fact, occasioned by that dreadful and wicked business of slavery, were the inhabitants of Great Britain to hear to tell of any other nation that murdered one hundred thousand innocent people annually, they would think them an exceeding inhuman, barbarous, and wicked people indeed, and that they would be surely punished by some signal judgment of Almighty God. But surely law and liberty, justice and equity, which are the proper foundations of the British government, and humanity the most amiable characteristic of the people, must be entirely fled from their land, if they can think a less punishment due to themselves, for supporting and carrying on such enormous wickedness, if they do not speedily relinquish and give it up. The very nature of that wickedness of enslaving of men is such, that were the traffic, which European nations carry on in it, a thousand times less than it is, it would be what no righteous nation would admit for the sake of any gain whatsoever. Wherefore as it is, what ought to be done? If there is any righteousness, any wisdom, any justice, or any humanity to be found, ought not the whole of it, and all the branches of such exceeding evil and wicked traffic, and all the iniquity of it to be relinquished, and root and branches to be speedily given up and put an end to?

> For while such monstrous iniquity, such deliberate barbarity and cruelty is carried on, whether it be considered as the crime of individuals, or as patronized and encouraged by the laws of the land, it holds forth an equal degree of enormity. And a crime founded in such a dreadful preeminence in wickedness, both of individuals and the nation, must sometime draw down upon them the heaviest judgments of Almighty God. On this occasion there seems already to be an interference of Divine Providence, though the obdurate and impenitent part of mankind may not regard it. The violent and supernatural agitations of all the elements, which for a series of years have prevailed in those European settlements where the unfortunate Africans are retained in a state of slavery, and which have brought unspeakable calamities to the inhabitants, and public losses to the states to which they severally belong, are so many awful visitations of God for this inhuman violation of his laws. And it is not perhaps unworthy of remark, that as the subjects of Great Britain have two-thirds of this impious commerce in their own hands, so they have suffered in the same proportion, or more severely than the rest. How far these misfortunes may appear to be acts of Providence, and to create an alarm to those who have been accustomed to refer every effect to its apparent cause; who have been habituated to stop there, and to overlook the finger of God, because it is slightly covered under the veil of secondary laws, we will not pretend to determine; but this we will assert with confidence, that the Europeans have richly deserved them all: the fear of sympathy that can hardly be restrained on other melancholy occasions, seems to forget to flow at the relation of these; and that we can never, with any shadow of justice, wish prosperity to the undertakers of those whose success must be the expense of the happiness of millions of their fellow creatures.*

*See the excellent Mr. Clarkson's *Essay on the Slavery and Commerce of the Human Species*; and, I must add, the amiable and indefatigable friend of mankind, Granville Sharp, Esq. from whose writings I have borrowed some of the following observations. I am also indebted to several others, whose intrinsic virtues will equally shine in the

For though this world is not the place of final retribution, yet there is an evidence maintained in the course of Divine Providence, that verily there is a God that judgeth in the earth. That nations may continue long, with a considerable degree of worldly prosperity, and without seeming to be distinguished by remarkable calamities. When their wickedness is become very great and prevalent; yet it is no way inconsistent to assert (and what sacred history warrants us to conclude), that their judgment slumbereth not. Had one been among the Canaanites a few years before the Israelites entered their country, or in Babylon a little before Cyrus encamped against it, he would have beheld a people in a state of great worldly prosperity, and in much security, notwithstanding that the judgments of God were ready to seize upon them. Great and destructive wars are kindled up from time to time, whereby multitudes of mankind are swept away from the face of the earth, and the wealth of nations are exhausted. Famine, pestilence and earthquakes have often spread terror, desolation and misery among the inhabitants of the world. Nor are there wanting instances of remarkable national distresses as a judgment for their wickedness, by a variety of other causes. Though men cannot easily be prevailed with to regard these as the operation of the hand of God, the scriptures, which contain the rules and history of Divine Providence, represent these as inflicted for the sins of nations, and not merely as casual things, for which no account can be given. And therefore some of these causes which may seem natural, and which have begun to make their appearance, and the annual destructions thereof, which are constantly heard of in some part or another, may be considered as tokens of God's judgments against the British empire, and a variety of them might be named; such as loss of territory and destructive wars, earthquakes and dreadful thunders, storms and hurricanes, blastings and destructive insects, inclement and unfruitful seasons, national debt and oppressions, poverty and distresses of individuals, etc. *For his own iniquity shall take the wicked himself;* and who can tell what dreadful calamities may yet befall to a people responsible for so great a share of iniquity as in that part which they carry on of the African slave trade alone. "And it is not known how soon a just national retribution of vengeance may burst forth against it; how soon the Almighty may think fit to recompense the British nation, according to the work, of their hands, for the horrible oppression of the poor Africans."

---

same amiable manner, while ever there is any virtue and humanity amongst men; and when those of the enslavers of men will sink into abhorrence forever.

"For national wickedness from the beginning of the world has generally been visited with national punishments; and surely no national wickedness can be more heinous in the sight of God than a public toleration of slavery, and sooner or later these kingdoms will be visited with some signal mark of his displeasure for the notorious oppression of the poor Africans, that are harassed and continually wearing out with a most shameful involuntary servitude in the British colonies, and by a public toleration under the sanction of laws, to which the monarch of England from time to time, by advice of their privy counselors, have given the royal assent, and thereby rendered themselves parties in the oppression, and it may be feared partakers in their guilt. And every man has ample reason to fear that God will make of this nation, in proportion to the magnitude of its guilt in the slave-dealing, a tremendous example of retribution to deter other nations from offending his external justice, if a sincere and speedy repentance does not avert it. For such notorious crimes the Almighty, even the Lord, hath sworn, *surely I will never forget any of these works.*" (See Amos 8.) But the judgments of God are often suspended and mitigated for the sake of the righteous; and nations are preserved from destruction in favor to them who remain faithful in times of general defection. ([See] Isaiah 1:9.) *"Except the Lord of Hosts had left us a very small remnant, we should have been as Sodom, and we should have been like unto Gomorrah."*

But while ever such a horrible business as the slavery and oppression of the Africans is carried on, there is not one man in all Great Britain and her colonies that knoweth anything of it, can be innocent and safe, unless he speedily riseth up with abhorrence of it in his own judgment, and, to avert evil, declare himself against it, and all such notorious wickedness. But should the contrary be adhered to, as it has been in the most shameful manner, by men of eminence and power; according to their eminence in station, the nobles and senators, and every man in office and authority, must incur a double load of guilt, and not only that burden of guilt in the oppression of the African stranger, but also in that of an impending danger and ruin to their country; and such a double load of iniquity must rest upon those guilty heads who withhold their testimony against the crying sin of tolerating slavery. The inhabitants in general who can approve of such inhuman barbarities, must themselves be a species of unjust barbarians and inhuman men. But the clergy of all denominations, whom we would consider as the devout messengers of righteousness, peace, and goodwill to all men, if we find any of them ranked with infidels and barbarians, we must consider them as particularly responsible, and, in some measure, guilty of the crimes of other wicked men in the highest degree. For it is their duty to warn every man, and to teach every man to know their errors; and if they do not, the crimes of those under their particular charge must rest upon themselves, and upon some of them, in such a case as this, that of the whole nation in general; and those (whatever their respective situation may be) who forbid others to assist them, must not be very sensible of their own duty, and the great extensiveness and importance of their own charge. And as it is their great duty to teach men righteousness and piety; this ought to be considered as sufficiently obvious unto them, and to all men, that nothing can be more contrary unto it, than the evil and very nature of enslaving men, and making merchandise of them like the brute creation. "For it is evident that no custom established among men was ever more impious; since it is contrary to reason, justice, nature, and principles of law and government, and the whole doctrine, in short, of natural religion, and the revealed voice of God. And, therefore, that it is both evident and expedient, that there is an absolute necessity to abolish the slave trade, and the West India slavery; and that to be in power, and to neglect even a day in endeavoring to put a stop to such monstrous iniquity and abandoned wickedness (as the tenure of every man's life, as well as the time of his being in office and power is very uncertain) must necessarily endanger a man's own eternal welfare, be he ever so great in temporal dignity."

The higher that any man is exalted in power and dignity, his danger is the more eminent, though he may not live to see the evil that may eventually be contributed to his country, because of his disobedience to the law and commandments of God. All men in authority, and kings in general, who are exalted to the most conspicuous offices of superiority, while they take upon themselves to be the administrators of righteousness and justice to others, they become equally responsible for admitting or suffering others under their authority to do wrong. Wherefore the highest offices of authority among men are not so desirable as some may be apt to conceive; it was so considered by the virtuous Queen Anne, when she was called to the royal dignity, as she declared to the council of the nation, that it was a heavy weight and burden brought upon her. For kings are the ministers of God, to do justice, and not to bear the sword in vain, but to revenge wrath upon them that do evil. But if they do not in such a case as this the cruel oppressions of thousands, and the blood of the murdered Africans who are slain by the sword of cruel avarice, must rest upon their own guilty heads in as eventually and plain a sense as it was David that murdered Uriah; and therefore they ought to let no companies of insidious merchants, or any guileful insinuations of wicked men prevail upon them to establish laws of iniquity, and to carry on a trade of oppression and injustice; but they ought to consider such as the worst of foes and rebels, and greater enemies than any that can rise up against their temporal dignity. From all such enemies, good Lord, deliver them! for it is even better to lose a temporal kingdom than only to endanger the happiness and enjoyment of an eternal one.

Nothing else can be conceived, but that the power of infernal wickedness has so reigned and pervaded over the enlightened nations, as to infatuate and lead on the great men, and the kings of Europe, to promote and establish such a horrible traffic of wickedness as the African slave trade and the West India slavery, and thereby to bring themselves under the guilty responsibility of such awful iniquity. The kings and governors of the nations in general have power to prevent their subjects and people from enslaving and oppressing others, if they will; but if they do not endeavor to do it, even if they could not effect that good purpose, they must then be responsible for their crimes; how much more, if they make no endeavors towards it, even when they can, and where no opposition, however plausible their pretenses might be, would dare to oppose them. Wherefore, if kings or nations or any men that dealeth unjustly with their fellow creatures to ensnare them, to enslave them, and to oppress them, or suffers others to do so, when they have it in their power to prevent it, and yet they do not, can it ever be thought that God will be well pleased with them? For can those which have no mercy on their fellow creatures expect to find mercy from the gracious Father of Men? Or will it not rather be said unto them as it is declared, *that he who leadeth into captivity shall be carried captive, and be bound in the cords of his own iniquity: Though hand join in hand the wicked shall not go unpunished; for sin and wickedness is the destruction of any people.* And should these nations in the most obnoxious and tenacious manner, still adhere to it as they have done, and continue to carry on in their colonies such works and purposes of iniquity, or oppression and injustice against the Africans, nothing else can be expected for them at last, but to meet with the fierce wrath of Almighty God, for such a combination of wickedness according to all the examples of his just retribution who cannot suffer such deliberate, such monstrous iniquity to go long unpunished.

There is good reason to suppose that it was far from the intention of Ferdinand, King of Spain, to use his new subjects in America in the brutal and barbarous manner that his people did; and happy for the credit of that nation, and the honor of mankind, even among the profligate adventurers which were sent to conquer and desolate the new world, there were some persons that retained some tincture of virtue and generosity and some men of the greatest reputation of both gentlemen and clergy, which did not only remonstrate, but protest against their measures then carried on. And since that iniquitous traffic of slavery has commenced and been carried on, many gentlemen of the most distinguished reputation, of different nations, and particularly in England, have protested and remonstrated against it. But the guileful insinuations of avaricious wicked men, which prevailed formerly have still been continued; and to answer the purposes of their own covetousness, the different nations have been fermented with jealousy to one another, lest another should have the advantage in any traffic: and while naturally emulous to promote their own ambition, they have embrewed their hands in that infamous commerce of iniquity; and by the insidious instigation of those whose private emolument depends on it, the various profligate adventurers, from time to time, have acquired the sanction of laws to support them, and have obtained the patronage of kings in their favor to encourage them, whereby that commerce of the most notorious injustice, and open violation of the laws of God, hath been carried on exceedingly to the shame of all the Christian nations, and greatly to the disgrace of all the monarchs of Europe. The fact speaks itself: *And destruction shall be to the workers of iniquity.* The bold and ostensive enslavers of men, who subject their fellow creatures to the rank of a brute, and the immolate value of a beast, are themselves the most abandoned slaves of infernal wickedness, the most obnoxious ruffians among men, the enemies of their country, and the disgrace of kings. Their iniquity is written in the light as with a sunbeam, and engraven on the hardest rock as with the point of a diamond, that cannot be easily wiped away: *But the wicked shall fall by their own wickedness.* And, nevertheless, by the insidious instigations of those who have forsaken the amiable virtues of men, and have acquired the cruel ferocity of tigers and wild beasts, they have not only polluted themselves with their iniquity, but their base treachery has brought shame and guilt upon some of the most exalted and most amiable characters in the world. And, therefore, that no evil may happen unto those who have been so shamefully beguiled and betrayed by the vile instigations of wicked, profligate, inhuman men, and that no shame and guilt may rest upon him, who standeth in the greatest eminence of responsibility, I would ever desire to pray; let all the prayers of the wise and pious be heard for the king, and for his wise counselors, and the great men that stand before him; for kings and great men stand in the most perilous situation of having the crimes of others imputed to them; wherefore kings have need of all your prayers, that the counsel of the wicked may not prevail against them, for these are the worst foes, and most terrible enemies, both to yourselves and to your sovereign. *Righteousness exalteth a nation, but sin is a reproach to any people.*

In this advanced era, when the kings of Europe are become more conspicuous for their manly virtues, than any before them have been, it is to be hoped that they will not any longer suffer themselves to be imposed upon, and be beguiled, and brought into guilt and shame, by any instigations of the cunning craftiness and evil policy of the avaricious and the vile profligate enslavers of men. And as their wisdom and understanding is great, and exalted as their high dignity, it is also to be hoped that they will exert themselves, in the cause of righteousness and justice, and be like the wisest and the greatest monarchs of old, to hearken to the counsel of the wise men that know the times, and to the righteous laws of God, and to deliver the oppressed, and to put an end to the iniquitous commerce and slavery of men. And as we hear tell of the kings of Europe having almost abolished the infernal invention of the bloody tribunal of the inquisition, and the Emperor and others making some grand reformations for the happiness and good of their subjects; it is to be hoped also that these exalted and liberal principles will lead them on to greater improvements in civilization and felicitation, and next to abolish that other diabolical invention of the bloody and cruel African slave trade, and the West Indian slavery.

But whereas the people of Great Britain having now acquired a greater share in that iniquitous commerce than all the rest together, they are the first that ought to set an example, lest they have to repent for their wickedness when it becomes too late; lest some impending calamity should speedily burst forth against them, and lest a just retribution for their enormous crimes, and a continuance in committing similar deeds of barbarity and injustice should involve them in ruin. For we may be assured that God will certainly avenge himself of such heinous transgressors of his law, and of all those planters and merchants, and of all others, who are the authors of the Africans' graves, severities, and cruel punishments and no plea of any absolute necessity can possibly excuse them. And as the inhabitants of Great Britain, and the inhabitants of the colonies, seem almost equally guilty of the oppression, there is great reason for both to dread the severe vengeance of Almighty God upon them, and upon all such notorious workers of wickedness; for it is evident that the legislature of Great Britain patronizes and encourages them, and shares in the infamous profits of the slavery of the Africans. It is therefore necessary that the inhabitants of the British nation should seriously consider these things for their own good and safety as well as for our benefit and deliverance, and that they may be sensible of their own error and danger, lest they provoke the vengeance of the Almighty against them. For what wickedness was there ever risen up so monstrous, and more likely to bring a heavy rod of destruction upon a nation, than the deeds committed by the West Indian slavery, and the African slave trade. And even in that part of it carried on by the Liverpool and Bristol merchants, the many shocking and inhuman instances of their barbarity and cruelty are such that everyone that heareth thereof has reason to tremble, and cry out. *Should not the land tremble for this, and everyone mourn that dwelleth therein?*

The vast carnage and murders committed by the British instigators of slavery is attended with a very shocking, peculiar, and almost unheard of conception, according to the notion of the perpetrators of it; they either consider them as their own property, that they may do with as they please, in life or death; or that taking away the life of a black man is of no more account than taking away the life of a beast. A very melancholy instance of this happened about the year 1780, as recorded in the courts of law; a master of a vessel bound to the Western Colonies, selected 132 of the most sickly of the black slaves, and ordered them to be thrown overboard into the sea in order to recover their value from the insurers, as he had perceived that he was too late to get a good market for them in the West Indies. On the trial, by the counsel for the owners of the vessel against the underwriters, their argument was that the slaves were to be considered the same as horses; and their plea for throwing them into the sea, was nothing better than that it might be more necessary to throw them overboard to lighten their vessel than goods of greater value or something to that effect. These poor creatures, it seems, were tied two and two together when they were thrown into the sea, lest some of them might swim a little for the last gasp of air, and, with the animation of their approaching exit, breathe their souls away to the gracious Father of spirits. Some of the last parcel, when they saw the fate of their companions, made their escape from trying by jumping overboard, and one was saved by means of a rope from some in the ship. The owners of the vessel, I suppose (inhuman connivers of robbery, slavery, murder and fraud) were rather a little defeated in this, by bringing their villainy to light in a court of law; but the inhuman monster of a captain was kept out of the way of justice from getting hold of him. Though such perpetrators of murder and fraud should have been sought after from the British Dan in the East Indies, to her Beershebah in the West.

But our lives are accounted of no value, we are hunted after as the prey in the desert, and doomed to destruction as the beasts that perish. And for this, should we appeal to the inhabitants of Europe, would they dare to say that they have not wronged us, and grievously injured us, and that the blood of millions do not cry out against them? And if we appeal to the inhabitants of Great Britain, can they justify the deeds of their conduct towards us? And is it not strange to think, that they who ought to be considered as the most learned and civilized people in the world, that they should carry on a traffic of the most barbarous cruelty and injustice, and that many even among them, are become so dissolute, as to think slavery, robbery and murder no crimes? But we will answer to this, that no man can, with impunity, steal, kidnap, buy or sell another man, without being guilty of the most atrocious villainy. And we will aver that every slaveholder that claims any property in slaves, or holds them in an involuntary servitude, are the most obnoxious and dissolute robbers among men; and that they have no more right, nor any better title to anyone of them than the most profligate and notorious robbers and thieves in the world, have to the goods which they have robbed and stolen from the right owners and lawful possessors thereof. But should the slaveholders say that they buy them; their title and claim is no better than that of the most notorious conniver, who buys goods from other robbers, knowing them to be stolen, and accordingly gives an inferior price for them. According to the laws of England, when such connivers are discovered, and the property of others unlawfully found in their possession the right owners thereof can oblige the connivers to restore back their property, and to punish them for their trespass. But the slaveholders, universally, are those connivers, they do not only rob men of some of their property, but they keep men from every property belonging to them, and compel them to their involuntary service and drudgery; and those whom they buy from other robbers, and keep in their possession, are greatly injured by them when compared to any species of goods whatsoever; and accordingly they give but a very inferior price for men, as all their vast estates in the West Indies is not sufficient to buy one of them, if the rightful possessor was to sell himself to them in the manner that they claim possession of him. Therefore let the inhabitants of any civilized nation determine whether if they were to be treated in the same manner that the Africans are, by various pirates, kidnappers, and slaveholders, and their wives, and their sons and daughters were to be robbed from them, or themselves violently taken away to a perpetual and intolerable slavery; or whether they would not think those robbers, who only took away their property, less injurious to them than the other. If they determine it so, as reason must tell every man, that himself is of more value than his property; then the executors of the laws of civilization ought to tremble at the inconsistency of passing judgment upon those whose crimes, in many cases, are less than what the whole legislature must be guilty of, when those of a far greater are encouraged and supported by it wherever slavery is tolerated by law, and consequently, that slavery can nowhere be tolerated with any consistency to civilization and the laws of justice among men; but if it can maintain its ground, to have any place at all, it must be among a society of barbarians and thieves, and where the law of their society is, for everyone to catch what he can. Then, when theft and robbery become no crimes, the man stealer and the conniving slaveholder might possibly get free.

But the several nations of Europe that have joined in that iniquitous traffic of buying, selling and enslaving men, must in course have left their own laws of civilization to adopt those of barbarians and robbers, and that they may say to one another, *When thou sawest a thief, then thou consentest with him, and hast been partaker with all the workers of iniquity.* But whereas every man, as a rational creature, is responsible for his actions, and he becomes not only guilty in doing evil himself, but in letting others rob and oppress their fellow creatures with impunity, or in not delivering the oppressed when he has it in his power to help them. And likewise that nation which may be supposed to maintain a very considerable degree of civilization, justice and equity within its own jurisdiction, is not in that case innocent, while it beholds another nation or people carrying on persecution, oppression and slavery, unless it remonstrates against that wickedness of the other nation, and makes use of every effort in its power to help the oppressed, and to rescue the innocent. For so it ought to be the universal rule of duty to all men that fear God and keep his commandments, to do good to all men wherever they can; and when they find any wronged and injured by others, they should endeavor to deliver the ensnared whatever their grievances may be; and should this sometimes lead them into war they might expect the protection and blessing of heaven. How far other motives may appear eligible for men to oppose one another with hostile force, it is not my business to inquire. But I should suppose the hardy veterans who engage merely about the purposes of envying one another concerning any different advantages of commerce, or for enlarging their territories and dominions, or for the end of getting riches by their conquest; that if they fall in the combat, they must generally die, as the fool dieth, vaunting in vain glory; and many of them be like to those who go out in darkness, never to see light; and should they come off alive, what more does their honor and fame amount to, but only to be like that antediluvian conqueror, *who had slain a man to his own wounding, and a young man to his hurt*. But those mighty men of renown in the days of old, because of their apostasy from God, and rebellion and wickedness to men, were at last all swallowed up by a universal deluge for their iniquity and crimes.

But again let me observe, that whatever civilization the inhabitants of Great Britain may enjoy among themselves, they have seldom maintained their own innocence in that great duty as a Christian nation towards others; and I may say, with respect to their African neighbors, or to any other wheresoever they may go by the way of commerce, they have not regarded them at all. And when they saw others robbing the Africans, and carrying them into captivity and slavery, they have neither helped them, nor opposed their oppressors in the least. But instead thereof they have joined in combination against them with the rest of other profligate nations and people, to buy, enslave and make merchandise of them, because they found them helpless and fit to suit their own purpose, and are become the head carriers-on of that iniquitous traffic. But the greater that any reformation and civilization is obtained by any nation, if they do not maintain righteousness, but carry on any course of wickedness and oppression, it makes them appear only the more inconsistent, and their tyranny and oppression the more conspicuous. Wherefore because of the great wickedness, cruelty and injustice done to the Africans, those who are greatest in the transgression give an evident and undubious warrant to all other nations beholding their tyranny and injustice to others, if those nations have any regard to their own innocence and virtue, and wish to maintain righteousness, and to remain clear of the oppression and blood of all men; it is their duty to chastise and suppress such unjust and tyrannical oppressors and enslavers of men. And should none of these be found among the enlightened and civilized nations, who maintain their own innocence and righteousness with regard to their duty unto all men; and that there may be none to chastise the tyrannical oppressors of others; and it may be feared, as it has often been, that fierce nations of various insects, and other annoyances, may be sent as a judgment to punish the wicked nations of men. For by some way or other every criminal nation, and all their confederates, who sin and rebel against God, and against his laws of nature and nations, will each meet with some awful retribution at last, unless they repent of their iniquity. And the greater advantages of light, learning, knowledge and civilization that any people enjoy, if they do not maintain righteousness, but do wickedly, they will meet with the more severe rebuke when the visitations of God's judgment cometh upon them. And the prophecy which was given to Moses, is still as much in force against the enlightened nations now for their wickedness, in going after the abominations of heathens and barbarians, for none else would attempt to enslave and make merchandise of men, as it was when denounced against the Israelitish nations of old, when they departed, or should depart, from the laws and statutes of the Most High. *The Lord shall bring a nation against thee, from far, from the ends of the earth, as swift as the eagle flieth, a nation whose tongue thou shalt not understand,* etc. (See Deut. 28.)

But lest any of these things should happen to the generous and respectful Britons, who are not altogether lost to virtue and consideration; let me say unto you, in the language of a wise and eminent Queen, as she did when her people were sold as a prey to their enemies: This it is not all your enemies (for they can be reckoned nothing else), the covetous instigators and carriers-on of slavery and wickedness, that can in any way countervail the damage to yourselves, to your king, and to your country; nor will all the infamous profits of the poor Africans avail you anything if it brings down the avenging hand of God upon you. We are not saying that we have not sinned, and that we are not deserving of the righteous judgments of God against us. But the enemies that have risen up against us are cruel, oppressive and unjust; and their haughtiness of insolence, wickedness and iniquity is like to that of Haman the son of Hammedatha; and who dare suppose, or even presume to think, that the inhuman ruffians and ensnarers of men, the vile negotiators and merchandisers of the human species, and the ostensive combinations of slaveholders in the West have done no evil? And should we be passive, as the suffering martyrs dying in the flames, whose blood crieth for vengeance on their persecutors and murderers; so the iniquity of our oppressors, enslavers and murderers rise up against them. For we have been hunted after as the wild beasts of the earth, and sold to the enemies of mankind as their prey; and should any of us have endeavored to get away from them, as a man would naturally fly from an enemy that waylaid him; we have been pursued after, and, by haughty mandates and laws of iniquity, overtaken, and murdered and slain, and the blood of millions cries out against them. And together with these that have been cruelly spoiled and slain, the very grievous afflictions that we have long suffered under, has been long crying for vengeance on our oppressors; and the great distress and wretchedness of human woe and misery, which we are yet lying under, is still rising up before that High and Sovereign Hand of Justice, where men, by all their oppression and cruelty, can no way prevent; their evil treatment of others may serve to increase the blow, but not to evade the stroke of His power, nor withhold the bringing down that arm of vengeance on themselves, and upon all their connivers and confederators, and the particular instigators of such willful murders and inhuman barbarity. The life of a black man is of as much regard in the sight of God, as the life of any other man; though we have been sold as a carnage to the market, and as a prey to profligate wicked men, to torture and lash us as they please, and as their caprice may think fit, to murder us at discretion.

And should any of the best of them plead, as they generally will do, and tell of their humanity and charity to those whom they have captured and enslaved, their tribute of thanks is but small; for what is it, but a little restored to the wretched and miserable whom they have robbed of their all; and only to be dealt with, like the spoils of those taken in the field of battle, where the wretched fugitives must submit to what they please. For as we have been robbed of our natural right as men, and treated as beasts, those who have injured us, are like to them who have robbed the widow, the orphans, the poor and the needy of their right, and whose children are rioting on the spoils of those who are begging at their doors for bread. And should they say that their fathers were thieves and connivers with ensnarers of men, and that they have been brought up to the iniquitous practice of slavery and oppression of their fellow creatures and they cannot live without carrying it on, and making their gain by the unlawful merchandise and cruel slavery of men, what is that to us, and where will it justify them? And some will be saying, that the Black People who are free in the West Indies are more miserable than the slaves; and well they may; for while they can get their work and drudgery done for nothing, it is not likely that they will employ those whom they must pay for their labor. But whatever necessity the enslavers of men may plead for their iniquitous practice of slavery, and the various advantages which they get by it, can only evidence their own injustice and dishonesty. A man that is truly honest, fears nothing so much as the very imputation of injustice; but those men who dare not face the consequence of acting uprightly in every case are detestable cowards, unworthy the name of men; for it is manifest that such men are more afraid of temporal inconveniences than they are of God: *And I say unto you, my friends, be not afraid of them that kill the body, and after that have no more that they can do; but I will forewarn you whom you shall fear: Fear him, who, after he hath killed, hath power to cast into hell.* (See Luke 12:4,5.)

But why should a total abolition, and a universal emancipation of slaves, and the enfranchisement of all the Black People employed in the culture of the Colonies, taking place as it ought to do, and without any hesitation, or delay for a moment, even though it might have some seeming appearance of loss either to government or to individuals, be feared at all? Their labor as freemen would be as useful in the sugar colonies as any other class of men that could be found; and should it even take place in such a manner that some individuals, at first, would suffer loss as a just reward for their wickedness in slave-dealing, what is that to the happiness and good of doing justice to others; and I must say, to the great danger, otherwise, that must eventually hang over the whole community? It is certain, that the produce of the labor of slaves, together with all the advantages of the West India traffic, bring in an immense revenue to government; but let that amount be what it will, there might be as much or more expected from the labor of an equal increase of free people, and without the implication of any guilt attending it, and which otherwise must be a greater burden to bear, and more ruinous consequences to be feared from it, than if the whole national debt was to sink at once, and to rest upon the heads of all that might suffer by it. Whereas, if a generous encouragement were to be given to a free people, peaceable among themselves, intelligent and industrious, who by art and labor would improve the most barren situations, and make the most of that which is fruitful; the free and voluntary labor of any, would soon yield to any government, many greater advantages than anything that slavery can produce. And this should be expected, wherever a Christian government is extended, and the true religion is embraced, that the blessings of liberty should be extended likewise, and that it should diffuse its influences first to fertilize the mind, and then the effects of its benignity would extend, and arise with exuberant blessings and advantages from all its operations. Was this to be the case, everything would increase and prosper at home and abroad, and ten thousand times greater and greater advantages would arise to the state, and more permanent and solid benefit to individuals from the service of freemen, than ever they can reap, or in any possible way enjoy, by the labor of slaves.

But why this diabolical traffic of slavery has not been abolished before now, and why it was introduced at all, as I have already inquired, must be greatly imputed to that powerful and pervading agency of infernal wickedness, which reigneth and prevaileth over the nations, and to that umbrageous image of iniquity established thereby; for had there been any truth and righteousness in that grand horn of delusion in the east, which may seem admirable to some, and be looked upon by its votaries as the fine burnished gold, and bright as the finest polished silver, then would not slavery, cruelty and oppression have been abolished wherever its influence came? And had the grand apostasy of its fellow horn, with all its lineaments been any better, and endowed with any real virtue and goodness, whom its devotees may behold as the finest polished diamond, and glistening as the finest forbidden wherever the beams of any Christianity arose? Then might we have expected to hear tidings of good, even from those who are gone to repose in the fabulous paradise of Mahomet? Then might we have looked for it from those who are now reclined to slumber in assimilation with the old dotards of Rome, or to those who are fallen asleep and become enamored with the scarlet couch of the abominable enchantress dyed in blood? And as well then might we not expect tenderness and compassion from those whom the goddess of avarice has so allured with her charms, that her heartsick lovers are become reversed to the feelings of human woe; and with the great hurry and bustle of the russet slaves employed in all the drudgeries of the western isles, and maritime shore, in the cruel and involuntary service of her voluptuousness, having so dazzled their eyes, and bereaved them of all sensibility, that their hearts are become callous as the nether millstone, fierce as the tigers, and devoid of the natural feelings of men? From all such enchantments we would turn away, and fly from them as from the ravenous beast of prey, as from the weeping crocodiles and the devouring reptiles, and as from the hoary monsters of the deep.

But we would look unto you, O ye multitude in the desert! against whom there is no enchantment, neither any divination whatever, that can prevail against you! for in your mouth there is no error or guile to be found, nor any fault before the throne of God. And what! though your dwellings be in all lands, and ye have no nation or kingdom on earth that ye can call your own, and your camp be surrounded with many enemies, yet you have a place of defense, an invincible fortress, the munitions of rocks for your refuge, and the shield of your anointed is Almighty; and behold his buckler is strong, and his scepter is exalted on high, and the throne of his dominion and power ruleth over all. But in the day that we shall be spoken for, if we find you a wall, we would build upon you a place of silver; and if you find us a door, enclose us with boards of cedar, for we long, and would to God that we longed more, to enter into your fortress, and follow you to your happy retreat. Then might we, like you, stand undaunted before our foes, and with more than heroic sullenness at all their cruel tortures, highly disdain their rage, and boldly dare them to do their worst. For you, O ye friends of the Most High, when you die, when ye are persecuted and slain, when you fall in the combat, when you die in the battle, it is you! only you, that come off conquerors, and more than conquerors through him that loved you! And should it yet be, as it has often been, that your foes might pursue you with their usual arrogance and persecuting rage, and cause you to die cruelly veiled in a curtain of blood, lo! your stains are all washed away, and your wounds and fears will soon be healed, and yourselves will be then invested with a robe of honor that will shine in whiteness forever new, and your blood that was shed by the terrific rage of your foes, will testify against them, and rise up in grandeur to you, as an infringement of gold floating in glory, and as his robe of honor which flames in eternal crimson through the heavens. But we envy no man, but wish them to do good, and not evil; and we want the prayers of the good, and wherever they can to help us; and the blessing of God be with all the promoters of righteousness and peace.

But wherefore, O beloved, should your watchmen sit still, when they hear tell that the enemy is invading all the outposts and camps of the British empire, where many of your dwellings are? Are they all fallen asleep, and lying down to slumber in assimilation with the workers of iniquity? Should not those who are awake, arise, and give the alarm, that others may arise and awake also? And should not they who feareth the name of the Lord, and worship in his holy temples, *Let judgment to run down as waters, and righteousness as a mighty stream?* But why think ye prayers in churches and chapels only will do ye good, if your charity do not extend to pity and regard your fellow creatures perishing through ignorance, under the heavy yoke of subjection and bondage, to the cruel and avaricious oppression of brutish profligate men; and when both the injured, and their oppressors, dwell in such a vicinity as equally to claim your regard? The injurers, oppressors, en-slavers, and murderers of others, eventually bring a curse upon them-selves, as far as they destroy, injure, and cruelly and basely treat those under their subjection and unlawful bondage. And where such a dreadful preeminence of iniquity abounds, as the admission of laws for tolerating slavery and wickedness, and the worst of robberies, not only of men's properties, but themselves; and the many inhuman mur-ders and cruelties occasioned by it: If it meets with your approbation, it is your sin, and you are then as a conniver and confederator with those workers of wickedness; and if you give it a sanction by your passive obedience, it manifests that you are gone over to those brutish enemies of mankind and can in no way be a true lover of your king and country.

Wherefore it ought to be the universal endeavor, and the ardent wish, of all the lovers of God as the Savior of men, and of all that de-light in his ways of righteousness, and of all the lovers of their country, and the friends of mankind, and of every real patriot in the land, and of every man and woman that dwelleth therein, and of all those that have any pretense to charity, generosity, sensibility and humanity, and whoever has any regard to innocence and virtue, to plead that slavery, with all its great and heinous magnitude of iniquity, might be abol-ished throughout all the British dominions; and from henceforth to hinder and prohibit the carrying on of that barbarous, brutish and in-human traffic of the slavery and commerce of the human species, wherever the power and influence of the British empire extends. And in doing this, and always in doing righteously, let the glory and honor of it be alone ascribed unto God Most High, for his great mercy and goodness to you; and that his blessings and unbounded beneficence may shine forth upon you, and upon all the promoters of it: and that it may with great honors and advantages of peace and prosperity be ever resting upon the noble Britons, and upon their most worthy, most eminent and august Sovereign, and upon all his government and the people under it; and that the streams thereof may run down in righteousness even to us, poor deplorable Africans.

And we that are particularly concerned would humbly join with all the rest of our brethren and countrymen in complexion, who have been grievously injured, and who jointly and separately, in all the language of grief and woe, are humbly imploring and earnestly entreating the most respectful and generous people of Great Britain, that they would consider us, and have mercy and compassion on us, and to take away that evil that your enemies, as well as our oppressors, are doing towards us, and cause them to desist from their evil treatment of the poor and despised Africans, before it be too late; and to restore that justice and liberty which is our natural right, that we have been unlawfully deprived and cruelly wronged of and to deliver us from that captivity and bondage which we now suffer under, in our present languishing state of exile and misery. And we humbly pray that God may put it into the minds of the noble Britons, that they may have the honor and advantage of doing so great good to many, and to extend their power and influence to do good afar; and that great good in abundance may come down upon themselves, and upon all their government and the people under it, in every place belonging to the British empire. But if the people and the legislature of Great Britain altogether hold their peace at such a time as this, and even laugh at our calamity as heretofore they have been wont to do, by making merchandise of us to enrich themselves with our misery and distress: we sit like the mourning Mordecai at their gates clothed in sackcloth; and, in this advanced era, we hope God in his Providence will rise up a deliverance for us some other way; and we have great reason to hope that the time of our deliverance is fast drawing nigh, and when the great Babylon of iniquity will fall.

And whereas we consider our case before God of the whole universe, the Gracious Father and Savior of men; we will look unto him for help and deliverance. The cry of our affliction is already gone up before him, and he will hearken to the voice of our distress; for he hears the cries and groans of the oppressed, and professes that if they cry at all unto him, he will hearken unto them, and deliver them. *For the oppression of the poor, for the sighing of the needy, now will I arise saith Jehovah, and will set him in safety from him that puffeth at him, or that would ensnare him.* (Ps. 12:5) *And I know that Jehovah will maintain the cause of the afflicted, and the right of the poor.* (Ps. 140:12) Wherefore it is our duty to look up to a greater deliverer than that of the British nation, or of any nation upon earth; for unless God gives them repentance, and peace towards him, we can expect no peace or deliverance from them. But still we shall have cause to trust, that God who made of one blood all the nations and children of men, and who gave to all equally a natural right to liberty; that he who ruleth over all the kingdoms of the earth with equal providential justice, shall then make enlargement and deliverance to arise to the grievously injured, and heavy oppressed Africans from another place.

And as we look for our help and sure deliverance to come from God Most High, should it not come in an apparent way from Great Britain, whom we consider as the Queen of nations, let her not think to escape more than others, if she continues to carry on oppression and injustice, and such preeminent wickedness against us: for we are only seeking that justice may be done to us, and what every righteous nation ought to do; and if it be not done, it will be adding iniquity to iniquity against themselves. But let us not suppose that the inhabitants of the British nation will adhere to the ways of the profligate: *For such is the way of an adulterous woman; she eateth, and wipeth her mouth; and saith, I have done no wickedness.* But rather let us suppose, *that whereas iniquity hath abounded, may righteousness much more abound.* For the wickedness that you have done is great, and wherever your traffic and colonies have been extended it is shameful; and the great injustice and cruelty done to the poor Africans crieth to heaven against you; and therefore that it may be forgiven unto you, it cries aloud for universal reformation and national repentance. But let it not suffice that a gracious call from the throne is inviting you, *To a religious observance of God's holy laws, as fearing, lest God's wrath and indignation, should be provoked against you;* but in your zeal for God's holy law, because of the shameful transgression thereof every man, every woman hath reason to mourn apart, and every one that dwelleth in the land ought to mourn and sigh for all the abominations done therein, and for the great wickedness carried on thereby.

And now that blessings may come instead of a curse, and that many beneficent purposes of good might speedily arise and flow from it, and be more readily promoted: I would hereby presume to offer the following considerations, as some outlines of a general reformation which ought to be established and carried on. And first, I would propose, that there ought to be days of mourning and fasting appointed to make inquiry into that great and preeminent evil for many years past carried on against the Heathen nations, and the horrible iniquity of making merchandise of us, and cruelly enslaving the poor Africans: and that you might seek grace and repentance, and find mercy and forgiveness before God Omnipotent; and that he may give you wisdom and understanding to devise what ought to be done.

Secondly, I would propose that a total abolition of slavery should be made and proclaimed; and that a universal emancipation of slaves should begin from the date thereof, and be carried on in the following manner: That a proclamation should be caused to be made, setting forth the anti-Christian unlawfulness of the slavery and commerce of the human species; and that it should be sent to all the courts and nations in Europe, to require their advice and assistance, and as they may find it unlawful to carry it on, let them whosoever will join to prohibit it. And if such a proclamation be found advisable to the British legislature, let them publish it, and cause it to be published, throughout all the British empire, to hinder and prohibit all men under their government to traffic either in buying or selling men; and, to prevent it, a penalty might be made against it of one thousand pounds, for any man either to buy or sell another man. And that it should require all slaveholders, upon the immediate information thereof, to mitigate the labor of their slaves to that of a lawful servitude, without tortures or oppression; and that they should not hinder, but cause and procure some suitable means of instruction for them in the knowledge of the Christian religion. And agreeable to the late *Royal Proclamation for the Encouragement of Piety and Virtue, and for the Preventing and Punishing of Vice, Profaneness and Immorality*; that by no means, under any pretense whatsoever, either for themselves or their masters, the slaves under their subjection should not be suffered to work on the Sabbath days, unless it be such works as necessity and mercy may require. But that those days, as well as some other hours selected for the purpose, should be appropriated for the time of their instruction; and that if any of their owners should not provide such suitable instructors for them, that those slaves should be taken away from them and given to others who would maintain and instruct them for their labor. And that it should be made known to the slaves that those who had been above seven years in the islands or elsewhere, if they had obtained any competent degree of knowledge of the Christian religion, and the laws of civilization, and had behaved themselves honestly and decently, that they should immediately become free; and that their owners should give them reasonable wages and maintenance for their labor, and not cause them to go away unless they could find some suitable employment elsewhere. And accordingly, from the date of their arrival to seven years, as they arrive at some suitable progress in knowledge, and behaved themselves honestly, that they should be getting free in the course of that time, and at the end of seven years to let every honest man and woman become free; for in the course of that time, they would have sufficiently paid their owners by their labor, both for their first purpose, and for the expenses attending their education. By being thus instructed in the course of seven years, they would become tractable and obedient, useful laborers, dutiful servants and good subjects; and Christian men might have the honor and happiness to see many of them vying with themselves to praise the God of their salvation. And it might be another necessary duty for Christians, in the course of that time, to make inquiry concerning some of their friends and relations in Africa: and if they found any intelligent persons amongst them, to give them as good education as they could; and find out a way of recourse to their friends; that as soon as they had made any progress in useful learning and the knowledge of the Christian religion, they might be sent back to Africa, to be made useful there as soon and as many of them as could be made fit for instructing others. The rest would become useful residentors in the colonies; where there might be employment enough given to all free people, with suitable wages according to their usefulness, in the improvement of land; and the more encouragement that could be given to agriculture, and every other branch of useful industry, would thereby increase the number of the inhabitants; without which any country, however blessed by nature, must continue poor.

And thirdly, I would propose that a fleet of some ships of war should be immediately sent to the coast of Africa, and particularly where the slave trade is carried on, with faithful men to direct that none should be brought from the coast of Africa without their own consent and the approbation of their friends, and to intercept all merchant ships that were bringing them away, until such a scrutiny was made, whatever nation they belonged to. And, I should suppose, if Great Britain was to do anything of this kind, that it would meet with the general approbation and assistance of other Christian nations; but whether it did or not, it could be very lawfully done at all the British forts and settlements on the coast of Africa; and particular remonstrances could be given to all the rest, to warn them of the consequences of such an evil and enormous wicked traffic as is now carried on. The Dutch have some crocodile settlers at the Cape, that should be called to a particular account for their murders and inhuman barbarities. But all the present governors of the British forts and factories should be dismissed, and faithful and good men appointed in their room; and those forts and factories, which at present are a den of thieves, might be turned into shepherd's tents, and have good shepherds sent to call the flocks to feed beside them. Then would doors of hospitality in abundance be opened in Africa to supply the weary travelers, and that immense abundance which they are enriched with, might be diffused afar; but the character of the inhabitants on the west coast of Africa, and the rich produce of their country, have been too long misrepresented by avaricious plunderers and merchants who deal in slaves; and if that country was not annually ravished and laid waste, there might be a very considerable profitable trade carried on with the Africans. And, should the noble Britons, who have often supported their own liberties with their lives and fortunes, extend their philanthropy to abolish the slavery and oppression of the Africans, they might have settlements and many kingdoms united in a friendly alliance with themselves, which might be made greatly to their own advantage, as well as they might have the happiness of being useful to promoting the prosperity and felicity of others, who have been cruelly injured and wrongfully dealt with. Were the Africans to be dealt with in a friendly manner, as by degrees they became to love learning, there would be nothing in their power, but what they would wish to render their service in return for the means of improving their understanding; and the present British factories, and other settlements, might be enlarged to a very great extent. And as Great Britain has been remarkable for ages past, for encouraging arts and sciences, and may now be put in competition with any nation in the known world, if they would take compassion on the inhabitants of the coast of Guinea, and to make use of such means as would be needful to enlighten their minds in the knowledge of Christianity, their virtue, in this respect, would have its own reward. And as the Africans became refined and established in light and knowledge, they would imitate their noble British friends, to improve their lands, and make use of that industry as the nature of their country might require, and to supply those that would trade with them with such productions as the nature of their climate would produce; and, in every respect, the fair Britons would have the preference with them to a very great extent; and, in another respect, they would become a kind of first ornament to Great Britain for her tender and compassionate care of such a set of distressed poor ignorant people. And were the noble Britons, and their august Sovereign, to cause protection and encouragement to be given to those Africans, they might expect in a short time, if need required it, to receive from thence great supplies of men in a lawful way, either for industry or defense; and of other things in abundance, from so great a source, where everything is luxurious and plenty, if not laid waste by barbarity and gross ignorance. Due encouragement being given to so great, so just, and such a noble undertaking, would soon bring more revenue in a righteous way to the British nation, that ten times its share in all the profits that slavery can produce;* and such a laudable example would inspire every generous and enterprising mind to imitate so great and worthy a nation, for establishing religion, justice, and equity to the Africans, and, in doing this, would be held in the highest esteem by all men, and be admired by all the world.

These three preceding considerations may suffice at present to show that some plan might be adopted in such a manner as effectually to relieve the grievances and oppression of the Africans, and to bring great honor and blessings to that nation, and to all men whosoever would endeavor to promote so great good to mankind; and it might render more conspicuous advantages to the noble Britons, as the first doers of it, and greater honor than the finding of America was at first to those that made the discovery: Though several difficulties may seem to arise at first, and the good to be sought after may appear as remote and unknown, as it was to explore the unknown region of the Western Ocean; should it be sought after, like the intrepid Columbus, if they do not find kingdoms of wealth by the way, they may be certain of finding treasures of happiness and peace in the end. But should there be any yet alive deserving the infamy and character of all the harsh things which I have ascribed to the insidious carriers-on of the slavery and commerce of the human species, they will certainly object to anything of this kind being proposed, or ever thought of, as doing so great a good to the base Black Negroes whom they make their prey. To

*A gentleman of my acquaintance told me that if ever he hears of anything of this kind taking place, he has a plan in contemplation, which would, in some equitable manner, produce from one million to fifteen million sterling to the British government annually, as it might be required; of which a due proportion of that revenue would be paid by the Africans; and that it would prevent all smuggling and illicit traffic; in a great measure, prevent running into debt, long imprisonment, and all unlawful bankruptcies; effectually prevent all dishonesty and swindling, and almost put an end to all robbery, fraud and theft.

such I must say again that it would be but a just commutation for what cannot be fully restored, in order to make restoration, as far as could be, for the injuries already done to them. And some may say that if they have wages to pay to the laborers for manufacturing the West India productions, that they would not be able to sell them at such a price as would suit the European market, unless all the different nations agreed to raise the price of their commodities in proportion. Whatever bad neighbors men may have to deal with, let the upright show themselves to be honest men, and that difficulty which some may fear would be but small as there can be no reason for men to do wrong because others do so; but as to what is consumed in Great Britain they could raise the price in proportion, and it would be better to sip the West India sweetness by paying a little more money for it (if it should be found needful) than to drink the blood of iniquity at a cheaper rate. I know several ladies in England who refuse to drink sugar in their tea, because of the cruel injuries done to the Black People employed in the culture of it at the West Indies. But should it cost the West Indians more money to have their manufactories carried by the labor of freemen than with slaves, it would be attended with greater blessings and advantages to them in the end. What the wages should be for the labor of freemen, is a question not so easily determined; yet I should think that it always ought to be something more than merely victuals and clothes; and if a man works by the day, he should have the three hundredth part of what might be estimated as sufficient to keep him in necessary clothes and provisions for a year, and, added to that, such wages of reward as their usefulness might require. Something of this kind should be observed in free countries, and then the price of provisions would be kept at such a rate as the industrious poor could live, without being oppressed and screwed down to work for nothing, but only barely to live. And were every civilized nation where they boast of liberty, so ordered by its government, that some general and useful employment were provided for every industrious man and woman, in such a manner that none should stand still and be idle, and have to say that they could not get employment, so long as there are barren lands enough at home and abroad sufficient to employ thousands and millions of people more than there are. This, in a great measure, would prevent thieves and robbers, and the labor of many would soon enrich a nation. But those employed by the general community should only have their maintenance either given or estimated in money, and half the wages of others, which would make them seek out for something else whenever they could, and half a loaf would be better than no bread. The men that were employed in this manner, would form a useful militia, and the women would be kept from a state of misery and want, and from following a life of dissolute wickedness. Liberty and Freedom, where people may starve for want, can do them but little good. We want many rules of civilization in Africa; but, in many respects, we may boast of some more essential liberties than any of the civilized nations in Europe enjoy; for the poorest amongst us are never in distress for want, unless some general and universal calamity happen to us. But if any nation or society of men were to observe the laws of God, and to keep his commandments, and walk in the way of righteousness, they would not need to fear the heat in sultry hot climates, nor the freezing inclemency of the cold, and the storms and hurricanes would not hurt them at all; they might soon see blessings and plenty in abundance showered down upon their mountains and valleys; and if his beneficence was sought after, who martials out the drops of the dew, and bids the winds to blow, and to carry the clouds on their wings to drop down their moisture and fatness on what spot soever he pleaseth, and who causeth the genial rays of the sun to warm and cherish the productions of the earth in every place according to that temperature which he sees meet; then might the temperate climes of Great Britain be seen to vie with the rich land of Canaan of old, which is now, because of the wickedness of its inhabitants, in comparison of what it was, as only a barren desert.

Particular thanks is due to every one of that humane society of worthy and respectful gentlemen, whose liberality hath supported many of the Black poor about London. *Those that honor their Maker have mercy on the poor; and many blessings are upon the head of the just: may the fear of the Lord prolong their days, and cause their memory to be blessed, and may their number be increased to fill their expectation with gladness;* for they have not only commiserated the poor in general, *but even those which are accounted as beasts, and imputed as vile in the sight of others.* The part that the British government has taken to cooperate with them has certainly a flattering and laudable appearance of doing some good; and the fitting out ships to supply a company of Black People with clothes and provisions, and to carry them to settle at Sierra Leone, in the West coast of Africa, as a free colony to Great Britain, in a peaceable alliance with the inhabitants, has every appearance of honor, and the approbation of friends. According to the plan, humanity hath made its appearance in a more honorable way of colonization, than any Christian nation have ever done before, and may be productive of much good, if they continue to encourage and support them. But after all there is some doubt whether their own flattering expectation in the manner as set forth to them, and the hope of their friends may not be defeated and rendered abortive; and there is some reason to fear, that they never will be settled as intended, in any permanent and peaceable way at Sierra Leone.

This prospect of settling a free colony to Great Britain in a peaceable alliance with the inhabitants of Africa at Sierra Leone, has neither altogether met with the credulous approbation of the Africans here, nor yet been sought after with any prudent and right plan by the promoters of it. Had a treaty of agreement been first made with the inhabitants of Africa, and the terms and nature of such a settlement fixed upon, and its situation and boundary pointed out; then might the Africans, and others here, have embarked with a good prospect of enjoying happiness and prosperity themselves, and have gone with a hope of being able to render their services, in return, of some advantage to their friends and benefactors of Great Britain. But as this was not done, and as they were to be hurried away at all events, come of them after what would; and yet, after all, to be delayed in the ships before they were set out from the coast, until many of them have perished with cold, and other disorders, and several of the most intelligent among them are dead, and others that, in all probability, would have been most useful for them were hindered from going, by means of some disagreeable jealousy of those who were appointed as governors, the great prospect of doing good seems all to be blown away. And so it appeared to some of those who are now gone, and at last, haphazard, were obliged to go; who endeavored in vain to get away by plunging into the water, that they might, if possible wade ashore, as dreading the prospect of their wretched fate, and as beholding their perilous situation, having every prospect of difficulty and surrounding danger.

What with the death of some of the original promoters and proposers of this charitable undertaking, and the death and deprivation of others that were to share the benefit of it, and by the adverse motives of those employed to be the conductors thereof, we think it will be more than what can be well expected, if we ever hear of any good in proportion to so great, well-designed, laudable and expensive charity. Many more of the Black People still in this country would have, with great gladness, embraced the opportunity, longing to reach their native land; but as the old saying is, A burnt child dreads the fire, some of these unfortunate sons and daughters of Africa have been severally unlawfully dragged away from their native abodes, under various pretenses, by the insidious treachery of others, and have been brought into the hands of barbarous robbers and pirates, and, like sheep to the market, have been sold into captivity and slavery, and thereby have been deprived of their natural liberty and property, and every connection that they held dear and valuable, and subjected to the cruel service of the hard-hearted brutes called planters. But some of them, by various services either to the public or to individuals, as more particularly in the course of [the] last war, have gotten their liberty again in this free country. They are thankful for the respite, but afraid of being ensnared again; for the European seafaring people in general, who trade to foreign parts, have such a prejudice against Black People, that they use them more like asses than men, so that a Black Man is scarcely ever safe among them. Much assiduity was made use to persuade the Black People in general to embrace the opportunity of going with this company of transports; but the wiser sort declined from all thoughts of it, unless they could hear of some better plan taking place for their security and safety. For as it seemed prudent and obvious to many of them taking heed to that sacred inquiry, *Doth a fountain send forth at the same place sweet water and bitter?* They were afraid that their doom would be to drink of the bitter water. For can it be readily conceived that government would establish a free colony for them nearly on the spot, while it supports its forts and garrisons, to ensnare, merchandise, and to carry others into captivity and slavery.

Above fifty years ago, P. Gordon, in his *Geography*, though he was no advocate against slavery, complains of the barbarities committed against the Heathen nations, and the base usage of the negro slaves subjected to bondage as brutes, and deprived of religion as men. His remark on the religion of the American islands, says: "As for the negro slaves, their lot has hitherto been, and still is, to serve such Christian masters who sufficiently declare what zeal they have for their conversion, by unkindly using a serious divine some time ago for only proposing to endeavor the same." This was above half a century ago, and their unchristian barbarity is still continued. Even in the little time that I was in Grenada, I saw a slave receive twenty-four lashes of a whip for being seen at a church on a Sunday, instead of going to work in the fields; and those whom they put the greatest confidence in are often served in the same manner. The noble proposals offered for instructing the heathen nations and people in his *Geography*, has been attended to with great supineness and indifference. The author wishes, that "sincere endeavors might be made to extend the limits of our Savior's kingdom with those of our own dominions; and to spread true religion as far as the British sails have done for traffic." And he adds, "Let our planters duly consider that to extirpate natives, is rather a supplanting than planting a new colony; and that it is far more honorable to overcome paganism in one than to destroy a thousand pagans. Each convert is a conquest."

To put an end to the nakedness of slavery and merchandising of men and to prevent murder, extirpation and dissolution is what every righteous nation ought to seek after; and to endeavor to diffuse knowledge and instruction to all the heathen nations wherever they can, is the grand duty of all Christian men. But while the horrible traffic of slavery is admitted and practiced, there can be but little hope of any good proposals meeting with success anywhere; for the abandoned carriers of it on have spread the poison of their iniquity wherever they come, at home and abroad. Were the iniquitous laws in support of it, and the whole of that oppression and injustice abolished, and the righteous laws of Christianity, equity, justice and humanity established in the room thereof, multitudes of nations would flock to the standard of truth, and instead of revolting away, they would count it their greatest happiness to be under the protection and jurisdiction of a righteous government. And in that respect, *in the multitude of the people is the King's Honor; but in the want of people, is the destruction of the Prince.*

We would wish to have the grandeur and fame of the British empire to extend far and wide; and the glory and honor of God to be promoted by it, and the interest of Christianity set forth among all the nations wherever its influence and power can extend; but not to be supported by the insidious pirates, depredators, murderers and slaveholders. And as it might diffuse knowledge and instruction to others, that it might receive a tribute of reward from all its territories, forts and garrisons, without being oppressive to any. But contrary to this the wickedness of many of the White People who keep slaves, and contrary to all the laws and duties of Christianity which the Scriptures teach, they have in general endeavored to keep the Black People in total ignorance as much as they can, which must be a great dishonor to any Christian government, and injurious to the safety and happiness of rulers.

But in order to diffuse any knowledge of Christianity to the unlearned Heathens, those who undertake to do anything therein ought to be wise and honest men. Their own learning, though the more the better, is not so much required as that they should be men of the same

mind and principles of the apostle Paul; men that would hate covetousness, and who would hazard their lives for the cause and gospel of
our Lord and Savior Jesus Christ. "I think it needless to express how
commendable such a design would be in itself and how desirable the
promotion thereof should be to all who style themselves Christians, of
what party or profession soever they are. Rational methods might be
taken to have the Scriptures translated into many foreign languages;
and a competent number of young students of theology might be educated at home in these foreign languages, to afford a constant supply of
able men, who might yearly go abroad, and be sufficiently qualified at
their first arrival to undertake the great work for which they were sent."
But as a hindrance to this, the many anti-Christian errors which are
gone abroad into the world, and all the popish superstition and non-
sense, and the various assimilations unto it, with the false philosophy
which abounds among Christians, seems to threaten with a universal
deluge; but God hath promised to fill the world with a knowledge of
himself, and he hath set up his bow in the rational heavens as well as in
the clouds, as a token that he will stop the proud ways of error and delusion, that hitherto they may come, and no farther. The holy arch of
truth is to be seen in the azure paths of the pious and wise, and con-
spicuously painted in crimson over the martyrs' tombs. These, with
the golden altars of truth, built up by the reformed churches, and
many pious, good and righteous men, are bulwarks that will ever stand
against all the forts of error. Teaching would be exceedingly necessary
to the pagan nations and ignorant people in every place and situation;
but they do not need any unscriptural forms and ceremonies to be
taught unto them; they can devise superstitions enough among themselves, and church government too, if ever they need any.

And hence we would agree in this one thing with that erroneous
philosopher, who has lately written *An Apology for Negro Slavery*, "But
if the slave is only to be made acquainted with the form, without the
substance; if he is only to be decked out with the external trappings of
religion; if he is only to be taught the uncheering principles of gloomy
superstition; or, if he is only to be inspired with the intemperate frenzy
of enthusiastic fanaticism, it were better that he remained in that dark
state, where he could not see good from ill." But these words *intemperate, frenzy, enthusiastic,* and *fanaticism* may be variously applied, and
often wrongfully; but, perhaps never better, or more fitly, than to be
ascribed as the genuine character of this author's brutish philoso-

phy; and he may subscribe to it, and the meaning of these words, with as much affinity to himself, as he bears a relation to a *Hume*, or to his friend *Tobin*. The poor negroes in the West Indies, have suffered enough by such religion as the philosophers of the North produce; Protestants, as they are called, are the most barbarous slaveholders, and there are none can equal the Scotch floggers and negro drivers, and the barbarous Dutch cruelties. Perhaps as the church of Rome begins to sink in its power, its followers may increase in virtue and humanity; so that many who are the professed adherents thereof, would even blush and abhor the very mention of the cruelty and bloody deeds that their ancestors have committed; and we find slavery itself more tolerable among them than it is in the Protestant countries.

But I shall add another observation which I am sorry to find among Christians, and I think it is a great deficiency among the clergy in general when covetous and profligate men are admitted amongst them, who either do not know or dare not speak the truth, but neglect their duty much or do it with such supineness that it becomes good for nothing. Sometimes an old woman selling matches will preach a better, and a more orthodox sermon than some of the clergy who are only decked out (as Mr. Turnbull calls it) with the external trappings of religion. Much of the great wickedness of others lieth at their door, and these words of the Prophet are applicable to them: *And first, saith the Lord, I will recompense their iniquity, and their sin double; because they have defiled my land, they have filled mine inheritance with the carcasses of their detestable and abominable things.* Such are the errors of men. Church signifies an assembly of people; but a building of wood, brick or stone where the people meet together is generally called so; and should the people be frightened away by the many abominable dead carcasses which they meet with they should follow the multitudes to the fields, to the valleys, to the mountains, to the islands, to the rivers, and to the ships, and compel them to come in, that the house of the Lord may be filled. But when we find some of the covetous connivers with slaveholders, in the West Indies, so ignorant as to dispute whether a Pagan can be baptized without giving him a Christian name, we cannot expect much from them or think that they will follow after much good. No name whether Christian or Pagan, has anything to do with baptism; if the requisite qualities of knowledge and faith be found in a man, he may be baptized, let his name be what it will. And Christianity does not require that we should be deprived of our own personal name, or the name of our ancestors; but it may very fitly add another name unto us, Christian, or one anointed. And it might as well be answered so to that question in the English liturgy, *What is your name?*—A Christian.

> *A Christian is the highest style of man!*
> *And is there, who the blessed cross wipes off*
> *As a foul blot, from his dishonor'd brow?*
> *If angels tremble, 'tis at such a sight:*
> *The wretch they quit desponding of their charge,*
> *More struck with grief or wonder who can tell?*

And let me now hope that you will pardon me in all that I have been thus telling you, O ye inhabitants of Great Britain! to whom I owe the greatest respect; to your king! to yourselves! and to your government! And tho' many things which I have written may seem harsh, it cannot be otherwise evaded when such horrible iniquity is transacted: and tho' to some what I have said may appear as the rattling leaves of autumn, that may soon be blown away and whirled in a vortex where few can hear and know: I must yet say, although it is not for me to determine the manner, that the voice of our complaint implies a vengeance because of the great iniquity that you have done, and because of the cruel injustice done unto us Africans; and it ought to sound in your ears as the rolling waves around your circumambient shores; and if it is not hearkened unto, it may yet arise with a louder voice, as the rolling thunder, and it may increase in the force of its volubility, not only to shake the leaves of the most stout in heart, but to rend the mountains before them and to cleave in pieces the rocks under them, and to go on with fury to smite the stoutest oaks in the forest; and even to make that which is strong and wherein you think that your strength lieth, to become as stubble and as the fibers of rotten wood, that will do you no good, and your trust in it will become a snare of infatuation to you!

THE

INTERESTING NARRATIVE

OF

THE LIFE

OF

OLAUDAH EQUIANO,

OR

GUSTAVUS VASSA,

THE AFRICAN

WRITTEN BY HIMSELF

Behold, God is my salvation; I will trust, and not be afraid, for the Lord Jehovah is my strength and my song; he also is become my salvation.
And in that day shall ye say, Praise the Lord, call upon his name, declare his doings among the people. Isa. 12:2.4.

EIGHTH EDITION ENLARGED.

NORWICH:
PRINTED FOR, AND SOLD BY THE AUTHOR.

1794.

PRICE FOUR SHILLINGS.
Formerly sold for 7s.

[*Entered at Stationers' Hall.*]

4

THE INTERESTING NARRATIVE

OF THE LIFE OF

OLAUDAH EQUIANO,

OR

GUSTAVUS VASSA,

THE AFRICAN,

WRITTEN BY HIMSELF

AN INVIDIOUS FALSEHOOD having appeared in the *Oracle* of the 25th, and the *Star* of the 27th of April 1792, with a view to hurt my character,* and to discredit and prevent the sale of my Narrative, asserting, that I was born in the Danish island of Santa Cruz, in the West Indies,[†] it is necessary that, in this edition, I should take notice thereof, and it is only needful for me to appeal to those numerous and respectable persons of character who knew me when I first arrived in England, and could speak no language but that of Africa.[‡]

Under this appeal, I now offer this edition of my Narrative to the candid reader, and to the friends of humanity, hoping it may still be the means, in its measure, of showing the enormous cruelties practiced on my sable brethren, and strengthening the generous emulation now prevailing in this country, to put a speedy end to a traffic both cruel and unjust.

Edinburgh, June 1792

LETTER

of Alexander Tillock to John Monteith, Esq. Glasgow

Dear Sir,
Your note of the 30th ult. I would have answered in course; but wished first to be able to inform you what paper we had taken the article from which respected Gustavus Vassa. By this day's post, have sent you a

---

* ————————"Speak of me as I am,
Nothing extenuate, nor set down aught
In malice."————
†   I may now justly say,
There is a lust in man no charm can tame,
Of loudly publishing his neighbor's shame;
On eagles wings immortal scandals fly,
But virtuous actions are but born and die.
    London. The *County Chronicle,* and *Weekly Advertiser* for Essex, Herts, Kent, Surry, Middlesex, etc. Tuesday, February 19th, 1788. (Postscript).
    "We are sorry the want of room prevents us from giving place to the favors of Gustavus Vassa on the slave trade. The zeal of this worthy African, in favor of this brethren, would do honor to any color, or to any cause."
‡ My friend Mrs. Baynes, formerly Miss Guerin, at Southampton, and many others of her friends. John Hill, Esq. Custom House, Dublin; Admiral Affleck; Admiral George

copy of the *Oracle* of Wednesday the 25th—in the last column of the 3d page, you will find the article from which we inserted the one in the *Star* of the 27th ult.—If it be erroneous, you will see it had not its origin with us. As to G.V. I know nothing about him.

After examining the paragraph in the *Oracle*, which immediately follows the one in question, I am inclined to believe that the one respecting G.V. may have been fabricated by some of the advocates for continuing the slave trade, for the purpose of weakening the force of the evidence brought against that trade; for, I believe, if they could, they would stifle the evidence altogether.

Having sent you the *Oracle*, we have sent all that we can say about the business. I am,

> Dear Sir,
> Your most humble servant,
> Alex. Tilloch
> Star Office, 5th May, 1792

LETTER
From the Rev. Dr. J. Baker, of May Fair Chapel, London,
to Mr. Gustavus Vassa, at David Dale's, Esq. Glasgow

Dear Sir,
I went after Mr. Millan (the printer of the *Oracle*), but he was not at home. I understood that an apology would be made to you, and I desired it might be a proper one, such as would give fair satisfaction, and take off any disadvantageous impressions which the paragraph alluded to may have made. Whether the matter will bear an action or not, I do not know, and have not inquired whether you can punish by law; because I think it is not worthwhile to go to the expense of a lawsuit, especially if a proper apology is made; for, can any man that reads your narrative believe that you are not a native of Africa?—I see therefore no good reason for not printing a fifth edition, on account of a scandalous paragraph in a newspaper.

> I remain,
> Dear Sir,
> Your sincere friend,
> J. Baker
> Grosvenor Street, May 14, 1792

Balfour, Portsmouth; Captain Gallia, Greenock; Mrs. Shaw, James Street, Covent Garden, London.

TO THE LORDS SPIRITUAL AND

TEMPORAL, AND THE COMMONS OF THE

PARLIAMENT OF GREAT BRITAIN.

My Lords and Gentlemen,

Permit me with the greatest deference and respect, to lay at your feet the following genuine Narrative; the chief design of which is to excite in your august assemblies a sense of compassion for the miseries which the slave trade has entailed on my unfortunate countrymen. By the horrors of that trade was I first torn away from all the tender connections that were naturally dear to my heart; but these, through the mysterious ways of Providence, I ought to regard as infinitely more than compensated by the introduction I have thence obtained to the knowledge of the Christian religion, and of a nation which, by its liberal sentiments, its humanity, the glorious freedom of its government, and its proficiency in arts and sciences, has exalted the dignity of human nature.

I am sensible I ought to entreat your pardon for addressing to you a work so wholly devoid of literary merit; but, as the production of an unlettered African, who is actuated by the hope of becoming an instrument towards the relief of his suffering countrymen, I trust that *such a man,* pleading in *such a cause,* will be acquitted of boldness and presumption.

May the God of Heaven inspire your hearts with peculiar benevolence on that important day when the question of Abolition is to be discussed, when thousands, in consequence of your determination, are to look for Happiness or Misery!

> I am,
> My Lords and Gentlemen,
> Your most obedient,
> And devoted humble servant,
> Olaudah Equiano,
> or
> Gustavus Vassa.
> March 1789

*To the Chairman of the Committees for
the Abolition of the Slave Trade*
Magdalen College, Cambridge, May 26, 1790

Gentlemen,
I take the liberty, as being joined with you in the same laudable endeavors to support the cause of humanity in the abolition of the Slave Trade, to recommend to your protection the bearer of this note Gustavus Vassa, an African; and to beg the favor of your assistance to him in the sale of this book.

> I am, with great respect,
> Gentlemen,
> Your most obedient servant,
> P. Peckard

Manchester, July 23, 1790

Thomas Walker has great pleasure in recommending the sale of the Narrative of Gustavus Vassa to the friends of justice and humanity, he being well entitled to their protection and support, from the united testimonies of the Rev. T. Clarkson, of London; Dr. Peckard, of Cambridge; and Sampson and Charles Lloyd, Esqrs. of Birmingham.

Sheffield, August 20, 1790

In consequence of the recommendation to Dr. Peckard of Cambridge; Messrs. Lloyd of Birmingham; the Rev. T. Clarkson of London; Thomas Walker, Thomas Cooper, and Isaac Moss, Esqrs. of Manchester; we beg leave also to recommend the sale of the Narrative of Gustavus Vassa to the friends of humanity in the town and neighborhood of Sheffield.

Dr. Brown,	Rev. Ja. Wilkinson,
Wm. Shore, Esq.,	Rev. Edw. Goodwin,
Samuel Marshall,	John Barlow.

Nottingham, 17th January, 1791

In consequence of the respectable recommendation of several gentlemen of the first character, who have borne testimony to the good sense, intellectual improvements, and integrity of Gustavus Vassa, lately of that injured and oppressed class of men, the injured Africans; and further convinced of the justice of his recommendations, from our own personal interviews with him, we take the liberty also to recommend the said Gustavus Vassa to the protection and assistance of the friends of humanity.

Rev. G. Walker,	F. Wakefield,
John Morris,	T. Bolton,
Joseph Rigsby, Rector, St. Peter's,	Thomas Hawksley,
Samuel Smith,	Francis Hart,
John Wright,	S. White, M. D.
	J. Hancock.

LETTER
To Mr. O'Brien, Carrickfergus
(Per favor of Mr. Gustavus Vassa)
Belfast, December 25, 1791

Dear Sir,
The bearer of this, Mr. Gustavus Vassa, an enlightened African, of good sense, agreeable manners, and of an excellent character, and who comes well recommended to this place, and noticed by the first people here, goes tomorrow for your town, for the purpose of vending some books, written by himself, which is a Narrative of his own Life and Sufferings, with some account of his native country and its inhabitants. He was torn from his relatives and country (by the more savage white men of England) at an early period in life; and during his residence in England, at which time I have seen him, during my agency for the American prisoners, with Sir William Dolben, Mr. Granville Sharp, Mr. Wilkes, and many other distinguished characters; he supported an irreproachable character, and was a principal instrument in bringing about the motion for a repeal of the Slave act. I beg leave to introduce him to your notice and civility; and if you can spare the time, your introduction of him personally to your neighbors may be of essential benefit to him.

I am,
Sir,
Your obedient humble servant,
Thos. Digges

LETTER
To Rowland Webster, Esq. Stockton
(Per favor of Mr. Gustavus Vassa)

Dear Sir,
I take the liberty to introduce to your knowledge Mr. Gustavus Vassa, an African of distinguished merit. He has recommendations to Stockton, and I am happy in adding to the number. To the principal supporters of the Bill for the Abolition of the slave trade he is well known; and he has, himself, been very instrumental in promoting a plan so truly conducive to the interests of Religion and Humanity. Mr. Vassa has published a Narrative which clearly delineates the iniquity of that unnatural and destructive commerce; and I am able to assert, from my own experience, that he has not exaggerated in a single particular. This work has been mentioned in very favorable terms by the Reviewers, and fully demonstrates that genius and worth are not limited to country or complexion. He has with him some copies for sale, and if you can conveniently assist him in the disposal thereof, you will greatly oblige,

> Dear Sir,
> Your friend and servant,
> William Eddis
> Durham, October 25, 1792

Hull, November 12, 1792

The bearer hereof, Mr. Gustavus Vassa, an African, is recommended to us by the Rev. Dr. Peckard, Dean of Peterborough, and by many other very respectable characters, as an intelligent and upright man; and as we have no doubt but the accounts we have received are grounded on the best authority, we recommend him to the assistance of the friends of humanity in this town, in promoting subscriptions to an interesting Narrative of his Life.

John Sykes, Mayor,	R. A. Harrison, Esq.
Thomas Clarke, Vicar,	Jos. R. Pease, Esq.
William Hornby, Esq.	of Gainsborough

LETTER
To William Hughes, Esq. Devizes

Dear Sir,
Whether you will consider my introducing to your acquaintance the bearer of this letter, Olaudah Equiano, the enlightened African (or Gustavus Vassa), as a liberty or a favor, I shall not anticipate.

He came recommended to me by men of distinguished talents and exemplary virtue, as an honest and benevolent man; and his conversation and manners as well as his book do more than justice to the recommendation.

The active part he took in bringing about the motion for a repeal of the Slave act, has given him much celebrity as a public man; and, in all the varied scenes of checkered life, through which he has passed, his private character and conduct have been irreproachable.

His *business* in your part of the world is to promote the sale of his book, and it is a part of *my business,* as a friend to the cause of humanity, to do all the little service that is in my poor power to a man who is engaged in so noble a cause as the freedom and salvation of his enslaved and unenlightened countrymen.

The simplicity that runs through his Narrative is singularly beautiful, and that beauty is heightened by the idea that it is *true*; this is all I shall say about this book, save only that I am sure those who buy it will not regret that they have laid out the price of it in the purchase.

Your notice, civility, and personal introduction of this fair-minded black man, to your friends in Devizes, will be gratifying to your own feelings, and laying a considerable weight of obligation on

           Dear Sir,
           Your most obedient and obliged servant,
           William Langworthy
           Bath, October 10th, 1793

MONTHLY REVIEW
for June 1789   Page 551

We entertain no doubt of the general authenticity of this very intelligent African's story; though it is not improbable that some English writer has assisted him in the compilement, or, at least, the correction of his book; for it is sufficiently well-written. The Narrative wears an honest face; and we have conceived a good opinion of the man, from the artless manner in which he has detailed the variety of adventures and vicissitudes which have fallen to his lot. His publication appears very seasonable, at a time when negro-slavery is the subject of public investigation; and it seems calculated to increase the odium that has been excited against the West India planters, on account of the cruelties that some are said to have exercised on their slaves, many instances of which are here detailed.

The sable author of this volume appears to be a very sensible man; and he is, surely, not the less worthy of credit from being a convert to Christianity. He is a Methodist, and has filled many pages towards the end of this work, with accounts of his dreams, visions, and divine influences; but all this, supposing him to have been under any delusive influence, only serves to convince us that he is guided by principle, and that he is not one of those poor converts, who having undergone the ceremony of baptism, have remained content with that portion only of the Christian religion; instances of which are said to be almost innumerable in America and the West Indies.

Gustavus Vassa appears to possess a very different character; and, therefore, we heartily wish success to his publication, which we are glad to see has been encouraged by a very respectable subscription.

THE *GENERAL MAGAZINE* AND *IMPARTIAL REVIEW*
for July 1789, characterizes this Work in the following Terms:

This is "a round unvarnished tale" of the checkered adventures of an African, who early in life, was torn from his native country, by those savage dealers in a traffic disgraceful to humanity, and which has fixed a stain on the legislature of Britain. The Narrative appears to be written with much truth and simplicity. The author's account of the manners of the natives of his own province (Eboe) is interesting and pleasing; and the reader, unless perchance he is either a West India planter, or Liverpool merchant, will find his humanity often severely wounded by the shameless barbarity practiced towards the author's hapless countrymen in all our colonies; if he feel, as he ought, the oppressed and the oppressors will equally excite his pity and indignation. That so unjust, so iniquitous a commerce may be abolished, is our ardent wish; and we heartily join in our author's prayer, "That the God of Heaven may inspire the hearts of our Representatives in Parliament, with peculiar benevolence on that important day when so interesting a question is to be discussed; when thousands, in consequence of their determination, are to look for happiness or misery!"

N.B. These letters, and the Reviewers' remarks, would not have appeared in the Narrative, were it not on the account of the false assertions of my enemies.

The kind reception which this Work has met with from many hundred persons, of all denominations, demands the Author's most sincere thanks to his numerous friends; and he most respectfully solicits the favor and encouragement of the candid and unprejudiced friends of the Africans.

CONTENTS

The Life of Gustavus Vassa

Chapter I

The Author's account of his country, and their manners and customs—Administration of justice—Embrenché—Marriage ceremony, and public entertainments—Mode of living—Dress—Manufactures—Buildings—Commerce—Agriculture—War and Religion—Superstition of the natives—Funeral ceremonies of the priests or magicians—Curious mode of discovering poison—Some hints concerning the origin of the author's countrymen, with the opinions of different writers on that subject.

I BELIEVE IT IS DIFFICULT for those who publish their own memoirs to escape the imputation of vanity; nor is this the only disadvantage under which they labor; it is also their misfortune, that whatever is uncommon is rarely, if ever, believed; and what is obvious we are apt to turn from with disgust, and to charge the writer with impertinence. People generally think those memoirs only worthy to be read or remembered which abound in great or striking events; those, in short, which in a high degree excite either admiration or pity: all others they consign to contempt and oblivion. It is, therefore, I confess, not a little hazardous, in a private and obscure individual, and a stranger too, thus to solicit the indulgent attention of the public; especially when I own I offer here the history of neither a saint, a hero, nor a tyrant. I believe there are a few events in my life which have not happened to many; it is true the incidents of it are numerous; and, did I consider myself a European, I might say my sufferings were great; but, when I compare my lot with that of most of my countrymen, I regard myself as a *particular favorite of Heaven,* and acknowledge the mercies of Providence in every occurrence of my life. If, then, the following narrative does not appear sufficiently interesting to engage general attention, let my motive be some excuse for its publication. I am not so foolishly vain as to expect from it either immortality or literary reputation. If it affords any satisfaction to my numerous friends, at whose request it has been written, or in the smallest degree promotes the interests of humanity, the ends for which it was undertaken will be fully

attained, and every wish of my heart gratified. Let it therefore be remembered that, in wishing to avoid censure, I do not aspire to praise.

That part of Africa, known by the name of Guinea, to which the
trade for slaves is carried on, extends along the coast above 3,400
miles, from Senegal to Angola, and includes a variety of kingdoms. Of
these the most considerable is the kingdom of Benin, both as to extent
and wealth, the richness and cultivation of the soil, the power of its
king, and the number and warlike disposition of the inhabitants. It is
situated nearly under the line, and extends along the coast above 170
miles, but runs back into the interior part of Africa, to a distance hitherto I believe unexplored by any traveler; and seems only terminated at
length by the empire of Abyssinia, near 1,500 miles from its beginning. This kingdom is divided into many provinces or districts: in one
of the most remote and fertile of which I was born, in the year 1745, situated in a charming fruitful vale, named Essaka.* The distance of this
province from the capital of Benin and the sea coast must be very considerable; for I had never heard of white men or Europeans, nor of the
sea; and our subjection to the king of Benin was little more than nominal; for every transaction of the government, as far as my slender observation extended, was conducted by the chiefs or elders of the place.
The manners and government of a people who have little commerce
with other countries are generally very simple; and the history of what
passes in one family or village, may serve as a specimen of the whole
nation. My father was one of those elders or chiefs I have spoken of,
and was styled *Embrenché*; a term, as I remember, importing the highest distinction, and signifying in our language a *mark* of grandeur.
This mark is conferred on the person entitled to it, by cutting the skin
across at the top of the forehead, and drawing it down to the eyebrows;
and, while it is in this situation, applying a warm hand, and rubbing it
until it shrinks up into a thick *weal* across the lower part of the forehead. Most of the judges and senators were thus marked; my father
had long borne it: I had seen it conferred on one of my brothers, and I
also was *destined* to receive it by my parents. Those Embrenché, or
chief men, decided disputes, and punished crimes; for which purpose
they always assembled together. The proceedings were generally

---

*See the observations on a Guinea voyage, in a series of letters addressed to the Rev. T.
Clarkson, by Jas. Field, Stanfield, in 1788, page 21—"I never saw a happier race of
people than those of the kingdom of Benin, seated in ease and plenty, the slave trade,
and its unavoidable bad effects excepted, everything bore the appearance of friendship, tranquility, and primitive independence."

short; and in most cases the law of retaliation prevailed. I remember a man was brought before my father, and the other judges, for kidnapping a boy; and, although he was the son of a chief, or senator, he was condemned to make recompense by a man and woman slave. Adultery, however, was sometimes punished with slavery or death; a punishment, which I believe is inflicted on it throughout most of the nations of Africa:★ so sacred among them is the honor of the marriage bed, and so jealous are they of the fidelity of their wives. Of this I recollect an instance—A woman was convicted before the judges of adultery, and delivered over, as the custom was, to her husband to be punished. Accordingly, he determined to put her to death; but, it being found, just before her execution, that she had an infant at her breast, and no woman being prevailed on to perform the part of a nurse, she was spared on account of the child. The men, however, do not preserve the same constancy to their wives which they expect from them; for they indulge in a plurality, though seldom in more than two. Their mode of marriage is thus: Both parties are usually betrothed when young by their parents (though I have known the males to betroth themselves). On this occasion a feast is prepared, and the bride and bridegroom stand up in the midst of all their friends, who are assembled for the purpose, while he declares she is thenceforth to be looked upon as his wife, and that no person is to pay any addresses to her. This is also immediately proclaimed in the vicinity, on which the bride retires from the assembly. Sometime after she is brought home to her husband, and then another feast is made, to which the relations of both parties are invited: her parents then deliver her to the bridegroom, accompanied with a number of blessings; and at the same time they tie round her waist a cotton string, of the thickness of a goose quill, which none but married women are permitted to wear; she is now considered as completely his wife; and at this time the dowry is given to the new married pair, which generally consists of portions of land, slaves, and cattle, household goods, and implements of husbandry. These are offered by the friends of both parties; besides which the parents of the bridegroom present gifts to those of the bride, whose property she is looked upon before marriage; but, after it, she is esteemed the sole property of the husband. The ceremony being now ended, the festival begins, which is celebrated with bonfires, and loud acclamations of joy, accompanied with music and dancing.

★See Benezet's *Account of Guinea* throughout.

We are almost a nation of dancers, musicians, and poets. Thus every great event, such as a triumphant return from battle, or other cause of public rejoicing, is celebrated in public dances, which are accompanied with songs and music suited to the occasion. The assembly is separated into four divisions, which dance either apart or in succession, and each with a character peculiar to itself. The first division contains the married men, who in their dances frequently exhibit feats of arms, and the representation of a battle. To these succeed the married women, who dance in the second division. The young men occupy the third; and the maidens the fourth. Each represents some interesting scene of real life, such as a great achievement, domestic employment, a pathetic story, or some rural sport; and as the subject is generally founded on some recent event, it is therefore ever new. This gives our dances a spirit and variety which I have scarcely seen elsewhere.* We have many musical instruments, particularly drums of different kinds, a piece of music which resembles a guitar, and another much like a stickado. These last are chiefly used by betrothed virgins, who play on them on all grand festivals.

As our manners are simple, our luxuries are few. The dress of both sexes [is] nearly the same. It generally consists of a long piece of calico, or muslin, wrapped loosely around the body, somewhat in the form of a highland plaid [kilt]. This is usually dyed blue, which is our favorite color. It is extracted from a berry, and is brighter and richer than any I have seen in Europe. Besides this, our women of distinction wear golden ornaments, which they dispose with some profusion on their arms and legs. When our women are not employed with the men in tillage, their usual occupation is spinning and weaving cotton, which they afterwards dye, and make into garments. They also manufacture earthen vessels, of which we have many kinds. Among the rest tobacco pipes, made after the same fashion, and used in the same manner, as those in Turkey.†

Our manner of living is entirely plain; for as yet the natives are unacquainted with those refinements in cookery which debauch the taste: Bullocks, goats, and poultry, supply the greatest part of their food. These constitute likewise the principal wealth of the country, and the chief articles of its commerce. The flesh is usually stewed in a

*When I was in Smyrna I have frequently seen the Greeks dance after this manner.
†The bowl is earthen, curiously figured, to which a long reed is fixed as a tube. This tube is sometimes so long as to be borne by one, and frequently, out of grandeur, by two boys.

pan. To make it savory we sometimes use also pepper and other spices; and we have salt made of wood ashes. Our vegetables are mostly plantains, eadas, yams, beans, and Indian corn. The head of the family usually eats alone; his wives and slaves have also their separate tables. Before we taste food, we always wash our hands; indeed our cleanliness on all occasions is extreme; but on this it is an indispensible ceremony. After washing, libation is made, by pouring out a small portion of the drink on the floor, and tossing a small quantity of the food in a certain place, for the spirits of departed relations, which the natives suppose to preside over their conduct, and guard them from evil. They are totally unacquainted with strong or spirituous liquors; and their principal beverage is palm wine.

This is got from a tree of that name, by tapping it at the top, and fastening a large gourd to it; and sometimes one tree will yield three or four gallons in a night. When just drawn, it is of a most delicious sweetness; but in a few days it acquires a tartish and more spirituous flavor: though I never saw anyone intoxicated by it. The same tree also produces nuts and oil. Our principal luxury is in perfumes; one sort of these is an odoriferous wood of delicious fragrance: the other a kind of earth; a small portion of which thrown into the fire diffuses a most powerful odor.* We beat this wood into powder, and mix it with palm oil; with which both men and women perfume themselves.

In our buildings we study convenience rather than ornament. Each master of a family has a large square piece of ground, surrounded with a moat or fence, or inclosed with a wall made of red earth tempered, which, when dry, is as hard as brick. Within this are his houses to accommodate his family and slaves; which, if numerous, frequently present the appearance of a village. In the middle stands the principal building, appropriated to the sole use of the master, and consisting of two apartments; in one of which he sits in the day with his family, the other is left apart for the reception of his friends. He has besides these a distinct apartment, in which he sleeps, together with his male children. On each side are the apartments of his wives, who have also their separate day and night houses. The habitations of the slaves and their families are distributed throughout the rest of the inclosure. These houses never exceed one story in height; they are always built of wood, or stakes driven into the ground, crossed with wattles, and neatly plas-

*When I was in Smyrna I saw the same kind of earth, and brought some of it with me to England; it resembles musk in strength, but is more delicious in scent, and is not unlike the smell of a rose.

tered within and without. The roof is thatched with reeds. Our day houses are left open at the sides; but those in which we sleep are always covered, and plastered in the inside with a composition mixed with cow dung, to keep off the different insects which annoy us during the night. The walls and floors also of these are generally covered with mats. Our beds consist of a platform, raised three or four feet from the ground, on which are laid skins, and different parts of a spongy tree called plantain. Our covering is calico or muslin, the same as our dress. The usual seats are a few logs of wood; but we have benches, which are generally perfumed, to accommodate strangers: these compose the greater part of our household furniture. Houses so constructed and furnished require but little skill to erect them. Every man is a sufficient architect for the purpose. The whole neighborhood affords their unanimous assistance in building them, and in return receive and expect no other recompense than a feast.

As we live in a country where nature is prodigal of her favors, our wants are few, and easily supplied; of course we have few manufactures. They consist for the most part of calicoes, earthenware, ornaments, and instruments of war and husbandry. But these make no part of our commerce, the principal articles of which, as I have observed, are provisions. In such a state money is of little use; however we have some small pieces of coin, if I may call them such. They are made something like an anchor; but I do not remember either their value or denomination. We have also markets, at which I have been frequently with my mother. These are sometimes visited by stout mahogany-colored men from the southwest of us: we call them *Oye-Eboe*, which term signifies red men living at a distance. They generally bring us firearms, gunpowder, hats, beads, and dried fish. The last we esteemed a great rarity, as our waters were only brooks and springs. These articles they barter with us for odoriferous woods and earth, and our salt of wood ashes. They always carry slaves through our land; but the strictest account is exacted of their manner of procuring them before they are suffered to pass. Sometimes indeed we sold slaves to them, but they were only prisoners of war, or such among us as had been convicted of kidnapping, or adultery, and some other crimes, which we esteemed heinous. This practice of kidnapping induces me to think that, notwithstanding all our strictness, their principal business among us was to trepan [trap] our people. I remember too they carried great sacks along with them, which not long after I had an opportunity of fatally seeing applied to that infamous purpose.

Our land is uncommonly rich and fruitful, and produces all kinds of vegetables in great abundance. We have plenty of Indian corn, and vast quantities of cotton and tobacco. Our pineapples grow without culture; they are about the size of the largest sugarloaf, and finely flavored. We have also spices of different kinds, particularly of pepper; and a variety of delicious fruits which I have never seen in Europe; together with gums of various kinds, and honey in abundance. All our industry is exerted to improve those blessings of nature. Agriculture is our chief employment; and everyone, even the children and women, are engaged in it. Thus we are all habituated to labor from our earliest years. Everyone contributes something to the common stock; and, as we are unacquainted with idleness, we have no beggars. The benefits of such a mode of living are obvious. The West India planters prefer the slaves of Benin or Eboe to those of any other part of Guinea, for their hardiness, intelligence, integrity, and zeal. Those benefits are felt by us in the general healthiness of the people, and in their vigor and activity; I might have added too in their comeliness. Deformity is indeed unknown amongst us, I mean that of shape. Numbers of the natives of Eboe, now in London, might be brought in support of this assertion; for, in regard to complexion, ideas of beauty are wholly relative. I remember while in Africa to have seen three negro children, who were tawny, and another quite white, who were universally regarded by myself and the natives in general, as far as related to their complexions, as deformed. Our women too were, in my eyes at least, uncommonly graceful, alert, and modest to a degree of bashfulness; nor do I remember to have ever heard of an instance of incontinence amongst them before marriage. They are also remarkably cheerful. Indeed cheerfulness and affability are two of the leading characteristics of our nation.

Our tillage is exercised in a large plain or common, some hours' walk from our dwellings, and all the neighbors resort thither in a body. They use no beasts of husbandry; and their only instruments are hoes, axes, shovels, and beaks, or pointed iron to dig with. Sometimes we are visited by locusts, which come in large clouds, so as to darken the air, and destroy our harvest. This however happens rarely, but when it does a famine is produced by it. I remember an instance or two wherein this happened. This common is often the theater of war; and therefore when our people go out to till their land, they not only go in a body, but generally take their arms with them, for fear of a surprise; and, when they apprehend an invasion, they guard the avenues to their dwellings, by driving sticks into the ground, which are so sharp at one

end as to pierce the foot, and are generally dipped in poison. From
what I can recollect of these battles, they appear to have been irrup-
tions of one little state or district on the other, to obtain prisoners or
booty. Perhaps they were incited to this by those traders who brought
the European goods I mentioned amongst us. Such a mode of ob-
taining slaves in Africa is common; and I believe more are procured
this way, and by kidnapping, than any other.* When a trader wants
slaves, he applies to a chief for them, and tempts him with his wares. It
is not extraordinary, if on this occasion he yields to the temptation
with as little firmness, and accepts the price of his fellow creature's
liberty with as little reluctance, as the enlightened merchant. Accordingly, he falls on his neighbors, and a desperate battle ensues. If he pre-
vails, and takes prisoners, he gratifies his avarice by selling them; but,
if his party be vanquished, and he falls into the hands of the enemy, he
is put to death: for, as he has been known to foment their quarrels, it is
thought dangerous to let him survive; and no ransom can save him,
though all other prisoners may be redeemed. We have firearms, bows
and arrows, broad two-edged swords and javelins; we have shields also,
which cover a man from head to foot. All are taught the use of these
weapons. Even our women are warriors, and march boldly out to fight
along with the men. Our whole district is a kind of militia: On a certain
signal given, such as the firing of a gun at night, they all rise in arms,
and rush upon their enemy. It is perhaps something remarkable, that,
when our people march to the field, a red flag or banner is borne before
them. I was once a witness to a battle in our common. We had been all
at work in it one day as usual, when our people were suddenly attacked.
I climbed a tree at some distance, from which I beheld the fight. There
were many women as well as men on both sides; among others my
mother was there, and armed with a broad sword. After fighting for a
considerable time with great fury, and many had been killed, our
people obtained the victory, and took their enemy's Chief prisoner. He
was carried off in great triumph; and, though he offered a large ransom
for his life, he was put to death. A virgin of note among our enemies
had been slain in the battle, and her arm was exposed in our market-
place, where our trophies were always exhibited. The spoils were divided according to the merit of the warriors. Those prisoners which
were not sold or redeemed we kept as slaves: but, how different was
their condition from that of the slaves in the West Indies! With us they

*See Benezet's *Account of Africa* throughout.

do no more work than other members of the community, even their master. Their food, clothing, and lodging, were nearly the same as theirs, except that they were not permitted to eat with those who were freeborn; and there were scarce any other difference between them than a superior degree of importance which the head of a family possesses in our state, and that authority which, as such, he exercises over every part of his household. Some of these slaves have even slaves under them, as their own property, and for their own use.

As to religion, the natives believe that there is one Creator of all things, and that he lives in the sun, and is girded round with a belt, that he may never eat or drink; but according to some, he smokes a pipe, which is our own favorite luxury. They believe he governs events, especially our deaths or captivity; but, as for the doctrine of eternity, I do not remember to have ever heard of it: some however believe in the transmigration of souls in a certain degree. Those spirits, which are not transmigrated, such as their dear friends or relations, they believe always attend them, and guard them from the bad spirits of their foes. For this reason, they always, before eating, as I have observed, put some small portion of the meat, and pour some of their drink, on the ground for them; and they often make oblations of the blood of beasts or fowls at their graves. I was very fond of my mother, and almost constantly with her. When she went to make these oblations at her mother's tomb, which was a kind of small solitary thatched house, I sometimes attended her. There she made her libations, and spent most of the night in cries and lamentation. I have been often extremely terrified on these occasions. The loneliness of the place, the darkness of the night, and the ceremony of libation, naturally awful and gloomy, were heightened by my mother's lamentations; and these concurring with the doleful cries of birds, by which these places were frequented, gave an inexpressible terror to the scene.

We compute the year from the day on which the sun crosses the line; and, on its setting that evening, there is a general shout throughout the land; at least, I can speak from my own knowledge, throughout our vicinity. The people at the same time make a great noise with rattles not unlike the basket rattles used by children here, though much larger, and hold up their hands to heaven for a blessing. It is then the greatest offerings are made; and those children whom our wise men foretell will be fortunate are then presented to different people. I remember many used to come to see me, and I was carried about to others for that purpose. They have many offerings, particularly at full moons, generally two at harvest, before the fruits are taken out of the ground: and, when any young animals are killed, sometimes they offer up part of them as a sacrifice. These offerings, when made by one of the heads of a family, serve for the whole. I remember we often had them at my father's and my uncle's, and their families have been present. Some of our offerings are eaten with bitter herbs. We had a saying among us to anyone of a cross temper, "That if they were to be eaten, they should be eaten with bitter herbs."

We practiced circumcision like the Jews, and made offerings of feasts on that occasion in the same manner as they did. Like them also our children were named from some event, some circumstance, or fancied foreboding, at the time of their birth. I was named *Olaudah*, which, in our language, signifies vicissitude, or fortunate also; one favored, and having a loud voice, and well spoken. I remember we never polluted the name of the object of our adoration; on the contrary, it was always mentioned with the greatest reverence; and we were totally unacquainted with swearing, and all those terms of abuse and reproach which find their way so readily and copiously into the language of more civilized people. The only expressions of that kind I remember were "May you rot," or "may you swell," or "may a beast take you."

I have before remarked, that the natives of this part of Africa are extremely cleanly. This necessary habit of decency was with us a part of religion, and therefore we had many purifications and washings; indeed almost as many, and used on the same occasions, if my recollection does not fail me, as the Jews. Those that touched the dead at any time were obliged to wash and purify themselves before they could enter a dwelling house. Every woman too, at certain times, was forbidden to come into a dwelling house, or touch any person, or anything we eat. I was so fond of my mother I could not keep from her, or avoid touching her at some of those periods, in consequence of which I was obliged to be kept out with her, in a little house made for that purpose, till offering was made, and then we were purified.

Though we had no places of public worship, we had priests and magicians, or wise men. I do not remember whether they had different offices, or whether they were united in the same persons, but they were held in great reverence by the people. They calculated our time, and foretold events, as their name imported, for we called them *Ah-affoe-way-cah*, which signifies calculators or yearly men, our year being called *Ah-affoe*. They wore their beards; and, when they died, they were succeeded by their sons. Most of their implements and things of value were interred along with them. Pipes and tobacco were also put into the grave with the corpse, which was always perfumed and ornamented; and animals were offered in sacrifice to them. None accompanied their funerals, but those of the same profession or tribe. These buried them after sunset, and always returned from the grave by a different way from that which they went.

These magicians were also our doctors or physicians. They practiced bleeding by cupping; and were very successful in healing wounds, and expelling poisons. They had likewise some extraordinary method of discovering jealousy, theft, and poisoning; the success of which no doubt they derived from the unbounded influence over the credulity and superstition of the people. I do not remember what those methods were, except that as to poisoning. I recollect an instance or two, which I hope it will not be deemed impertinent here to insert, as it may serve as a kind of specimen of the rest, and is still used by the negroes in the West Indies. A young woman had been poisoned, but it was not known by whom: the doctors ordered the corpse to be taken up by some persons, and carried to the grave. As soon as the bearers had raised it on their shoulders, they seemed seized with some sudden impulse,* and ran to and fro, unable to stop themselves. At last, after having passed through a number of thorns and prickly bushes unhurt, the corpse fell from them close to a house, and defaced it in the fall: and the owner being taken up, he immediately confessed the poisoning.†

The natives are extremely cautious about poison. When they buy any eatable, the seller kisses it all round before the buyer, to show him it is not poisoned; and the same is done when any meat or drink is presented, particularly to a stranger. We have serpents of different kinds, some of which are esteemed ominous when they appear in our houses,

---

*See also *Lieutenant Matthew's Voyage*, p. 123.

†An instance of this kind happened at Montserrat, in the West Indies, in the year 1763. I then belonged to the ship *Charming Sally*, Capt. Doran.—The chief mate, Mr. Mansfield, and some of the crew being one day on shore, were present at the burying of a poisoned negro girl. Though they had often heard of the circumstance of the running in such cases, and had even seen it, they imagined it to be a trick of the corpse bearers. The mate therefore desired two of the sailors to take up the coffin, and carry it to the grave. The sailors, who were all of the same opinion, readily obeyed; but they had scarcely raised it to their shoulders before they began to run furiously about, quite unable to direct themselves, until at last, without intention, they came to the hut of him who had poisoned the girl. The coffin then immediately fell from their shoulders against the hut, and damaged part of the wall. The owner of the hut was taken into custody on this, and confessed the poisoning—I give this story as it was related by the mate and crew on their return to the ship. The credit which is due to it I leave with the reader.

and these we never molest. I remember two of those ominous snakes, each of which was as thick as the calf of a man's leg, and in color resembling a dolphin in the water, crept at different times into my mother's night house, where I always lay with her, and coiled themselves into folds, and each time they crowed like a cock. I was desired by some of our wise men to touch these, that I might be interested in the good omens, which I did, for they are quite harmless, and would tamely suffer themselves to be handled; and then they were put into a large open earthen pan, and set on one side of the highway. Some of our snakes, however, were poisonous. One of them crossed the road one day as I was standing on it, and passed between my feet, without offering to touch me, to the great surprise of many who saw it; and these incidents were accounted, by the wise men, and likewise by my mother and the rest of the people, as remarkable omens in my favor.

Such is the imperfect sketch my memory has furnished me with of the manners and customs of a people among whom I first drew my breath. And here I cannot forbear suggesting what has long struck me very forcibly, namely, the strong analogy which even by this sketch, imperfect as it is, appears to prevail in the manners and customs of my countrymen, and those of the Jews, before they reached the Land of Promise, and particularly the patriarchs, while they were yet in that pastoral state which is described in Genesis—an analogy which alone would induce me to think that the one people had sprung from the other.* Indeed this is the opinion of Dr. Gill, who, in his *Commentary on Genesis,* very ably deduces the pedigree of the Africans from Afer and Afra, the descendants of Abraham by Keturah his wife and concubine (for both these titles are applied to her). It is also conformable to the sentiments of Dr. John Clarke, formerly Dean of Sarum, in his *Truth of the Christian Religion:* Both these authors concur in ascribing to us this original. The reasonings of those gentlemen are still further confirmed by the *Scripture Chronology* of the Reverend Arthur Bedford; and, if any further corroboration were required, this resemblance in so many respects, is a strong evidence in support of the opinion. Like the Israelites in their primitive state, our government was conducted by our chiefs, our judges, our wise men, and elders; and the head of a family with us enjoyed a similar authority over his household with that which is ascribed to Abraham and the other patriarchs. The law of retaliation obtained almost universally with us as with

*See 1 Chron. 1:33. Also John Brown's *Dictionary of the Bible* on the same verse.

them; and even their religion appeared to have shed upon us a ray of its glory, though broken and spent in its passage, or eclipsed by the cloud with which time, tradition, and ignorance might have enveloped it; for we had our circumcision (a rule I believe peculiar to that people); we had also our sacrifices and burnt offerings, our washings and purifications, on the same occasions as they had.

As to the difference of color between the Eboan Africans and the modern Jews, I shall not presume to account for it. It is a subject which has engaged the pens of men of both genius and learning, and is far above my strength. The most able and Reverend Mr. T. Clarkson, however, in his much-admired *Essay on the Slavery and Commerce of the Human Species,* has ascertained the cause in a manner that at once solves every objection on that account, and, on my mind at least, has produced the fullest conviction. I shall therefore refer to that performance for the theory,* contenting myself with extracting a fact as related by Dr. Mitchel.† "The Spaniards who have inhabited America under the torrid zone, for any time, are become as dark colored as our native Indians of Virginia, of which *I myself have been a witness.*" There is also another instance‡ of a Portuguese settlement at Mitomba, a river in Sierra Leone, where the inhabitants are bred from a mixture of the first Portuguese discoverers with the natives, and are now become, in their complexion, and in the woolly quality of their hair, *perfect negroes,* retaining, however, a smattering of the Portuguese language.

These instances, and a great many more which might be adduced, while they show how the complexions of the same persons vary in different climates, it is hoped may tend also to remove the prejudice that some conceive against the natives of Africa on account of their color. Surely the minds of the Spaniards did not change with their complexions! Are there not causes enough to which the apparent inferiority of an African may be ascribed, without limiting the goodness of God, and supposing he forebore to stamp understanding on certainly his own image, because "carved in ebony"? Might it not naturally be ascribed to their situation? When they come among Europeans, they are ignorant of their language, religion, manners, and customs. Are any pains taken to teach them these? Are they treated as men? Does not slavery itself depress the mind, and extinguish all its fire, and every noble sentiment? But, above all, what advantages do not a refined

*Pages 178 to 216.
†Philos. Trans. No. 476. Sect. 4. cited by the Rev. Mr. Clarkson, p. 205.
‡Same page.

people possess over those who are rude and uncultivated? Let the polished and haughty European recollect, that *his* ancestors were once, like the Africans, uncivilized, and even barbarous. Did Nature make *them* inferior to their sons? and should *they too* have been made slaves? Every rational mind answers, No. Let such reflections as these melt the pride of their superiority into sympathy for the wants and miseries of their sable brethren, and compel them to acknowledge, that understanding is not confined to feature or color. If, when they look round the world, they feel exultation, let it be tempered with benevolence to others, and gratitude to God, "who hath made of one blood all nations of men for to dwell on all the face of the earth;* and whose wisdom is not our wisdom, neither are our ways his ways."

Chapter II

The Author's birth and parentage—His being kidnapped with his sister—Their separation—Surprise at meeting again—Are finally separated—Account of the different places and incidents the Author met with and his arrival on the coast—The effect the sight of a slave ship had on him—He sails for the West Indies—Horrors of a slave ship—Arrives at Barbados, where the cargo is sold and dispersed.

I HOPE THE READER will not think I have trespassed on his patience in introducing myself to him with some account of the manners and customs of my country. They had been implanted in me with great care, and made an impression on my mind which time could not erase, and which all the adversity and variety of fortune I have since experienced served only to rivet and record; for, whether the love of one's country be real or imaginary, or a lesson of reason, or an instinct of nature, I still look back with pleasure on the first scenes of my life, though that pleasure has been for the most part mingled with sorrow.

I have already acquainted the reader with the time and place of my birth. My father, besides many slaves, had a numerous family, of which seven lived to grow up, including myself and a sister, who was the only daughter. As I was the youngest of the sons, I became, of course, the greatest favorite with my mother, and was always with her; and she used to take particular pains to form my mind. I was trained

*Acts 17:26.

up from my earliest years in the arts of agriculture and war: my daily exercise was shooting and throwing javelins; and my mother adorned me with emblems, after the manner of our greatest warriors. In this way I grew up till I was turned the age of eleven, when an end was put to my happiness in the following manner. Generally, when the grown people in the neighborhood were gone far in the fields to labor, the children assembled together in some of the neighbors' premises to play; and commonly some of us used to get up a tree to look out for any assailant, or kidnapper that might come upon us; for they sometimes took these opportunities of our parents' absence, to attack and carry off as many as they could seize. One day, as I was watching at the top of a tree in our yard, I saw one of those people come into the yard of our next neighbor but one, to kidnap, there being many stout young people in it. Immediately on this, I gave the alarm of the rogue, and he was surrounded by the stoutest of them, who entangled him with cords, so that he could not escape till some of the grown people came and secured him. But alas! ere [before] long it was my fate to be thus attacked, and to be carried off, when none of the grown people were nigh. One day, when all our people were gone out to their works as usual, and only I and my dear sister were left to mind the house, two men and a woman got over our walls, and in a moment seized us both; and, without giving us time to cry out, or make resistance, they stopped our mouths, tied our hands, and ran off with us into the nearest wood: and continued to carry us as far as they could, till night came on, when we reached a small house, where the robbers halted for refreshment, and spent the night. We were then unbound, but were unable to take any food; and, being quite overpowered by fatigue and grief, our only relief was some sleep, which allayed our misfortune for a short time. The next morning we left the house, and continued traveling all the day. For a long time we had kept the woods, but at last we came into a road which I believed I knew. I had now some hopes of being delivered; for we had advanced but a little way before I discovered some people at a distance, on which I began to cry out for their assistance; but my cries had no other effect than to make them tie me faster, and stop my mouth, and then they put me into a large sack. They also stopped my sister's mouth, and tied her hands; and in this manner we proceeded till we were out of the sight of these people.—When we went to rest the following night they offered us some victuals; but we refused them; and the only comfort we had was in being in one another's arms all that night, and bathing each other with our tears. But alas! we were soon deprived of even the smallest comfort of weeping together. The next day proved a day of greater sorrow than I had yet experienced; for my sister and I were then separated, while we lay clasped in each other's arms; it was in vain that we besought them not to part us: she was torn from me, and immediately carried away, while I was left in a state of distraction not to be described. I cried and grieved continually; and for several days did not eat anything but what they forced into my mouth. At length, after many days traveling, during which I had often changed masters, I got into the hands of a chieftain, in a very pleasant country. This man had two wives and some children, and they all used me extremely well, and did all they could to comfort me; particularly the first wife, who was something like my mother. Although I was a great many days' journey from my father's house, yet these people spoke exactly the same language with us. This first master of mine, as I may call him, was a smith, and my principal employment was working his bellows, which was the same kind as I had seen in my vicinity. They were in some respects not unlike the stoves here in gentlemen's kitchens; and were covered over with leather; and in the middle of that leather a stick was fixed, and a person stood up and worked it, in the same manner as is done to pump water out of a cask with a hand pump. I believe it was gold he worked, for it was of a lovely bright yellow color, and was worn by the women on their wrists and ankles. I was there I suppose about a month, and they at last used to trust me some little distance from the house. This liberty I used in embracing every opportunity to inquire the way to my own home: and I also sometimes, for the same purpose, went with the maidens, in the cool of the evenings, to bring pitchers of water from the springs for the use of the house. I had also remarked where the sun rose in the morning, and set in the evening, as I had traveled along; and I had observed that my father's house was towards the rising of the sun. I therefore determined to seize the first opportunity of making my escape, and to shape my course for that quarter; for I was quite oppressed and weighed down by grief after my mother and friends; and my love of liberty, ever great, was strengthened by the mortifying circumstance of not daring to eat with the freeborn children, although I was mostly their companion.

While I was projecting my escape one day, an unlucky event happened, which quite disconcerted my plan, and put an end to my hopes. I used to be sometimes employed in assisting an elderly woman slave to cook and take care of the poultry; and one morning, while I was feeding some chickens, I happened to toss a small pebble at one of them, which hit it on the middle, and directly killed it. The old slave, having soon after missed the chicken, inquired after it; and on my relating the accident (for I told her the truth, because my mother would never suffer me to tell a lie) she flew into a violent passion, threatening that I should suffer for it; and, my master being out, she immediately went and told her mistress what I had done. This alarmed me very much, and I expected an instant flogging, which to me was uncommonly dreadful; for I had seldom been beaten at home. I therefore resolved to fly; and accordingly I ran into a thicket that was hard by, and hid myself in the bushes. Soon afterwards my mistress and the slave returned, and, not seeing me, they searched all the house, but not finding me, and I not making answer when they called to me, they thought I had run away, and the whole neighborhood was raised in the pursuit of me. In that part of the country (as well as ours) the houses and villages were skirted with woods or shrubberies, and the bushes were so thick, that a man could readily conceal himself in them, so as to elude the strictest search. The neighbors continued the whole day looking for me, and several times many of them came within a few yards of the place where I lay hid. I expected every moment, when I heard a rustling among the trees, to be found out, and punished by my master; but they never discovered me, though they were often so near that I even heard their conjectures as they were looking about for me; and I now learned from them that any attempt to return home would be hopeless. Most of them supposed I had fled towards home; but the distance was so great, and the way so intricate, that they thought I could never reach it, and that I should be lost in the woods. When I heard this I was seized with a violent panic, and abandoned myself to despair. Night too began to approach, and aggravated all my fears. I had before entertained hopes of getting home, and had determined when it should be dark to make the attempt; but I was now convinced it was fruitless, and began to consider that, if possibly I could escape all other animals, I could not those of the human kind; and that, not knowing the way, I must perish in the woods.—Thus was I like the hunted deer:

Ev'ry leaf, and ev'ry whispering breath
Convey'd a foe, and ev'ry foe a death.

I heard frequent rustlings among the leaves; and being pretty sure they were snakes, I expected every instant to be stung by them.—This increased my anguish; and the horror of my situation became now quite insupportable. I at length quitted the thicket, very faint and hungry, for I had not eaten or drank anything all the day, and crept to my master's kitchen, from whence I set out at first, and which was an open shed, and laid myself down in the ashes, with an anxious wish for death to relieve me from all my pains. I was scarcely awake in the morning when the old woman slave who was the first up, came to light the fire, and saw me in the fireplace. She was very much surprised to see me, and could scarcely believe her own eyes. She now promised to intercede for me, and went for her master, who soon after came, and, having slightly reprimanded me, ordered me to be taken care of, and not ill treated.

Soon after this my master's only daughter and child by his first wife sickened and died, which affected him so much that for some time he was almost frantic, and really would have killed himself had he not been watched and prevented. However, in a small time afterwards he recovered, and I was again sold. I was now carried to the left of the sun's rising, through many dreary wastes and dismal woods, amidst the hideous roarings of wild beasts.—The people I was sold to used to carry me very often, when I was tired, either on their shoulders or on their backs. I saw many convenient well-built sheds along the roads, at proper distances, to accommodate the merchants and travelers, who lay in those buildings along with their wives, who often accompany them; and they always go well armed.

From the time I left my own nation I always found somebody that understood me till I came to the sea coast. The languages of different nations did not totally differ, nor were they so copious as those of the Europeans, particularly the English. They were therefore easily learned; and, while I was journeying thus through Africa, I acquired two or three different tongues. In this manner I had been traveling for a considerable time, when one evening, to my great surprise, whom should I see brought to the house where I was but my dear sister. As soon as she saw me she gave a loud shriek, and ran into my arms.—I was quite overpowered; neither of us could speak, but, for a considerable time, clung to each other in mutual embraces, unable to do anything but weep. Our meeting affected all who saw us; and indeed I must acknowledge, in honor of those sable destroyers of human rights, that I never met with any ill treatment, or saw any offered to their slaves, except tying them, when necessary, to keep them from running away. When these people knew we were brother and sister, they indulged us to be together; and the man, to whom I supposed we belonged, lay with us, he in the middle, while she and I held one another by the hands across his breast all night; and thus for a while we forgot our misfortunes in the joy of being together; but even this small comfort was soon to have an end; for scarcely had the fatal morning appeared, when she was again torn from me forever! I was now more miserable, if possible, than before. The small relief which her presence gave me from pain was gone, and the wretchedness of my situation was redoubled by my anxiety after her fate, and my apprehensions lest her sufferings should be greater than mine, when I could not be with her to alleviate them. Yes, thou dear partner of all my childish sports! thou sharer of my joys and sorrows! happy should I have ever esteemed myself to encounter every misery for you, and to procure your freedom by the sacrifice of my own! Though you were early forced from my arms, your image has been always riveted in my heart, from which neither *time nor fortune* have been able to remove it: so that while the thoughts of your sufferings have damped my prosperity, they have mingled with adversity, and increased its bitterness. To that heaven which protects the weak from the strong, I commit the care of your innocence and virtues, if they have not already received their full reward; and if your youth and delicacy have not long since fallen victims to the violence of the African trader, the pestilential stench of a Guinea ship, the seasoning in the European colonies, or the lash and lust of a brutal and unrelenting overseer.

I did not long remain after my sister. I was again sold, and carried through a number of places, till, after traveling a considerable time, I came to a town called Timnah, in the most beautiful country I had yet seen in Africa. It was extremely rich, and there were many rivulets which flowed through it; and supplied a large pond in the center of the town, where the people washed. Here I first saw and tasted coconuts, which I thought superior to any nuts I had ever tasted before; and the trees, which were loaded, were also interspersed amongst the houses, which had commodious shades adjoining, and were in the same manner as ours, the insides being neatly plastered and whitewashed. Here I also saw and tasted for the first time sugarcane. Their money consisted of little white shells, the size of the fingernail: they are known in this country by the name of *core*. I was sold here for one hundred and seventy-two of them by a merchant who lived and brought me there. I had been about two or three days at his house, when a wealthy widow, a neighbor of his, came there one evening, and brought with her an only son, a young gentleman about my own age and size. Here they saw me; and having taken a fancy to me, I was bought of the merchant, and went home with them. Her house and premises were situated close to one of those rivulets I have mentioned, and were the finest I ever saw in Africa: they were very extensive, and she had a number of slaves to attend her. The next day I was washed and perfumed, and when mealtime came, I was led into the presence of my mistress, and ate and drank before her with her son. This filled me with astonishment: and I could scarce help expressing my surprise that the young gentleman should suffer me who was bound to eat with him who was free; and not only so, but that he would not at any time either eat or drink till I had taken first, because I was the eldest, which was agreeable to our custom. Indeed everything here, and all their treatment of me, made me forget that I was a slave. The language of these people resembled ours so nearly, that we understood each other perfectly. They had also the very same customs as we. There were likewise slaves daily to attend us, while my young master and I, with other boys, sported with our darts and bows and arrows, as I had been used to do at home. In this resemblance to my former happy state, I passed about two months, and I now began to think I was to be adopted into the family, and was beginning to be reconciled to my situation, and to forget by degrees my misfortunes, when all at once the delusion vanished; for, without the least previous knowledge, one morning early, while my dear master and companion was still asleep, I was awakened out of my reverie to fresh sorrow, and hurried away even among the uncircumcised.

Thus, at the very moment I dreamed of the greatest happiness, I found myself most miserable: and seemed as if fortune wished to give me this taste of joy only to render the reverse more poignant. The change I now experienced was as painful as it was sudden and unexpected. It was a change indeed from a state of bliss to a scene which is inexpressible by me, as it discovered to me an element I had never before beheld, and till then had no idea of, and wherein such instances of hardship and fatigue continually occurred as I can never reflect on but with horror.

All the nations and people I had hitherto passed through resembled our own in their manners, customs and language; but I came at length to a country, the inhabitants of which differed from us in all those particulars. I was very much struck with this difference, especially when I came among a people who did not circumcise, and ate without washing their hands. They cooked also in iron pots, and had European cutlasses and crossbows, which were unknown to us, and fought with their fists among themselves. Their women were not so modest as ours, for they ate, and drank, and slept with their men. But, above all, I was amazed to see no sacrifices or offerings among them. In some of those places the people ornamented themselves with scars, and likewise filed their teeth very sharp. They wanted sometimes to ornament me in the same manner, but I would not suffer them; hoping that I might sometime be among a people who did not thus disfigure themselves, as I thought they did. At last, I came to the banks of a large river, which was covered with canoes, in which the people appeared to live with their household utensils and provisions of all kinds. I was beyond measure astonished at this, as I had never before seen any water larger than a pond or a rivulet; and my surprise was mingled with no small fear, when I was put into one of these canoes, and we began to paddle and move along the river. We continued going on thus till night; and, when we came to land, and made fires on the banks, each family by themselves, some dragged their canoes on shore, others stayed and cooked in theirs, and lay in them all night. Those on the land had mats, of which they made tents, some in the shape of little houses: In these we slept; and, after the morning meal, we embarked again, and proceeded as before. I was often very much astonished to see some of the women, as well as the men, jump into the water, dive to the bottom, come up again, and swim about. Thus I continued to travel, sometimes by land, sometimes by water, through different countries, and various nations, till, at the end of six or seven months after I had been kidnapped, I arrived at the sea coast. It would be tedious and uninteresting to relate all the incidents which befell me during this journey, and which I have not yet forgotten; of the various lands I passed through, and the manners and customs of all the different people among whom I lived: I shall therefore only observe, that, in all the places where I was; the soil was exceedingly rich; the pomkins [pumpkins], eadas, plantains, yams, etc., etc. were in great abundance, and of incredible size. There were also large quantities of different gums, though not used for any purpose; and everywhere a great deal of tobacco. The cotton even grew quite wild; and there was plenty of red wood. I saw no mechanics whatever in all the way, except such as I have mentioned. The chief employment in all these countries was agriculture, and both the males and females, as with us, were brought up to it, and trained in the arts of war.

The first object which saluted my eyes when I arrived on the coast was the sea, and a slave ship, which was then riding at anchor, and waiting for its cargo. These filled me with astonishment, which was soon converted into terror, which I am yet at a loss to describe, nor the then feelings of my mind. When I was carried on board I was immediately handled, and tossed up, to see if I were sound, by some of the crew; and I was now persuaded that I had got into a world of bad spirits, and that they were going to kill me. Their complexions too differing so much from ours, their long hair, and the language they spoke, which was very different from any I had ever heard, united to confirm me in this belief. Indeed, such were the horrors of my views and fears at the moment, that, if ten thousand worlds had been my own, I would have freely parted with them all to have exchanged my condition with that of the meanest slave in my own country. When I looked round the ship too, and saw a large furnace or copper boiling, and a multitude of black people of every description chained together, every one of their countenances expressing dejection and sorrow, I no longer doubted of my fate, and, quite overpowered with horror and anguish, I fell motionless on the deck and fainted. When I recovered a little, I found some black people about me, who I believed were some of those who brought me on board, and had been receiving their pay; they talked to me in order to cheer me, but all in vain. I asked them if we were not to be eaten by those white men with horrible looks, red faces, and long hair? They told me I was not; and one of the crew brought me a small portion of spirituous liquor in a wine glass; but, being afraid of him, I would not take it out of his hand. One of the blacks therefore took it from him, and gave it to me, and I took a little down my palate, which, instead of reviving me, as they thought it would, threw me into the greatest consternation at the strange feeling it produced having never tasted any such liquor before. Soon after this, the blacks who brought me on board went off, and left me abandoned to despair. I now saw myself deprived of all chance of returning to my native country, or even the least glimpse of hope of gaining the shore, which I now considered as friendly: and I even wished for my former slavery, in preference to my present situation, which was filled with horrors of every kind, still heightened by my ignorance of what I was to undergo. I was not long suffered to indulge my grief; I was soon put down under the decks, and there I received such a salutation in my nostrils as I had never experienced in my life; so that, with the loathsomeness of the stench, and crying together, I became so sick and low that I was not able to eat, nor had I the least desire to taste anything. I now wished for the last friend, Death, to relieve me; but soon, to my grief, two of the white men offered me eatables; and, on my refusing to eat, one of them held me fast by the hands, and laid me across, I think, the windlass, and tied my feet, while the other flogged me severely. I had never experienced anything of this kind before; and although not being used to the water, I naturally feared that element the first time I saw it; yet, nevertheless, could I have got over the nettings, I would have jumped over the side; but I could not; and, besides, the crew used to watch us very closely who were not chained down to the decks, lest we should leap into the water; and I have seen some of these poor African prisoners most severely cut for attempting to do so, and hourly whipped for not eating. This indeed was often the case with myself. In a little time after, amongst the poor chained men, I found some of my own nation, which in a small degree gave ease to my mind. I inquired of them what was to be done with us? they give me to understand we were to be carried to these white people's country to work for them. I then was a little revived, and thought, if it were no worse than working, my situation was not so desperate: but still I feared I should be put to death, the white people looked and acted, as I thought, in so savage a manner; for I had never seen among any people such instances of brutal cruelty; and this not only shown towards us blacks, but also to some of the whites themselves. One white man in particular I saw, when we were permitted to be on deck, flogged so unmercifully with a large rope near the foremast, that he died in consequence of it; and they tossed him over the side as they would have done a brute. This made me fear these people the more; and I expected nothing less than to be treated in the same manner. I could not help expressing my fears and apprehensions to some of my countrymen: I asked them if these people had no country, but lived in this hollow place the ship? they told me they did not, but came from a distant one. "Then," said I, "how comes it in all our country we never heard of them?" They told me, because they lived so very far off. I then asked, where were their women? had they any like themselves? I was told they had: "And why," said I, "do we not see them?" they answered, because they were left behind. I asked how the vessel could go? they told me they could not tell; but that there were cloths put upon the masts by the help of the ropes I saw, and then the vessel went on; and the white men had some spell or magic they put in the water when they liked in order to stop the vessel. I was exceedingly amazed at this account, and really thought they were spirits. I therefore wished much to be from amongst them, for I expected they would sacrifice me: but my wishes were vain; for we were so quartered that it was impossible for any of us to make our escape. While we stayed on the coast I was mostly on deck; and one day, to my great astonishment, I saw one of these vessels coming in with the sails up. As soon as the whites saw it, they gave a great shout, at which we were amazed; and the more so as the vessel appeared larger by approaching nearer. At last she came to an anchor in my sight, and when the anchor was let go, I and my countrymen who saw it were lost in astonishment to observe the vessel stop; and were now convinced it was done by magic. Soon after this the other ship got her boats out, and they came on board of us, and the people of both ships seemed very glad to see each other. Several of the strangers also shook hands with us black people, and made motions with their hands, signifying, I suppose, we were to go to their country; but we did not understand them. At last, when the ship we were in had got in all her cargo, they made ready with many fearful noises, and we were all put under deck, so that we could not see how they managed the vessel. But this disappointment was the least of my sorrow. The stench of the hold while we were on the coast was so intolerably loathsome, that it was dangerous to remain there for any time, and some of us had been permitted to stay on the deck for the fresh air; but now that the whole ship's cargo were confined together, it became absolutely pestilential. The closeness of the place, and the heat of the climate, added to the number in the ship, which was so crowded that each had scarcely room to turn himself, almost suffocated us. This produced copious perspirations, so that the air soon became unfit for respiration, from a variety of loathsome smells, and brought on a sickness among the slaves, of which many died, thus falling victims to the improvident avarice, as I may call it, of their purchasers. This wretched situation was again aggravated by the galling of the chains, now become insupportable; and the filth of the necessary tubs, into which the children often fell, and were almost suffocated. The shrieks of the women, and the groans of the dying, rendered the whole a scene of horror almost inconceivable. Happily perhaps for myself I was soon reduced so low here that it was thought necessary to keep me almost always on deck; and from my extreme youth I was not put in fetters. In this situation I expected every hour to share the fate of my companions, some of whom were almost daily brought upon deck at the point of death, which I began to hope would soon put an end to my miseries. Often did I think many of the inhabitants of the deep much more happy than myself; I envied them the freedom they enjoyed, and as often wished I could change my condition for theirs. Every circumstance I met with served only to render my state more painful, and heighten my apprehensions and my opinion of the cruelty of the whites. One day they had taken a number of fishes; and when they had killed and satisfied themselves with as many as they thought fit, to our astonishment who were on the deck, rather than give any of them to us to eat, as we expected, they tossed the remaining fish into the sea again, although we begged and prayed for some as well as we could, but in vain; and some of my countrymen, being pressed by hunger, took an opportunity, when they thought no one saw them, of trying to get a little privately; but they were discovered, and the attempt procured them some very severe floggings. One day, when we had a smooth sea, and moderate wind, two of my wearied countrymen, who were chained together (I was near them at the time), preferring death to such a life of misery, somehow made through the nettings, and jumped into the sea; immediately another quite dejected fellow, who, on account of his illness, was suffered to be out of irons, also followed their example; and I believe many more would very soon have done the same, if they had not been prevented by the ship's crew, who were instantly alarmed. Those of us that were the most active were in a moment put down under the deck; and there was such a noise and confusion amongst the people of the ship as I never heard before, to stop her, and get the boat out to go after the slaves. However, two of the wretches were drowned, but they got the other, and afterwards flogged him unmercifully, for thus attempting to prefer death to slavery. In this manner we continued to undergo more hardships than I can now relate; hardships which are inseparable from this accursed trade. —Many a time we were near suffocation, from the want of fresh air, which we were often without for whole days together. This, and the stench of the necessary tubs, carried off many. During our passage I first saw flying fishes, which surprised me very much: they used frequently to fly across the ship, and many of them fell on the deck. I also now first saw the use of the quadrant. I had often with astonishment seen the mariners make observations with it, and I could not think what it meant. They at last took notice of my surprise; and one of them willing to increase it, as well as to gratify my curiosity, made me one day look through it. The clouds appeared to me to be land, which disappeared as they passed along. This heightened my wonder: and I was now more persuaded than ever that I was in another world, and that everything about me was magic. At last, we came in sight of the island of Barbados, at which the whites on board gave a great shout, and made many signs of joy to us. We did not know what to think of this; but, as the vessel drew nearer, we plainly saw the harbor, and other ships of different kinds and sizes: and we soon anchored among them off Bridgetown. Many merchants and planters now came on board, though it was in the evening. They put us in separate parcels, and examined us attentively. They also made us jump, and pointed to the land, signifying we were to go there. We thought by this we should be eaten by these ugly men, as they appeared to us; and when, soon after we were all put down under the deck again, there was much dread and trembling among us, and nothing but bitter cries to be heard all the night from these apprehensions, insomuch that at last the white people got some old slaves from the land to pacify us. They told us we were not to be eaten, but to work, and were soon to go on land, where we should see many of our country people. This report eased us much; and sure enough, soon after we landed, there came to us Africans of all languages. We were conducted immediately to the merchant's yard, where we were all pent up together like so many sheep in a fold, without regard to sex or age. As every object was new to me, everything I saw filled me with surprise. What struck me first was, that the houses were built with bricks, in stories, and in every other respect different from those I have seen in Africa: But I was still more astonished on seeing people on horseback. I did not know what this could mean; and indeed I thought these people were full of nothing but magical arts. While I was in this astonishment, one of my fellow prisoners spoke to a countryman of his about the horses, who said they were the same kind they had in their country. I understood them, though they were from a distant part of Africa, and I thought it odd I had not seen any horses there; but afterwards, when I came to converse with different Africans, I found they had many horses amongst them, and much larger than those I then saw. We were not many days in the merchant's custody before we were sold after their usual manner, which is this: On a signal given, (as the beat of a drum), the buyers rush at once into the yard where the slaves are confined, and make choice of that parcel they like best. The noise and clamor with which this is attended, and the eagerness visible in the countenances of the buyers, serve not a little to increase the apprehension of the terrified Africans, who may well be supposed to consider them as the ministers of that destruction to which they think themselves devoted. In this manner, without scruple, are relations and friends separated, most of them never to see each other again. I remember in the vessel in which I was brought over, in the men's apartment, there were several brothers who, in the sale, were sold in different lots; and it was very moving on this occasion to see and hear their cries at parting. O, ye nominal Christians! might not an African ask you, learned you this from your God? who says unto you, Do unto all men as you would men should do unto you. Is it not enough that we are torn from our country and friends to toil for your luxury and lust of gain? Must every tender feeling be likewise sacrificed to your avarice? Are the dearest friends and relations, now rendered more dear by their separation from their kindred, still to be parted from each other, and thus prevented from cheering the gloom of slavery with the small comfort of being together, and mingling their sufferings and sorrows? Why are parents to lose their children, brothers their sisters, or husbands their wives? Surely this is a new refinement in cruelty, which, while it has no advantage to atone for it, thus aggravates distress, and adds fresh horrors even to the wretchedness of slavery.

Chapter III

The Author is carried to Virginia—His distress—Surprise at seeing a picture and a watch—Is bought by Captain Pascal, and sets out for England—His terror during the voyage—Arrives in England—His wonder at a fall of snow—Is sent to Guernsey, and in some time goes on board a ship of war with his master—Some account of the expedition against Louisbourgh, under the command of Admiral Boscawen in 1758.

I NOW TOTALLY LOST the small remains of comfort I had enjoyed in conversing with my countrymen; the women too, who used to wash and take care of me, were all gone different ways, and I never saw one of them afterwards.

I stayed in this island for a few days; I believe it could not be above a fortnight; when I and some few more slaves that were not saleable among the rest, from very much fretting, were shipped off in a sloop for North America. On the passage we were better treated than when we were coming from Africa, and we had plenty of rice and fat pork. We were landed up a river a good way from the sea, about Virginia county, where we saw few or none of our native Africans, and not one soul who could talk to me. I was a few weeks weeding grass and gathering stones in a plantation, and at last all my companions were distributed different ways, and only myself was left. I was now exceedingly miserable, and thought myself worse off than any of the rest of my companions; for they could talk to each other, but I had no person to speak to that I could understand. In this state I was constantly grieving and pining, and wishing for death, rather than anything else. While I was in this plantation, the gentleman to whom I supposed the estate belonged being unwell, I was one day sent for to his dwelling house to fan him: when I came into the room where he was, I was very much affrighted at some things I saw, and the more so, as I had seen a black woman slave as I came through the house, who was cooking the dinner, and the poor creature was cruelly loaded with various kinds of iron machines; she had one particularly on her head, which locked her mouth so fast that she could scarcely speak, and could not eat nor drink. I was much astonished and shocked at this contrivance, which I afterwards learned was called the iron muzzle. Soon after I had a fan put into my hand, to fan the gentleman while he slept; and so I did indeed with great fear. While he was fast asleep I indulged myself a great deal in looking about the room, which to me appeared very fine and curious. The first object that engaged my attention was a watch which hung on the chimney, and was going. I was quite surprised at the noise it made, and was afraid it would tell the gentleman anything I might do amiss: and when I immediately after observed a picture hanging in the room, which appeared constantly to look at me, I still more affrighted, having never seen such things as these before. At one time I thought it was something relative to magic; and not seeing it move, I thought it might be some way the whites had to keep their great men when they died, and offer them libations as we used to do our friendly spirits. In this state of anxiety I remained till my master awoke, when I was dismissed out of the room, to my no small satisfaction and relief, for I thought that these people were all made of wonders. In this place I was called Jacob; but on board the *African Snow* I was called Michael. I had been some time in this miserable, forlorn, and much dejected state, without having anyone to talk to, which made my life a burden, when the kind and unknown hand of the Creator (who in very deed leads the blind in a way they know not) now began to appear, to my comfort; for one day the captain of a merchant ship, called the *Industrious Bee*, came on some business to my master's house. This gentleman, whose name was Michael Henry Pascal, was a lieutenant in the royal navy, but now commanded this trading ship, which was somewhere in the confines of the county many miles off. While he was at my master's house it happened that he saw me, and liked me so well that he made a purchase of me. I think I have often heard him say he gave thirty or forty pounds sterling for me; but I do not now remember which. However, he meant me for a present to some of his friends in England; and I was sent accordingly from the house of my then master (one Mr. Campbell) to the place where the ship lay; I was conducted on horseback by an elderly black man (a mode of traveling which appeared very odd to me). When I arrived I was carried on board a fine large ship, loaded with tobacco, etc. and just ready to sail for England. I now thought my condition much mended; I had sails to lie on, and plenty of good victuals to eat; and everybody on board used me very kindly, quite contrary to what I had seen of any white people before; I therefore began to think that they were not all of the same disposition. A few days after I was on board we sailed for England. I was still at a loss to conjecture my destiny. By this time, however, I could smatter a little imperfect English; and I wanted to know as well as I could where we were going. Some of the people of the ship used to tell me they were going to carry me back to my own country, and this made me very happy. I was quite rejoiced at the idea of going back; and thought if I should get home what wonders I should have to tell. But I was reserved for another fate, and was soon undeceived when we came within sight of the English coast. When I was on board this ship my captain and master named me *Gustavus Vassa*. I at that time began to understand him a little, and refused to be called so, and told him as well as I could that I would be called Jacob; but he said I should not, and still called me Gustavus: and when I refused to answer to my new name, which at first I did, it gained me many a cuff; so at length I submitted, and by which name I have been known ever since. The ship had a very long passage; and on that account we had very short allowance of provisions. Towards the last we had only one pound and a half of bread per week, and about the same quantity of meat, and one quart of water a day. We spoke with only one vessel the whole time we were at sea, and but once we caught a few fishes. In our extremities the captain and people told me, in jest, they would kill and eat me, but I thought them in earnest, and was depressed beyond measure, expecting every moment to be my last. While I was in this situation one evening they caught with a good deal of trouble, a large shark, and got it on board. This gladdened my poor heart exceedingly, as I thought it would serve the people to eat instead of their eating me; but very soon, to my astonishment, they cut off a small part of the tail, and tossed the rest over the side. This renewed my consternation; and I did not know what to think of these white people; I very much feared they would kill and eat me. There was on board the ship a young lad who had never been at sea before, about four or five years older than myself: his name was Richard Baker. He was a native of America, had received an excellent education, and was of a most amiable temper. Soon after I went on board he showed me a great deal of partiality and attention, and in return I grew extremely fond of him. We at length became inseparable; and for the space of two years, he was of very great use to me, and was my constant companion and instructor. Although this dear youth had many slaves of his own, yet he and I have gone through many sufferings together on shipboard; and we have many nights lain in each other's bosoms when we were in great distress. Thus such a friendship was cemented between us as we cherished till his death, which to my very great sorrow happened in the year 1759, when he was up the Archipelago, on board his majesty's ship the *Preston*: an event which I have never ceased to regret, as I lost at once a kind interpreter, an agreeable companion, and a faithful friend; who, at the age of fifteen, discovered a mind superior to prejudice; and who was not ashamed to notice, to associate with, and to be the friend and instructor of one who was ignorant, a stranger of a different complexion, and a slave! My master had lodged in his mother's house in America: he respected him very much, and made him always eat with him in the cabin. He used often to tell him jocularly that he would kill and eat me. Sometimes he would say to me—the black people were not good to eat, and would ask me if we did not eat people in my country. I said, no: then he said he would kill Dick (as he always called him) first, and afterwards me. Though this hearing relieved my mind a little as to myself, I was alarmed for Dick, and whenever he was called I used to be very much afraid he was to be killed; and I would peep and watch to see if they were going to kill him: nor was I free from this consternation till we made the land. One night we lost a man overboard; and the cries and noise were so great and confused, in stopping the ship, that I, who did not know what was the matter, began, as usual, to be very much afraid, and to think they were going to make an offering with me, and perform some magic; which I still believed they dealt in. As the waves were very high, I thought the ruler of the seas was angry, and I expected to be offered up to appease him. This filled my mind with agony, and I could not anymore that night close my eyes again to rest. However, when daylight appeared, I was a little eased in my mind; but still every time I was called I used to think it was to be killed. Sometime after this, we saw some very large fish, which I afterwards found were called grampusses. They looked to me extremely terrible, and made their appearance just at dusk, and were so near as to blow the water on the ship's deck. I believed them to be the rulers of the sea; and, as the white people did not make any offerings at any time, I thought they were angry with them; and, at last, what confirmed my belief was, the wind just then died away, and a calm ensued, and, in consequence of it, the ship stopped going. I supposed that the fish had performed this, and I hid myself in the forepart of the ship, through fear of being offered up to appease them, every minute peeping and quaking; but my good friend Dick came shortly towards me, and I took an opportunity to ask him, as well as I could, what these fish were? not being able to talk much English, I could but just make him understand my question; and not at all, when I asked him if any offerings were to be made to them? However, he told me these fish would swallow anybody; which sufficiently alarmed me. Here he was called away by the captain, who was leaning over the quarterdeck railing and looking at the fish; and most of the people were busied in getting a barrel of pitch to light, for them to play with. The captain now called me to him, having learned some of my apprehensions from Dick; and having diverted himself and others for some time with my fears, which appeared ludicrous enough in my crying and trembling, he dismissed me. The barrel of pitch was now lighted and put over the side into the water: by this time it was just dark, and the fish went after it; and, to my great joy, I saw them no more.

However, all my alarms began to subside when we got sight of land; and at last the ship arrived at Falmouth, after a passage of thirteen weeks. Every heart on board seemed gladdened on our reaching the shore, and none more than mine. The captain immediately went on shore, and sent on board some fresh provisions, which we wanted very much: we made good use of them, and our famine was soon turned into feasting, almost without ending. It was about the beginning of the spring 1757 when I arrived in England, and I was near twelve years of age at that time. I was very much struck with the buildings and the pavement of the streets in Falmouth; and, indeed, every object I saw filled me with new surprise. One morning, when I got upon deck, I saw it covered all over with the snow that fell overnight: as I had never seen anything of the kind before, I thought it was salt; so I immediately ran down to the mate, and desired him, as well as I could, to come and see how somebody in the night had thrown salt all over the deck. He, knowing what it was, desired me to bring some of it down to him: accordingly I took up a handful of it, which I found very cold indeed; and

when I brought it to him he desired me to taste it. I did so, and I was surprised beyond measure. I then asked him what it was? he told me it was
snow: but I could not in any wise understand him. He asked me if we
had no such thing in my country? and I told him, No. I then asked him
the use of it, and who made it; he told me a great man in the heavens,
called God: but here again I was to all intents and purposes at a loss to
understand him; and the more so, when a little after I saw the air filled
with it, in a heavy shower, which fell down on the same day. After this
I went to church; and having never been at such a place before, I was
again amazed at seeing and hearing the service. I asked all I could
about it; and they gave me to understand it was worshipping God, who
made us and all things. I was still at a great loss, and soon got into an
endless field of inquiries, as well as I was able to speak and ask about
things. However, my little friend Dick used to be my best interpreter;
for I could make free with him, and he always instructed me with pleasure: and from what I could understand by him of this God, and in
seeing these white people did not sell one another as we did, I was
much pleased; and in this I thought they were much happier than we
Africans. I was astonished at the wisdom of the white people in all
things I saw; but was amazed at their not sacrificing or making any
offerings, and eating with unwashed hands, and touching the dead. I
likewise could not help remarking the particular slenderness of their
women, which I did not at first like; and I thought they were not so
modest and shamefaced as the African women.

I had often seen my master and Dick employed in reading; and I had
great curiosity to talk to the books, as I thought they did; and so to learn
how all things had a beginning: for that purpose I have often taken up
a book, and have talked to it, and then put my ears to it, when alone, in
hopes it would answer me; and I have been very much concerned when
I found it remained silent.

My master lodged at the house of a gentleman in Falmouth, who
had a fine little daughter about six or seven years of age, and she grew
prodigiously fond of me; insomuch that we used to eat together, and
had servants to wait on us. I was so much caressed by this family that it
often reminded me of the treatment I had received from my little noble
African master. After I had been here a few days, I was sent on board of
the ship; but the child cried so much after me that nothing could pacify
her till I was sent for again. It is ludicrous enough, that I began to fear I
should be betrothed to this young lady; and when my master asked me
if I would stay there with her behind him, as he was going away with

the ship, which had taken in the tobacco again, I cried immediately, and said I would not leave him. At last, by stealth, one night I was sent on board the ship again; and in a little time we sailed for Guernsey, where she was in part owned by a merchant, one Nicholas Doberry. As I was now amongst a people who had not their faces scarred, like some of the African nations where I had been, I was very glad I did not let them ornament me in that manner when I was with them. When we arrived at Guernsey, my master placed me to board and lodge with one of his mates; who had a wife and family there; and some months afterwards he went to England, and left me in the care of this mate, together with my friend Dick. This mate had a little daughter, aged about five or six years, with whom I used to be much delighted. I had often observed, that, when her mother washed her face, it looked very rosy; but, when she washed mine, it did not look so; I therefore tried oftentimes myself if I could not by washing make my face of the same color as my little playmate (Mary), but it was all in vain; and I now began to be mortified at the difference in our complexions. This woman behaved to me with great kindness and attention; and taught me everything in the same manner as she did her own child, and indeed in every respect treated me as such. I remained here till the summer of the year 1757, when my master, being appointed first lieutenant of his majesty's ship the *Roebuck,* sent for Dick and me, and his old mate: On this we all left Guernsey, and set out for England in a sloop bound for London. As we were coming up towards the Nore, where the *Roebuck* lay, a man-of-war's boat came alongside to press our people, on which each man ran to hide himself. I was very much frightened at this, though I did not know what it meant, or what to think or do. However, I went and hid myself also under a hencoop. Immediately the press gang came on board with their swords drawn, and searched all about, pulled the people out by force, and put them into the boat. At last I was found out also; the man that found me held me up by the heels while they all made their sport of me, I roaring and crying out all the time most lustily; but at last the mate, who was my conductor, seeing this, came to my assistance, and did all he could to pacify me; but all to very little purpose, till I had seen the boat go off. Soon afterwards we came to the Nore, where the *Roebuck* lay; and, to our great joy, my master came on board to us, and brought us to the ship. I was amazed indeed to see the quantity of men and the guns. However my surprise began to diminish, as my knowledge increased; and I ceased to feel those apprehensions and alarms which had taken such strong possession of me when I first came among the Europeans, and for some time after. I began now to pass to an opposite extreme; I was so far from being afraid of anything new which I saw, that, after I had been some time in this ship, I even began to long for an engagement. My griefs too, which in young minds are not perpetual, were now wearing away; and I soon enjoyed myself pretty well, and felt tolerably easy in my present situation. There was a number of boys on board, which still made it more agreeable; for we were always together, and a great part of our time was spent in play. I remained in this ship a considerable time, during which we made several cruises, and visited a variety of places; among others we were twice in Holland, and brought over several persons of distinction from it, whose names I do not now remember. On the passage, one day, for the diversion of those gentlemen, all the boys were called on the quarterdeck, and were paired proportionably, and then made to fight; after which the gentlemen gave the combatants from five to nine shillings each. This was the first time I ever fought with a white boy, and I never knew what it was to have a bloody nose before. This made me fight most desperately; I suppose considerably more than an hour: and at last, both of us being weary, we were parted. I had a great deal of this kind of sport afterwards, in which the captain and the ship's company used very much to encourage me. Sometime afterwards the ship went to Leith, in Scotland, from thence to the Orkneys, where I was surprised in seeing scarcely any night; and from thence we sailed with a great fleet, full of soldiers, for England. All this time we had never come to an engagement, though we were frequently cruising off the coast of France; during which we chased many vessels, and took in all seventeen prizes. I had been learning many of the maneuvers of the ship during our cruise; and I was several times made to fire the guns.

One evening, off Le Havre-de-Grâce, just as it was growing dark, we were standing off shore, and met with a fine large French-built frigate. We got all things immediately ready for fighting, and I now expected I should be gratified in seeing an engagement, which I had so long wished for in vain. But the very moment the word of command was given to fire, we heard those on board the other ship cry "Haul down the jib"; and in that instant she hoisted English colors. There was instantly with us an amazing cry of "Avast!" or "stop firing"; and I think one or two guns had been let off, but happily they did no mischief. We had hailed them several times; but they not hearing, we received no answer, which was the cause of our firing. The boat was then sent on board of her, and she proved to be the *Ambuscade* man-of-war, to my no small disappointment. We returned to Portsmouth, without having been in any action, just as the trial of Admiral Byng (whom I saw several times during it); and my master having left the ship and gone to London for promotion, Dick and I were put on board the *Savage* sloop of war, and we went in her to assist in bringing off the *St. George* man-of-war, that had run ashore somewhere on the coast. After staying a few weeks on board the *Savage*, Dick and I were sent on shore at Deal, where we remained some short time, till my master sent for us to London, the place I had long desired exceedingly to see. We therefore both with great pleasure got into a wagon, and came to London, where we were received by a Mr. Guerin, a relation of my master. This gentleman had two sisters, very amiable ladies, who took much notice and great care of me. Though I had desired so much to see London, when I arrived in it I was unfortunately unable to gratify my curiosity; for I had at this time the chilblains to such a degree, that I could not stand for several months, and I was obliged to be sent to St. George's Hospital. There I grew so ill, that the doctors wanted to cut my leg off at different times, apprehending a mortification; but I always said I would rather die than suffer it: and happily (I thank God) I recovered without the operation. After being there several weeks, and just as I had recovered, the smallpox broke out on me, so that I was again confined: and I thought myself now particularly unfortunate. However, I soon recovered again: and by this time my master having been promoted to be first lieutenant of the *Preston* man-of-war of fifty guns, then new at Deptford, Dick and I were sent on board her, and soon after we went to Holland to bring over the late Duke of Cumberland to England. While I was in this ship an incident happened, which though trifling, I beg leave to relate, as I could not help taking particular notice of it, and considering it then as a judgment of God. One morning a young man was looking up to the foretop, and in a wicked tone, common on shipboard, d—d his eyes about something. Just at the moment some small particles of dirt fell into his left eye, and by the evening it was very much inflamed. The next day it grew worse, and within six or seven days he lost it. From this ship my master was appointed a lieutenant on board the *Royal George*. When he was going he wished me to stay on board the *Preston*, to learn the French horn; but the ship being ordered for Turkey, I could not think of leaving my master, to whom I was very warmly attached; and I told him, if he left me behind it would break my heart. This prevailed on him to take me with him; but he left Dick on board the *Preston*, whom I embraced at parting for the last time. The *Royal George* was the largest ship I had ever seen; so that when I came on board of her I was surprised at the number of people, men, women, and children, of every denomination; and the largeness of the guns, many of them also of brass, which I had never seen before. Here were also shops or stalls of every kind of goods, and people crying their different commodities about the ship as in a town. To me it appeared a little world, into which I was again cast without a friend, for I had no longer my dear companion Dick. We did not stay long here. My master was not many weeks on board before he got an appointment to be sixth lieutenant of the *Namur,* which was then at Spithead, fitting up for Vice Admiral Boscawen, who was going with a large fleet on an expedition against Louisbourgh. The crew of the *Royal George* were turned over to her, and the flag of that gallant Admiral was hoisted on board, the blue at the main-topgallant masthead. There was a very great fleet of men-of-war of every description assembled together for this expedition, and I was in hopes soon to have an opportunity of being gratified with a sea fight. All things being now in readiness, this mighty fleet (for there was also Admiral Cornish's fleet in company, destined for the East Indies) at last weighed anchor, and sailed. The two fleets continued in company for several days, and then parted; Admiral Cornish, in the *Lenox,* having first saluted our Admiral in the *Namur,* which he returned. We then steered for America; but, by contrary winds, we were driven off Tenerife, where I was struck with its noted peak. Its prodigious height, and its form, resembling a sugarloaf, filled me with wonder. We remained in sight of this island some days, and then proceeded for America, which we soon made, and got into a very commodious harbor called St. George, in Halifax, where we had fish in great plenty, and all other fresh provisions. We were here joined by different men-of-war and transport ships with soldiers; after which, our fleet being increased to a prodigious number of ships of all kinds, we sailed for Cape Breton in Nova Scotia. We had the good and gallant General Wolfe on board our ship, whose affability made him highly esteemed and beloved by all the men. He often honored me as well as other boys, with marks of his notice; and saved me once a flogging for fighting with a young gentleman. We arrived at Cape Breton in the summer of 1758; and here the soldiers were to be landed, in order to make an attack upon Louisbourgh. My master had some part in superintending the landing; and here I was in a small measure gratified in seeing an encounter between our men and the enemy. The French were posted on the shore to receive us, and disputed our landing for a long time: but at last they were driven from their trenches, and a complete landing was effected. Our troops pursued them as far as the town of Louisbourgh. In this action many were killed on both sides. One thing remarkable I saw this day; a lieutenant of the *Princess Amelia,* who, as well as my master, superintended the landing, was giving the word of command, and while his mouth was open a musket ball went through it, and passed out at his cheek. I had that day in my hand the scalp of an Indian king, who was killed in the engagement: the scalp had been taken off by a Highlander. I saw this king's ornaments too, which were very curious, and made of feathers.

Our land forces laid siege to the town of Louisbourgh, while the French men-of-war were blocked up in the harbor by the fleet, the batteries at the same time playing upon them from the land. This they did with such effect, that one day I saw some of the ships set on fire by the shells from the batteries, and I believe two or three of them were quite burnt. At another time, about fifty boats belonging to the English men-of-war, commanded by Captain George Balfour of the *Aetna* fireship, and Mr. Laforey, another junior captain, attacked and boarded the only two remaining French men-of-war in the harbor. They also set fire to a seventy-gun ship, but they brought off a sixty-four, called the *Bienfaisant.* During my stay here I had often an opportunity of being near Captain Balfour, who was pleased to notice me, and liked me so much that he often asked my master to let him have me, but he would not part with me; and no consideration would have induced me to leave him. At last Louisbourgh was taken, and the English men-of-war came into the harbor before it, to my very great joy; for I had now more liberty of indulging myself, and I went often on shore. When the ships were in the harbor, we had the most beautiful procession on the water I ever saw. All the admirals and captains of the men-of-war, full dressed, and in their barges, well ornamented with pendants, came alongside of the *Namur.* The Vice Admiral then went on shore in his barge, followed by the other officers in order of seniority, to take possession, as I suppose, of the town and fort. Sometime after this, the French governor and his lady, and other persons of note, came on board our ship to dine. On this occasion our ships were dressed with colors of all kinds, from the topgallant masthead to the deck; and this, with the firing of guns, formed a most grand and magnificent spectacle.

As soon as everything here was settled, Admiral Boscawen sailed with part of the fleet for England, leaving some ships behind with Rear

Admirals Sir Charles Hardy and Durell. It was now winter; and one evening, during our passage home, about dusk, when we were in the channel, or near soundings, and were beginning to look for land, we descried seven sail of large men-of-war, which stood off shore. Several people on board of our ship said, as the two fleets were (in forty minutes from the first sight) within hail of each other, that they were English men-of-war; and some of our people even began to name some of the ships. By this time both fleets began to mingle, and our admiral ordered his flag to be hoisted. At that instant the other fleet, which [was] French, hoisted their ensigns, and gave us a broadside as they passed by. Nothing could create greater surprise and confusion among us than this. The wind was high, the sea rough, and we had our lower and middle deck guns housed in, so that not a single gun on board was ready to be fired at any of the French ships. However, the *Royal William* and the *Somerset*, being our sternmost ships, became a little prepared, and each gave the French ships a broadside as they passed by. I afterwards heard this was a French squadron, commanded by Monsieur Conflans; and certainly had the Frenchman known our condition, and had a mind to fight us, they might have done us great mischief. But we were not long before we were prepared for an engagement. Immediately many things were tossed overboard; the ships were made ready for fighting as soon as possible; and, about ten at night, we had bent a new mainsail, the old one being split. Being now in readiness for fighting, we wore ship, and stood after the French fleet, who were one or two ships in number more than we. However, we gave them chase, and continued pursuing them all night; and at daylight we saw six of them, all large ships of the line, and an English East Indiaman, a prize they had taken. We chased them all day till between three and four o'clock in the evening, when we came up with, and passed within a musket shot of one seventy-four gunship, and the Indiaman also, who now hoisted her colors, but immediately hauled them down again. On this we made a signal for the other ships to take possession of her; and, supposing the man-of-war would likewise strike, we cheered, but she did not; though, if we had fired into her, from being so near, we must have taken her. To my utter surprise, the *Somerset*, which was the next ship astern of the *Namur*, made way likewise; and, thinking they were sure of this French ship, they cheered in the same manner, but still continued to follow us. The French Commodore was about a gunshot ahead of all, running from us with all speed; and about four o'clock he carried his fore-topmast overboard. This caused another loud cheer with us; and a little after the topmast came close by us; but to our great surprise, instead of coming up with her, we found she went as fast as ever, if not faster. The sea grew now much smoother; and the wind lulling, the seventy-four gunship we had passed came again by us in the very same direction, and so near, that we heard her people talk as she went by; yet not a shot was fired on either side; and about five or six o'clock, just as it grew dark, she joined her Commodore. We chased all night: but the next day we were out of sight, so that we saw no more of them; and we only had the old India-man (called *Carnarvon* I think) for our trouble. After this, we stood in for the channel, and soon made the land; and, about the close of the year 1758–9 we got safe to St. Helen's; here the *Namur* ran aground; and also another large ship astern of us; but, by starting our water, and tossing many things overboard to lighten her, we got the ships off without any damage. We stayed but a short time at Spithead, and then went into Portsmouth harbor to refit; from whence the Admiral went to London; and my master and I soon followed, with a press-gang, as we wanted some hands to complete our complement.

Chapter IV

The Author is baptized—Narrowly escapes drowning—Goes on an expedition to the Mediterranean—Incidents he met with there—Is witness to an engagement between some English and French ships—A particular account of the celebrated engagement between Admiral Boscawen and Monsieur Le Clue, off Cape Logas, in August 1759—Dreadful explosion of a French ship—The Author sails for England—His master appointed to the command of a fire ship—Meets a negro boy, from whom he experiences much benevolence—Prepares for an expedition against Belle Isle—A remarkable story of a disaster which befell his ship—Arrives at Belle Isle—Operations of the landing and siege—The Author's danger and distress, with his manner of extricating himself—Surrender of Belle Isle—Transactions afterwards on the coast of France—Remarkable instance of kidnapping—The Author returns to England—Hears a talk of peace, and expects his freedom—His ship sails for Deptford to be paid off, and when he arrives there he is suddenly seized by his master, and carried forcibly on board a West India ship, and sold.

IT WAS NOW BETWEEN three and four years since I first came to England, a great part of which I had spent at sea; so that I became inured to that service, and began to consider myself as happily situated; for my master treated me always extremely well; and my attachment and gratitude to him were very great. From the various scenes I had beheld on shipboard, I soon grew a stranger to terror of every kind, and was, in that respect at least almost an Englishman. I have often reflected with surprise that I never felt half the alarm at any of the numerous dangers I have been in, that I was filled with at the first sight of the Europeans, and at every act of theirs, even the most trifling; when I first came among them, and for sometime afterwards. That fear, however, which was the effect of my ignorance, wore away as I began to know them. I could now speak English tolerably well, and I perfectly understood everything that was said. I not only felt myself quite easy with these new countrymen, but relished their society and manners. I no longer looked upon them as spirits but as men superior to us; and therefore I had the stronger desire to resemble them: to imbibe their spirit, and imitate their manners; I therefore embraced every occasion of improvement; and every new thing that I observed I treasured up in my memory. I had long wished to be able to read and write; and for this purpose I took every opportunity to gain instruction, but had made as yet very little progress. However, when I went to London with my master, I had soon an opportunity of improving myself, which I gladly embraced. Shortly after my arrival, he sent me to wait upon the Miss Guerins, who had treated me with much kindness when I was there before; and they sent me to school.

While I was attending these ladies, their servants told me I could not go to heaven unless I was baptized. This made me very uneasy; for I had now some faint idea of a future state: Accordingly I communicated my anxiety to the eldest Miss Guerin, with whom I was become a favorite, and pressed her to have me baptized; when to my great joy, she told me I should. She had formerly asked my master to let me be baptized, but he had refused; however, she now insisted on it; and he, being under some obligation to her brother, complied with her request; so I was baptized in St. Margaret's Church, Westminster, in February 1759, by my present name. The clergyman, at the same time, gave me a book, called *A Guide to the Indians,* written by the Bishop of Sodor and Man. On this occasion, Miss Guerin and her brother did me the honor to stand as godfather and godmother, and afterwards gave me a treat. I used to attend these ladies about the town, in which service I was extremely happy; as I had thus many opportunities of seeing London, which I desired of all things. I was sometimes, however, with my master at his rendezvous house, which was at the foot of Westminster Bridge. Here I used to enjoy myself in playing about the bridge stairs, and often in the watermen's wherries, with other boys. On one of these occasions there was another boy with me in a wherry, and we went out into the current of the river: while we were there two more stout boys came to us in another wherry, and, abusing us for taking the boat desired me to get into the other wherry boat. Accordingly I went to get out of the wherry I was in; but just as I had got one of my feet into the other boat, the boys shoved it off, so that I fell into the Thames; and, not being able to swim, I should unavoidably have been drowned, but for the assistance of some watermen, who providentially came to my relief.

The *Namur* being again got ready for sea, my master with his gang, was ordered on board; and, to my no small grief, I was obliged to leave my schoolmaster, whom I liked very much, and always attended while I stayed in London, to repair on board with my master, nor did I leave my kind patronesses, the Miss Guerins, without uneasiness and regret. They often used to teach me to read, and took great pains to instruct me in the principles of religion and the knowledge of God. I therefore parted from those amiable ladies with reluctance; after receiving from them many friendly cautions how to conduct myself, and some valuable presents.

When I came to Spithead, I found we were destined for the Mediterranean, with a large fleet, which was now ready to put to sea. We only waited for the arrival of the admiral, who soon came on board; and about the beginning of the spring 1759, having weighed anchor and got under way, sailed for the Mediterranean; and in eleven days, from the Land's End, we got to Gibraltar. While we were here I used to be often on shore, and got various fruits in great plenty, and very cheap.

I had frequently told several people, in my excursions on shore, the story of my being kidnapped with my sister, and of our being separated, as I have related before; and I had as often expressed my anxiety for her fate, and my sorrow at having never met her again. One day, when I was on shore, and mentioning these circumstances to some persons, one of them told me he knew where my sister was, and, if I would accompany him, he would bring me to her. Improbable as this story was, I believed it immediately, and agreed to go with him, while my heart leaped for joy; and, indeed, he conducted me to a black young woman, who was so like my sister that at first sight I really thought it was her; but I was quickly undeceived; and, on talking to her, I found her to be of another nation.

While we lay here the *Preston* came in from the Levant. As soon as she arrived, my master told me I should now see my old companion Dick, who was gone in her when she sailed for Turkey. I was much rejoiced at this news, and expected every minute to embrace him; and when the captain came on board of our ship, which he did immediately after, I ran to inquire about my friend; but, with inexpressible sorrow, I learned from the boat's crew that the dear youth was dead! and that they had brought his chest, and all his other things, to my master: these he afterwards gave to me, and I regarded them as a memorial of my friend, whom I loved and grieved for as a brother.

While we were at Gibraltar I saw a soldier hanging by the heels at one of the moles.* I thought this a strange sight, as I had seen a man hanged in London by his neck. At another time I saw the master of a frigate towed to shore on a grating, by several of the men-of-war's boats, and discharged [from] the fleet, which I understood was a mark of disgrace for cowardice. On board the same ship there was also a sailor hung up at the main yardarm.

After lying at Gibraltar for some time, we sailed up the Mediterranean a considerable way above the Gulf of Lyons: where we were one night overtaken with a terrible gale of wind, much greater than any I had ever yet experienced. The sea ran so high that, though all the guns were well-housed, there was great reason to fear their getting loose, the ship rolled so much; and if they had it must have proved our destruction. After we had cruised here for a short time, we came to Barcelona, a Spanish seaport, remarkable for its silk manufactories. Here the ships were all to be watered; and my master, who spoke different languages, and used often to interpret for the admiral, superintended the watering of ours. For that purpose he and the officers of the other ships, who were on the same service, had tents pitched in the bay; and the Spanish soldiers were stationed along the shore, I suppose to see that no depredations were committed by our men.

I used constantly to attend my master, and I was charmed with this place. All the time we stayed it was like a fair with the natives who brought us fruits of all kinds, and sold them to us much cheaper than I

*He had drowned himself in endeavoring to desert.

got them in England. They used also to bring wine down to us in hog-
and sheepskins, which diverted me very much. The Spanish officers
here treated our officers with great politeness and attention; and some
of them, in particular, used to come often to my master's tent to visit
him; where they would sometimes divert themselves by mounting me
on the horses or mules, so that I could not fall, and setting them off at
full gallop; my imperfect skill in horsemanship all the while affording
them no small entertainment. After the ships were watered, we returned to our old station of cruising off Toulon, for the purpose of in-
tercepting a fleet of French men-of-war that lay there. One Sunday, in
our cruise, we came off a place where there were two small French frigates lying in shore; and our admiral, thinking to take or destroy them,
sent two ships in after them—the *Culloden* and the *Conqueror.* They
soon came up to the Frenchmen, and I saw a smart fight here, both by
sea and land: for the frigates were covered by batteries, and they played
upon our ships most furiously, which they as furiously returned, and
for a long time a constant firing was kept up on all sides at an amazing
rate. At last one frigate sunk; but the people escaped, though not without much difficulty: and a little after some of the people left the other
frigate also, which was a mere wreck. However, our ships did not venture to bring her away, they were so much annoyed from the batteries,
which raked them both in going and coming; their topmasts were shot
away, and they were otherwise so much shattered, that the admiral was
obliged to send in many boats to tow them back to the fleet. I afterwards sailed with a man who fought in one of the French batteries during the engagement, and he told me our ships had done considerable
mischief that day on shore, and in the batteries.

   After this we sailed for Gibraltar, and arrived there about August
1759. Here we remained with all our sails unbent, while the fleet was
watering and doing other necessary things. While we were in this situation, one day the admiral, with most of the principal officers, and
many people of all stations, being on shore, about seven o'clock in the
evening we were alarmed by signals from the frigates stationed for that
purpose; and in an instant there was a general cry that the French fleet
was out, and just passing through the straits. The admiral immediately
came on board with some other officers; and it is impossible to describe the noise, hurry, and confusion, throughout the whole fleet, in
bending their sails and flipping their cables; many people and ship's
boats were left on shore in the bustle. We had two captains on board of
our ship, who came away in the hurry and left their ships to follow. We

showed lights from the gunwales to the main-topmasthead; and all our lieutenants were employed amongst the fleet to tell the ships not to wait for their captains, but to put the sails to the yards, flip their cables, and follow us; and in this confusion of making ready for fighting, we set out for sea in the dark after the French fleet. Here I could have exclaimed with Ajax,

> *Oh Jove! O father! if it be thy will*
> *That we must perish, we thy will obey,*
> *But let us perish by the light of day.*

They had got the start of us so far that we were not able to come up with them during the night; but at daylight we saw seven sail of ships of the line some miles ahead. We immediately chased them till about four o'clock in the evening, when our ships came up with them; and though we were about fifteen large ships, our gallant admiral only fought them with his own division, which consisted of seven: so that we were just ship for ship. We passed by the whole of the enemy's fleet in order to come at their commander, Monsieur La Clue, who was in the *Ocean*, an eighty-four-gun ship: as we passed they all fired on us; and at one time three of them fired together, continuing to do so for some time. Notwithstanding which our admiral would not suffer a gun to be fired at any of them, to my astonishment; but made us lie on our bellies on the deck till we came quite close to the *Ocean*, who was ahead of them all; when we had orders to pour the whole three tiers into her at once.

The engagement now commenced with great fury on both sides: the *Ocean* immediately returned our fire, and we continued engaged with each other for some time; during which I was frequently stunned with the thundering of the great guns, whose dreadful contents hurried many of my companions into awful eternity. At last the French line was entirely broken, and we obtained the victory, which was immediately proclaimed with loud huzzas and acclamations. We took three prizes, *La Modeste,* of sixty-four guns, and *Le Temeraire* and *Centaur,* of seventy-four guns each. The rest of the French ships took to flight with all the sail they could crowd. Our ship being very much damaged, and quite disabled from pursuing the enemy, the admiral immediately quitted her, and went in the broken and only boat we had left on board the *Newark,* with which, and some other ships, he went after the French. The *Ocean,* and another large French ship called the *Redoutable,* endeavoring to escape, ran ashore at Cape Logas, on the coast of Portugal; and the French admiral and some of the crew got ashore; but we, finding it impossible to get the ships off, set fire to them both. About midnight I saw the *Ocean* blow up, with a most dreadful explosion. I never beheld a more awful scene. About the space of a minute, the midnight seemed turned into day by the blaze, which was attended with a noise louder and more terrible than thunder, that seemed to rend every element around us.

My station during the engagement was on the middle deck, where I was quartered with another boy, to bring powder to the aftermost gun; and here I was witness of the dreadful fate of many of my companions, who, in the twinkling of an eye, were dashed in pieces, and launched into eternity. Happily I escaped unhurt, though the shot and splinters flew thick about me during the whole fight. Towards the latter part of it my master was wounded, and I saw him carried down to the surgeon; but, though I was much alarmed for him, and wished to assist him, I dared not leave my post. At this station my gun mate (a partner in bringing powder for the same gun) and I ran a very great risk for more than half an hour of blowing up the ship. For, when we had taken the cartridges out of the boxes, the bottoms of many of them proving rotten, the powder ran all about the deck, near the match tub: we scarcely had water enough at last to throw on it. We were also, from our employment, very much exposed to the enemy's shots; for we had to go through nearly the whole length of the ship to bring the powder. I expected therefore every minute to be my last; especially when I saw our men fall so thick about me; but, wishing to guard as much against the dangers as possible, at first I thought it would be fastest not to go for the powder till the Frenchmen had fired their broadside; and then, while they were charging, I could go and come with my powder; but immediately afterwards I thought this caution was fruitless; and, cheering myself with the reflection that there was a time allotted for me to die as well as to be born, I instantly cast off all fear or thought whatever of death, and went through the whole of my duty with alacrity; pleasing myself with the hope, if I survived the battle, of relating it and the dangers I had escaped to the Miss Guerins, and others, when I should return to London.

Our ship suffered very much in this engagement; for, besides the number of our killed and wounded, she was almost torn to pieces, and our rigging so much shattered, that our mizzenmast, main yard, etc. hung over the side of the ship; so that we were obliged to get many carpenters and others, from some of the ships of the fleet, to assist in setting us in some tolerable order; and, notwithstanding which, it took us some time before we were completely refitted; after which we left Admiral Broderick to command, and we, with the prizes, steered for England. On the passage, and as soon as my master was something recovered of his wounds, the admiral appointed him captain of the *Aetna* fireship, on which he and I left the *Namur,* and went on board of her at sea. I liked this little ship very much. I now became the captain's steward; in which situation I was very happy, for I was extremely well treated by all on board, and I had leisure to improve myself in reading and writing. The latter I had learned a little of before I left the *Namur,* as there was a school on board. When we arrived at Spithead, the *Aetna* went into Portsmouth harbor to refit, which being done, we returned to Spithead, and joined a large fleet that was thought to be intended against Havana; but about that time the king died; whether that prevented the expedition I know not; but it caused our ship to be stationed at Cowes, in the Isle of Wight, till the beginning of the year sixty-one. Here I spent my time very pleasantly; I was much on shore all about this delightful island, and found the inhabitants very civil.

While I was here, I met with a trifling incident which surprised me agreeably. I was one day in a field belonging to a gentleman who had a black boy about my own size; this boy having observed me from his master's house, was transported at the sight of one of his own countrymen, and ran to meet me with the utmost haste. I not knowing what he was about, turned a little out of his way at first, but to no purpose: he soon came close to me, and caught hold of me in his arms as if I had been his brother, though we had never seen each other before. After we had talked together for some time, he took me to his master's house, where I was treated very kindly. This benevolent boy and I were very happy in frequently seeing each other, till about the month of March 1761, when our ship had orders to fit out again for another expedition. When we got ready we joined a very large fleet at Spithead, commanded by Commodore Keppel, which was destined against Belle Isle; and, with a number of transport ships with troops on board, to make a descent on the place, we sailed once more in quest of fame. I longed to engage in new adventures and see fresh wonders.

I had a mind on which everything uncommon made its full impression, and every event which I considered as marvellous. Every extraordinary escape, or signal deliverance, either of myself or others, I looked upon to be effected by the interposition of Providence. We had not been above ten days at sea before an incident of this kind happened;

which, whatever credit it may obtain from the reader, made no small impression on my mind.

We had on board a gunner, whose name was John Mondle, a man of very indifferent morals. This man's cabin was between the decks, exactly over where I lay, abreast of the quarterdeck ladder. One night, the 5th of April, being terrified with a dream, he awoke in so great a fright that he could not rest in his bed any longer, nor even remain in his cabin; and he went upon deck about four o'clock in the morning extremely agitated. He immediately told those on the deck of the agonies of his mind, and the dream which occasioned it; in which he said he had seen many things very awful, and had been warned by St. Peter to repent, who told him his time was short. This he said had greatly alarmed him, and he was determined to alter his life. People generally mock the fears of others when they are themselves in safety; and some of his shipmates who heard him only laughed at him. However, he made a vow that he never would drink strong liquors again; and he immediately got a light, and gave away his sea stores of liquor. After which, his agitation still continuing, he began to read the scriptures, hoping to find some relief; and soon afterwards he laid himself down again on his bed, and endeavored to compose himself to sleep, but to no purpose; his mind still continuing in a state of agony. By this time it was exactly half after seven in the morning; I was then under the half deck at the great cabin door; and all at once I heard the people in the waist cry out, most fearfully "The Lord have mercy upon us! We are all lost! The Lord have mercy upon us!" Mr. Mondle hearing the cries, immediately ran out of his cabin; and we were instantly struck by the *Lynne,* a forty-gun ship, Captain Clerk, which nearly ran us down. This ship had just put about, and was by the wind, but had not got full headway, or we must all have perished; for the wind was brisk. However, before Mr. Mondle had got four steps from his cabin door, she struck our ship with her cutwater, right in the middle of his bed and cabin, and ran it up to the combings of the quarterdeck hatchway, and above three feet below water, and in a minute there was not a bit of wood to be seen where Mr. Mondle's cabin stood; and he was so near being killed, that some of the splinters tore his face. As Mr. Mondle must inevitably have perished from this accident, had he not been alarmed in the very extraordinary way I have related, I could not help regarding this as an awful interposition of Providence for his preservation. The two ships for some time swinged alongside of each other; for ours being a fireship, our grappling irons caught the *Lynne* every way, and the yards and rigging went at an astonishing rate. Our ship was in such a shocking condition that we all thought she would instantly go down, and everyone ran for their lives, and got as well as they could on board the *Lynne*; but our lieutenant being the aggressor, he never quitted the ship. However, when we found she did not sink immediately, the captain came on board again, and encouraged our people to return and try to save her. Many of them came back, but some would not venture. Some of the ships in the fleet, seeing our situation, immediately sent their boats to our assistance, but it took us the whole day to save the ship with all their help. And by using every possible means, particularly frapping her together with many hawsers, and putting a great quantity of tallow below water where she was damaged, she was kept together; but it was well we did not meet with any gales of wind, or we must have gone to pieces; for we were in such a crazy condition that we had ships to attend us till we arrived at Belle Isle, the place of our destination; and then we had all things taken out of the ship, and she was properly repaired. This escape of Mr. Mondle, which he, as well as myself, always considered as a singular act of Providence, I believe had a great influence on his life and conduct ever afterwards.

Now that I am on this subject, I beg leave to relate another instance or two which strongly raised my belief of the particular interposition of heaven, and which might not otherwise have found a place here, from their insignificance. I belonged for a few days, in the year 1758, to the *Jason,* of fifty-four guns, at Plymouth; and one night, when I was on board, a woman, with a child at her breast, fell from the upper deck down into the hold, near the keel. Everyone thought that the mother and child must be both dashed to pieces; but, to our great surprise, neither of them was hurt. I myself one day fell headlong from the upper deck of the *Aetna* down the afterhold, when the ballast was out; and all who saw me fall cried out I was killed; but I received not the least injury. And in the same ship a man fell from the masthead on the deck without being hurt. In these, and in many more instances, I thought I could plainly trace the hand of God, without whose permission a sparrow cannot fall. I began to raise my fear from man to him alone, and to call daily on his holy name with fear and reverence: and I trust he heard my supplications, and graciously condescended to answer me according to his holy word, and to implant the seeds of piety in me, even one of the meanest of his creatures.

When we had refitted our ship, and all things were in readiness for attacking the place, the troops on board the transports were ordered to disembark; and my master, as a junior captain, had a share in the command of the landing. This was on the 12th of April. The French were drawn up on the shore, and had made every disposition to oppose the landing of our men, only a small part of them this day being able to effect it; most of them, after fighting with great bravery, were cut off; and General Crawford, with a number of others, were taken prisoners. In this day's engagement we had also our lieutenant killed.

On the 21st of April we renewed our efforts to land the men, while all the men-of-war were stationed along the shore to cover it, and fired at the French batteries and breastworks, from early in the morning till about four o'clock in the evening, when our soldiers effected a safe landing. They immediately attacked the French; and, after a sharp encounter, forced them from the batteries. Before the enemy retreated, they blew up several of them, lest they should fall into our hands. Our men now proceeded to besiege the citadel, and my master was ordered on shore to superintend the landing of all the materials necessary for carrying on the siege; in which service I mostly attended him. While I was there I went about to different parts of the island; and one day, particularly, my curiosity almost cost me my life. I wanted very much to see the mode of charging the mortars, and letting off the shells, and for that purpose I went to an English battery that was but very few yards from the walls of the citadel. There indeed I had an opportunity of completely gratifying myself in seeing the whole operation, and that not without running a very great risk, both from the English shells that burst while I was there, but likewise from those of the French. One of the largest of their shells burst within nine or ten yards of me: there was a single rock close by, about the size of a butt; and I got instant shelter under it in time to avoid the fury of the shell. Where it burst the earth was torn in such a manner that two or three butts might easily have gone into the hole it made, and it threw great quantities of stones and dirt to a considerable distance. Three shots were also fired at me, and another boy who was along with me, one of them in particular seemed

Winged with red lightning and impetuous rage;

for, with a most dreadful sound, it hissed close by me, and struck a rock at a little distance, which it shattered to pieces. When I saw what perilous circumstances I was in, I attempted to return the nearest way I could find, and thereby I got between the English and the French sentinels. An English sergeant, who commanded the outposts, seeing me, and surprised how I came there (which was by stealth along the seashore), reprimanded me very severely for it, and instantly took the sentinel off his post into custody, for his negligence in suffering me to pass the lines. While I was in this situation I observed at a little distance a French horse belonging to some islanders, which I thought I would now mount, for the greater expedition of getting off. Accordingly, I took some cord which I had about me, and making a kind of bridle of it, I put it round the horse's head, and the tame beast very quietly suffered me to tie him thus and mount him. As soon as I was on the horse's back I began to kick and beat him, and try every means to make him go quick, but all to very little purpose: I could not drive him out of a slow pace. While I was creeping along, still within reach of the enemy's shot, I met with a servant well mounted on an English horse. I immediately stopped; and, crying, told him my case, and begged of him to help me; and this he effectually did; for, having a fine large whip, he began to lash my horse with it so severely, that he set off full speed with me towards the sea, while I was quite unable to hold or manage him. In this manner I went along till I came to a craggy precipice. I now could not stop my horse; and my mind was filled with apprehensions of my deplorable fate, should he go down the precipice, which he appeared fully disposed to do: I therefore thought I had better throw myself off him at once, which I did immediately, with a great deal of dexterity, and fortunately escaped unhurt. As soon as I found myself at liberty, I made the best of my way for the ship, determined I would not be so foolhardy again in a hurry.

We continued to besiege the citadel till June, when it surrendered. During the siege I have counted above sixty shells and carcasses in the air at once. When this place was taken I went through the citadel, and in the bombproofs under it, which were cut in the solid rock; and I thought it a surprising place both for strength and building: notwithstanding which our shots and shells had made amazing devastation, and ruinous heaps all around it.

After the taking of this island, our ships, with some others commanded by Commodore Stanhope in the *Swiftsure*, went to Basse Road, where we blocked up a French fleet. Our ships were there from June till February following; and in that time I saw a great many scenes of war, and stratagems on both sides, to destroy each other's fleet. Sometimes we would attack the French with some ships of the line; at other times with boats; and frequently we made prizes. Once or twice the French attacked us, by throwing shells with their bomb-vessels; and one day, as a French vessel was throwing shells at our ships, she broke from her springs behind the Isle of Rhe: the tide being complicated, she came within a gunshot of the *Nassau*; but the *Nassau* could not bring a gun to bear upon her, and thereby the Frenchman got off. We were twice attacked by their fire-floats, which they chained together, and then let them float down with the tide; but each time we sent boats with grapplings, and towed them safe out of the fleet.

We had different commanders while we were at this place, Commodores Stanhope, Dennis, Lord Howe, etc. From thence, before the Spanish war began, our ship, and the *Wasp* sloop, were spent to St. Sebastian, in Spain, by Commodore Stanhope; and Commodore Dennis afterwards sent our ship as a cartel* to Bayonne in France;† after which we went in February 1762, to Belle Isle, and there stayed till the summer, then we left it, and returned to Portsmouth.

After our ship was fitted out again for service, in September she went to Guernsey, where I was very glad to see my old hostess, who was now a widow, and my former little charming companion her daughter. I spent some time here very happily with them, till October, when we had orders to repair to Portsmouth. We parted from each other with a great deal of affection, and I promised to return soon, and see them again, not knowing what all-powerful fate had determined for me. Our ship having arrived at Portsmouth, we went into the harbor, and remained there till the latter end of November, when we heard great talk about peace; and, to our very great joy, in the beginning of December we had orders to go up to London with our ship to be paid off. We received this news with loud huzzas, and every other demonstration of gladness; and nothing but mirth was to be seen throughout every part of the ship. I too was not without my share of the general joy on this occasion. I thought now of nothing but being freed, and working for myself, and thereby getting money to enable me to get a good education; for I always had a great desire to be able at least to read and write; and

---

*Among others whom we brought from Bayonne, were two gentlemen who had been in the West Indies, where they sold slaves; and they confessed they had made at one time a false bill of sale, and sold two Portuguese white men among a lot of slaves.

†Some people have it, that sometimes shortly before persons die, their ward has been seen; that is, some spirit, exactly in their likeness, though they are themselves at other places at the same time. One day while we were at Bayonne, Mr. Mondle saw one of our men, as he thought, in the gun room; and a little after, coming on the quarterdeck, he spoke of the circumstance of this man to some of the officers. They told him that this man was then out of the ship, in one of the boats with the lieutenant; but Mr. Mondle would not believe it, and we searched the ship, when we found the man was actually out of her; and when the boat returned sometime afterwards, we found the man had been drowned the very time Mr. Mondle thought he saw him.

while I was on shipboard I had endeavored to improve myself in both. While I was in the *Aetna* particularly, the captain's clerk taught me to write, and gave me a smattering of arithmetic as far as the rule of three. There was also one Daniel Queen, about forty years of age, a man very well educated, who messed with me on board this ship, and he likewise dressed and attended the captain. Fortunately this man soon became very much attached to me, and took very great pains to instruct me in many things. He taught me to shave and dress hair a little, and also to read in the Bible, explaining many passages to me, which I did not comprehend. I was wonderfully surprised to see the laws and rules of my own country written almost exactly here; a circumstance which I believe tended to impress our manners and customs more deeply on my memory. I used to tell him of this resemblance; and many a time we had sat up the whole night together at this employment. In short, he was like a father to me; and some even used to call me after his name; they also styled me the black Christian. Indeed I almost loved him with the affection of a son. Many things I have denied myself that he might have them; and when I used to play at marbles or any other game, and won a few halfpence, or got any little money, which I sometimes did for shaving anyone, I used to buy him a little sugar or tobacco, as far as my stock of money would go. He used to say, that he and I never should part; and that when our ship was paid off, and I was as free as himself or any other man on board, he would instruct me in his business, by which I might gain a good livelihood. This gave me new life and spirits, and my heart burned within me, while I thought the time long till I obtained my freedom: for though my master had not promised it to me, yet besides the assurances I had received that he had no right to detain me, he always treated me with the greatest kindness, and reposed in me an unbounded confidence; he even paid attention to my morals; and would never suffer me to deceive him, or tell lies, of which he used to tell me the consequences; and that if I did so, God would not love me; so that from all this tenderness I had never once supposed, in all my dreams of freedom, that he would think of detaining me any longer than I wished.

In pursuance of our orders we sailed from Portsmouth for the Thames, and arrived at Deptford the 10th of December, where we cast anchor just as it was high water. The ship was up about half an hour, when my master ordered the barge to be manned; and all in an instant, without having before given me the least reason to suspect anything of the matter, he forced me into the barge, saying I was going to leave him, but he would take care I should not. I was so struck with the unexpectedness of this proceeding, that for some time I did not make a reply, only I made an offer to go for my books and chest of clothes, but he swore I should not move out of his sight; and if I did he would cut my throat, at the same time taking his hanger. I began, however, to collect myself: and, plucking up courage, I told him I was free, and he could not by law serve me so. But this only enraged him the more; and he continued to swear, and said he would soon let me know whether he would or not, and at that instant sprung himself into the barge from the ship, to the astonishment and sorrow of all on board. The tide, rather unluckily for me, had just turned downward, so that we quickly fell down the river along with it, till we came among some outward-bound West Indiamen; for he was resolved to put me on board the first vessel he could get to receive me. The boat's crew, who pulled against their will, became quite faint at different times, and would have gone ashore, but he would not let them. Some of them strove then to cheer me, and told me he could not sell me, and that they would stand by me, which revived me a little, and [I] still entertained hopes; for as they pulled along he asked some vessels to receive me, and they would not. But, just as we had got a little below Gravesend, we came alongside of a ship which was going away the next tide for the West Indies; her name was the *Charming Sally*, Captain James Doran; and my master went on board and agreed with him for me; and in a little time I was sent for into the cabin. When I came there, Captain Doran asked me if I knew him? I answered that I did not; "Then," said he, "you are now my slave." I told him my master could not sell me to him, nor to anyone else. "Why," said he, "did not your master buy you?" I confessed he did. "But I have served him," said I, "many years, and he has taken all my wages and prize money, for I only got one sixpence during the war; besides this I have been baptized; and by the laws of the land no man has a right to sell me": and I added, that I had heard a lawyer and others at different times tell my master so. They both then said that those people who told me so were not my friends: but I replied, "It was very extraordinary that other people did not know the law as well as they." Upon this Captain Doran said I talked too much English; and if I did not behave myself well, and be quiet, he had a method on board to make me. I was too well convinced of his power over me to doubt what he said: and my former sufferings in the slave ship presenting themselves to my mind, the recollection of them made me shudder. However, before I retired, I told them that as I could not get any right among men here, I hoped I should hereafter in Heaven; and I immediately left the cabin, filled with resentment and sorrow. The only coat I had with me my master took away with him, and said, "If your prize money had been 10,000 pounds I had a right to it all, and would have taken it." I had about nine guineas, which during my long sea-faring life, I had scraped together from trifling perquisites and little ventures; and I hid it that instant, lest my master should take that from me likewise, still hoping that by some means or other I should make my escape to the shore, and indeed some of my old shipmates told me not to despair, for they would get me back again; and that, as soon as they could get their pay, they would immediately come to Portsmouth to me, where this ship was going: but, alas! all my hopes were baffled, and the hour of my deliverance was as yet far off. My master, having soon concluded his bargain with the captain, came out of the cabin, and he and his people got into the boat, and put off; I followed them with aching eyes as long as I could, and when they were out of sight I threw myself on the deck, with a heart ready to burst with sorrow and anguish.

Chapter V

The Author's reflections on his situation—Is deceived by a promise of being delivered—His despair at sailing for the West Indies—Arrives at Montserrat, where he is sold to Mr. King—Various interesting instances of oppression, cruelty, and extortion, which the Author saw practiced upon the slaves in the West Indies during his captivity, from the year 1763 to 1766—Address on it to the planters.

THUS, AT THE MOMENT I EXPECTED all my toils to end, was I plunged, as I supposed, in a new slavery: in comparison of which all my service hitherto had been perfect freedom; and whose horrors, always present to my mind, now rushed on it with tenfold aggravation. I wept very bitterly for some time: and began to think that I must have done something to displease the Lord, that he thus punished me so severely. This filled me with painful reflections on my past conduct; I recollected that on the morning of our arrival at Deptford I had rashly sworn that as soon as we reached London I would spend the night in rambling and sport. My conscience smote me for this unguarded expression: I felt that the Lord was able to disappoint me in all things, and immediately considered my present situation as a judgment of heaven on account of my presumption in swearing: I therefore, with contrition of heart, acknowledged my transgression to God, and poured out my soul before him with unfeigned repentance, and with earnest supplications I besought him not to abandon me in my distress, nor cast me from his mercy forever. In a little time my grief, spent with its own violence, began to subside; and after the first confusion of my thoughts was over, I reflected with more calmness on my present condition: I considered that trials and disappointments are sometimes for our good, and I thought God might perhaps have permitted this in order to teach me wisdom and resignation; for he had hitherto shadowed me with the wings of his mercy, and by his invisible but powerful hand brought me the way I knew not. These reflections gave me a little comfort, and I arose at last from the deck with dejection and sorrow in my countenance, yet mixed with some faint hope that the *Lord would appear* for my deliverance.

Soon afterwards as my new master was going on shore, he called me to him, and told me to behave myself well, and do the business of the ship the same as any of the rest of the boys, and that I should fare the better for it; but I made him no answer. I was then asked if I could swim, and I said, no. However I was made to go under the deck, and was well watched. The next tide the ship got under way, and soon after arrived at the Mother Bank, Portsmouth; where she waited a few days for some of the West India convoy. While I was here I tried every means I could devise among the people of the ship to get me a boat from the shore, as there was none suffered to come alongside of the ship; and their own, whenever it was used, was hoisted in again immediately. A sailor on board took a guinea from me on pretense of getting me a boat; and promised me, time after time, that it was hourly to come off. When he had the watch upon deck I watched also; and looked long enough, but all in vain; I could never see either the boat or my guinea again. And what I thought was still the worst of all, the fellow gave information, as I afterwards found, all the while to the mates of my intention to go off, if I could in any way do it; but, roguelike, he never told them he had got a guinea from me to procure my escape. However, after we had sailed, and his trick was made known to the ship's crew, I had some satisfaction in seeing him detested and despised by them all for his behavior to me. I was still in hopes that my old shipmates would not forget their promise to come for me at Portsmouth: and they did at last, but not till the day before we sailed, some of them did come there, and sent me off some oranges, and other tokens of their regard. They also sent me word they would come off to me themselves the next day or the day after; and a lady also, who lived in Gosport, wrote to me that she would come and take me out of the ship at the same time. This lady had been once very intimate with my former master; I used to sell and take care of a great deal of property for her in different ships; and in return she always showed great friendship for me; and used to tell my master that she would take me away to live with her: but unfortunately, for me, a disagreement soon afterwards took place between them; and she was succeeded in my master's good graces by another lady, who appeared sole mistress of the *Aetna,* and mostly lodged on board. I was not so great a favorite with this lady as with the former; she had conceived a pique against me on some occasion when she was on board, and she did not fail to instigate my master to treat me in the manner he did.★

However, the next morning, the 30th of December, the wind being brisk and easterly, the *Aeolus* frigate, which was to escort the convoy, made a signal for sailing. All the ships then got up their anchors; and, before any of my friends had an opportunity to come off to my relief, to my inexpressible anguish our ship had got under way. What tumultuous emotions agitated my soul when the convoy got under sail, and I, a prisoner on board, now without hope! I kept my swimming eyes upon the land in a state of unutterable grief; not knowing what to do, and despairing how to help myself. While my mind was in this situation, the fleet sailed on, and in one day's time I lost sight of the wished-for land. In the first expressions of my grief I reproached my fate, and wished I had never been born. I was ready to curse the tide that bore us, the gale that wafted my prison, and even the ship that conducted us; and I called on death to relieve me from the horrors I felt and dreaded, that I might be in that place

> *Where slaves are free, and men oppress no more.*
> *Fool that I was, inur'd so long to pain,*
> *To trust to hope, or dream of joy again.*
> *Now dragg'd once more beyond the western main,*
> *To groan beneath some dastard planter's chain;*
> *Where my poor countrymen in bondage wait*

★Thus was I sacrificed to the envy and resentment of this woman, for knowing that the lady whom she had succeeded in my master's good graces designed to take me into her service; which, had I once got on shore, she would not have been able to prevent. She felt her pride alarmed at the superiority of her rival in being attended by a black servant: it was not less to prevent this than to be revenged on me, that she caused the captain to treat me thus cruelly.

The long enfranchisement of a ling'ring fate:
Hard lingering fate! while, ere the dawn of day,
Rous'd by the lash, they go their cheerless way;
And as their soul with shame and anguish burn,
Salute with groans unwelcome morn's return,
And, chiding ev'ry hour the slow-pac'd sun,
Pursue their toils till all his race is run.
No eye to mark their suff'rings with a tear;
No friend to comfort, and no hope to cheer:
Then, like the dull unpity'd brutes, repair
To stalls as wretched, and as coarse a fare;
Thank heaven one day of mis'ry was o'er,
Then sink to sleep, and wish to wake no more. *

The turbulence of my emotions, however, naturally gave way to calmer thoughts, and I soon perceived what fate had decreed no mortal on earth could prevent. The convoy sailed on without any accident, with a pleasant gale and smooth sea, for six weeks, till February, when one morning the *Aeolus* ran down a brig, one of the convoy, and she instantly went down and was engulfed in the dark recesses of the ocean. The convoy was immediately thrown into great confusion till it was daylight; and the *Aeolus* was illuminated with lights to prevent any further mischief. On the 13th of February 1763, from the masthead, we descried our destined island Montserrat, and soon after I beheld those

Regions of sorrow, doleful shades, where peace
And rest can rarely dwell. Hope never comes
That comes to all, but torture without end
Still urges.

At the sight of this land of bondage, a fresh horror ran through all my frame, and chilled me to the heart. My former slavery now rose in dreadful review to my mind, and displayed nothing but misery, stripes, and chains; and, in the first paroxysm of my grief, I called upon God's thunder, and his avenging power, to direct the stroke of death to

*"The Dying Negro," a poem originally published in 1773. Perhaps it may not be deemed impertinent here to add, that this elegant and pathetic little poem was occasioned, as appears by the advertisement prefixed to it, by the following incident: "A black, who a few days before, had ran away from his master, and got himself christened, with intent to marry a white woman, his fellow servant, being taken, and sent on board a ship in the Thames, took an opportunity of shooting himself through the head."

me, rather than permit me to become a slave, and to be sold from lord to lord.

In this state of my mind our ship came to an anchor, and soon after discharged her cargo. I now knew what it was to work hard; I was made to help to unload and load the ship. And, to comfort me in my distress in that time, two of the sailors robbed me of all my money, and ran away from the ship. I had been so long used to a European climate, that at first I felt the scorching West India sun very painful, while the dashing surf would toss the boat and the people in it frequently above high-water mark. Sometimes our limbs were broken with this, or even attended with instant death, and I was day by day mangled and torn.

About the middle of May, when the ship was got ready to sail for England, I all the time believing that Fate's blackest clouds were gathering over my head, and expecting their bursting would mix me with the dead, Captain Doran sent for me ashore one morning, and I was told by the messenger that my fate was then determined. With trembling steps and fluttering heart I came to the captain, and found with him one Mr. Robert King, a Quaker and the first merchant in the place. The captain then told me my former master had sent me there to be sold; but that he had desired him to get me the best master he could, as he told him, I was a very deserving boy, which Captain Doran said he found to be true, and if he were to stay in the West Indies, he would be glad to keep me himself; but he could not venture to take me to London, for he was very sure that when I came there I would leave him. I at that instant burst out a-crying, and begged much of him to take me to England with him, but all to no purpose. He told me he had got me the very best master in the whole island, with whom I should be as happy as if I were in England, and for that reason he chose to let him have me, though he could sell me to his own brother-in-law for a great deal more money than what he got from this gentleman. Mr. King, my new master, then made a reply, and said, the reason he had bought me was on account of my good character; and, as he had not the least doubt of my good behavior, I should be very well off with him. He also told me he did not live in the West Indies, but at Philadelphia, where he was going soon; and, as I understood something of the rules of arithmetic, when we got there he would put me to school, and fit me for a clerk. This conversation relieved my mind a little, and I left those gentlemen considerably more at ease in myself than when I came to them; and I was very thankful to Captain Doran, and even to my old master, for the character they had given me; a character which I afterwards found of infinite service to me. I went on board again, and took leave of all my shipmates; and the next day the ship sailed. When she weighed anchor I went to the waterside and looked at her, with a very wishful and aching heart, and followed her with my eyes until she was totally out of sight. I was so bowed down with grief that I could not hold up my head for many months; and if my new master had not been kind to me, I believe I should have died under it at last. And indeed I soon found that he fully deserved the good character which Captain Doran had given me of him; for he possessed a most amiable disposition and temper, and was very charitable and humane. If any of his slaves behaved amiss, he did not beat or use them ill, but parted with them. This made them afraid of disobliging him; and as he treated his slaves better than any other man on the island, so he was better and more faithfully served by them in return. By this kind treatment I did at last endeavor to compose myself; and with fortitude, though moneyless, determined to face whatever fate had decreed for me. Mr. King soon asked me what I could do; and at the same time said he did not mean to treat me as a common slave. I told him I knew something of seamanship, and could shave and dress hair pretty well; and I could refine wines, which I had learned on shipboard where I had often done it; and that I could write, and understood arithmetic tolerably well as far as the Rule of Three. He then asked me if I knew anything of gauging; and, on my answering that I did not, he said one of his clerks should teach me to gauge.

Mr. King dealt in all manner of merchandise, and kept from one to six clerks. He loaded many vessels in a year; particularly to Philadelphia, where he was born, and was connected with a great mercantile house in that city. He had, besides many vessels, droggers of different sizes, which used to go about the island and other places to collect rum, sugar, and other goods. I understood pulling and managing those boats very well; and this hard work, which was the first that he set me to, in the sugar seasons, used to be my constant employment. I have rowed the boat, and slaved at the oars, from one hour to sixteen in the twenty-four; during which I had fifteen pence sterling per day to live on, though sometimes only ten pence. However, this was considerably more than was allowed to other slaves that used to work often with me, and belonged to other gentlemen on the island: these poor souls had never more than nine pence a day, and seldom more than six pence, from their masters or owners, though they earned them three or four pisterines* a day: for it is a a common practice in the West Indies, for men to purchase slaves though they have not plantations themselves, in order to let them out to planters and merchants at so much apiece by the day, and they give what allowance they choose out of this produce of their daily work to their slaves for subsistence; this allowance is often very scanty. My master often gave the owners of these slaves two and a half of these pieces per day, and found the poor fellows in victuals himself, because he thought their owners did not feed them well enough according to the work they did. The slaves used to like this very well, and as they knew my master to be a man of feeling, they were always glad to work for him in preference to any other gentleman; some of whom, after they had been paid for these poor people's labors, would not give them their allowance out of it. Many times have I seen these unfortunate wretches beaten for asking for their pay; and often severely flogged by their owners if they did not bring them their daily or weekly money exactly to the time; though the poor creatures were obliged to wait on the gentlemen they had worked for, sometimes more than half the day, before they could get their pay; and this generally on Sundays, when they wanted the time for themselves. In particular, I knew a countryman of mine, who once did not bring the weekly money directly that it was earned; and though he brought it the same day to his master, yet he was staked to the ground for his pretended negligence, and was just going to receive a hundred lashes, but for a gentleman who begged him off fifty. This poor man was very industrious, and by his frugality had saved so much money, by working on shipboard, that he had got a white man to buy him a boat, unknown to his master. Some time after he had this little estate, the governor wanted a boat to bring his sugar from different parts of the island; and, knowing this to be a negro man's boat, he seized upon it for himself, and would not pay the owner a farthing. The man on this went to his master, and complained to him of this act of the governor; but the only satisfaction he received was to be damned very heartily by his master, who asked him how dared any of his negroes to have a boat. If the justly merited ruin of the governor's fortune could be any gratification to the poor man he had thus robbed, he was not without consolation. Extortion and rapine are poor providers; and sometime after this the governor died in the King's Bench, in England, as I was told, in great poverty. The last war favored this poor negro man, and he found some

---

*These pisterines are of the value of a shilling.

means to escape from his Christian master; he came to England, where I saw him afterwards several times. Such treatment as this often drives these miserable wretches to despair, and they run away from their masters at the hazard of their lives. Many of them, in this place, unable to get their pay when they have earned it, and fearing to be flogged, as usual, if they return home without it, run away where they can for shelter, and a reward is often offered to bring them in dead or alive. My master used sometimes in these cases, to agree with their owners, and to settle with them himself; and thereby he saved many of them a flogging.

Once, for a few days, I was let out to fit a vessel, and I had no victuals allowed me by either party; at last I told my master of this treatment, and he took me away from him. In many of the estates, on the different islands where I used to be sent for rum or sugar, they would not deliver it to me, or any other negro; he was therefore obliged to send a white man along with me to those places; and then he used to pay him from six to ten pisterines a day. From being thus employed, during the time I served Mr. King, in going about the different estates on the island, I had all the opportunity I could wish for, to see the dreadful usage of the poor men; usage that reconciled me to my situation, and made me bless God for the hands into which I had fallen.

I had the good fortune to please my master in every department in which he employed me; and there was scarcely any part of his business, or household affairs, in which I was not occasionally engaged. I often supplied the place of a clerk, in receiving and delivering cargos to the ships, in tending stores, and delivering goods: and, besides this, I used to shave and dress my master when convenient, and take care of his horse; and when it was necessary, which was very often, I worked likewise on board of different vessels of his. By these means I became very useful to my master, and saved him, as he used to acknowledge, above a hundred pounds a year. Nor did he scruple to say I was of more advantage to him than any of his clerks; though their usual wages in the West Indies are from sixty to a hundred pounds current a year.

I have sometimes heard it asserted, that a negro cannot earn his master the first cost; but nothing can be further from the truth. I suppose nine-tenths of the mechanics throughout the West Indies are negro slaves; and I well know the coopers among them earn two dollars a day; the carpenters the same, and oftentimes more; as also the masons, smiths, and fishermen, etc., and I have known many slaves whose masters would not take a thousand pounds current for them. But surely this assertion refutes itself; for, if it be true, why do the planters and merchants pay such a price for slaves? And, above all, why do those who make this assertion exclaim the most loudly against the abolition of the slave trade? So much are we blinded, and to such inconsistent arguments are they driven by mistaken interest! I grant, indeed, that slaves are sometimes, by half-feeding, half-clothing, overworking, and stripes, reduced so low, that they are turned out as unfit for service, and left to perish in the woods, or expire on a dunghill.

My master was several times offered by different gentlemen one hundred guineas for me; but he always told them he would not sell me, to my great joy: and I used to double my diligence and care for fear of getting into the hands of those men who did not allow a valuable slave the common support of life. Many of them even used to find fault with my master for feeding his slaves so well as he did; although I often went hungry, and an Englishman might think my fare very indifferent; but he used to tell them he always would do it, because the slaves thereby looked better and did more work.

While I was thus employed by my master, I was often a witness to cruelties of every kind, which were exercised on my unhappy fellow slaves. I used frequently to have different cargos of new negroes in my care for sale; and it was almost a constant practice with our clerks, and other whites, to commit violent depredations on the chastity of the female slaves; and these I was, though with reluctance, obliged to submit to at all times, being unable to help them. When we have had some of these slaves on board my master's vessels to carry them to other islands, or to America, I have known our mates to commit these acts most shamefully, to the disgrace, not of Christians only, but of men. I have even known them [to] gratify their brutal passion with females not ten years old; and these abominations some of them practiced to such scandalous excess, that one of our captains discharged the mate and others on that account. And yet in Montserrat I have seen a negro man staked to the ground, and cut most shockingly, and then his ears cut off bit by bit, because he had been connected with a white woman who was a common prostitute: as if it were no crime in the whites to rob an innocent African girl of her virtue; but most heinous in a black man only to gratify a passion of nature, where the temptation was offered by one of a different color, though the most abandoned woman of her species.

One Mr. Drummond told me that he had sold 41,000 negroes, and that he once cut off a negro man's leg for running away—I asked him, if the man had died in the operation, how he as a Christian could answer for the horrid act before God? and he told me, answering was a thing of another world; what he thought and did were policy. I told him that the Christian doctrine taught us to do unto others as we would that others should do unto us. He then said that his scheme had the desired effect—it cured that man and some others of running away.

Another negro man was half-hanged, and then burnt, for attempting to poison a cruel overseer. Thus by repeated cruelties are the wretches first urged to despair, and then murdered, because they still retain so much of human nature about them as to wish to put an end to their misery, and retaliate on their tyrants! These overseers are indeed for the most part persons of the worst character of any denomination of men in the West Indies. Unfortunately, many humane gentlemen, by not residing on their estates, are obliged to leave the management of them in the hands of these human butchers, who cut and mangle the slaves in a shocking manner on the most trifling occasions, and altogether treat them in every respect like brutes. They pay no regard to the situation of pregnant women, nor the least attention to the lodging of the field negroes. Their huts, which ought to be well covered, and the place dry where they take their little repose, are often open sheds, built in damp places; so that, when the poor creatures return tired from the toils of the field, they contract many disorders from being exposed to the damp air in this uncomfortable state, while they are heated, and their pores are open. This neglect certainly conspires with many others to cause a decrease in the births as well as in the lives of the grown negroes. I can quote many instances of gentlemen who reside on their estates in the West Indies and then the scene is quite changed; the negroes are treated with lenity and proper care, by which their lives are prolonged, and their masters profited. To the honor of humanity, I knew several gentlemen who managed their estates in this manner; and they found that benevolence was their true interest. And, among many I could mention in several of the islands, I knew one in Montserrat* whose slaves looked remarkably well, and never needed any fresh supplies of negroes; and there are many other estates, especially in Barbados, which, from such judicious treatment, need no fresh stock of negroes at any time. I have the honor of knowing a most worthy and humane gentleman, who is a native of Barbados, and has estates there.† This gentleman has written a treatise on the usage of his

*Mr. Dubury, and many others, in Monserrat.
† Sir Philip Gibbes, Bart, Barbados.

own slaves. He allows them two hours for refreshment at midday, and many other indulgences and comforts, particularly in their lying; and, besides this, he raises more provisions on his estate than they can destroy; so that by these attentions he saves the lives of his negroes, and keeps them healthy, and as happy as the condition of slavery can admit. I myself, as shall appear in the sequel, managed an estate, where, by those attentions, the negroes were uncommonly cheerful and healthy, and did more work by half than by the common mode of treatment they usually do. For want, therefore, of such care and attention to the poor negroes, and otherwise oppressed as they are, it is no wonder that the decrease should require 20,000 new negroes annually to fill up the vacant places of the dead.

Even in Barbados, notwithstanding those humane exceptions which I have mentioned, and others I am acquainted with, which justly make it quoted as a place where slaves meet with the best treatment, and need fewest recruits of any in the West Indies, yet this island requires 1,000 negroes annually to keep up the original stock, which is only 80,000. So that the whole term of a negro's life may be said to be there but sixteen years!* and yet the climate here is in every respect the same as that from which they are taken, except in being more wholesome. Do the British colonies decrease in this manner? And yet what a prodigious difference is there between an English and West India climate!

While I was in Montserrat, I knew a negro man, named Emanuel Sankey, who endeavored to escape from his miserable bondage, by concealing himself on board of a London ship: But fate did not favor the poor oppressed man; for, being discovered when the vessel was under sail, he was delivered up again to his master. This *Christian master* immediately pinned the wretch down to the ground, at each wrist and ankle, and then took some sticks of sealing wax, and lighted them, and dropped it all over his back. There was another master who was noted for cruelty, and I believe he had not a slave but what had been cut, and had pieces fairly taken out of the flesh: and after they had been punished thus, he used to make them get into a long wooden box or case he had for that purpose, in which he shut them up during [his] pleasure. It was just about the height and breadth of a man; and the poor wretches had no room when in the case to move.

It was very common in several of the islands, particularly in St.

---

*Benezet's *Account of Guinea,* p. 16.

Kitt's, for the slaves to be branded with the initial letters of their master's name, and a load of heavy iron hooks hung about their necks. Indeed, on the most trifling occasions they were loaded with chains, and often other instruments of torture were added. The iron muzzle, thumbscrews, etc. are so well known as not to need a description, and were sometimes applied for the slightest faults. I have seen a negro beaten till some of his bones were broken, for only letting a pot boil over. It is not uncommon after a flogging to make slaves go on their knees, and thank their owners, and pray, or rather say, God bless them. I have often asked many of the men slaves (who used to go several miles to their wives, and late in the night, after having been wearied with a hard day's labor) why they went so far for wives, and why they did not take them of their own master's negro women, and particularly those who lived together as household slaves? Their answers have ever been—"Because when the master or mistress choose to punish the women, they make the husbands flog their own wives, and that they could not bear to do." Is it surprising that usage like this should drive the poor creatures to despair, and make them seek a refuge in death from those evils which render their lives intolerable—while

> *With shudd'ring horror pale, and eyes aghast,*
> *They view their lamentable lot, and find*
> *No rest!*

This they frequently do. A negro man on board a vessel of my master's, while I belonged to her, having been put in irons for some trifling misdemeanor, and kept in that state for some days, being weary of life, took an opportunity of jumping overboard into the sea; however, he was picked up without being drowned. Another, whose life was also a burden to him, resolved to starve himself to death, and refused to eat any victuals: this procured him a severe flogging; and he also, on the first occasion which offered, jumped overboard at Charleston [S.C.], but was saved.

Nor is there any greater regard shown to the little property than there is to the persons and lives of the negroes. I have already related an instance or two of particular oppression out of many which I have witnessed; but the following is frequent in all the islands. The wretched field slaves, after toiling all the day for an unfeeling owner, who gives them but little victuals, steal sometimes a few moments from rest or refreshment to gather some small portion of grass, according as their time will admit. This they commonly tie up in a parcel; either a bit's worth (six pence) or half a bit's worth; and bring it to town, or to the market to sell. Nothing is more common than for the white people on this occasion to take the grass from them without paying for it; and not only so, but too often also to my knowledge, our clerks, and many others, at the same time, have committed acts of violence on the poor, wretched, and helpless females, whom I have seen for hours stand crying to no purpose, and get no redress or pay of any kind. Is not this one common and crying sin, enough to bring down God's judgment on the islands? He tells us the oppressor and the oppressed are both in his hands; and if these are not the poor, the broken-hearted, the blind, the captive, the bruised, which our Savior speaks of, who are they? One of these depredators once, in St. Eustatius, came on board of our vessel, and bought some fowls and pigs of me; and a whole day after his departure with the things, he returned again, and wanted his money back: I refused to give it, and, not seeing my captain on board, he began the common pranks with me; and swore he would even break open my chest and take my money. I therefore expected, as my captain was absent, that he would be as good as his word; and he was just proceeding to strike me, when fortunately a British seaman on board, whose heart had not been debauched by a West India climate, interposed and prevented him. But had the cruel man struck me, I certainly should have defended myself at the hazard of my life; for what is life to a man thus oppressed? He went away, however, swearing; and threatened that whenever he caught me on shore he would shoot me, and pay for me afterwards.

The small account in which the life of a negro is held in the West Indies, is so universally known, that it might seem impertinent to quote the following extract, if some people had not been hardy enough of late to assert, that negroes are on the same footing in that respect as Europeans. By the 329th Act, page 125, of the Assembly of Barbados, it is enacted, "That if any negro, or other slave, under punishment by his master, or his order, for running away, or any other crime or misdemeanor towards his said master, unfortunately shall suffer in life or member, no person whatsoever shall be liable to a fine; but if any man shall out of *wantonness, or only of bloody-mindedness or cruel intention, willfully kill a negro or other slave, of his own, he shall pay into the public treasury fifteen pounds sterling.*" And it is the same in most, if not all, of the West India islands. Is not this one of the many acts of the island, which call loudly for redress? And do not the Assembly which enacted it, deserve the appellation of savages and brutes rather than of Christians and men? It is an act at once unmerciful, unjust, and unwise; which for cruelty would disgrace an assembly of those who are called barbarians; and for its injustice and *insanity* would shock the morality and common sense of a Samiade or Hottentot.

Shocking as this and many other acts of the bloody West India code at first view appear, how is the iniquity of it heightened when we consider to whom it may be extended. Mr. James Tobin, a zealous laborer in the vineyard of slavery, gives an account* of a French planter of his acquaintance in the island of Martinique, who showed him many mulattoes working in the fields like beasts of burden; and he told Mr. Tobin, these were all the produce of his own loins! And I myself have known similar instances. Pray, reader, are these sons and daughters of the French planter less his children by being begotten on black women! And what must be the virtue of those legislators, and the feelings of those fathers, who estimate the lives of their sons, however begotten, at no more than fifteen pounds, though they should be murdered, as the act says, *out of wantonness and bloody-mindedness!* But is not the slave trade entirely at war with the heart of man? And surely that which is begun, by breaking down the barriers of virtue, involves in its continuance destruction to every principle, and buries all sentiments in ruin!

I have often seen slaves, particularly those who were meager, in different islands, put into scales and weighed, and then sold from three pence to six pence or nine pence a pound. My master, however, whose humanity was shocked at this mode, used to sell such by the lump. And at or after a sale, even those negroes born in the islands, it is not uncommon to see taken from their wives, wives taken from their husbands, and children from their parents, and sent off to other islands, and wherever else their merciless lords choose; and probably never more during life see each other! Oftentimes my heart has bled at these partings; when the friends of the departed have been at the waterside, and with sighs and tears have kept their eyes fixed on the vessel till it went out of sight.

A poor Creole negro I knew well, who, after having often been thus transported from island to island, at last resided at Montserrat. This man used to tell me many melancholy tales of himself. Generally, after he had done working for his master, he used to employ his few leisure moments to go a-fishing. When he had caught any fish, his master

*In his "Cursory Remarks."

would frequently take them from him without paying him; and at other times some other white people would serve him in the same manner. One day he said to me, very movingly, "Sometimes when a white man take away my fish, I go to my master, and he get me my right; and when my master by strength take away my fishes, what me must do? I can't go to anybody to be righted"; then, said the poor man, looking up above, "I must look up to God Mighty in the top for right." This artless tale moved me much, and I could not help feeling the just cause Moses had in redressing his brother against the Egyptian. I exhorted the man to look up still to the God on the top, since there was no redress below. Though I little thought then that I myself should more than once experience such imposition, and need the same exhortation hereafter, in my own transactions in the islands; and that even this poor man and I should sometime after suffer together in the same manner, as shall be related hereafter.

Nor was such usage as this confined to particular places or individuals; for in all the different islands in which I have been (and I have visited no less than fifteen) the treatment of the slaves was nearly the same; so nearly indeed, that the history of an island, or even a plantation, with a few such exceptions as I have mentioned, might serve for a history of the whole. Such a tendency has the slave trade to debauch men's minds, and harden them to every feeling of humanity! For I will not suppose that the dealers in slaves are born worse than other men— No! it is the fatality of this mistaken avarice that it corrupts the milk of human kindness, and turns it into gall. And, had the pursuits of those men been different, they might have been as generous, as tenderhearted, and just, as they are unfeeling, rapacious, and cruel. Surely this traffic cannot be good, which spreads like a pestilence, and taints what it touches! which violates that first natural right of mankind, equality and independency, and gives one man a dominion over his fellows which God could never intend! For it raises the owner to a state as far above man as it depresses the slave below it; and, with all the presumption of human pride, sets a distinction between them, immeasurable in extent, and endless in duration! Yet how mistaken is the avarice even of the planters! Are slaves more useful by being thus humbled to the condition of brutes, than they would be if suffered to enjoy the privileges of men? The freedom which diffuses health and prosperity throughout Britain answers you—no. When you make men slaves, you deprive them of half their virtue, you set them in your own conduct an example of fraud, rapine, and cruelty, and compel them to live with you in a state of war; and yet you complain that they are not honest and faithful! You stupefy them with stripes, and think it necessary to keep them in a state of ignorance; and yet you assert that they are incapable of learning; that their minds are such a barren soil or moor, that culture would be lost on them; and that they come from a climate, where nature (though prodigal of her bounties in a degree unknown to yourselves) has left man alone scant and unfinished, and incapable of enjoying the treasures she had poured out for him! An assertion at once impious and absurd.★ Why do you use those instruments of torture? Are they fit to be applied by one rational being to another? And are you not struck with shame and mortification, to see the partakers of your nature reduced so low? But, above all, are there no dangers attending this mode of treatment? Are you not hourly in dread of an insurrection? Nor would it be surprising: for when

> *No peace is given*
> *To us enslav'd, but custody severe;*
> *And stripes and arbitrary punishment*
> *Inflicted—What peace can we return?*
> *But to our power, hostility and hate;*
> *Untam'd reluctance, and revenge tho' slow,*
> *Yet ever plotting how the conqueror least*
> *May reap his conquest, and may least rejoice*
> *In doing what we most in suf'ring feel.*

But by changing your conduct, and treating your slaves as men, every cause of fear would be banished. They would be faithful, honest, intelligent, and vigorous; and peace, prosperity, and happiness would attend you.

Chapter VI

Some account of Brimstone Hill in Montserrat—The Author surprised by two earthquakes—Favorable change in the Author's situation—He commences merchant with three pence—His various success in dealing in the different islands, and America, and the impositions he meets with

★See the *Observations on a Guinea Voyage,* in a series of letters to the Rev. T. Clarkson, by James Field, Stanfield, in 1788, p. 21, 22.—"The subjects of the king of Benin, at Gatoe, where I was, had their markets regular and well stocked; they teemed with luxuries unknown to the Europeans."

in his transactions with white people—A curious imposition on human nature—Danger of the surfs in the West Indies—Remarkable instance of kidnapping a free mulatto—The Author is nearly murdered by Dr. Perkins, in Savannah.

IN THE PRECEDING CHAPTER I have set before the reader a few of those many instances of oppression, extortion, and cruelty, which I have been a witness to in the West Indies; but, were I to enumerate them all, the catalogue would be tedious and disgusting. The punishments of the slaves, on every trifling occasion, are so frequent, and so well known, together with the different instruments with which they are tortured, that it cannot any longer afford novelty to recite them; and they are too shocking to yield delight either to the writer or the reader. I shall therefore hereafter only mention such as incidently befell myself in the course of my adventures.

In the variety of departments in which I was employed by my master, I had an opportunity of seeing many curious scenes in different islands; but, above all, I was struck with a celebrated curiosity called Brimstone Hill, which is a high and steep mountain, some few miles from the town of Plymouth, in Montserrat. I had often heard of some wonders that were to be seen on this hill, and I went once with some white and black people to visit it. When we arrived at the top, I saw under different cliffs great flakes of brimstone, occasioned by the steams of various little ponds, which were then boiling naturally in the earth. Some of these ponds were as white as milk, some quite blue, and many others of different colors. I had taken some potatoes with me, and I put them into different ponds, and in a few minutes they were well boiled. I tasted some of them, but they were very sulfurous; and the silver shoe buckles, and all the other things of that metal we had among us, were in a little time turned as black as lead.

Whilst I was in the island, one night I felt a strange sensation, namely, I was told that the house where I lived was haunted by spirits. And once, at midnight, as I was sleeping on a large chest, I felt the whole building shake in an uncommon and astonishing manner; so much so, that it shook me off the chest where I then lay. I was exceedingly frightened, and thought it was indeed the visitation of the spirits. It threw me into such a tremor as is not to be described. I instantly covered my head all over as I lay, and did not know what to think or do; and in this consternation, a gentleman who lay in the next room just by me came out, and I was glad to hear him, and made a sham cough, and he asked me if I felt the earthquake. I told him I was shook off the chest where I lay, but did not know what occasioned it; and he told me it was an earthquake, and shook him out of his bed. At hearing this I became easy in my mind.

At another time a circumstance of this kind happened, when I was on board of a vessel at Montserrat Road, at midnight, as we were asleep, and it shook the vessel in the most unaccountable manner imaginable, and to me it seemed as when a vessel or a boat runs on gravel, as near as I can describe it. Many things on board were moved out of their places, but happily no damage was done.

About the end of the year 1763, kind Providence seemed to appear rather more favorable to me. One of my master's vessels, a Bermuda sloop, about sixty tons burden, was commanded by one Captain Thomas Farmer, an Englishman, a very alert and active man, who gained my master a great deal of money by his good management in carrying passengers from one island to another; but very often his sailors used to get drunk, and run away with the vessel's boat, which hindered him in his business very much. This man had taken a liking to me; and many different times begged of my master to let me go a trip with him as a sailor: but he would tell him he could not spare me, though the vessel sometimes could not go for want of hands, for sailors were generally very scarce in the island. However, at last, from necessity or force, my master was prevailed on, though very reluctantly, to let me go with this captain; but he gave him great charge to take care that I did not run away; for if I did, he would make him pay for me. This being the case, the captain had for some time a sharp eye upon me whenever the vessel anchored: and as soon as she returned I was sent for on shore again. Thus was I slaving, as it were for life, sometimes at one thing, and sometimes at another; so that the captain and I were nearly the most useful men in my master's employment. I also became so useful to the captain on shipboard, that many times, when he used to ask me to go with him, though it should be but for twenty-four hours to some of the islands near us, my master would answer he could not spare me; at which the captain would swear, and would not go the trip, and tell my master I was better to him on board than any three white men he had; for they used to behave ill in many respects, particularly in getting drunk, and then frequently got the boat stove, so as to hinder the vessel from coming back so soon as she might have done. This my master knew very well; and, at last, by the captain's constant entreaties, after I had been several times with him, one day, to my great joy, told me the captain would not let him rest, and asked whether I would go aboard as a sailor, or stay on shore and mind the stores, for he could not bear any longer to be plagued in this manner. I was very happy at this proposal, for I immediately thought I might in time stand some chance by being on board to get a little money, or possibly make my escape if I should be used ill: I also expected to get better food, and in greater abundance; for I had oftentimes felt much hunger, though my master treated his slaves, as I have observed, uncommonly well; I therefore, without hesitation, answered him, that I would go and be a sailor if he pleased. Accordingly I was ordered on board directly. Nevertheless, between the vessel and the shore, when she was in port, I had little or no rest, as my master always wished to have me along with him. Indeed he was a very pleasant gentleman, and but for my expectations on ship-board I should not have thought of leaving him. But the captain liked me also very much, and I was entirely his right-hand man. I did all I could to deserve his favor, and in return I received better treatment from him than any other I believe ever met with in the West Indies in my situation.

After I had been sailing for some time with this captain, I at length endeavored to try my luck, and commence merchant. I had but a very small capital to begin with; for one single half-bit, which is equal to three pence in England, made up my whole stock. However, I trusted to the Lord to be with me; and at one of our trips to St. Eustatius, a Dutch island, I bought a glass tumbler with my half-bit, and when I came to Montserrat I sold it for a bit, or six pence. Luckily we made several successive trips to St. Eustatius (which was a general mart for the West Indies, about twenty leagues from Montserrat), and in our next, finding my tumbler so profitable, with this one bit I bought two tumblers more; and when I came back I sold them for two bits equal to a shilling sterling. When we went again, I bought with these two bits four more of these glasses, which I sold for four bits on our return to Montserrat; and in our next voyage to St. Eustatius, I bought two glasses with one bit, and with the other three I bought a jug of Geneva, nearly about three pints in measure. When we came to Montserrat, I sold the gin for eight bits, and the tumblers for two, so that my capital now amounted in all to a dollar, well husbanded and acquired in the space of a month or six weeks, when I blessed the Lord that I was so rich. As we sailed to different islands, I laid this money out in various things occasionally and it used to turn to very good account, especially when we went to Guadaloupe, Grenada, and the rest of the French islands. Thus was I going all about the islands upwards of four years, and ever trading as I went, during which I experienced many instances of ill usage, and have seen many injuries done to other negroes in our dealings with whites; and, amidst our recreations, when we have been dancing and merrymaking, they without cause, have molested and insulted us. Indeed I was more than once obliged to look up to God on high, as I had advised the poor fisherman sometime before. And I had not been long trading for myself in the manner I have related above, when I experienced the like trial in company with him as follows: This man being used to the water, was, upon an emergency, put on board of us by his master to work as another hand, on a voyage to Santa Cruz; and at our sailing he had brought his little all for a venture, which consisted of six bits' worth of limes and oranges in a bag; I had also my whole stock; which was about twelve bits' worth of the same kind of goods, separate in two bags; for we had heard these fruits sold well in that island. When we came there, in some little convenient time, he and I went ashore with our fruits to sell them; but we had scarcely landed, when we were met by two white men, who presently took our three bags from us. We could not at first guess what they meant to do, and for some time we thought they were jesting with us; but they too soon let us know otherwise: for they took our ventures immediately to a house hard by, and adjoining the fort, while we followed all the way begging of them to give us our fruits, but in vain. They not only refused to return them, but swore at us, and threatened if we did not immediately depart, they would flog us well. We told them these three bags were all we were worth in the world; that we brought them with us to sell, and that we came from Montserrat, and showed them the vessel. But this was rather against us, as they now saw we were strangers as well as slaves. They still therefore swore, and desired us to be gone; and even took sticks to beat us; while we, seeing they meant what they said, went off in the greatest confusion and despair. Thus, in the very minute of gaining more by three times than I ever did by any venture in my life before, was I deprived of every farthing I was worth. An insupportable misfortune! but how to help ourselves we knew not. In our consternation we went to the commanding officer of the fort, and told him how we had been served by some of his people; but we obtained not the least redress: he answered our complaints only by a volley of imprecations against us, and immediately took a horsewhip, in order to chastise us, so that we were obliged to turn out much faster than we came in. I now, in the agony of distress and indignation, wished that the ire of God, in his forked lightning, might transfix these cruel oppressors among the dead. Still, however, we persevered; went back again to the house, and begged and besought them again and again for our fruits, till at last some other people that were in the house asked if we would be contented if they kept one bag, and gave us the other two. We, seeing no remedy whatever, consented to this; and they, observing one bag to have both kinds of fruit in it, which belonged to my companion, kept that; and the other two, which were mine, they gave us back. As soon as I got them, I ran as fast as I could and got the first negro man I could to help me off; my companion, however, stayed a little longer to plead; he told them the bag they had was his, and likewise all that he was worth in the world; but this was of no avail, and he was obliged to return without it. The poor old man, wringing his hands, cried bitterly for his loss; and, indeed, he then did look up to God on high, which so moved me with pity for him, that I gave him nearly one third of my fruits. We then proceeded to the market to sell them; and Providence was more favorable to us than we could have expected, for we sold our fruits uncommonly well; I got for mine about thirty-seven bits. Such a surprising reverse of fortune in so short a space of time seemed like a dream, and proved no small encouragement for me to trust the Lord in any situation. My captain afterwards frequently used to take my part, and get me my right when I have been plundered or used ill by these tender Christian depredators; among whom I have shuddered to observe the unceasing blasphemous execrations which are wantonly thrown out by persons of all ages and conditions; not only without occasion, but even as if they were indulgences and pleasures.

At one of our trips to St. Kitt's, I had eleven bits of my own; and my friendly captain lent me five more, with which I bought a Bible. I was very glad to get this book, which I scarcely could meet with anywhere. I think there was none sold in Montserrat; and, much to my grief, from being forced out of the *Aetna* in the manner I have related, my Bible, and the *Guide to the Indians,* the two books I loved above all others, were left behind.

While I was in this place, St. Kitt's, a very curious imposition on human nature took place: A white man wanted to marry in the church a free black woman that had land and slaves in Montserrat: but the clergyman told him it was against the law of the place to marry a white and a black in the church. The man then asked to be married on the water, to which the parson consented, and the two lovers went in one boat, and the parson and clerk in another, and thus the ceremony was performed. After this the loving pair came on board our vessel, and my captain treated them extremely well, and brought them safe to Montserrat.

The reader cannot but judge of the irksomeness of this situation to a mind like mine, in being daily exposed to new hardships and impositions, after having seen many better days, and been, as it were, in a state of freedom and plenty; added to which, every part of the world I had hitherto been in seemed to me a paradise in comparison of the West Indies. My mind was therefore hourly replete with inventions and thoughts of being freed, and, if possible, by honest and honorable means; for I always remembered the old adage, and I trust it has ever been my ruling principle, "that honesty is the best policy"; and likewise that other golden precept—"To do unto all men as I would they should do unto me." However, as I was from early years a predestinarian, I thought whatever fate had determined must ever come to pass; and therefore, if ever it were my lot to be freed, nothing could prevent me, although I should at present see no means or hope to obtain my freedom; on the other hand, if it were my fate not to be freed, I never should be so, and all my endeavors for that purpose would be fruitless. In the midst of these thoughts I therefore looked up with prayers anxiously to God for my liberty; and at the same time used every honest means, and did all that was possible on my part to obtain it. In process of time I became master of a few pounds, and in a fair way of making more, which my friendly captain knew very well: this occasioned him sometimes to take liberties with me; but whenever he treated me waspishly, I used plainly to tell him my mind, and that I would die before I would be imposed upon as other negroes were, and that to me life had lost its relish when liberty was gone. This I said, although I foresaw my then well-being or future hopes of freedom (humanly speaking) depended on this man. However, as he could not bear the thoughts of my not sailing with him, he always became mild on my threats: I therefore continued with him; and, from my great attention to his orders and his business, I gained him credit, and through his kindness to me I at last procured my liberty. While I thus went on, filled with the thoughts of freedom, and resisting oppression as well as I was able, my life hung daily in suspense, particularly in the surfs I have formerly mentioned, as I could not swim. These are extremely violent throughout the West Indies, and I was ever exposed to their howling rage and devouring fury in all the islands. I have seen them strike and toss a boat right up on end, and maim several on board. Once in the island of Grenada, when I and about eight others were pulling a large boat with two puncheons of water in it, a surf struck us, and drove the boat and all in it about half a stone's throw, among some trees, and above the high-water mark. We were obliged to get all the assistance we could from the nearest estate to mend the boat, and launch it into the water again. At Montserrat one night, in pressing hard to get off the shore on board, the punt was over-set with us four times; the first time I was very near being drowned; however the jacket I had on kept me above water a little space of time, while I called on a man near me who was a good swimmer, and told him I could not swim; he then made haste to me, and, just as I was sink-ing, he caught hold of me, and brought me to sounding, and then he went and brought the punt also. As soon as we had turned the water out of her, lest we should be used ill for being absent, we attempted again three times more, and as often the horrid surfs served us as at first: but at last, the fifth time we attempted, we gained our point, at the immi-nent hazard of our lives. One day also, at Old Road, in Montserrat, our captain, and three men besides myself, were going in a large canoe in quest of rum and sugar, when a single surf tossed the canoe an amaz-ing distance from the water, and some of us near a stone's throw from each other; most of us were very much bruised; so that I and many more often said, and really thought, that there was not such another place under the heavens as this. I longed, therefore, much to leave it, and daily wished to see my master's promise performed of going to Philadelphia.

While we lay in this place, a very cruel thing happened on board of our sloop, which filled me with horror; though I found afterward such practices were frequent. There was a very clever and decent free young mulatto man who sailed a long time with us; he had a free woman for his wife, by whom he had a child; and she was then living on shore, and all very happy. Our captain and mate, and other people on board, and several elsewhere, even the natives of Bermuda, then with us, all knew this young man from a child that he was always free, and no one had ever claimed him as their property: however, as might too often over-comes right in these parts, it happened that a Bermuda captain, whose vessel lay there for a few days in the road, came on board us, and seeing the mulatto man, whose name was Joseph Clipson, he told him he was not free, and that he had orders from his master to bring him to Ber-muda. The poor man could not believe the captain to be in earnest; but he was very soon undeceived, his men laying violent hands on him; and although he showed a certificate of his being born free in St. Kitt's, and most people on board knew that he served his time to boat-building, and always passed for a freeman, yet he was forcibly taken out of our vessel. He then asked to be carried ashore before the secretary or magistrates, and these infernal invaders of human rights promised him he should; but, instead of that, they carried him on board of the other vessel: and the next day, without giving the poor man any hearing on shore, or suffering him even to see his wife or child, he was carried away, and probably doomed never more in this world to see them again. Nor was this the only instance of this kind of barbarity I was a witness to. I have since often seen in Jamaica, and other islands, freemen, whom I have known in America, thus villainously trepanned and held in bondage. I have heard of two similar practices even in Philadelphia: and were it not for the benevolence of the Quakers in that city, many of the sable race, who now breathe the air of liberty, would, I believe, be groaning indeed under some planter's chains. These things opened my mind to a new scene of horror, to which I had been before a stranger. Hitherto I had thought only slavery dreadful; but the state of a free negro appeared to me now equally so at least, and in some respects even worse, for they live in constant alarm for their liberty, which is but nominal, for they are universally insulted and plundered, without the possibility of redress; for such is the equity of the West Indian laws, that no free negro's evidence will be admitted in their courts of justice. In this situation is it surprising that slaves, when mildly treated, should prefer even the misery of slavery to such a mockery of freedom? I was now completely disgusted with the West Indies, and thought I should never be entirely free until I had left them.

> *With thoughts like these my anxious boding mind*
> *Recall'd those pleasing scenes I left behind;*
> *Scenes where fair Liberty in bright array*
> *Makes darkness bright, and e'en illumines day;*
> *Where no complexion, wealth or station, can*
> *Protect the wretch who makes a slave of man.*

I determined to make every exertion to obtain my freedom, and to return to old England. For this purpose, I thought a knowledge of navigation might be of use to me; for, though I did not intend to run away, unless I should be ill used, yet, in such a case, if I understood navigation, I might attempt my escape in our sloop, which was one of the swiftest sailing vessels in the West Indies, and I could be at no loss for hands to join me: and, if I should make this attempt, I had intended to have gone for England; but this, as I said, was only to be in the event of my meeting with any ill usage. I therefore employed the mate of our vessel to teach me navigation, for which I agreed to give him twenty-four dollars, and actually paid him part of the money down; though, when the captain, sometime after, came to know that the mate was to have such a sum for teaching me, he rebuked him, and said it was a shame for him to take any money from me. However, my progress in this useful art was much retarded, by the constancy of our work. Had I wished to run away, I did not want opportunities, which frequently presented themselves; and particularly at one time, soon after this. When we were at the island of Guadaloupe, there was a large fleet of merchantmen bound for old France; and, seamen then being very scarce, they gave from fifteen to twenty pounds a man for the run. Our mate, and all the white sailors, left our vessel on this account, and went on board of the French ships. They would have had me also to go with them, for they regarded me, and swore to protect me if I would go; and, as the fleet was to sail the next day, I really believe I could have got safe to Europe at that time. However, as my master was kind, I would not attempt to leave him; still remembering the old maxim, that "honesty is the best policy," I suffered them to go without me. Indeed my captain was much afraid of my leaving him and the vessel at that time, as I had so fair an opportunity: but, I thank God, this fidelity of mine turned out much to my advantage hereafter, when I did not in the least think of it; and made me so much in favor with the captain, that he used now and then to teach me some parts of navigation himself; but some of our passengers, and others, seeing this, found much fault with him for it, saying, it was a very dangerous thing to let a negro know navigation; thus I was hindered again in my pursuits. About the latter end of the year 1764, my master bought a larger sloop, called the *Prudence,* about seventy or eighty tons, of which my captain had the command. I went with him into this vessel, and we took a load of new slaves for Georgia and Charleston. My master now left me entirely to the captain, though he still wished for me to be with him; but I, who always much wished to lose sight of the West Indies, was not a little rejoiced at the thoughts of seeing any other country. Therefore, relying on the goodness of my captain, I got ready all the little venture I could; and, when the vessel was ready, we sailed to my great joy. When we got to our destined places, Georgia and Charleston, I expected I should have an opportunity of selling my little property to advantage; but here, particularly in Charleston, I met with buyers, white men, who imposed on me as in other places. Notwithstanding, I was resolved to have fortitude, thinking no lot or trial too hard when kind heaven is the rewarder.

We soon got loaded again, and returned to Montserrat; and there, among the rest of the islands, I sold my goods well; and in this manner I continued trading during the year 1764; meeting with various scenes of imposition, as usual. After this, my master fitted out his vessel for Philadelphia, in the year 1765; and during the time we were loading her, and getting ready for the voyage, I worked with redoubled alacrity, from the hope of getting money enough by these voyages to buy my freedom, if it should please God; and also to see the city of Philadelphia, which I had heard a great deal about for some years past; besides which, I had always longed to prove my master's promise the first day I came to him. In the midst of these elevated ideas, and while I was about getting my little merchandise in readiness, one Sunday my master sent for me to his house. When I came there I found him and the captain together; and, on my going in, I was struck with astonishment at his telling me he heard that I meant to run away from him when I got to Philadelphia: "And therefore," said he, "I must sell you again: you cost me a great deal of money, no less than forty pounds sterling; and it will not do to lose so much. You are a valuable fellow," continued he, "and I can get any day for you one hundred guineas, from many gentlemen in this island." And then he told me of Captain Doran's brother-in-law, a severe master, who ever wanted to buy me to make me his overseer. My captain also said he could get much more than a hundred guineas for me in Carolina. This I knew to be a fact: for the gentleman that wanted to buy me came off several times on board of us, and spoke to me to live with him, and said he would use me well. When I asked what work he would put me to, he said, as I was a sailor, he would make me a captain of one of his rice vessels. But I refused; and fearing, at the same time, by a sudden turn I saw in the captain's temper, he might mean to sell me, I told the gentleman I would not live with him on any condition, and that I certainly would run away with his vessel: but he said he did not fear that, as he would catch me again; and then he told me how cruelly he would serve me if I should do so. My captain, however, gave him to understand that I knew something of navigation: so he thought better of it; and, to my great joy, he went away. I now told my master I did not say I would run away in Philadelphia; neither did I mean it, as he did not use me ill, nor yet the captain: for if they did, I certainly would have made some attempts before now;

but as I thought that if it were God's will I ever should be freed it would be so; and, on the contrary, if it was not his will, it would not happen; so I hoped, if ever I were freed, whilst I was used well, it should be by honest means; but as I could not help myself, he must do as he pleased! I could only hope and trust to the God of heaven; and at that instant my mind was big with inventions, and full of schemes to escape. I then appealed to the captain, whether ever he saw any sign of my making the least attempt to run away; and asked him if I did not always come on board according to the time for which he gave me liberty; and, more particularly, when all our men left us at Guadaloupe, and went on board of the French fleet, and advised me to go with them, whether I might not, and that he could not have got me again. To my no small surprise, and very great joy, the captain confirmed every syllable that I had said, and even more; for he said he had tried different times to see if I would make any attempt of this kind, both at St. Eustatius and in America, and he never found that I made the smallest; but, on the contrary, I always came on board according to his orders; and he did really believe, if I ever meant to run away, that, as I could never have had a better opportunity, I would have done it the night the mate and all the people left our vessel at Guadaloupe. The captain then informed my master, who had been thus imposed on by our mate (though I did not know who was my enemy), the reason the mate had for imposing this lie upon him; which was, because I had acquainted the captain of the provisions the mate had given away, or taken out of the vessel. This speech of the captain's was like life to the dead to me, and instantly my soul glorified God; and still more so on hearing my master immediately say that I was a sensible fellow, and he never did intend to use me as a common slave; and that, but for the entreaties of the captain, and his character of me, he would not have let me go from the stores about as I had done; that also, in so doing, he thought by carrying one little thing or other to different places to sell I might make money. That he also intended to encourage me in this, by crediting me with half a puncheon of rum and half a hogshead of sugar at a time; so that, from being careful, I might have money enough, in some time, to purchase my freedom; and, when that was the case, I might depend upon it he would let me have it for forty pounds sterling money, which was only the same price he gave for me. This sound gladdened my poor heart beyond measure; though indeed it was no more than the very idea I had formed in my mind of my master long before, and I immediately made him this reply: "Sir, I always had that very thought of you, indeed I had, and that made me so diligent in serving you." He then gave me a large piece of silver coin, such as I had never seen or had before, and told me to get ready for the voyage, and he would credit me with a tierce of sugar and another of rum; he also said that he had two amiable sisters in Philadelphia, from whom I might get some necessary things. Upon this my noble captain desired me to go aboard; and, knowing the African mettle, he charged me not to say anything of this matter to anybody; and he promised that the lying mate should not go with him anymore. This was a change indeed; in the same hour to feel the most exquisite pain, and in the turn of a moment the fullest joy. It caused in me such sensations as I was only able to express in my looks; my heart was so overpowered with gratitude, that I could have kissed both of their feet. When I left the room, I immediately went, or rather flew, to the vessel, which being loaded, my master, as good as his word, trusted me with a tierce of rum, and another of sugar; when we sailed, and arrived safe at the elegant city of Philadelphia. I soon sold my goods here pretty well; and in this charming place I found everything plentiful and cheap.

While I was in this place a very extraordinary occurrence befell me. I had been told one evening of a *wise* woman, a Mrs. Davis, who revealed secrets, foretold events, etc. I put little faith in this story at first, as I could not conceive that any mortal could foresee the future disposals of Providence, nor did I believe in any other revelation than that of the Holy Scriptures; however, I was greatly astonished at seeing this woman in a dream that night, though a person I never before beheld in my life; this made such an impression on me, that I could not get the idea the next day out of my mind, and I then became as anxious to see her as I was before indifferent; accordingly, in the evening, after we left off working, I inquired where she lived, and, being directed to her, to my inexpressible surprise, beheld the very woman in the very same dress she appeared to me to wear in the vision. She immediately told me I had dreamed of her the preceding night; related to me many things that had happened with a correctness that astonished me; and finally told me I should not be long a slave; this was the more agreeable news, as I believed it the more readily from her having so faithfully related the past incidents of my life. She said I should be twice in very great danger of my life within eighteen months, which, if I escaped, I should afterwards go on well; so giving me her blessing, we parted. After staying here some time till our vessel was loaded, and I had brought in my little traffic, we sailed from this agreeable spot for Montserrat, once more to encounter the raging surfs.

We arrived safe at Montserrat, where we discharged our cargo, and I sold my things well. Soon after that we took slaves on board for St. Eustatius, and from thence to Georgia. I had always exerted myself, and did double work, in order to make our voyage as short as possible; and from thus overworking myself while we were at Georgia I caught a fever and ague. I was very ill eleven days, and near dying; eternity was now exceedingly impressed on my mind, and I feared very much that awful event. I prayed the Lord therefore to spare me; and I made a promise in my mind to God, that I would be good if ever I should recover. At length, from having an eminent doctor to attend me, I was restored again to health: and soon after we got the vessel loaded, and set off for Montserrat. During the passage, as I was perfectly restored, and had much business of the vessel to mind, all my endeavors to keep up my integrity, and perform my promise to God, began to fail; and in spite of all I could do, as we drew nearer and nearer to the islands, my resolutions more and more declined, as if the very air of that country or climate seemed fatal to piety. When we were safe arrived at Montserrat, and I had got ashore, I forgot my former resolutions.—Alas! how prone is the heart to leave that God it wishes to love! and how strongly do the things of this world strike the senses and captivate the soul!—After our vessel was discharged, we soon got her ready, and took in, as usual, some of the poor oppressed natives of Africa, and other negroes; we then set off again for Georgia and Charleston. We arrived at Georgia, and, having landed part of our cargo, proceeded to Charleston with the remainder. While we were there I saw the town illuminated, the guns were fired, and bonfires and other demonstrations of joy shown, on account of the repeal of the Stamp Act. Here I disposed of some goods on my own account; the white men buying them with smooth promises and fair words, giving me, however, but very indifferent payment. There was one gentleman particularly who bought a puncheon of rum of me, which gave me a great deal of trouble; and although I used the interest of my friendly captain, I could not obtain anything for it; for, being a negro man, I could not oblige him to pay me. This vexed me much, not knowing how to act; and I lost some time in seeking after this Christian; and though, when the Sabbath came (which the negroes usually make their holiday) I was much inclined to go to public worship, but instead of that I was obliged to hire some black men to help me to pull a boat across the water to go in quest of this gentleman. When I found him, after much entreaty, both from myself and my worthy captain, he at last paid me in dollars; some of them however, were copper, and of consequence of no value; but he took advantage of my being a negro man, and obliged me to put up with those or none, although I objected to them. Immediately after, as I was trying to pass them in the market amongst other white men, I was abused for offering to pass bad coin; and though I showed them the man I had got them from, I was within one minute of being tied up and flogged without either judge or jury; however, by the help of a good pair of heels, I ran off, and so escaped the bastinadoes I should have received. I got on board as fast as I could, but still continued in fear of them until we sailed, which, I thank God, we did not long after; and I have never been amongst them since.

We soon came to Georgia, where we were to complete our lading: and here worse fate than ever attended me: For one Sunday night, as I was with some negroes in their master's yard in the town of Savannah, it happened that their master, one Doctor Perkins, who was a very severe and cruel man, came in drunk; and not liking to see any strange negroes in his yard, he, and a ruffian of a white man he had in his service, beset me in an instant, and both of them struck me with the first weapons they could get hold of. I cried out as long as I could for help and mercy; but, though I gave a good account of myself, and he knew my captain, who lodged hard by him, it was to no purpose. They beat and mangled me in a shameful manner, leaving me near dead. I lost so much blood from the wounds I received, that I lay quite motionless, and was so benumbed that I could not feel anything for many hours. Early in the morning they took me away to the jail. As I did not return to the ship all night, my captain not knowing where I was, and being uneasy that I did not then make my appearance, he made inquiry after me; and, having found where I was, immediately came to me. And soon as the good man saw me so cut and mangled, he could not forbear weeping; he soon got me out of jail to his lodgings, and immediately sent for the best doctors in the place, who at first declared it as their opinion that I could not recover. My captain on this went to all the lawyers in the town for their advice, but they told him they could do nothing for me as I was a negro. He then went to Doctor Perkins, the hero who had vanquished me, and menaced him, swearing he would be revenged of him, and challenged him to fight. But cowardice is ever the companion of cruelty—and the Doctor refused. However by the skillfulness of one Doctor Brady of that place, I began at last to amend; but, although I was so sore and bad with the wounds I had all over me that I could not rest in any posture, yet I was in more pain on account of the captain's uneasiness about me than I otherwise should have been. The worthy man nursed and watched me all the hours of the night; and I was, through his attention, and that of the Doctor, able to get out of bed in about sixteen or eighteen days. All this time I was very much wanted on board, as I used frequently to go up and down the river for rafts, and other parts of our cargo, and stow them, when the mate was sick or absent. In about four weeks I was able to go on duty; and in a fortnight after, having got in all our lading, our vessel set sail for Montserrat; and in less than three weeks we arrived there safe, towards the end of the year. This ended my adventures in 1765; for I did not leave Montserrat again till the beginning of the following year.

Chapter VII

The Author's disgust at the West Indies—Forms schemes to obtain his freedom—Ludicrous disappointment he and his captain meet with in Georgia—At last, by several successful voyages, he acquires a sum of money sufficient to purchase it—Applies to his master, who accepts it, and grants his manumission, to his great joy—He afterwards enters as a freeman on board one of Mr. King's ships, and sails for Georgia—Impositions on free negroes as usual—His venture of turkeys—Sails for Montserrat, and on his passage his friend the Captain falls ill and dies.

EVERY DAY NOW brought me nearer my freedom, and I was impatient till we proceeded again to sea, that I might have an opportunity of getting a sum large enough to purchase it. I was not long ungratified; for in the beginning of the year 1766, my master bought another sloop, named the *Nancy,* the largest I had ever seen. She was partly laden, and was to proceed to Philadelphia; our captain had his choice of three, and I was well pleased he chose this, which was the largest: for, from his having a large vessel, I had more room, and could carry a larger quantity of goods with me. Accordingly, when we had delivered our old vessel, the *Prudence,* and completed the lading of the *Nancy,* having made near three hundred percent by four barrels of pork I brought from Charleston, I laid in as large a cargo as I could, trusting to God's providence to prosper my undertaking. With these views I sailed for Philadelphia. On our passage, when we drew near the land, I was for the first time surprised at the sight of some whales, having never seen any such large sea monsters before; and, as we sailed by the land, one morning I saw a puppy whale close by the vessel; it was about the length of a wherry boat, and it followed us all the day until we got within the Capes. We arrived safe and in good time at Philadelphia, and I sold my goods there chiefly to the Quakers. They always appeared to be a very honest discreet sort of people, and never attempted to impose on me; I therefore liked them, and ever after chose to deal with them in preference to any others.

One Sunday morning, while I was here, as I was going to church, I chanced to pass a meetinghouse. The doors being open, and the house full of people, it excited my curiosity to go in. When I entered the house, to my great surprise, I saw a very tall woman standing in the midst of them, speaking in an audible voice something which I could not understand. Having never seen anything of this kind before, I stood and stared about me for some time, wondering at this odd scene. As soon as it was over, I took an opportunity to make inquiry about the place and people, when I was informed they were called Quakers. I particularly asked what that woman I saw in the midst of them had said, but none of them were pleased to satisfy me; so I quitted them, and soon after, as I was returning, I came to a church crowded with people; the churchyard was full likewise, and a number of people were even mounted on ladders, looking in at the windows. I thought this a strange sight, as I had never seen churches, either in England or the West Indies, crowded in this manner before. I therefore made bold to ask some people the meaning of all this, and they told me the Reverend Mr. George Whitfield was preaching. I had often heard of this gentleman, and had wished to see and hear him; but I had never before had an opportunity. I now therefore resolved to gratify myself with the sight, and pressed in amidst the multitude. When I got into the church I saw this pious man exhorting the people with the greatest fervor and earnestness, and sweating as much as I ever did while in slavery at Montserrat beach. I was very much struck and impressed with this; I thought it strange I had never seen divines exert themselves in this manner before, and was no longer at a loss to account for the thin congregations they preached to.

When we had discharged our cargo here, and were loaded again, we left this fruitful land once more, and set sail for Montserrat. My traffic had hitherto succeeded so well with me, that I thought, by selling my goods when we arrived at Montserrat, I should have money enough to purchase my freedom. But as soon as our vessel arrived there, my master came on board, and gave orders for us to go to St. Eustatius, and discharge our cargo there, and from thence proceed to Georgia. I was much disappointed at this; but thinking, as usual, it was of no use to murmur at the decrees of fate, I submitted without repining, and we went to St. Eustatius. After we had discharged our cargo there we took in a live cargo (as we call a cargo of slaves). Here I sold my goods tolerably well; but, not being able to lay out all my money in this small island to as much advantage as in many other places, I laid out only part, and the remainder I brought away with me neat. We sailed from hence for Georgia, and I was glad when we got there, though I had not much reason to like the place from my last adventure in Savannah; but I longed to get back to Montserrat and procure my freedom, which I expected to be able to purchase when I returned. As soon as we arrived here I waited on my careful doctor, Mr. Brady, to whom I made the most grateful acknowledgments in my power for his former kindness and attention during my illness.

While we were here, an odd circumstance happened to the captain and me, which disappointed us both a good deal. A silversmith, whom we had brought to this place some voyages before, agreed with the captain to return with us to the West Indies, and promised at the same time to give the captain a great deal of money, having pretended to take a liking to him, and being as we thought very rich. But while we stayed to load our vessel this man was taken ill in a house where he worked, and in a week's time became very bad. The worse he grew, the more he used to speak of giving the captain what he had promised him, so that he expected something considerable from the death of this man, who had no wife or child, and he attended him day and night. I used also to go with the captain, at his own desire, to attend him; especially when we saw there was no appearance of his recovery; and, in order to recompense me for my trouble, the captain promised me ten pounds, when he should get the man's property. I thought this would be of great service to me, although I had nearly money enough to purchase my freedom, if I should get safe this voyage to Montserrat. In this expectation I laid out above eight pounds of my money for a suit of superfine blue clothes to dance in at my freedom, which I hoped was then at hand. We still continued to attend this man, and were with him even on the last day he lived, till very late at night, when we went on board. After we were got to bed, about one or two o'clock in the morning, the captain was sent for, and informed the man was dead. On this he came to my bed, and, waking me, informed me of it, and desired me to get up and procure a light, and immediately go with him. I told him I was very sleepy, and wished he would take somebody else with him; or else, as the man was dead, and could want no further attendance, to let all things remain as they were till the next morning. "No, no," said he, "we will have the money tonight, I cannot wait till tomorrow; so let us go." Accordingly I got up and struck a light, and away we both went and saw the man as dead as we could wish. The captain said he would give him a grand burial, in gratitude for the promised treasure; and desired that all the things belonging to the deceased might be brought forth. Among others, there was a nest of trunks of which he had kept the keys whilst the man was ill, and when they were produced we opened them with no small eagerness and expectation; and as there were a great number within one another, with much impatience we took them one out of the other. At last, when we came to the smallest, and had opened it, we saw it was full of papers, which we supposed to be notes; at the sight of which our hearts leapt for joy; and that instant the captain, clapping his hands, cried out, "Thank God! here it is." But when we took up the trunk, and began to examine the supposed treasure and long-looked-for bounty, (alas! alas! how uncertain and deceitful are all human affairs!) what had we found? While we thought we were embracing a substance, we grasped an empty nothing!! The whole amount that was in the nest of trunks was only one dollar and a half; and all that the man possessed would not pay for his coffin. Our sudden and exquisite joy was now succeeded by as sudden and exquisite pain; and my captain and I exhibited, for some time, most ridiculous figures—pictures of chagrin and disappointment! We went away greatly mortified, and left the deceased to do as well as he could for himself, as we had taken so good care of him when alive for nothing. We set sail once more for Montserrat, and arrived there safe, but much out of humor with our friend the silversmith. When we had unladen the vessel, and I had sold my venture, finding myself master of about forty-seven pounds—I consulted my true friend, the captain, how I should proceed in offering my master the money for my freedom. He told me to come on a certain morning, when he and my master would be at breakfast together. Accordingly, on that morning, I went, and met the captain there, as he had appointed. When I went in I made my obeisance to my master, and with my money in my hand, and many fears in my heart, I prayed him to be as good as his offer to me, when he was pleased to promise me my freedom as soon as I could purchase it. This speech seemed to confound him; he began to recoil; and my heart sunk that instant within me. "What!" said he, "give you your freedom? Why, where did you get the money? Have you got forty pounds sterling?" "Yes, sir," I answered. "How did you get it?" replied he; I told him, "Very honestly." The captain then said he knew I got the money very honestly, and with much industry, and that I was particularly careful. On which my master replied, I got money much faster than he did; and said he would not have made the promise he did if he had thought I should have got money so soon. "Come, come," said my worthy captain, clapping my master on the back, "Come, Robert, (which was his name), I think you must let him have his freedom; you have laid your money out very well; you have received good interest for it all this time, and here is now the principal at last. I know Gustavus [has] earned you more than a hundred a year, and he will still save you money, as he will not leave you: Come, Robert, take the money." My master then said, he would not be worse than his promise; and, taking the money, told me to go to the secretary at the Register Office, and get my commission drawn up. These words of my master were like a voice from heaven to me; in an instant all my trepidation was turned into unuttered bliss; and I most reverently bowed myself with gratitude, unable to express my feelings, but by the overflowing of my eyes, and a heart replete with thanks to God; while my true and worthy friend the captain congratulated us both with a peculiar degree of heartfelt pleasure. As soon as the first transports of my joy were over, and I had expressed my thanks to these my worthy friends in the best manner I was able, I rose with a heart full of affection and reverence, and left the room in order to obey my master's joyful mandate of going to the Register Office. As I was leaving the house, I called to mind the words of the Psalmist, in the 126th Psalm, and like him, "I glorified God in my heart, in whom I trusted." These words had been impressed on my mind from the very day I was forced from Deptford to the present hour, and I now saw them, as I thought, fulfilled and verified. My imagination was all rapture as I flew to the Register Office; and, in this respect, like the apostle Peter,* (whose deliverance from prison was so sudden and extraordinary, that he thought he was in a vision), I could scarcely believe I was awake. Heavens! who could do justice to my feel-

*Acts 12:9.

ings at this moment? Not conquering heroes themselves, in the midst of a triumph—Not the tender mother who has just regained her long-lost infant, and presses it to her heart—Not the weary hungry mariner, at the sight of the desired friendly port—Not the lover, when he once more embraces his beloved mistress, after she has been ravished from his arms!—All within my breast was tumult, wildness, and delirium! My feet scarcely touched the ground, for they were winged with joy, and, like Elijah as he rose to Heaven, they "were with lightning sped as I went on." Everyone I met I told of my happiness, and blazed about the virtue of my amiable master and captain.

When I got to the office, and acquainted the Register with my errand, he congratulated me on the occasion, and told me he would draw up my manumission for half-price, which was a guinea. I thanked him for his kindness; and, having received it, and paid him, I hastened to my master to get him to sign it, that I might fully be released. Accordingly he signed the manumission that day; so that, before night, I who had been a slave in the morning, trembling at the will of another, now became my own master, and completely free. I thought this was the happiest day I had ever experienced; and my joy was still heightened by the blessings and prayers of many of the sable race, particularly the aged, to whom my heart had ever been attached with reverence.

As the form of my manumission has something peculiar in it, and expresses the absolute power and dominion one man claims over his fellow, I shall beg leave to present it before my readers at full length:

> *Montserrat.*—To all men unto whom these presents shall come: I Robert King, of the parish of St. Anthony, in the said island, merchant, send greeting: Know ye, that I the aforesaid Robert King, for, and in consideration of the sum of seventy pounds current money of the said island, to me in hand paid, and to the intent that a negro man slave, named Gustavus Vasa, shall and may become free, have manumitted, emancipated, enfranchised, and set free, and by these presents do manumit, emancipate, enfranchise, and set free the aforesaid negro man slave named Gustavus Vasa, forever; hereby giving, granting, and releasing unto him, the said Gustavus Vasa, all right, title, dominion, sovereignty and property, which, as lord and master over the aforesaid Gustavus Vasa, I have had, or which I now have, or by any means whatsoever I may or can hereafter possibly have over him the aforesaid Negro, forever. In witness

whereof, I the above said Robert King, have unto these presents set my hand and seal, this tenth day of July, in the year of our Lord one thousand seven hundred and sixty-six.

ROBERT KING.

Signed, sealed, and delivered in the presence of Terry Legay.

Montserrat,
Registered the within manumission, at full length, this eleventh day of July, 1766, in liber D.

TERRY LEGAY, Register.

In short, the fair as well as black people immediately styled me by a new appellation, to me the most desirable in the world, which was Freeman, and at the dances I gave, my Georgia superfine blue clothes made no indifferent appearance, as I thought. Some of the sable females, who formerly stood aloof, now began to relax, and appear less coy, but my heart was still fixed on London, where I hoped to be ere long. So that my worthy captain, and his owner my late master, finding that the bent of my mind was towards London, said to me, "We hope you won't leave us, but that you will still be with the vessels." Here gratitude bowed me down; and none but the generous mind can judge of my feelings, struggling between inclination and duty. However, notwithstanding my wish to be in London, I obediently answered my benefactors that I would go in the vessel, and not leave them; and from that day I was entered on board as an able-bodied sailor, at thirty-six shillings per month, besides what perquisites I could make. My intention was to make a voyage or two, entirely to please these my honored patrons; but I determined that the year following, if it pleased God, I would see old England once more, and surprise my old master, Capt. Pascal, who was hourly in my mind; for I still loved him, notwithstanding his usage to me, and I pleased myself with thinking of what he would say when he saw what the Lord had done for me in so short a time, instead of being, as he might perhaps suppose, under the cruel yoke of some planter. With these kinds of reveries I often used to entertain myself, and shorten the time till my return: and now, being as in my original free African state, I embarked on board the *Nancy*, after having got all things ready for our voyage. In this state of serenity we sailed for St. Eustatius; and having smooth seas and calm weather we soon arrived there: after taking our cargo on board, we proceeded to Savannah in Georgia, in August 1766. While we were there, as usual, I used to go for the cargo up the rivers in boats: and when on this business have been frequently beset by alligators, which were very numerous on that coast and river; and shot many of them when they have been near getting into our boats; which we have with great difficulty sometimes prevented, and have been very much frightened at them. I have seen a young one sold alive in Georgia for six pence.

During our stay at this place, one evening a slave belonging to Mr. Read, a merchant of Savannah, came near our vessel, and began to use me very ill. I entreated him, with all the patience I was master of, to desist, as I knew there was little or no law for a free negro here; but the fellow, instead of taking my advice, persevered in his insults, and even struck me. At this I lost all temper, and fell on him and beat him soundly. The next morning his master came to our vessel as we lay alongside the wharf, and desired me to come ashore that he might have me flogged all round the town, for beating his negro slave. I told him he had insulted me, and had given the provocation, by first striking me. I had told my captain also the whole affair that morning, and wished him to have gone along with me to Mr. Read, to prevent bad consequences; but he said that it did not signify, and if Mr. Read said anything, he would make matters up, and desired me to go to work, which I accordingly did. The captain being on board when Mr. Read came and applied to him to deliver me up, he said he knew nothing of the matter, I was a freeman. I was astonished and frightened at this, and thought I had better keep where I was, than go ashore and be flogged round the town, without judge or jury. I therefore refused to stir, and Mr. Read went away, swearing he would bring all the constables in the town, for he would have me out of the vessel. When he was gone, I thought his threat might prove too true to my sorrow; and I was confirmed in this belief, as well by the many instances I had seen of the treatment of free negroes, as from a fact that had happened within my own knowledge here a short time before.

There was a free black man, a carpenter, that I knew, who for asking a gentleman that he worked for, for the money he had earned, was put into gaol; and afterwards this oppressed man was sent from Georgia, with false accusations, of an intention to set the gentleman's house on fire, and run away with his slaves. I was therefore much embarrassed, and very apprehensive of a flogging at least. I dreaded, of all things, the thoughts of being stripped, as I never in my life had the marks of any violence of that kind. At that instant a rage seized my soul, and for a little I determined to resist the first man that should offer to lay violent hands on me, or basely use me without a trial; for I would sooner die like a freeman, than suffer myself to be scourged by the hands of ruffians, and my blood drawn like a slave. The Captain and others, more cautious, advised me to make haste and conceal myself; for they said Mr. Read was a very spiteful man, and he would soon come on board with constables, and take me. At first I refused this counsel, being determined to stand my ground; but at length, by the prevailing entreaties of the Captain and Mr. Dixon, with whom he lodged, I went to Mr. Dixon's house, which was a little out of the town, at a place called *Yea-ma-chra*. I was but just gone, when Mr. Read, with the constables, came for me, and searched the vessel, but not finding me there, he swore he would have me dead or alive. I was secreted above five days; however, the good character which my Captain always gave me, as well as some other gentlemen who also knew me, procured me some friends. At last some of them told my Captain that he did not use me well, in suffering me thus to be imposed upon, and said they would see me redressed, and get me on board some other vessel. My Captain, on this, immediately went to Mr. Read, and told him, that ever since I eloped from the vessel, his work had been neglected, and he could not go on with her loading, himself and mate not being well; and, as I had managed things on board for them, my absence must have retarded his voyage, and consequently hurt the owner; he therefore begged of him to forgive me, as he said he never heard any complaint of me before, during the several years I had been with him. After repeated entreaties, Mr. Read said I might go to hell, and that he would not meddle with me; on which my Captain came immediately to me at his lodging, and, telling me how pleasantly matters had gone on, desired me to go on board.

Some of my other friends then asked him if he had got the constables' warrants from them? the Captain said, no. On this I was desired by them to stay in the house; and they said they would get me on board of some other vessel before the evening. When the Captain heard this, he became almost distracted. He went immediately for the warrants, and, after using every exertion in his power, he at last got them from my hunters; but I had all the expenses to pay.

After I had thanked all my friends for their kindness, I went on board again to my work, of which I had always plenty. We were in haste to complete our lading, and were to carry twenty head of cattle with us to the West Indies, where they are a very profitable article. In order to encourage me in working, and to make up for the time I had lost, my

Captain promised me the privilege of carrying two bullocks of my own with me; and this made me work with redoubled ardor. As soon as I had got the vessel loaded, in doing which I was obliged to perform the duty of the mate as well as my own work, and when the bullocks were near coming on board, I asked the captain leave to bring my two, according to his promise; but, to my great surprise, he told me there was no room for them. I then asked him to permit me to take one; but he said he could not. I was a good deal mortified at this usage, and told him I had no notion that he intended thus to impose on me: nor could I think well of any man that was so much worse than his word. On this we had some disagreement, and I gave him to understand that I intended to leave the vessel. At this he appeared to be very much dejected; and our mate, who had been very sickly, and whose duty had long devolved upon me, advised him to persuade me to stay: in consequence of which he spoke very kindly to me, making many fair promises, telling me that as the mate was so sickly, he could not do without me; and that as the safety of the vessel and cargo depended greatly upon me, he therefore hoped that I would not be offended at what had passed between us, and swore he would make up all matters to me when we arrived in the West Indies, so I consented to slave on as before. Soon after this, as the bullocks were coming on board, one of them ran at the captain, and butted him so furiously in the breast, that he never recovered of the blow. In order to make me some amends for this treatment about the bullocks, the captain now pressed me very much to take some turkeys, and other fowls, with me, and gave me liberty to take as many as I could find room for; but I told him he knew very well I had never carried any turkeys before, as I always thought they were such tender birds that they were not fit to cross the seas. However, he continued to press me to buy them for once; and, what seemed very surprising to me, the more I was against it, the more he urged my taking them, insomuch that he insured me from all losses that might happen by them, and I was prevailed on to take them; but I thought this very strange, as he had never acted so with me before. This, and not being able to dispose of my paper money in any other way, induced me at length to take four dozen. The turkeys, however, I was so dissatisfied about, that I determined to make no more voyages to this quarter, nor with this captain; and was very apprehensive that my free voyage would be the worst I had ever made.

We set sail for Montserrat. The captain and mate had been both complaining of sickness when we sailed, and as we proceeded on our voyage they grew worse. This was about November, and we had not been long at sea before we began to meet with strong northerly gales and rough seas; and in about seven or eight days all the bullocks were near being drowned, and four or five of them died. Our vessel, which had not been tight at first, was much less so now: and, though we were but nine in the whole, including five sailors and myself, yet we were obliged to attend to the pump, every half or three-quarters of an hour. The captain and mate came on deck as often as they were able, which was now but seldom; for they declined so fast, that they were not well enough to make observations above four or five times the whole passage. The whole care of the vessel rested therefore upon me; and I was obliged to direct her by mere dint of reason, not being able to work a traverse. The Captain was now very sorry he had not taught me navigation, and protested, if ever he should get well again, he would not fail to do so: but in about seventeen days his illness increased so much, that he was obliged to keep his bed, continuing sensible, however, till the last, constantly having the owner's interest at heart; for this just and benevolent man ever appeared much concerned about the welfare of what he was entrusted with. When this dear friend found the symptoms of death approaching, he called me by my name; and, when I came to him, he asked (with almost his last breath) if he had ever done me any harm? "God forbid I should think so," I replied, "I should then be the most ungrateful of wretches to the best of benefactors." While I was thus expressing my affection and sorrow by his bedside, he expired without saying another word, and the day following we committed his body to the deep. Every man on board loved him, and regretted his death; but I was exceedingly affected at it, and found that I did not know till he was gone, the strength of my regard for him. Indeed I had every reason in the world to be attached to him; for, besides that he was in general mild, affable, generous, faithful, benevolent, and just, he was to me a friend and a father; and had it pleased Providence, that he had died but five months before, I verily believe I should not have obtained my freedom when I did; and it is not improbable that I might not have been able to get it at any rate afterwards.

The captain being dead, the mate came on the deck and made such observations as he was able, but to no purpose. In the course of a few days more, the bullocks that remained, were found dead; but the turkeys I had, though on the deck, and exposed to so much wet and bad weather, did well, and I afterwards gained near three hundred percent on the sale of them; so that in the event it proved a happy circumstance for me that I had not bought the bullocks I intended, for they must have perished with the rest; and I could not help looking on this, otherwise trifling circumstance, as a particular providence of God, and was thankful accordingly. The care of the vessel took up all my time, and engaged my attention entirely. As we were now out of the variable winds, I thought I should not be much puzzled to hit the islands. I was persuaded I steered right for Antigua, which I wished to reach, as the nearest to us; and in the course of nine or ten days we made this island to our great joy; and the day after we came safe to Montserrat.

Many were surprised when they heard of my conducting the sloop into the port, and I now obtained a new appellation, and was called captain. This elated me not a little, and it was quite flattering to my vanity to be thus styled by as high a title as any sable freeman in this place possessed. When the death of the captain became known, he was much regretted by all who knew him; for he was a man universally respected. At the same time the sable captain lost no fame; for the success I had met with increased the affection of my friends in no small measure; and I was offered, by a gentleman of the place, the command of his sloop to go amongst the islands, but I refused.

BAHAMA BANKS. 1767.

They ran the ship aground, and the fore part stuck fast, and remained unmoveable, but the hinder part was broken by the violence of the waves.

Acts 27:41.

Howbeit we must be cast upon a certain island; Wherefore, sirs, be of good cheer; for I believe God, that it shall be even as it was told me.

Acts 27:25, 26.

And so it came to pass that they escaped all safe to the land.

Acts 27:44.

Now a thing was secretly brought to me, and mine ear received a little thereof.

In thoughts from the visions of the night, when dead sleep falleth on men.

Job 4:12, 13.

Lo, all these things worketh God oftentimes with man.

To bring back his soul from the pit, to be enlightened with the light of the living.

Job 33:29, 30.

Chapter VIII

The Author, to oblige Mr. King, once more embarks for Georgia in the
Nancy—*A new captain is appointed—They sail, and steer a new*
course—Three remarkable dreams—The vessel is shipwrecked on the
Bahama Bank, but the crew are preserved, principally by means of the
Author—He sets out from the island, with the captain in a small boat, in
quest of a ship—Their distress—Meet with a wrecker—Sail for Provi-
dence—Are overtaken again by a terrible storm, and are all near per-
ishing—Arrive at New Providence—The Author, after some time, sails
from thence to Georgia—Meets with another storm, and is obliged to put
back and refit—Arrives at Georgia—Meets new impositions—Two
white men attempt to kidnap him—Officiates as a parson at a funeral
ceremony—Bids adieu to Georgia, and sails for Martinique.

AS I HAD NOW, by the death of my captain, lost my great benefactor
and friend, I had little inducement to remain longer in the West Indies,
except my gratitude to Mr. King, which I thought I had pretty well discharged in bringing back his vessel safe, and delivering his cargo to his
satisfaction. I began to think of leaving this part of the world, of which
I had been long tired, and returning to England, where my heart had
always been; but Mr. King still pressed me very much to stay with his
vessel; and he had done so much for me, that I found myself unable to
refuse his requests, and consented to go another voyage to Georgia, as
the mate from his ill state of health, was quite useless in the vessel. Accordingly, a new captain was appointed, whose name was William
Phillips, an old acquaintance of mine; and, having refitted our vessel,
and taken several slaves on board, we set sail for St. Eustatius, where we
stayed but a few days; and on the 30th of January 1767, we steered for
Georgia. Our new captain boasted strangely of his skill in navigating
and conducting a vessel; and, in consequence of this, he steered a new
course, several points more to the westward than we ever did before;
this appeared to me very extraordinary.

On the 4th of February, which was soon after we had got into our
new course, I dreamt the ship was wrecked amidst the surfs and rocks,
and that I was the means of saving everyone on board; and on the night
following I dreamed the very same dream. Those dreams, however,
made no impression on my mind; and the next evening, it being my
watch below, I was pumping the vessel a little after eight o'clock, just
before I went off the deck, as is the custom, and being weary with the

duty of the day, and tired at the pump (for we made a good deal of water), I began to express my impatience, and uttered with an oath, "Damn the vessel's bottom out." But my conscience instantly smote me for the expression. When I left the deck I went to bed, and had scarcely fallen asleep when I dreamed the same dream again about the ship as I had dreamt the two preceding nights. At twelve o'clock the watch was changed; and, as I had always the charge of the captain's watch, I then went upon deck. At half after one in the morning, the man at the helm saw something under the leebeam that the sea washed against, and he immediately called to me that there was a grampus, and desired me to look at it. Accordingly I stood up and observed it for some time; but when I saw the sea wash up against it again and again, I said it was not a fish but a rock. Being soon certain of this, I went down to the captain, and, with some confusion, told him the danger we were in, and desired him to come upon deck immediately. He said it was very well, and I went up again. As soon as I was upon deck, the wind, which had been pretty high, having abated a little, the vessel began to be carried sideways towards the rock, by means of the current. Still the captain did not appear. I therefore went to him again and told him the vessel was then near a large rock, and desired he would come up with all speed. He said he would, and I returned on the deck. When I was upon the deck again I saw we were not above a pistol shot from the rock, and I heard the noise of the breakers all around us. I was exceedingly alarmed at this; and the captain not having yet come on the deck I lost all patience; and, growing quite enraged, I ran down to him again, and asked him, why he did not come up, and what he could mean by all this? "The breakers," said I, "are around us, and the vessel is almost on the rock." With that he came on the deck with me, and tried to put the vessel about, and get her out of the current, but all to no purpose, the wind being very small. We then called all hands up immediately; and after a little we got up one end of a cable, and fastened it to the anchor. By this time the surf foamed round us, and made a dreadful noise on the breakers, and the very moment we let the anchor go, the vessel struck against the rocks. One swell now succeeded another, as it were one wave calling on its fellow: The roaring of the billows increased, and, with one single heave of the swells, the sloop was pierced and transfixed among the rocks! In a moment a scene of horror presented itself to my mind, such as I never had conceived or experienced before. All my sins stared me in the face; and especially I thought that God had hurled his direful vengeance on my guilty head for cursing the vessel on which my life depended. My spirits at this forsook me, and I expected every moment to go to the bottom: I determined if I should still be saved, that I would never swear again. And in the midst of my distress, while the dreadful surfs were dashing with unremitting fury among the rocks, I remembered the Lord, though fearful that I was undeserving of forgiveness, and I thought that as he had often delivered, he might yet deliver; and calling to mind the many mercies he had shown me in times past, they gave me some small hope that he might still help me. I then began to think how we might be saved; and, I believe no mind was ever like mine so replete with inventions and confused with schemes, though how to escape death I knew not. The captain immediately ordered the hatches to be nailed down on the slaves in the hold, where there were above twenty, all of whom must unavoidably have perished if he had been obeyed. When he desired the men to nail down the hatches I thought that my sin was the cause of this, and that God would charge me with these people's blood. This thought rushed upon my mind that instant with such violence, that it quite overpowered me, and I fainted. I recovered just as the people were about to nail down the hatches; perceiving which, I desired them to stop. The captain then said it must be done; I asked him why? He said, that everyone would endeavor to get into the boat, which was but small, and thereby we should be drowned; for it would not have carried above ten at the most. I could no longer restrain my emotion, and I told him he deserved drowning for not knowing how to navigate the vessel; and I believe the people would have tossed him overboard if I had given them the least hint of it. However, the hatches were not nailed down; and, as none of us could leave the vessel then on account of the darkness, and as we knew not where to go, and were convinced besides that the boat could not survive the surfs, and besides being broken, we all said we would remain on the dry part of the vessel, and trust to God till daylight appeared, when we should know better what to do.

I then advised to get the boat prepared against morning, and some of us began to set about it; but others abandoned all care of the ship, and themselves, and fell to drinking. Our boat had a piece out of her bottom near two feet long, and we had no materials to mend her; however, necessity being the mother of invention, I took some pump-leather, and nailed it to the broken part, and plastered it over with tallow-grease. And, thus prepared, with the utmost anxiety of mind, we watched for daylight, and thought every minute an hour, till it appeared. At last it saluted our longing eyes, and kind Providence accompanied its approach with what was no small comfort to us; for the dreadful swells began to subside; and the next thing that we discovered to raise our drooping spirits, was a small key, or desolate island, about five or six miles off; but a barrier soon presented itself; for there was not water enough for our boat to go over the reefs, and this threw us again into a sad consternation; but there was no alternative, we were therefore obliged to put but few things in the boat at once; and, what was still worse, all of us were frequently under the necessity of getting out to drag and lift it over the reefs. This cost us much labor and fatigue; and, what was yet more distressing, we could not avoid having our legs cut and torn very much with the rocks. There were only four people that would work with me at the oars; and they consisted of three black men and a Dutch creole sailor; and, though we went with the boat five times that day, we had no others to assist us. But, had we not worked in this manner, I really believe the people could not have been saved; for not one of the white men did anything to preserve their lives; indeed they soon got so drunk that they were not able, but lay about the deck like swine, so that we were at last obliged to lift them into the boat, and carry them on shore by force. This want of assistance made our labor intolerably severe; insomuch that, by going on shore so often that day, the skin was partly stript off my hands.

However, we continued all the day to toil and strain our exertions, till we had brought all on board safe to the shore; so that out of thirty-two people we lost not one.

My dream now returned upon my mind with all its force; it was fulfilled in every part; for our danger was the same I had dreamt of; and I could not help looking on myself as the principal instrument in effecting our deliverance: for, owing to some of our people getting drunk, the rest of us were obliged to double our exertions; and it was fortunate we did, for in a very little time longer the patch of leather on the boat would have been worn out, and she would have been no longer fit for service. Situated as we were, who could think that men should be so careless of the danger they were in? for, if the wind had but raised the swell as it was when the vessel struck, we must have bid a final farewell to all hopes of deliverance; and though I warned the people who were drinking, and entreated them to embrace the moment of deliverance, nevertheless they persisted, as if not possessed of the least spark of reason. I could not help thinking, that if any of these people had been lost, God would charge me with their lives, which, perhaps, was one cause of my laboring so hard for their preservation, and indeed every one of them afterwards seemed so sensible of the service I had rendered them, that while we were on the key, I was a kind of chieftain amongst them. I brought some limes, oranges, and lemons ashore; and, finding it to be a good soil where we were, I planted several of them as a token to anyone that might be cast away hereafter. This key, as we afterwards found, was one of the Bahama islands, which consist of a cluster of large islands, with smaller ones or keys, as they are called, interspersed among them. It was about a mile in circumference, with a white sandy beach running in a regular order along it. On that part of it where we first attempted to land, there stood some very large birds, called flamingos: these, from the reflection of the sun, appeared to us, at a little distance, as large as men; and, when they walked backwards, and forwards, we could not conceive what they were: our captain swore they were cannibals. This created a great panic among us; and we held a consultation how to act. The captain wanted to go to a key that was within sight, but a great way off; but I was against it, as in so doing we should not be able to save all the people; "And therefore," said I, "let us go on shore here, and perhaps these cannibals may take to the water." Accordingly, we steered toward them: and when we approached them, to our very great joy and no less wonder, they walked off one after the other very deliberately; and at last they took flight, and relieved us entirely from our fears. About the key there were turtles and several sorts of fish in such abundance that we caught them without bait, which was a great relief to us after the salt provisions on board. There was also a large rock on the beach, about ten feet high, which was in the form of a punch bowl at the top; this we could not help thinking Providence had ordained to supply us with rainwater; and it was something singular, that, if we did not take the water when it rained, in some little time after it would turn as salt as seawater.

Our first care, after refreshment, was, to make ourselves tents to lodge in, which we did as well as we could with some sails we had brought from the ship. We then began to think how we might get from this place, which was quite uninhabited; and we determined to repair our boat, which was very much shattered, and to put to sea in quest of a ship, or some inhabited island. It took us up, however, eleven days before we could get the boat ready for sea, in the manner we wanted it, with a sail and other necessaries. When we had got all things prepared, the captain wanted me to stay on shore, while he went to sea in quest of a vessel to take all the people off the key; but this I refused; and the captain and myself, with five more, set off in the boat towards New

Providence. We had no more than two musket loads of gunpowder with us, if anything should happen; and our stock of provisions consisted of three gallons of rum, four of water, some salt beef, some biscuit; and in this manner we proceeded to sea.

On the second day of our voyage, we came to an island called Abaco, the largest of the Bahama islands. We were much in want of water; for by this time our water was expended, and we were exceedingly fatigued in pulling two days in the heat of the sun; and it being late in the evening, we hauled the boat ashore to try for water, and remain during the night: when we came ashore we searched for water, but could find none. When it was dark, we made a fire around us for fear of the wild beasts, as the place was an entire thick wood, and we took it by turns to watch. In this situation we found very little rest, and waited with impatience for the morning. As soon as the light appeared we set off again with our boat, in hopes of finding assistance during the day. We were now much dejected and weakened by pulling the boat; for our sail was of no use, and we were almost famished for want of fresh water to drink. We had nothing left to eat but salt beef, and that we could not use without water. In this situation we toiled all day in sight of the island, which was very long; in the evening, seeing no relief, we made shore again, and fastened our boat. We then went to look for fresh water, being quite faint for the want of it; and we dug and searched about for some all the remainder of the evening, but could not find one drop, so that our dejection at this period became excessive, and our terror so great, that we expected nothing but death to deliver us. We could not touch our beef, which was salt as brine, without fresh water; and we were in the greatest terror from the apprehension of wild beasts. When unwelcome night came, we acted as on the night before; and the next morning we set off again from the island in hopes of seeing some vessel. In this manner we toiled as well as we were able till four o'clock, during which we passed several keys, but could not meet with a ship; and, still famishing with thirst, went ashore on one of those keys again, in hopes of finding some water. Here we found some leaves with a few drops of water on them, which we lapped with much eagerness; we then dug in several places, but without success. As we were digging holes in search of water, there came forth some very thick and black stuff; but none of us could touch it, except the poor Dutch creole, who drank about a quart of it, as eagerly as if it had been wine. We tried to catch fish, but could not: and we now began to repine at our fate, and abandon ourselves to despair; when, in the midst of our mur-

muring, the captain, all at once cried out, "A sail! a sail! a sail!" This gladdening sound was like a reprieve to a convict, and we all instantly turned to look at it; but in a little time some of us began to be afraid it was not a sail. However, at a venture, we embarked, and steered after it; and, in half an hour, to our unspeakable joy, we plainly saw that it was a vessel. At this our drooping spirits revived, and we made towards her with all the speed imaginable. When we came near to her, we found she was a little sloop, about the size of a Gravesend hoy, and quite full of people; a circumstance which we could not make out the meaning of. Our captain, who was a Welshman, swore that they were pirates, and would kill us. I said, be that as it might, we must board her if we were to die by it; and, if they should not receive us kindly, we must oppose them as well as we could: for there was no alternative between their perishing and ours. This counsel was immediately taken; and I really believe that the captain, myself, and the Dutchman, would then have faced twenty men. We had two cutlasses and a musket, that I brought in the boat; and in this situation we rowed alongside, and immediately boarded her. I believe there were about forty hands on board; but how great was our surprise, as soon as we got on board, to find that the major part of them were in the same predicament as ourselves.

They belonged to a whaling schooner that was wrecked two days before us about nine miles to the north of our vessel. When she was wrecked, some of them had taken to their boats, and had left some of their people and property on a key, in the same manner as we had done; and were going, like us, to New Providence in quest of a ship, when they met with this little sloop, called a wrecker; their employment in those seas being to look after wrecks. They were then going to take the remainder of the people belonging to the schooner; for which the wrecker was to have all things belonging to the vessel, and likewise their people's help to get what they could out of her, and were then to carry the crew to New Providence.

We told the people of the wrecker the condition of our vessel, and we made the same agreement with them as the schooner's people; and, on their complying, we begged of them to go to our key directly, because our people were in want of water. They agreed, therefore, to go along with us first; and in two days we arrived at the key, to the inexpressible joy of the people that we had left behind, as they had been reduced to great extremities for want of water in our absence. Luckily for us, the wrecker had now more people on board than she could carry or victual for any moderate length of time; they therefore hired the schooner's people to work on the wreck, and we left them our boat, and embarked for New Providence.

Nothing could have been more fortunate than our meeting with this wrecker, for New Providence was at such a distance that we never could have reached it in our boat. The island of Abaco was much longer than we expected; and it was not till after sailing for three or four days that we got safe to the farther end of it, towards New Providence. When we arrived there, we watered and got a good many lobsters and other shellfish, which proved a great relief to us, as our provisions and water were almost exhausted. We then proceeded on our voyage; but the day after we left the island, late in the evening, and whilst we were yet amongst the Bahama keys, we were overtaken by a violent gale of wind, so that we were obliged to cut away the mast. The vessel was very near foundering; for she parted from her anchors, and struck several times on the shoals. Here we expected every minute that she would have gone to pieces, and each moment to be our last; so much so, that my old captain and sickly useless mate, and several others, fainted; and death stared us in the face on every side. All the swearers on board now began to call on the God of Heaven to assist them: and sure enough, beyond our comprehension he did assist us, and in a miraculous manner delivered us! In the very height of our extremity the wind lulled for a few minutes; and, although the swell was high beyond expression, two men who were expert swimmers, attempted to go to the buoy of the anchor, which we still saw in the water, at some distance, in a little punt that belonged to the wrecker, which was not large enough to carry more than two. She filled at different times in their endeavors to get into her alongside of our vessel; and they saw nothing but death before them, as well as we; but they said they might as well die that way as any other. A coil of very small rope, with a little buoy, was put along with them; and, at last, with great hazard, they got the punt clear from the vessel; and these two intrepid water heroes paddled away for life towards the buoy of the anchor. Our eyes were fixed on them all the time, expecting every minute to be their last; and the prayers of all those that remained in their senses were offered up to God, on their behalf, for a speedy deliverance, and for our own, which depended on them; and he heard and answered us! These two men at last reached the buoy; and having fastened the punt to it, they tied one end of their rope to the small buoy that they had in the punt, and sent it adrift towards the vessel. We on board observing this, threw out boathooks and leads fastened to lines, in order to catch the buoy; at last we caught it, and fastened a hawser to the end of the small rope; we then gave them a sign to pull, and they pulled the hawser to them, and fastened it to the buoy: which being done, we hauled for our lives, and, through the mercy of God, we got again from the shoals into deep water, and the punt got safe to the vessel. It is impossible for any to conceive our heartfelt joy at this second deliverance from ruin, but those who have suffered the same hardships. Those whose strength and senses were gone, came to themselves, and were now as elated as they were before depressed. Two days after this the wind ceased, and the water became smooth. The punt then went on shore, and we cut down some trees; and having found our mast and mended it, we brought it on board, and fixed it up. As soon as we had done this we got up the anchor, and away we went once more for New Providence, which in three days more we reached safe, after having been above three weeks in a situation in which we did not expect to escape with life. The inhabitants here were very kind to us; and, when they learned our situation showed us a great deal of hospitality and friendship. Soon after this, every one of my old fellow sufferers that were free, parted from us, and shaped their course where their inclination led them. One merchant, who had a large sloop, seeing our condition, and knowing we wanted to go to Georgia, told four of us that his vessel was going there; and if we would work on board and load her, he would give us our passage free. As we could not get any wages whatever, and found it very hard to get off the place, we were obliged to consent to his proposal; and we went on board and helped to load the sloop, though we had only our victuals allowed us. When she was entirely loaded, he told us she was going to Jamaica first, where we must go if we went in her. This, however, I refused; but my fellow sufferers not having any money to help themselves with, necessity obliged them to accept of the offer, and to steer that course, though they did not like it.

We stayed in New Providence about seventeen or eighteen days; during which time I met with many friends, who gave me encouragement to stay there with them, but I declined it; though, had not my heart been fixed on England, I should have stayed, as I liked the place extremely, and there were some free black people here who were very happy, and we passed our time pleasantly together, with the melodious sound of the catguts, under the lime and lemon trees. At length Captain Phillips hired a sloop to carry him and some of the slaves that he could not sell here, to Georgia; and I agreed to go with him in this vessel, meaning now to take my farewell of that place. When the vessel was ready, we all embarked; and I took my leave of New Providence, not without regret. We sailed about four o'clock in the morning, with a fair wind, for Georgia; and, about eleven o'clock the same morning, a sudden and short gale sprung up and blew away most of our sails; and, as we were still among the keys, in a very few minutes it dashed the sloop against the rocks. Luckily for us the water was deep; and the sea was not so angry, but that, after having for some time labored hard, and being many in number, we were saved through God's mercy; and, by using our greatest exertions, we got the vessel off. The next day we returned to Providence, where we soon got her again refitted. Some of the people swore that we had spells set upon us, by somebody in Montserrat; and others said that we had witches and wizards amongst the poor helpless slaves; and that we never should arrive safe at Georgia. But these things did not deter me; I said, "Let us again face the winds and seas, and swear not, but trust to God, and he will deliver us." We therefore once more set sail; and with hard labor, in seven days' time arrived safe at Georgia.

After our arrival we went up to the town of Savannah; and the same evening I went to a friend's house to lodge, whose name was Mosa, a black man. We were very happy at meeting each other; and, after supper we had a light till it was between nine and ten o'clock at night. About that time the watch or patrol came by, and, discerning a light in the house, they knocked at the door; we opened it, and they came in and sat down, and drank some punch with us; they also begged some limes of me, as they understood I had some, which I readily gave them. A little after this they told me I must go to the watch-house with them; this surprised me a good deal, after our kindness to them; and I asked them, why so? They said that all negroes who had a light in their houses after nine o'clock were to be taken into custody, and either pay some dollars, or be flogged. Some of these people knew that I was a freeman; but, as the man of the house was not free, and had his master to protect him, they did not take the same liberty with him they did with me. I told them that I was a freeman, and just arrived from Providence; that we were not making any noise, and that I was not a stranger in that place, but was very well known there: "Besides," said I, "what will you do with me?"—"That you shall see," replied they, "but you must go to the watch-house with us." Now, whether they meant to get money from me or not, I was at a loss to know; but I thought immediately of the oranges and limes at Santa Cruz: and seeing that nothing would pacify them, I went with them to the watch-house, where I remained during the night. Early the next morning these imposing ruffians flogged a negro man and woman that they had in the watch-house, and then they told me that I must be flogged too; I asked why? and if there was no law for freemen? and told them if there was I would have it put in force against them. But this only exasperated them the more, and they instantly swore they would serve me as Doctor Perkins had done; and were going to lay violent hands on me; when one of them, more humane than the rest, said, that as I was a freeman they could not justify stripping me by law. I then immediately sent for Doctor Brady, who was known to be an honest and worthy man; and on his coming to my assistance they let me go.

This was not the only disagreeable incident I met with while I was in this place; for, one day, while I was a little way out of the town of Savannah, I was beset by two white men, who meant to play their usual tricks with me in the way of kidnapping. As soon as these men accosted me, one of them said to the other, "This is the very fellow we are looking for, that you lost": and the other swore immediately that I was the identical person. On this they made up to me, and were about to handle me; but I told them to be still and keep off, for I had seen those kind of tricks played upon other free blacks, and they must not think to serve me so. At this they paused a little, and one said to the other—it will not do; and the other answered that I talked too good English. I replied, I believed I did; and I had also with me a revengeful stick equal to the occasion; and my mind was likewise good. Happily however it was not used; and, after we had talked together a little in this manner, the rogues left me.

I stayed in Savannah some time, anxiously trying to get to Montserrat once more to see Mr. King, my old master, and then to take a final farewell of the American quarter of the globe. At last I met with a sloop called the *Speedwell*, Captain John Bunton, which belonged to Grenada, and was bound to Martinique, a French island, with a cargo of rice; and I shipped myself on board of her.

Before I left Georgia, a black woman who had a child lying dead, being very tenacious of the church burial service, and not able to get any white person to perform it, applied to me for that purpose. I told her I was no parson; and, besides, that the service over the dead did not affect the soul. This however did not satisfy her; she still urged me very hard; I therefore complied with her earnest entreaties, and at last consented to act the parson for the first time in my life. As she was much respected, there was a great company both of white and black people at the grave. I then accordingly assumed my new vocation, and performed the funeral ceremony to the satisfaction of all present; after which I bade adieu to Georgia, and sailed for Martinique.

Chapter IX

The Author arrives at Martinique—Meets with new difficulties—Gets to Montserrat, where he takes leave of his old master, and sails for England—Meets Captain Pascal—Learns the French horn—Hires himself with Doctor Irving, where he learns to freshen sea water—Leaves the Doctor and goes a voyage to Turkey and Portugal; and afterwards goes a voyage to Grenada, and another to Jamaica—Returns to the Doctor, and they embark together on a voyage to the North Pole, with the Honorable Captain Phipps—Some account of that voyage, and the dangers the Author was in—He returns to England.

I THUS TOOK A FINAL LEAVE of Georgia; for the treatment I had received in it disgusted me very much against the place; and when I left it and sailed for Martinique, I determined never more to revisit it. My new captain conducted his vessel safer than my former one; and, after an agreeable voyage we got safe to our intended port. While I was on this island I went about a good deal, and found it very pleasant: in particular, I admired the town of St. Pierre, which is the principal one in the island, and built more like a European town than any I had seen in the West Indies. In general also, slaves were better treated, had more holidays, and looked better than those in the English islands. After we had done our business here, I wanted my discharge, which was necessary; for it was then the month of May, and I wished much to be at Montserrat to bid farewell to Mr. King, and all my other friends there, in time to sail for old England in the July fleet. But, alas! I had put a great stumbling block in my own way, by which I was near losing my passage that season to England. I had lent my captain some money, which I now wanted, to enable me to prosecute my intentions. This I told him; but when I applied for it, though I urged the necessity of my occasion, I met with so much shuffling from him, that I began at last to be afraid of losing my money, as I could not recover it by law; for I have already mentioned, that throughout the West Indies no black man's testimony is admitted, on any occasion, against any white person whatever, and therefore my own oath would have been of no use. I was obliged therefore, to remain with him till he might be disposed to return it to me. Thus, we sailed from Martinique for the Grenades [Grenada]. I frequently pressing the captain for my money, to no purpose; and, to render my condition worse, when we got there, the captain and his owners quarreled; so that my situation became daily more irksome: for besides that we on board had little or no victuals allowed us, and I could not get my money nor wages, as I could then have gotten my passage free to Montserrat had I been able to accept it. The worst of all was, that it was growing late in July, and the ships in the islands must sail by the 26th of that month. At last, however, with a great many entreaties, I got my money from the captain, and took the first vessel I could meet with for St. Eustatius. From thence I went in another to Basseterre in St. Kitt's, where I arrived on the 19th of July. On the 22d, having met with a vessel bound to Montserrat, I wanted to go in her; but the captain and others would not take me on board until I should advertise myself, and give notice of my going off the island. I told them of my haste to be in Montserrat, and that the time then would not admit of advertising, it being late in the evening, and the vessel about to sail; but he insisted it was necessary, and otherwise he said he would not take me. This reduced me to great perplexity; for if I should be compelled to submit to this degrading necessity, which every black freeman is under, of advertising himself like a slave, when he leaves an island, and which I thought a gross imposition upon any freedom, I feared I should miss that opportunity of going to Montserrat, and then I could not get to England that year. The vessel was just going off, and no time could be lost; I immediately therefore set about with a heavy heart, to try who I could get to befriend me in complying with the demands of the captain. Luckily I found, in a few minutes, some gentlemen of Montserrat whom I knew; and, having told them my situation I requested their friendly assistance in helping me off the island. Some of them, on this, went with me to the captain, and satisfied him of my freedom; and, to my very great joy, he desired me to go on board. We then set sail, and the next day, 2d, I arrived at the wished-for place, after an absence of six months, in which I had more than once experienced the delivering hand of Providence, when all human means of escaping destruction seemed hopeless. I saw my friends with a gladness of heart, which was increased by my absence, and the dangers I had escaped, and I was received with great friendship by them all, but particularly by Mr. King, to whom I related the fate of his sloop, the

Nancy, and the causes of her being wrecked. I now learned with extreme sorrow, that his house was washed away during my absence, by the bursting of a pond at the top of a mountain that was opposite the town of Plymouth. It swept [a] great part of the town away, and Mr. King lost a great deal of property from the inundation, and nearly his life. When I told him I intended to go to London that season, and that I had come to visit him before my departure, the good man expressed a great deal of affection for me, and sorrow that I should leave him, and warmly advised me to stay there; insisting, as I was much respected by all the gentlemen in the place, that I might do very well, and in a short time have land and slaves of my own. I thanked him for this instance of his friendship; but, as I wished very much to be in London, I declined remaining any longer there, and begged he would excuse me. I then requested he would be kind enough to give me a certificate of my behavior while in his service, which he very readily complied with, and gave me the following:

Montserrat, 26th of July, 1767.
The bearer hereof, Gustavus Vasa, was my slave for upwards of three years, during which he has always behaved himself well, and discharged his duty with honesty and assiduity.

ROBERT KING.
To all whom this may concern.

Having obtained this, I parted from my kind master, after many sincere professions of gratitude and regard, and prepared for my departure for London. I immediately agreed to go with one Captain John Hunter, for seven guineas (the passage to London), on board a ship called the *Andromache*; and on the 24th and 25th, I had free dances, as they are called, with some of my friends and countrymen, previous to my setting off; after which I took leave of all my friends, and on the 26th I embarked for London, exceedingly glad to see myself once more on board of a ship, and still more so, in steering the course I had long wished for. With a light heart I bade Montserrat farewell, and never had my feet on it since; and with it I bade adieu to the sound of the cruel whip, and all other dreadful instruments of torture! Adieu to the offensive sight of the violated chastity of the sable females, which has too often accosted my eyes! Adieu to oppressions (although to me less severe than to most of my countrymen!) And adieu to the angry howling dashing surfs! I wished for a grateful and thankful heart to praise the Lord God on high for all his mercies! In this ecstasy I steered the ship all night.

We had a most prosperous voyage, and, at the end of seven weeks, arrived at Cherrygarden Stairs. Thus were my longing eyes once more gratified with a sight of London, after having been absent from it above four years. I immediately received my wages, and I never had earned seven guineas so quick in my life before; I had thirty-seven guineas in all when I got cleared of the ship. I now entered upon a scene quite new to me, but full of hope. In this situation my first thoughts were to look out for some of my former friends, and amongst the first of those were the Miss Guerins. As soon as I had regaled myself I went in quest of those kind ladies, whom I was very impatient to see; and, with some difficulty and perseverance, I found them at May's Hill, Greenwich. They were most agreeably surprised to see me, and I was quite over-joyed at meeting with them. I told them my history, at which they expressed great wonder, and freely acknowledged it did their cousin, Captain Pascal, no honor. He then visited there frequently; and I met him, four or five days after, in Greenwich Park. When he saw me, he appeared a good deal surprised, and asked me how I came back? I answered, "In a ship." To which he replied dryly, "I suppose you did not walk back to London on the water." As I saw, by his manner, that he did not seem to be sorry for his behavior to me, and that I had not much reason to expect any favor from him, I told him that he had used me very ill, after I had been such a faithful servant to him for so many years; on which, without saying anymore, he turned about and went away. A few days after this I met Captain Pascal at Miss Guerin's house, and asked him for my prize money. He said there was none due to me; for if my prize money had been 10,000 pounds he had a right to it all. I told him I was informed otherwise: on which he bade me defiance, and, in a bantering tone, desired me to commence a lawsuit against him for it: "There are lawyers enough," said he, "that will take the cause in hand, and you had better try it." I told him then, that I would try it, which enraged him very much; however, out of regard to the ladies, I remained still, and never made any further demand of my right. Some time afterwards, these friendly ladies asked me what I meant to do with myself, and how they could assist me. I thanked them, and said, if they pleased, I would be their servant; but if not I had thirty-seven guineas, which would support me for some time, and I would be much obliged to them to recommend me to some person who would teach me a business whereby I might earn my living. They answered me very politely, that they were sorry it did not suit them to take me as their servant, and asked me what business I should like to learn? I said, hairdressing. They then promised to assist me in this; and soon after, they recommended me to a gentleman whom I had known before, one Captain O'Hara, who treated me with much kindness, and procured me a master, a hairdresser, in Coventry Court, Haymarket, with whom he placed me. I was with this man from September till the February following. In that time we had a neighbor in the same court, who taught the French horn. He used to blow it so well, that I was charmed with it, and agreed with him to teach me to blow it. Accordingly he took me in hand, and began to instruct me, and I soon learned all the three parts. I took great delight in blowing on this instrument, the evenings being long; and besides that I was fond of it, I did not like to be idle, and it filled up my vacant hours innocently. At this time also I agreed with the Reverend Mr. Gregory, who lived in the same court, where he kept an academy and an evening school, to improve me in arithmetic. This he did as far as barter and aligation; so that all the time I was there I was entirely employed. In February 1768, I hired myself to Doctor Charles Irving, in Pall Mall, so celebrated for his successful experiments in making seawater fresh; and here I had plenty of hairdressing to improve my hand. This gentleman was an excellent master; he was exceedingly kind and good-tempered; and allowed me in the evenings to attend my schools, which I esteemed a great blessing; therefore I thanked God and him for it, and used all my diligence to improve the opportunity. This diligence and attention recommended me to the notice and care of my three preceptors, who on their parts bestowed a great deal of pains in my instruction, and besides were all very kind to me. My wages, however, which were by two-thirds less than ever I had in my life (for I had only 12 pounds per annum), I soon found would not be sufficient to defray this extraordinary expense of masters, and my own necessary expenses; my old thirty-seven guineas had by this time worn all away to one. I thought it best, therefore, to try the sea again in quest of more money, as I had been bred to it, and had hitherto found the profession of it successful. I had also a very great desire to see Turkey, and I now determined to gratify it. Accordingly, in the month of May 1768, I told the Doctor my wish to go to sea again, to which he made no opposition; and we parted on friendly terms. The same day I went into the city in quest of a master. I was extremely fortunate in my inquiry, for I soon heard of a gentleman who had a ship going to Italy and Turkey, and he wanted a man who could dress hair well. I was overjoyed at this, and went immediately on board of his ship, as I had been directed, which I found to be fitted up with great taste, and I already foreboded no small pleasure in sailing in her. Not finding the gentleman on board, I was directed to his lodgings, where I met with him the next day, and gave him a specimen of my dressing. He liked it so well that he hired me immediately, so that I was perfectly happy, for the ship, master, and voyage, were entirely to my mind. The ship was called the *Delawar,* and my master's name was John Jolly, a neat, smart, good-humored man, just such a one as I wished to serve. We sailed from England in July following, and our voyage was extremely pleasant. We went to Villefranche, Nice, and Leghorn; and in all these places I was charmed with the richness and beauty of the countries, and struck with the elegant buildings with which they abound. We had always in them plenty of extraordinary good wines and rich fruits, which I was very fond of; and I had frequent occasions of gratifying both my taste and curiosity; for my Captain always lodged on shore in those places, which afforded me opportunities to see the country around. I also learned navigation of the mate, which I was very fond of. When we left Italy, we had delightful sailing among the Archipelago islands, and from thence to Smyrna in Turkey. This is a very ancient city; the houses are built of stone, and most of them have graves adjoining to them; so that they sometimes present the appearance of churchyards. Provisions are very plentiful in this city, and good wine less than a penny a pint. The grapes, pomegranates, and many other fruits, were also the richest and largest I ever saw or tasted. The natives are well-looking, and strong made, and treated me always with great civility. In general I believe they are fond of black people; and several of them gave me pressing invitations to stay amongst them, although they keep the Franks, or Christians, separate, and do not suffer them to dwell immediately amongst them. I was astonished in not seeing women in any of their shops, and very rarely any in the streets; and whenever I did they were covered with a veil from head to foot, so that I could not see their faces, except when any of them out of curiosity uncovered them to look at me, which they sometimes did. I was surprised to see how the Greeks are, in some measure, kept under by the Turks, as the negroes are in the West Indies by the white people. The less refined Greeks, as I have already hinted, dance here in the same manner as we do in our nation.

On the whole, during our stay here, which was about five months, I liked the place and the Turks extremely well. I could not help observing one very remarkable circumstance there: the tails of the sheep are flat, and so very large, that I have known the tail even of a lamb to weigh from eleven to thirteen pounds. The fat of them is very white and rich,

and is excellent in puddings, for which it is much used. Our ship being at length richly loaded with silk and other articles, we sailed for
England.

In May 1769, soon after our return from Turkey, our ship made a
delightful voyage to Oporto, in Portugal, where we arrived at the time
of the carnival. On our arrival, there were sent on board of us thirty-six
articles to observe, with very heavy penalties if we should break any of
them; and none of us even dared to go on board any other vessel, or on
shore, till the Inquisition had sent on board and searched for everything illegal, especially bibles. All we had were produced, and certain
other things were sent on shore till the ships were going away; and any
person, in whose custody a bible was found concealed, was to be im-
prisoned and flogged, and sent into slavery for ten years. I saw here
many very magnificent sights, particularly the garden of Eden, where
many of the clergy and laity went in procession in their several orders
with the host, and sung *Te Deum*. I had a great curiosity to go into some
of their churches, but could not gain admittance without using the
necessary sprinkling of holy water at my entrance. From curiosity, and
a wish to be holy, I therefore complied with this ceremony, but its virtues were lost upon me, for I found myself nothing the better for it.
This place abounds with plenty of all kinds of provisions. The town is
well built and pretty, and commands a fine prospect. Our ship having
taken in a load of wine, and other commodities, we sailed for London,
and arrived in July following.

Our next voyage was to the Mediterranean. The ship was again got
ready, and we sailed in September for Genoa. This is one of the finest
cities I ever saw; some of the edifices were of beautiful marble, and
made a most noble appearance; and many had very curious fountains
before them. The churches were rich and magnificent, and curiously
adorned both in the inside and out. But all this grandeur was, in my
eyes, disgraced by the galley slaves, whose condition both there and in
other parts of Italy is truly piteous and wretched. After we had stayed
there some weeks, during which we bought many different things we
wanted, and got them very cheap, we sailed to Naples, a charming city,
and remarkably clean. The bay is the most beautiful I ever saw; the
moles for shipping are excellent. I thought it extraordinary to see
grand operas acted here on Sunday nights, and even attended by their
Majesties. I too, like these great ones, went to those sights, and vainly
served God in the day while I thus served mammon effectually at
night. While we remained here, there happened an eruption of Mount

Vesuvius, of which I had a perfect view. It was extremely awful; and we were so near that the ashes from it used to be thick on our deck. After we had transacted our business at Naples, we sailed with a fair wind once more for Smyrna, where we arrived in December. A *seraskier*, or officer, took a liking to me here, and wanted me to stay, and offered me two wives; however I refused the temptation, thinking one was as much as some could manage, and more than others would venture on. The merchants here travel in caravans in large companies. I have seen many caravans from India, with some hundreds of camels laden with different goods. The people of these caravans are quite brown. Among other articles, they brought with them a great quantity of locusts, which are a kind of pulse, sweet and pleasant to the palate, and in shape resembling French beans, but longer. Each kind of goods is sold in a street by itself, and I always found the Turks very honest in their dealings. They let no Christians into their mosques, or churches, for which I was very sorry; as I was always fond of going to see the different modes of worship of the people wherever I went. The plague broke out while we were in Smyrna, and we stopped taking goods into the ship till it was over. She was then richly laden, and we sailed in about March 1770 for England. One day in our passage we met with an accident which was near burning the ship. A black cook, in melting some fat, overset the pan into the fire under the deck, which immediately began to blaze, and the flame went up very high under the foretop. With the fright, the poor cook became almost white, and altogether speechless. Happily, however, we got the fire out without doing much mischief. After various delays in this passage, which was tedious, we arrived in Standgate Creek in July; and at the latter end of the year, some new event occurred, so that my noble captain, the ship, and I, all separated.

In April 1771, I shipped myself as a steward with Captain William Robertson of the ship *Grenada Planter*, once more to try my fortune in the West Indies; and we sailed from London for Madeira, Barbados, and the Grenadas. When we were at this last place, having some goods to sell, I met once more with my former kind of West India customers.

A white man, an islander, bought some goods of me to the amount of some pounds, and made me many fair promises as usual, but without any intention of paying me. He had likewise bought goods from some more of our people, whom he intended to serve in the same manner; but he still amused us with promises. However, when our ship was loaded and near sailing, this honest buyer discovered no intention or sign of paying for anything he had bought of us; but on the contrary, when I asked him for my money he threatened me and another black man he had bought goods of, so that we found we were like to get more blows than payment. On this we went to complain to one Mr. McIntosh, a justice of the peace; we told his worship of the man's villainous tricks, and begged that he would be kind enough to see us redressed: but being negroes, although free, we could not get any remedy; and our ship being then just upon the point of sailing, we knew not how to help ourselves, though we thought it hard to lose our property in this manner. Luckily for us, however, this man was also indebted to three white sailors, who could not get a farthing from him; they therefore readily joined us, and we all went together in search of him. When we found where he was, we took him out of a house and threatened him with vengeance; on which, finding he was likely to be handled roughly, the rogue offered each of us some allowance, but nothing near our demands. This exasperated us much; and some were for cutting his ears off; but he begged hard for mercy, which was at last granted him, after we had entirely stripped him. We then let him go, for which he thanked us, glad to get off so easily, and ran into the bushes, after having wished us a good voyage. We then repaired on board, and shortly after set sail for England. I cannot help remarking here a very narrow escape we had from being blown up, owing to a piece of negligence of mine. Just as our ship was under sail, I went down under the cabin to do some business, and had a lighted candle in my hand, which, in my hurry, without thinking, I held in a barrel of gunpowder. It remained in the powder until it was near catching fire, when fortunately I observed it, and snatched it out in time, and providentially no harm happened; but I was so overcome with terror that I immediately fainted at this deliverance.

In twenty-eight days' time we arrived in England, and I got clear of this ship. But, being still of a roving disposition, and desirous of seeing as many different parts of the world as I could, I shipped myself soon after, in the same year, as steward on board of a fine large ship, called the *Jamaica,* Captain David Watt; and we sailed from England in December 1771 for Nevis and Jamaica. I found Jamaica to be a very fine, large island, well peopled, and the most considerable of the West India islands. There [was] a vast number of negroes here, whom I found, as usual, exceedingly imposed upon by the white people, and the slaves punished as in the other islands. There are negroes whose business it is to flog slaves; they go about to different people for employment, and, the usual pay is from one to four bits. I saw many cruel punishments inflicted on the slaves in the short time I stayed here. In particular I was present when a poor fellow was tied up and kept hanging by the wrists at some distance from the ground, and then some half-hundred weights were fixed to his ankles, in which posture he was flogged most unmercifully. There were also, as I heard, two different masters noted for cruelty on the island, who had staked up two negroes naked, and in two hours the vermin stung them to death. I heard a gentleman, I well knew, tell my captain that he passed sentence on a negro man to be burnt alive for attempting to poison an overseer. I pass over numerous other instances, in order to relieve the reader by a milder scene of roguery. Before I had been long on the island, one Mr. Smith, at Port Morant, bought goods of me to the amount of twenty-five pounds sterling; but when I demanded payment from him, he was going each time to beat me, and threatened that he would put me in gaol. One time he would say I was going to set his house on fire; at another he would swear I was going to run away with his slaves. I was astonished at this usage from a person who was in the situation of a gentleman, but I had no alternative, and was therefore obliged to submit. When I came to Kingston, I was surprised to see the number of Africans who were assembled together on Sundays; particularly at a large commodious place called Spring Path. Here each different nation of Africa meet and dance after the manner of their own country. They still retain most of their native customs: they bury their dead, and put victuals, pipes and tobacco, and other things in the grave with the corpse, in the same manner as in Africa. Our ship having got her loading, we sailed for London, where we arrived in the August following. On my return to London, I waited on my old and good master, Doctor Irving, who made me an offer of his service again. Being now tired of the sea I gladly accepted it. I was very happy in living with this gentleman once more; during which time we were daily employed in reducing old Neptune's dominions by purifying the briny element, and making it fresh. Thus I went on till May 1773, when I was roused by the sound of fame to seek new adventures, and find, towards the North Pole, what our Creator never intended we should, a passage to India. An expedition was now fitting out to explore a northeast passage, conducted by the Honorable Constantine John Phipps, late Lord Mulgrave, in his Majesty's sloop of war the *Race Horse*. My master being anxious for the reputation of this adventure, we therefore prepared everything for our voyage, and I attended him on board the *Race Horse,* the 24th day of May 1773. We proceeded to Sheerness, where we were joined by his Majesty's sloop the *Carcass,* commanded by Captain Lutwidge. On the 4th of June we sailed towards our destined place, the pole; and on the 15th of the same month we were off Shetland. On this day I had a great and unexpected deliverance from an accident which was near blowing up the ship, and destroying the crew, which made me ever after during the voyage uncommonly cautious. The ship was so filled that there was very little room on board for anyone, which placed me in a very awkward situation. I had resolved to keep a journal of this singular and interesting voyage; and I had no other place for this purpose but a little cabin, or the doctor's storeroom, where I slept. This little place was stuffed with all manner of combustibles, particularly with tow and aqua fortis, and many other dangerous things. It happened in the evening, as I was writing my journal, that I had occasion to take the candle out of the lantern, and a spark unfortunately having touched a single thread of the tow, all the rest caught the flame, and immediately the whole was in a blaze. I saw nothing but present death before me, and expected to be the first to perish in the flames. In a moment the alarm was spread and many people who were near ran to assist in putting out the fire. All this time I was in the very midst of the flames; my shirt, and the handkerchief on my neck, were burnt, and I was almost smothered with the smoke. However, through God's mercy, as I was nearly giving up all hopes, some people brought blankets and mattresses, and threw them on the flames, by which means, in a short time, the fire was put out. I was severely reprimanded and menaced by such of the officers who knew it, and strictly charged never more to go there with a light: and, indeed, even my own fears made me give heed to this command for a little time; but at last, not being able to write my journal in any other part of the ship, I was tempted again to venture by stealth with a light in the same cabin, though not without considerable fear and dread on my mind. On the 20th of June we began to use Doctor Irving's apparatus for making saltwater fresh; I used to attend the distillery; I frequently purified from twenty-six to forty gallons a day. The water thus distilled was perfectly pure, well tasted, and free from salt; and was used on various occasions on board the ship. On the 28th of June, being in latitude 78, we made Greenland, where I was surprised to see the sun did not set. The weather now became extremely cold; and as we sailed between north and east, which was our course, we saw many very high and curious mountains of ice; and also a great number of very large whales, which used to come close to our ship, and blow the water up to a very great height in the air. One morning we had vast quantities of sea horses [walruses] about the ship, which neighed exactly like any other horses. We fired some harpoon guns amongst them in order to take some, but we could not get any. The 30th, the captain of a Greenland ship came on board, and told us of three ships that were lost in the ice; however we still held on our course till July the 11th, when we were stopped by one compact impenetrable body of ice. We ran along it from east to west above ten degrees; and on the 27th we got as far north as 80, 37; and in 19 or 20 degrees east longitude from London. On the 29th and 30th of July, we saw one continued plain of smooth unbroken ice, bounded only by the horizon; and we fastened to a piece of ice that was eight yards eleven inches thick. We had generally sunshine, and constant daylight; which gave cheerfulness and novelty to the whole of this striking, grand, and uncommon scene; and to heighten it still more, the reflection of the sun from the ice gave the clouds a most beautiful appearance. We killed many different animals at this time, and, among the rest, nine bears. Though they had nothing in their paunches but water yet they were all very fat. We used to decoy them to the ship sometimes by burning feathers or skins. I thought them coarse eating, but some of the ship's company relished them very much. Some of our people once, in a boat, fired at and wounded a sea horse, which dived immediately; and in a little time after brought up with it a number of others. They all joined in an attack upon the boat, and were with difficulty prevented from staving or oversetting her; but a boat from the *Carcass* having come to assist ours, and joined it, they dispersed, after having wrested an oar from one of the men. One of the ship's boats had before been attacked in the same manner, but happily no harm was done. Though we wounded several of these animals we never got but one. We remained hereabouts until the 1st of August; when the two ships got completely fastened in the ice, occasioned by the loose ice that set in from the sea. This made our situation very dreadful and alarming; so that on the 7th day we were in very great apprehension of having the ships squeezed to pieces. The officers now held a council to know what was best for us to do in order to save our lives; and it was determined that we should endeavor to escape by dragging our boats along the ice towards the sea; which, however, was farther off than any of us thought. This determination filled us with extreme dejection, and confounded us with despair; for we had very little prospect of escaping with life. However, we sawed some of the ice about the ships, to keep it from hurting them; and thus kept them in a kind of pond. We then began to drag the boats as well as we could towards the sea; but, after two or three days' labor, we made very little progress; so that some of our hearts totally failed us, and I really began to give up myself for lost, when I saw our surrounding calamities. While we were at this hard labor, I once fell into a pond we had made amongst some loose ice, and was very near being drowned; but providentially some people were near, who gave me immediate assistance, and thereby I escaped drowning. Our deplorable condition, which kept up the constant apprehension of our perishing in the ice, brought me gradually to think of eternity in such a manner as I never had done before. I had the fears of death hourly upon me, and shuddered at the thought of meeting the grim king of terrors in the *natural* state I then was in, and was exceedingly doubtful of a happy eternity if I should die in it. I had no hopes of my life being prolonged for any time; for we saw that our existence could not be long on the ice after leaving the ships, which were now out of sight, and some miles from the boats. Our appearance now became truly lamentable; pale dejection seized every countenance; many, who had been before blasphemers, in this our distress began to call on the good God of heaven for his help; and in the time of our utter need he heard us, and against hope, or human probability, delivered us! It was the eleventh day of the ship's being thus fastened, and the fourth of our drawing the boats in this manner, that the wind changed to the east-northeast. The weather immediately became mild and the ice broke towards the sea, which was to the southwest of us. Many of us on this got on board again, and with all our might we hove the ships into every open water we could find, and made all the sail on them in our power: now, having a prospect of success, we made signals for the boats and the remainder of the people. This seemed to us like a reprieve from death; and happy was the man who could first get on board of any ship, or the first boat he could meet. We then proceeded in this manner till we got into open water again, which we accomplished in about thirty hours, to our infinite joy and gladness of heart. As soon as we were out of danger, we came to anchor and refitted; and on the 19th of August we sailed from this uninhabited extremity of the world, where the inhospitable climate affords neither food nor shelter, and not a tree or shrub of any kind grows amongst its barren rocks, but all is one desolate and expanded waste of ice, which even the constant beams of the sun for six months in the year cannot penetrate or dissolve. The sun now being on the decline the days shortened as we sailed to the southward; and, on the 28th, in latitude 78, it was dark by ten o'clock at night. September the 10th, in latitude

58–59, we met a very severe gale of wind and high seas, and shipped a great deal of water in the space of ten hours. This made us work exceedingly hard at all our pumps a whole day; and one sea, which struck the ship with more force than anything I ever met with of the kind before, laid her under water for some time so that we thought she would have gone down. Two boats were washed from the booms, and the longboat from the chucks: all other moveable things on the decks were also washed away, among which were many curious things of different kinds, which we had brought from Greenland; and we were obliged, in order to lighten the ship, to toss some of our guns overboard. We saw a ship at the same time in very great distress, and her masts were gone; but we were unable to assist her. We now lost sight of the *Carcass* till the 26th, when we saw land about Orfordness, off which place she joined us. From thence we sailed for London, and on the 30th came up to Deptford. And thus ended our Arctic voyage, to the no small joy of all on board, after having been absent four months; in which time, at the imminent hazard of our lives, we explored nearly as far towards the Pole as 81 degrees north, and 20 degrees east longitude; being much farther, by all accounts, than any navigator had ever ventured before; in which we fully proved the impracticability of finding a passage that way to India.

Chapter X

The Author leaves Doctor Irving, and engages on board a Turkey ship—Account of a black man's being kidnapped on board, and sent to the West Indies, and the Author's fruitless endeavors to procure his freedom—Some account of the manner of the Author's conversion to the Faith of Jesus Christ.

OUR VOYAGE TO THE NORTH POLE being ended, I returned to London with Doctor Irving, with whom I continued for some time, during which I began seriously to reflect on the dangers I had escaped, particularly those of my last voyage, which made a lasting impression on my mind; and, by the grace of God, proved afterwards a mercy to me: it caused me to reflect deeply on my eternal state, and to seek the Lord with full purpose of heart ere it be too late. I rejoiced greatly; and heartily thanked the Lord for directing me to London, where I was determined to work out my own salvation, and, in so doing, procure a title to heaven; being the result of a mind blinded by ignorance and sin.

In process of time I left my master, Doctor Irving, the purifier of waters. I lodged in Coventry Court, Haymarket, where I was continually oppressed and much concerned about the salvation of my soul, and was determined (in my own strength) to be a first-rate Christian. I used every means for this purpose; and, not being able to find any person amongst those with whom I was then acquainted that acquiesced with me in point of religion, or, in scripture language, that would show me any good, I was much dejected, and knew not where to seek relief; however, I first frequented the neighboring churches, St. James's, and others, two or three times a day, for many weeks: still I came away dissatisfied: something was wanting that I could not obtain, and I really found more heartfelt relief in reading my bible at home than in attending the church; and, being resolved to be saved, I pursued other methods. First I went among the people called Quakers, whose meeting at times was in silence, and I remained as much in the dark as ever. I then searched into the Roman Catholic principles, but was not in the least edified. I at length had recourse to the Jews, which availed me nothing, as the fear of eternity daily harassed my mind and I knew not where to seek shelter from the wrath to come. However, this was my conclusion, at all events, to read the four evangelists, and whatever sect or party I found adhering thereto, such I would join. Thus I went on heavily without any guide to direct me the way that leadeth to eternal life. I asked different people questions about the manner of going to heaven, and was told different ways. Here I was much staggered, and could not find any at that time more righteous than myself, or indeed so much inclined to devotion. I thought we should not all be saved (this is agreeable to the Holy Scriptures), nor would all be damned. I found none among the circle of my acquaintance that kept holy the Ten Commandments. So righteous was I in my own eyes, that I was convinced I excelled many of them in that point, by keeping eight out of ten; and finding those, who in general termed themselves Christians, not so honest or so good in their morals as the Turks. I really thought the Turks were in a safer way of salvation than my neighbors; so that between hopes and fears I went on, and the chief comforts I enjoyed were in the musical French horn, which I then practiced, and also dressing of hair. Such was my situation some months, experiencing the dishonesty of many people here. I determined at last to set out for Turkey, and there to end my days. It was now early in the spring

1774. I sought for a master, and found a Captain John Hughes, commander of a ship called *Anglicama,* fitting out in the river Thames, and bound to Smyrna in Turkey. I shipped myself with him as a steward; at the same time I recommended to him a very clever black man, John Annis, as a cook. This man was on board the ship near two months doing his duty: he had formerly lived many years with Mr. William Kirkpatrick, a gentleman of the island of St. Kitt's, from whom he parted by consent, though he afterwards tried many schemes to inveigle the poor man. He had applied to many captains, who traded to St. Kitt's, to trepan him; and when all their attempts and schemes of kidnapping proved abortive, Mr. Kirkpatrick came to our ship at Union Stairs, on Easter Monday, April the 4th, with two wherry boats and six men, having learned that the man was on board, and tied, and forcibly took him away from the ship, in the presence of the crew and the chief mate, who had detained him after he had information to come away. I believe this was a combined piece of business; but, be that as it may, it certainly reflected great disgrace on the mate, and captain also, who, although they had desired the oppressed man to stay on board, yet notwithstanding this vile act on the man who had served him, he did not in the least assist to recover him, or pay me a farthing of his wages, which was about five pounds. I proved the only friend he had, who attempted to regain him his liberty, if possible, having known the want of liberty myself. I sent as soon as I could to Gravesend, and got knowledge of the ship in which he was; but unluckily she had sailed the first tide after he was put on board. My intention was then immediately to apprehend Mr. Kirkpatrick, who was about setting off for Scotland; and, having obtained a *habeas corpus* for him, and got a tipstaff to go with me to St. Paul's Churchyard, where he lived, he, suspecting something of this kind, set a watch to look out. My being known to them, obliged me to use the following deception: I whitened my face that they might not know me, and this had the desired effect. He did not go out of his house that night, and next morning I contrived a well-plotted stratagem, notwithstanding he had a gentleman in his house to personate him. My direction to the tipstaff had the desired effect; he got admittance into the house, and conducted him to a judge according to the writ. When he came there, his plea was, that he had not the body in custody, on which he was admitted to bail. I proceeded immediately to that well-known philanthropist, Granville Sharp, Esq., who received me with the utmost kindness, and gave me every instruction that was needful on the occasion. I left him in full hope that I should gain the unhappy man his liberty, with the warmest sense of gratitude towards Mr. Sharp for his kindness; but, alas! my attorney proved unfaithful; he took my money, lost me many months employ, and did not do the least good in the cause; and when the poor man arrived at St. Kitt's, he was, according to custom, staked to the ground with four pins through a cord, two on his wrists, and two on his ankles, was cut and flogged most unmercifully, and afterwards loaded cruelly with irons about his neck. I had two very moving letters from him while he was in this situation; and I made attempts to go after him at a great hazard, but was sadly disappointed: I also was told of it by some very respectable families now in London, who saw him in St. Kitt's in the same state, in which he remained till kind death released him out of the hands of his tyrants. During this disagreeable business, I was under strong convictions of sin, and thought that my state was worse than any man's; my mind was unaccountably disturbed; I often wished for death, though at the same time convinced I was altogether unprepared for that awful summons: suffering much by villains in the late cause, and being much concerned about the state of my soul, these things (but particularly the latter) brought me very low; so that I became a burden to myself, and viewed all things around me as emptiness and vanity, which could give no satisfaction to a troubled conscience. I was again determined to go to Turkey, and resolved, at that time, never more to return to England. I engaged as steward on board a Turkeyman (the *Wester Hall*, Captain Lina), but was prevented by means of my late captain, Mr. Hughes, and others. All this appeared to be against me, and the only comfort I then experienced was in reading the Holy Scriptures, where I saw that "there is no new thing under the sun," (Eccles. 1:9); and what was appointed for me I must submit to. Thus I continued to travel in much heaviness, and frequently murmured against the Almighty, particularly in his providential dealings; and, awful to think! I began to blaspheme, and wished often to be anything but a human being. In these severe conflicts the Lord answered me by awful "visions of the night, when deep sleep falleth upon men, in slumberings upon the bed." (Job 33:15) He was pleased, in much mercy, to give me to see, and in some measure understand, the great and awful scene of the judgment day, that "no unclean person, no unholy thing, can enter into the kingdom of God." (Eph. 5:5) I would then, if it had been possible, have changed my nature with the meanest worm on the earth, and was ready to say to the mountains and rocks, "fall on me," (Rev. 6:16); but all in vain. I then, in the greatest agony, requested the divine

Creator, that he would grant me a small space of time to repent of my follies and vile iniquities, which I felt were grievous. The Lord, in his manifold mercies, was pleased to grant my request, and being yet in a state of time, the sense of God's mercies were so great on my mind when I awoke, that my strength entirely failed me for many minutes, and I was exceedingly weak. This was the first spiritual mercy I ever was sensible of, and being on praying ground, as soon as I recovered a little strength, and got out of bed and dressed myself, I invoked heaven from my inmost soul, and fervently begged that God would never again permit me to blaspheme his most holy name. The Lord, who is long-suffering, and full of compassion to such poor rebels as we are, condescended to hear and answer. I felt that I was altogether unholy, and saw clearly what a bad use I had made of the faculties I was endowed with: they were given me to glorify God with; I thought, therefore, I had better want them here, and enter into life eternal, than abuse them and be cast into hellfire. I prayed to be directed, if there were any holier persons than those with whom I was acquainted, that the Lord would point them out to me. I appealed to the Searcher of Hearts, whether I did not wish to love him more, and serve him better. Notwithstanding all this, the reader may easily discern, if a believer, that I was still in nature's darkness. At length I hated the house in which I lodged, because God's most holy name was blasphemed in it; then I saw the word of God verified, namely, "Before they call, I will answer; and while they are yet speaking, I will hear."

I had a great desire to read the Bible the whole day at home; but not having a convenient place for retirement, I left the house in the day, rather than stay amongst the wicked ones; and that day, as I was walking, it pleased God to direct me to a house where there was an old seafaring man, who experienced much of the love of God shed abroad in his heart. He began to discourse with me; and, as I desired to love the Lord, his conversation rejoiced me greatly; and indeed I had never heard before the love of Christ to believers set forth in such a manner, and in so clear a point of view. Here I had more questions to put to the man than his time would permit him to answer: and in that memorable hour there came in a Dissenting Minister; he joined our discourse, and asked me some few questions; among others, where I heard the Gospel preached? I knew not what he meant by hearing the gospel; I told him I had read the gospel: and he asked me where I went to church, or whether I went at all, or not? To which I replied, "I attended St. James's, St. Martin's, and St. Ann's, Soho." "So," said he, "you are a churchman?" I answered, I was. He then invited me to a love feast at his chapel that evening. I accepted the offer, and thanked him; and soon after he went away. I had some further discourse with the old Christian, added to some profitable reading, which made me exceedingly happy. When I left him he reminded me of coming to the feast; I assured him I would be there. Thus we parted, and I weighed over the heavenly conversation that had passed between these two men, which cheered my then heavy and drooping spirit more than anything I had met with for many months. However, I thought the time long in going to my supposed banquet. I also wished much for the company of these friendly men; their company pleased me much; and I thought the gentleman very kind in asking me, a stranger, to a feast; but how singular did it appear to me, to have it in a chapel! When the wished for hour came I went, and happily the old man was there, who kindly seated me, as he belonged to the place. I was much astonished to see the place filled with people, and no signs of eating and drinking. There were many ministers in the company. At last they began by giving out hymns, and between the singing, the ministers engaged in prayer: in short, I knew not what to make of this sight, having never seen anything of the kind in my life before now. Some of the guests began to speak their experience, agreeable to what I read in the Scriptures: much was said by every speaker of the providence of God, and his unspeakable mercies to each of them. This I knew in a great measure, and could most heartily join them. But when they spoke of a future state, they seemed to be altogether certain of their calling and election of God; and that no one could ever separate them from the love of Christ, or pluck them out of his hands. This filled me with utter consternation intermingled with admiration. I was so amazed as not to know what to think of the company; my heart was attracted, and my affections were enlarged; I wished to be as happy as them, and was persuaded in my mind that they were different from the world "that lieth in wickedness." (1 John 5:19) Their language and singing, etc. did well harmonize; I was entirely overcome, and wished to live and die thus. Lastly, some persons in the place produced some neat baskets full of buns, which they distributed about; and each person communicated with his neighbor, and sipped water out of different mugs, which they handed about to all who were present. This kind of Christian fellowship I had never seen, nor ever thought of seeing on earth; it fully reminded me of what I had read in the Holy Scriptures of the primitive Christians, who loved each other and broke bread; in partaking of it, even from house to house. This entertainment (which lasted about four hours) ended in singing and prayer. It was the first soul feast I ever was present at. This last twenty-four hours produced me things, spiritual and temporal, sleeping and walking, judgment and mercy, that I could not but admire the goodness of God, in directing the blind, blasphemous sinner in the path that he knew not, even among the just; and instead of judgment he has showed mercy, and will hear and answer the prayers and supplications of every returning prodigal;

> *O! to grace how great a debtor*
> *Daily I'm constrain'd to be.*

After this I was resolved to win heaven, if possible; and if I perished, I thought it should be at the feet of Jesus, in praying to him for salvation. After having been an eyewitness to some of the happiness which attended those who feared God, I knew not how, with any propriety, to return to my lodgings, where the name of God was continually profaned, at which I felt the greatest horror; I paused in my mind for some time, not knowing what to do; whether to hire a bed elsewhere, or go home again. At last, fearing an evil report might arise, I went home, with a farewell to card-playing and vain-jesting, etc. I saw that time was very short, eternity long, and very near; and I viewed those persons alone blessed, who were found ready at midnight call, or when the judge of all, both quick and dead, cometh.

The next day I took courage, and went to Holborn, to see my new and worthy acquaintance, the old man, Mr. C———; he, with his wife, a gracious woman, were at work at silk-weaving; they seemed mutually happy, and both quite glad to see me, and I more so to see them. I sat down, and we conversed much about soul matters, etc. Their discourse was amazingly delightful, edifying, and pleasant. I knew not at last how to leave this agreeable pair, till time summoned me away. As I was going they lent me a little book, entitled *The Conversion of an Indian*. It was in questions and answers. The poor man came over the sea to London, to inquire after the Christian's God, who (through rich mercy) he found, and had not his journey in vain. The above book was of great use to me, and at that time was a means of strengthening my faith; however, in parting, they both invited me to call on them when I pleased. This delighted me, and I took care to make all the improvement from it I could; and so far I thanked God for such company and desires. I prayed that the many evils I felt within might be done away, and that I might be weaned from my former carnal acquaintances.

This was quickly heard and answered, and I was soon connected with those whom the Scripture calls the excellent of the earth. I heard the gospel preached, and the thoughts of my heart and actions were laid open by the preachers, and the way of salvation by Christ alone was evidently set forth. Thus I went on happily for near two months; and I once heard during this period, a reverend gentleman (Mr. Green) speak of a man who had departed this life in full assurance of his going to glory. I was much astonished at the assertion; and did very deliberately inquire how he could get at this knowledge. I was answered fully, agreeably to what I read in the oracles of truth; and was told also, that if I did not experience the new birth, and the pardon of my sins, through the blood of Christ, before I died, I could not enter the kingdom of heaven. I knew not what to think of this report, as I thought I kept eight commandments out of ten; then my worthy interpreter told me I did not do it, nor could I; and he added, that no man ever did or could keep the commandments, without offending in one point. I thought this sounded every strange, and puzzled me much for many weeks; for I thought it a hard saying. I then asked my friend, Mr. L——d, who was a clerk of a chapel, why the commandments of God were given, if we could not be saved by them? To which he replied, "The law is a schoolmaster to bring us to Christ," who alone could, and did keep the commandments, and fulfilled all their requirements for his elect people, even those to whom he had given a living faith, and the sins of those chosen vessels *were already* atoned for and forgiven them while living;* and if I did not experience the same before my exit, the Lord would say at that great day to me, "Go, ye cursed," etc. etc., for God would appear faithful in his judgments to the wicked, as he would be faithful in showing mercy to those who were ordained to it before the world was; therefore Christ Jesus seemed to be all in all to that man's soul. I was much wounded at this discourse, and brought into such a dilemma as I never expected. I asked him, if *he* was to die that moment, whether he was sure to enter the kingdom of God; and added, "Do you *know* that your sins are forgiven you?" he answered in the affirmative. Then confusion, anger, and discontent seized me, and I staggered much at this sort of doctrine; it brought me to a stand, not knowing which to believe, whether salvation by works, or by faith only in Christ. I requested him to tell me how I might know when my sins were forgiven me. He assured me he could not, and that none but God alone could do this. I told him it was very mysterious; but he said it was

*Rom. 8:1, 2, 3.

really matter of fact, and quoted many portions of Scripture immediately to the point, to which I could make no reply. He then desired me to pray to God to show me these things. I answered that I prayed to God every day. He said, "I perceive you are a churchman." I answered, I was. He then entreated me to beg of God, to show me what I was, and the true state of my soul. I thought the prayer very short and odd; so we parted for that time. I weighed all these things well over, and could not help thinking how it was possible for a man to know that his sins were forgiven him in this life. I wished that God would reveal this selfsame thing unto me. In a short time after this I went to Westminster chapel; the late Reverend Doctor Peckwell preached from Lamentations 3:39. It was a wonderful sermon; he clearly showed that a living man had no cause to complain for the punishments of his sins; he evidently justified the Lord in all his dealings with the sons of men; he also showed the justice of God in the eternal punishment of the wicked and impenitent. The discourse seemed to me like a two-edged sword cutting all ways; it afforded me much joy, intermingled with many fears about my soul; and when it was ended, he gave it out that he intended, the ensuing week, to examine all those who meant to attend the Lord's Table. Now I thought much of my good works, and at the same time was doubtful of my being a proper object to receive the sacrament: I was full of meditation till the day of examining. However, I went to the chapel, and, though much distressed, I addressed the reverend gentleman, thinking, if I was not right, he would endeavor to convince me of it. When I conversed with him, the first thing he asked me was, what I knew of Christ? I told him I believed in him, and had been baptized in his name. "Then," said he, "when were you brought to the knowledge of God; and how were you convinced of sin?" I knew not what he meant by these questions; I told him I kept eight commandments out of ten; but that I sometimes swore on board ship, and sometimes when on shore, and broke the Sabbath. He then asked me if I could read; I answered, "Yes."—"Then," said he, "do you not read in the Bible, he that offends in one point is guilty of all?" I said, "Yes." Then he assured me, that one sin unattoned for was as sufficient to damn a soul, as one leak was to sink a ship. Here I was struck with awe; for the minister exhorted me much, and reminded me of the shortness of time, and the length of eternity, and that no unregenerate soul, or anything unclean, could enter the kingdom of heaven.

He did not admit me as a communicant; but recommended me to read the Scriptures, and hear the word preached; not to neglect fervent prayer to God, who has promised to hear the supplications of those who seek him in godly sincerity; so I took my leave of him, with many thanks, and resolved to follow his advice, so far as the Lord would condescend to enable me. During this time I was out of employ, nor was I likely to get a situation suitable for me, which obliged me to go once more to sea. I engaged as steward of a ship called the *Hope,* Captain Richard Strange, bound from London to Cadiz in Spain. In a short time after I was on board, I heard the name of God much blasphemed, and I feared greatly lest I should catch the horrible infection. I thought if I sinned again, after having life and death set evidently before me, I should certainly go to hell. My mind was uncommonly chagrined, and I murmured much at God's providential dealings with me, and was discontented with the commandments, that I could not be saved by what I had done; I hated all things, and wished I had never been born; confusion seized me, and I wished to be annihilated. One day I was standing on the very edge of the stern of the ship, thinking to drown myself; but this Scripture was instantly impressed on my mind, "That no murderer hath eternal life abiding in him." (I John 3:15) Then I paused, and thought myself the unhappiest man living. Again, I was convinced that the Lord was better to me than I deserved, and I was better off in the world than many. After this I began to fear death; I fretted, mourned, and prayed, till I became a burden to others, but more so to myself. At length I concluded to beg my bread on shore, rather than go again to sea amongst a people who feared not God, and I entreated the captain three different times to discharge me; he would not, but each time gave me greater and greater encouragement to continue with him, and all on board showed me very great civility: notwithstanding all this, I was unwilling to embark again. At last some of my religious friends advised me, by saying it was my lawful calling, consequently it was my duty to obey, and that God was not confined to place, etc., particularly Mr. G. Smith, the governor of Tothill Fields Bridewell, who pitied my case, and read the eleventh chapter of the Hebrews to me, with exhortations. He prayed for me, and I believe that he prevailed on my behalf, as my burden was then greatly removed, and I found a heartfelt resignation to the will of God. The good man gave me a pocket Bible, and Alleine's *Alarm to the Unconverted.* We parted, and the next day I went on board again. We sailed for Spain, and I found favor with the captain. It was the fourth of the month of September when we sailed from London: we had a delightful voyage to Cadiz, where we arrived the twenty-third of the same month. The place is strong, commands a fine prospect, and is very rich. The Spanish galleons frequent that port, and some arrived whilst we were there.

I had many opportunities of reading the Scriptures. I wrestled hard with God in fervent prayers, who had declared in his word that he would hear the groanings and deep sighs of the poor in spirit. I found this verified to my utter astonishment and comfort in the following manner: On the morning of the 6th of October (I pray you to attend) all that day, I thought that I should either see or hear something supernatural. I had a secret impulse on my mind of something that was to take place,* which drove me continually for that time to a throne of grace. It pleased God to enable me to wrestle with him, as Jacob did: I prayed that if sudden death were to happen, and I perished, it might be at Christ's feet.

In the evening of the same day, as I was reading and meditating on the fourth chapter of the Acts, twelfth verse, under the solemn apprehensions of eternity, and reflecting on my past actions, I began to think I had lived a moral life, and that I had a proper ground to believe I had an interest in the divine favor; but still meditating on the subject, not knowing whether salvation was to be had partly for our own good deeds, or solely as the sovereign gift of God:—in this deep consternation the Lord was pleased to break in upon my soul with his bright beams of heavenly light; and in an instant, as it were, removing the veil and letting light into a dark place. (Isa. 25:7) I saw clearly, with the eye of faith, the crucified Savior, bleeding on the cross on Mount Calvary: the Scriptures became an unsealed book, I saw myself a condemned criminal under the law, which came with its full force to my conscience, and when "the commandment came sin revived, and I died." I saw the Lord Jesus Christ in his humiliation, loaded and bearing my reproach, sin, and shame. I then clearly perceived, that by the deeds of the law no flesh living could be justified. I was then convinced, that by the first Adam sin came, and by the second Adam (the Lord Jesus Christ) all that are saved must be made alive. It was given me at that time to know what it was to be born again. (John 3:5) I saw the eighth chapter to the Romans, and the doctrines of God's decrees, verified agreeable to his eternal, everlasting, and unchangeable purposes. The word of God was sweet to my taste, yea sweeter than honey and the honeycomb. Christ was revealed to my soul as the chiefest among ten thousand. These heavenly moments were really as life to the dead, and what John calls an earnest of the Spirit.† This was indeed unspeakable, and, I firmly believe, undeniable by many. Now every leading providential circumstance that happened to me, from the day I was taken

*See page 243.
†John 16:13, 14, etc.

from my parents to that hour, was then in my view, as if it had but just then occurred. I was sensible of the invisible hand of God, which guided and protected me when in truth I knew it not: still the Lord pursued me although I slighted and disregarded it; this mercy melted me down. When I considered my poor wretched state, I wept, seeing what a great debtor I was to sovereign free grace. Now the Ethiopian was willing to be saved by Jesus Christ, the sinner's only surety, and also to rely on none other person or thing for salvation. Self was obnoxious, and good works he had none, for it is God that worketh in us both to will and to do. Oh! the amazing things of that hour can never be told—it was joy in the Holy Ghost! I felt an astonishing change; the burden of sin, the gaping jaws of hell, and the fears of death, that weighed me down before, now lost their horror; indeed I thought death would now be the best earthly friend I ever had. Such were my grief and joy, as, I believe, are seldom experienced. I was bathed in tears, and said, what am I, that God should thus look on me the vilest of sinners? I felt a deep concern for my mother and friends, which occasioned me to pray with fresh ardor; and, in the abyss of thought, I viewed the unconverted people of the world in a very awful state, being without God and without hope.

It pleased God to pour out on me the spirit of prayer and the grace of supplication, so that in loud acclamations I was enabled to praise and glorify his most holy name. When I got out of the cabin, and told some of the people what the Lord had done for me, alas! who could understand me or believe my report! None but to whom the arm of the Lord was revealed. I became a barbarian to them in talking of the love of Christ: his name was to me as ointment poured forth; indeed it was sweet to my soul, but to them a rock of offense. I thought my case singular, and every hour a day until I came to London, for I much longed to be with some to whom I could tell of the wonders of God's love towards me, and join in prayer to him whom my soul loved and thirsted after. I had uncommon commotions within, such as few can tell aught about. Now the Bible was my only companion and comfort; I prized it much, with many thanks to God that I could read it for myself, and was not left to be tossed about or led by man's devices and notions. The worth of a soul cannot be told.—May the Lord give the reader an understanding in this. Whenever I looked in the Bible I saw things new, and many texts were immediately applied to me with great comfort; for I knew that to me was the word of salvation sent. Sure I was that the Spirit which indited the word opened my heart to receive the truth of it as it is in Jesus—that the same Spirit enabled me to act with faith upon the promises which were precious to me, and enabled me to believe to the salvation of my soul. By free grace I was persuaded that I had a part and lot in the first resurrection, and was enlightened with the "light of the living." (Job 33:30) I wished for a man of God, with whom I might converse; my soul was like the chariots of Aminadab, Canticles 6:12. These, among others, were the precious promises that were so powerfully applied to me: "All things whatsoever ye shall ask in prayer, believing, ye shall receive." (Matt. 21:22) "Peace I leave with you, my peace I give unto you." (John 14:27) I saw the blessed Redeemer to be the fountain of life, and the well of salvation. I experienced him to be all in all; he had brought me by a way that I knew not, and he had made crooked paths straight. Then in his name I set up my Ebenezer, saying, hitherto he had helped me: and could say to the sinners about me, behold what a Savior I have. Thus I was, by the teaching of that all-glorious Deity, the great One in Three, and Three in One, confirmed in the truths of the Bible; those oracles of everlasting truth, on which every soul living must stand or fall eternally, agreeable to Acts 4:12. "Neither is there salvation in any other, for there is no other name under heaven given among men whereby we must be saved, but only Jesus Christ." May God give the reader a right understanding in these facts! "To him that believeth, all things are possible, but to them that are unbelieving, nothing is pure." (Titus 1:15)

During this period we remained at Cadiz until our ship got laden. We sailed about the 4th of November; and, having a good passage, we arrived in London the month following, to my comfort, with heartfelt gratitude to God, for his rich and unspeakable mercies.

On my return I had but one text which puzzled me, or that the devil endeavored to buffet me with, namely Romans 11:6, and as I had heard of the Reverend Mr. Romaine, and his great knowledge in the Scriptures, I wished much to hear him preach. One day I went to Blackfriars Church, and, to my great satisfaction and surprise he preached from that very text. He very clearly showed the difference between human works and free election, which is according to God's sovereign will and pleasure. These glad tidings set me entirely at liberty, and I went out of the church rejoicing, seeing my spots were those of God's children. I went to Westminster chapel, and saw some of my old friends, who were glad when they perceived the wonderful change that the Lord had wrought in me, particularly Mr. G. Smith, my worthy acquaintance, who was a man of a choice spirit, and had great zeal for the Lord's service. I enjoyed his correspondence till he died in the year 1784. I was again examined in that same chapel, and was received into church fel-

lowship amongst them: I rejoiced in spirit, making melody in my heart
to the God of all my mercies. Now my whole wish was to be dissolved,
and to be with Christ—but, alas! I must wait mine appointed time.

Miscellaneous Verses

Or,

REFLECTIONS ON THE STATE OF MY MIND DURING MY FIRST CON-
VICTIONS OF THE NECESSITY OF BELIEVING THE TRUTH, AND EXPE-
RIENCING THE INESTIMABLE BENEFITS OF CHRISTIANITY.

> *Well may I say my life has been*
> *One scene of sorrow and of pain;*
> *From early days I griefs have known,*
> *And as I grew my griefs have grown.*
>
> *Dangers were always in my path;*
> *And fear of wrath and sometimes death;*
> *While pale dejection in me reign'd*
> *I often wept, by grief constrain'd.*
>
> *When taken from my native land,*
> *By an unjust and cruel band,*
> *How did uncommon dread prevail!*
> *My sighs no more I could conceal.*
>
> *To ease my mind I often strove,*
> *And tried my trouble to remove:*
> *I sung and utter'd sighs between—*
> *Assay'd to stifle guilt with sin.*
>
> *But O! not all that I could do*
> *Would stop the current of my woe;*
> *Conviction still my vileness show'd;*
> *How great my guilt—how lost to good.*
>
> *Prevented, that I could not die,*
> *Nor could to one sure refuge fly;*
> *An orphan state I had to mourn,—*
> *Forsook by all, and left forlorn.*

Those who beheld my downcast mien,
Could not guess at my woes unseen:
They by appearance could not know
The troubles that I waded through.

Lust, anger, blasphemy, and pride,
With legions of such ills beside,
Troubled my thoughts, while doubts and fears
Clouded and darken'd most my years.

Sighs now no more would be confin'd—
They breath'd the trouble of my mind:
I wish'd for death, but check'd the word,
And often pray'd unto the Lord.

Unhappy, more than some on earth,
I thought the place that gave me birth—
Strange thoughts oppress'd—while I replied,
"Why not in Ethiopia died?"

And why thus spar'd when nigh to hell!—
God only knew—I could not tell!—
A tott'ring fence, a bowing wall,
I thought myself e'er since the fall.

Oft times I mus'd, and nigh despair,
While birds melodious fill'd the air;
Thrice happy songsters, ever free,
How blest were they, compar'd to me!

Thus all things added to my pain;
While grief compell'd me to complain;
When sable clouds began to rise,
My mind grew darker than the skies.

The English nation forc'd to leave,
How did my breast with sorrow heave!
I long'd for rest—cried "Help me, Lord,
Some mitigation, Lord, afford."

Yet on, dejected, still I went—
Heart-throbbing woes within me pent;
Nor land, nor sea, could comfort give,
Nor aught my anxious mind relieve.

Weary with troubles yet unknown
To all but God and self alone,
Numerous months for peace I strove,
Numerous foes I had to prove.

Inur'd to dangers, grief, and woes,
Train'd up 'midst perils, death, and foes,
I said, "Must it thus ever be?
No quiet is permitted me."

Hard hap, and more than heavy lot!
I pray'd to God, "Forget me not—
What thou ordain'st help me to bear;
But, O! deliver from despair!"

Strivings and wrestling seem'd in vain;
Nothing I did could ease my pain:
Then gave I up my work and will,
Confess'd and own'd my doom was hell!

Like some poor pris'ner at the bar,
Conscious of guilt, of sin and fear,
Arraign'd, and self-condemn'd I stood—
"Lost in the world and in my blood!"

Yet here, 'midst blackest clouds confin'd,
A beam from Christ, the day star shin'd;
Surely, thought I, if Jesus please,
He can at once sign my release.

I, ignorant of his righteousness,
Set up my labors in its place;
Forgot for why his blood was shed,
And pray'd and fasted in his stead.

He dy'd for sinners—I am one;
Might not his blood for me atone?
Tho' I am nothing else but sin,
Yet surely he can make me clean!

Thus light came in, and I believ'd;
Myself forgot, and help receiv'd!
My Savior then I know I found,
For, eas'd from guilt, no more I groan'd.

O, happy hour, in which I ceas'd
To mourn, for then I found a rest!
My soul and Christ were now as one—
Thy light, O Jesus, in me shone!

Bless'd be thy name, for now I know
I and my works can nothing do;
"The Lord alone can ransom man—
For this the spotless Lamb was slain!"

When sacrifices, works, and pray'r,
Prov'd vain, and ineffectual were,
"Lo, then I come!" the Savior cry'd,
And bleeding, bow'd his head and dy'd.

He dy'd for all who ever saw
No help in them, nor by the law:
I this have seen; and gladly own
"Salvation is by Christ alone!" *

Chapter XI

The Author embarks on board a ship bound for Cadiz—Is near being shipwrecked—Goes to Malaga—Remarkable fine cathedral there— The Author disputes with a Popish priest—Picks up eleven miserable men at sea in returning to England—Engages again with Doctor Irving to accompany him to Jamaica and the Miskito shore—Meets with an Indian prince on board—The Author attempts to instruct him in the truths of the gospel—Frustrated by the bad example of some in the ship— They arrive on the Miskito shore with some slaves they purchased at Jamaica, and begin to cultivate a plantation—Some account of the manners and customs of the Miskito Indians—Successful device of the Author to quell a riot among them—Curious entertainment giv[en] by them to Doctor Irving and the Author, who leaves the shore, and goes for Jamaica—Is barbarously treated by a man with whom he engaged for his passage—Escapes, and goes to the Miskito admiral, who treats him kindly—He gets another vessel, and goes on board—Instances of bad treatment—Meets Doctor Irving—Gets to Jamaica—Is cheated by his captain—Leaves the doctor, and sails for England.

*Acts 4:12.

WHEN OUR SHIP was got ready for sea again, I was entreated by the captain to go in her once more; but, as I felt myself as happy as I could wish to be in this life, I for some time refused; however, the advice of my friends at last prevailed; and, in full resignation to the will of God, I again embarked for Cadiz in March, 1775. We had a very good passage, without any material accident, until we arrived off the Bay of Cadiz; when one Sunday, just as we were going into the harbor, the ship struck against a rock, and knocked off a garboard plank, which is the next to the keel. In an instant all hands were in the greatest confusion, and began with loud cries to call on God to have mercy on them. Although I could not swim, and saw no way of escaping death, I felt no dread in my then situation, having no desire to live. I even rejoiced in spirit, thinking this death would be sudden glory. But the fullness of time was not yet come. The people near to me were much astonished in seeing me thus calm and resigned; but I told them of the peace of God, which through sovereign grace I enjoyed, and these words were that instant in my mind:

> *Christ is my pilot wise, my compass is his word;*
> *My soul each storm defies, while I have such a Lord.*
>   *I trust his faithfulness and power,*
>   *To save me in the trying hour.*
>
> *Though rocks and quicksands deep through all my passage lie,*
> *Yet Christ shall safely keep and guide me with his eye.*
>   *How can I sink with such a prop,*
>   *That bears the world and all things up.*

At this time there were many large Spanish flukers or passage vessels full of people crossing the channel, who, seeing our condition, a number of them came alongside of us. As many hands as could be employed began to work; some at our three pumps, and the rest unloading the ship as fast as possible. There being only a single rock, called the Porpus, on which we struck, we soon got off it, and providentially it was then high water; we therefore run the ship ashore at the nearest place to keep her from sinking. After many tides, with a great deal of care and industry, we got her repaired again. When we had dispatched our business at Cadiz, we went to Gibraltar, and from thence to Malaga, a very pleasant and rich city, where there is one of the finest cathedrals I had ever seen. It had been above fifty years in building, as I heard, though it was not then quite finished; great part of the inside, however, was completed, and highly decorated with the richest marble columns and many superb paintings; it was lighted occasionally by an amazing number of wax tapers of different sizes, some of which were as thick as a man's thigh; these, however, were only used on some of their grand festivals.

I was very much shocked at the custom of bullbaiting, and other diversions which prevailed here on Sunday evenings, to the great scandal of Christianity and morals. I used to express my abhorrence of it to a priest whom I met with. I had frequent contests about religion with the reverend father, in which he took great pains to make a proselyte of me to his church; and I no less to convert him to mine. On these occasions I used to produce my bible, and show him in what points his church erred. He then said he had been in England, and that every person there read the bible, which was very wrong; but I answered him, that Christ desired us to search the Scriptures. In his zeal for my conversion, he solicited me to go to one of the universities in Spain, and declared that I should have my education free; and told me, if I got myself made a priest, I might in time become even a Pope; and he said that Pope Benedict was a black man. As I was ever desirous of learning, I paused some time upon this temptation, and thought by being crafty (by going to the university), I might catch some with guile; but again I began to think it would only be hypocrisy in me to embrace his offer, as I could not in conscience conform to the opinions of his church. I was therefore enabled to regard the word of God, which says, "Come out from amongst them," and refused Father Vincent's offer. So we parted without conviction on either side.

Having taken at this place some fine wines, fruits, and money, we proceeded to Cadiz, where we took about two tons more of money, etc. and then sailed for England in the month of June. When we were about the north latitude 42, we had contrary wind for several days, and the ship did not make in that time above six or seven miles straight course. This made the captain exceedingly fretful and peevish; and I was very sorry to hear God's most holy name often blasphemed by him. One day, as he was in that impious mood, a young gentleman on board, who was a passenger, reproved him, and said he acted wrong, for we ought to be thankful to God for all things, as we were not in want of anything on board; and though the wind was contrary for us, yet it was fair for some others, who perhaps stood in more need of it than we. I immediately seconded this young gentleman with some boldness, and said we had not the least cause to murmur, for that the Lord was better to us than we deserved, and that he had done all things well. I expected that the captain would be very angry with me for speaking, but he replied not a word. However, before that time, or hour, on the following day, being the 21st of June, much to our great joy and astonishment, we saw the providential hand of our benign Creator, whose ways with his blind creatures are past finding out. The preceding night I dreamed that I saw a boat immediately off the starboard main shrouds; and exactly at half-past one o'clock the following day at noon, while I was below, just as we had dined in the cabin, the man at the helm cried out, A boat! which brought my dream that instant into my mind. I was the first man that jumped on the deck; and looking from the shrouds onward, according to my dream, I descried a little boat at some distance; but, as the waves were high, it was as much as we could do sometimes to discern her: we, however, stopped the ship's way, and the boat which was extremely small, came alongside with eleven miserable men, whom we took on board immediately. To all human appearance these people must have perished in the course of one hour, or less; the boat being small, it barely contained them. When we took them up they were half-drowned, and had no victuals, compass, water, or any other necessary whatsoever, and had only one bit of an oar to stir with, and that right before the wind; so that they were obliged to trust entirely to the mercy of the waves. As soon as we got them all on board, they bowed themselves on their knees, and, with hands and voices lifted up to heaven, thanked God for their deliverance; and I trust that my prayers were not wanting amongst them at the same time. This mercy of the Lord quite melted me, and I recollected his words, which I saw thus verified in the 107th Psalm,

O give thanks unto the Lord, for he is good, for his mercy endureth forever. Hungry and thirsty, their souls fainted in them. They cried unto the Lord in their trouble, and he delivered them out of their distresses. And he led them forth by the right way, that they might go to a city of habitation. O that men would praise the Lord for his goodness, and for his wonderful works to the children of men! For he satisfieth the longing soul, and filleth the hungry soul with goodness.

Such as sit in darkness and in the shadow of death:

Then they cried unto the Lord in their trouble, and he saved them out of their distresses. They that go down to the sea in ships; that do business in great waters; these see the works of the Lord, and his wonders in the deep. Whoso is wise and will observe these things, even they shall understand the loving kindness of the Lord.

The poor distressed captain said, "that the Lord is good; for, seeing that I am not fit to die, he therefore gave me a space of time to repent." I was very glad to hear this expression, and took an opportunity, when convenient, of talking to him on the providence of God. They told us they were Portuguese, and were in a brig loaded with corn, which shifted that morning at five o'clock, owing to which the vessel sunk that instant with two of the crew; and how these eleven got into the boat (which was lashed to the deck) not one of them could tell. We provided them with every necessary, and brought them all safe to London: and I hope the Lord gave them repentance unto eternal life.

At our arrival, I was happy once more amongst my friends and brethren till November, when my old friend, the celebrated Doctor Irving, bought a remarkable fine sloop, about 150 tons. He had a mind for a new adventure, in cultivating a plantation at Jamaica and the Miskito shore; asked me to go with him, and said that he would trust me with his estate in preference to anyone. By the advice, therefore, of my friends, I accepted of the offer, knowing that the harvest was fully ripe in those parts, and hoped to be an instrument, under God, of bringing some poor sinner to my well-beloved master, Jesus Christ. Before I embarked, I found with the Doctor four Miskito Indians, who were chiefs in their own country, and were brought here by some English traders for some selfish ends. One of them was the Miskito king's son, a youth of about eighteen years of age; and whilst he was here he was baptized by the name of George. They were going back at the government's expense, after having been in England about twelve months, during which they learned to speak pretty good English. When I came to talk to them, about eight days before we sailed, I was very much mortified in finding that they had not frequented any churches since they were here, and were baptized, nor was any attention paid to their morals. I was very sorry for this mock Christianity, and had just an opportunity to take some of them once to church before we sailed. We embarked in the month of November 1775, on board of the sloop *Morning Star,* Captain David Miller, and sailed for Jamaica. In our passage I took all the pains that I could to instruct the Indian prince in the doctrines of Christianity, of which he was entirely ignorant; and, to my great joy, he was quite attentive, and received with gladness the truths that the Lord enabled me to set forth to him. I taught him in the compass of eleven days all the letters, and he could put even two or three of them together, and spell them. I had Fox's *Martyrology* with cuts, and he used to be very fond of looking into it, and would ask many questions about the papal cruelties he saw depicted there, which I explained to him. I made such progress with this youth, especially in religion, that when I used to go to bed at different hours of the night, if he was in his bed, he would get up on purpose to go to prayer with me, without any other clothes than his shirt; and before he would eat any of his meals amongst the gentlemen in the cabin, he would first come to me to pray, as he called it. I was well pleased at this, and took great delight in him, and used much supplication to God for his conversion. I was in full hope of seeing daily every appearance of that change which I could wish; not knowing the devices of Satan, who had many of his emissaries to sow his tares as fast as I sowed the good seed, and pull down as fast as I built up. Thus we went on nearly four-fifths of our passage, when Satan at last got the upper hand. Some of his messengers, seeing this poor heathen much advanced in piety, began to ask him whether I had converted him to Christianity, laughed and made their jest at him, for which I rebuked them as much as I could; but this treatment caused the prince to halt between two opinions. Some of the true sons of Belial, who did not believe that there was any hereafter, told him never to fear the devil, for there was none existing; and if ever he came to the prince, they desired he might be sent to them. Thus they teased the poor innocent youth, so that he would not learn his book anymore! He would not drink nor carouse with these ungodly actors, nor would he be with me even at prayers. This grieved me very much. I endeavored to persuade him as well as I could, but he would not come; and entreated him very much to tell me his reasons for acting thus. At last he asked me, "How comes it that all the white men on board who can read and write, and observe the sun, and know all things, yet swear, lie, and get drunk, only excepting yourself?" I answered him, the reason was, that they did not fear God; and that if any one of them died so they could not go to, or be happy with God. He replied, that if a certain person went to hell he would go to hell too! I was sorry to hear this; and, as he sometimes had the toothache, and also some other persons in the ship at the same time, I asked him if their toothache made his easy? he said, no. Then I told him, if he and these people went to hell together, their pains would not make his any lighter. This had great weight with him: it depressed his spirits much; and he became ever after, during the passage, fond of being alone. When we were in the latitude of Martinique, and near making the land, one morning we had a brisk gale of wind, and, carrying too much sail, the mainmast went over the side. Many people were then all about the deck, and the yards, masts, and rigging, came tumbling all about us, yet there was not one of us the least hurt, although some were within a hair's breadth of being killed; and, particularly, I saw two men, who, by the providential hand of God, were most miraculously preserved from being smashed to pieces. On the 5th of January we made Antigua and Montserrat, and ran along the rest of the islands: and on the fourteenth we arrived at Jamaica. One Sunday, while we were there, I took the Miskito, Prince George, to church, where he saw the sacrament administered. When we came out we saw all kinds of people, almost from the church door for the space of half a mile down to the waterside, buying and selling all kinds of commodities: and these acts afforded me great matter of exhortation to this youth, who was much astonished. Our vessel being ready to sail for the Miskito shore, I went with the Doctor on board a Guinea-man, to purchase some slaves to carry with us, and cultivate a plantation; and I chose them all of my own countrymen, some of whom came from Libya.* On the 12th of February we sailed from Jamaica, and on the eighteenth arrived at the Miskito shore, at a place called Dupeupy. All our Indian guests now, after I had admonished them, and a few cases of liquor given them by the Doctor, took an affectionate leave of us, and went ashore, where they were met by the Miskito king, and we never saw one of them afterwards. We then sailed to the southward of the shore, to a place called Cape Gracias a Dios, where there was a large lagoon or lake, which received the emptying of two or three very fine large rivers, and abounded much in fish and land tortoise. Some of the native Indians came on board of us here; and we used them well, and told them we were come to dwell amongst them, which they seemed pleased at. So the Doctor and I, with some others, went with them ashore; and they took us to different places to view the land, in order to choose a place to make a plantation of. We fixed on a spot near a river's bank, in a rich soil; and, having got our necessaries out of the sloop, we began to clear away the woods, and plant different kinds of vegetables, which had a quick growth. While we were employed in this manner, our vessel went northward to Black River to trade. While she was there, a Spanish *guarda costa* met with and took her. This proved very hurtful, and a great embarrassment to us. How-

*See John Brown's *Scripture Dictionary*, I Chron. 1: 33. Also Purver's Bible, with Notes on Gen. 25:4.

ever, we went on with the culture of the land. We used to make fires every night all around us, to keep off wild beasts, which, as soon as it was dark, set up a most hideous roaring. Our habitation being far up in the woods, we frequently saw different kinds of animals; but none of them ever hurt us, except poisonous snakes, the bite of which the Doctor used to cure by giving to the patient, as soon as possible, about half a tumbler of strong rum, with a good deal of Cayenne pepper in it. In this manner he cured two natives, and one of his own slaves. The Indians were exceedingly fond of the Doctor, and they had good reason for it; for I believe they never had such a useful man amongst them. They came from all quarters to our dwelling; and some *woolwow* or flat-headed Indians, who lived fifty or sixty miles above our river, and this side of the South Sea, brought us a good deal of silver in exchange for our goods. The principal articles we could get from our neighboring Indians were turtle oil, and shells, little silk grass, and some provisions; but they would not work at anything for us, except fishing; and a few times they assisted to cut some trees down, in order to build us houses; which they did exactly like the Africans, by the joint labor of men, women and children. I do not recollect any of them to have had more than two wives. These always accompanied their husbands when they came to our dwelling, and then they generally carried whatever they brought to us, and always squatted down behind their husbands. Whenever we gave them anything to eat, the men and their wives ate separate. I never saw the least sign of incontinence amongst them. The women are ornamented with beads, and fond of painting themselves; the men also paint, even to excess, both their faces and shirts: their favorite color is red. The women generally cultivate the ground, and the men are all fishermen and canoe makers. Upon the whole, I never met any nation that were so simple in their manners as these people, or had so little ornament in their houses. Neither had they, as I ever could learn, one word expressive of an oath. The worst word I ever heard amongst them when they were quarreling, was one that they had got from the English, which was, "you rascal." I never saw any mode of worship among them, but in this they were not worse than their European brethren or neighbors, for I am sorry to say that there was not one white person in our dwelling, nor anywhere else, that I saw, in different places I was at on the shore, that was better or more pious than those unenlightened Indians; but they either worked or slept on Sundays; and, to my sorrow, working was too much Sunday's employment with ourselves; so much so, that in some length of time we really did not know one day from another. This mode of living laid the foundation of my decamping at last. The natives are well made and warlike; and they particularly boast of having never been conquered by the Spaniards. They are great drinkers of strong liquors when they can get them. We used to distill rum from pineapples, which were very plentiful here; and then we could not get them away from our place. Yet they seemed to be singular, in point of honesty, above any other nation I was ever amongst. The country being hot, we lived under an open shed, where we had all kinds of goods, without a door or lock to any one article; yet we slept in safety, and never lost anything, or were disturbed. This surprised us a good deal; and the Doctor, myself, and others, used to say if we were to lie in that manner in Europe we should have our throats cut the first night. The Indian Governor goes once in a certain time all about the province or district, and has a number of men with him as attendants and assistants. He settles all the differences among the people, like the judges here, and is treated with very great respect. He took care to give us timely notice before he came to our habitation, by sending his stick as a token, for rum, sugar, and gunpowder, which we did not refuse sending; and at the same time we made the utmost preparations to receive his honor and his train. When he came with his tribe, and all our neighboring chieftains, we expected to find him a grave reverend judge, solid and sagacious; but, instead of that, before he and his gang came in sight, we heard them very clamorous; and they even had plundered some of our good neighboring Indians, having intoxicated themselves with our liquor. When they arrived we did not know what to make of our new guests, and would gladly have dispensed with the honor of their company. However, having no alternative, we feasted them plentifully all the day till the evening; when the Governor, getting quite drunk, grew very unruly, and struck one of our most friendly chiefs, who was our nearest neighbor, and also took his gold-laced hat from him. At this a great commotion took place; and the Doctor interfered to make peace, as we could all understand one another, but to no purpose; and at last they became so outrageous, that the Doctor, fearing he might get into trouble, left the house, and made the best of his way to the nearest wood, leaving me to do as well as I could among them. I was so enraged with the Governor, that I could have wished to have seen him tied fast to a tree, and flogged for his behavior; but I had not people enough to cope with his party. I therefore thought of a stratagem to appease the riot. Recollecting a passage I had read in the *Life of Columbus,* when he was amongst the

Indians in Mexico or Peru, where, on some occasion, he frightened them, by telling them of certain events in the heavens, I had recourse to the same expedient, and it succeeded beyond my most sanguine expectations. When I had formed my determination, I went in the midst of them, and taking hold of the Governor, I pointed up to the heavens. I menaced him and the rest: I told them God lived there, and that he was angry with them, and they must not quarrel so; that they were all brothers, and if they did not leave off and go away quietly, I would take the book (pointing to the bible), read, and *tell* God to make them dead. This operated on them like magic. The clamor immediately ceased, and I gave them some rum and a few other things; after which they went away peaceably; and the Governor afterwards gave our neighbor, who was called Captain Plasmyah, his hat again. When the Doctor returned, he was exceedingly glad at my success in thus getting rid of our troublesome guests. The Miskito people within our vicinity, out of respect to the Doctor, myself, and his people, made entertainments of the grand kind, called in their tongue *tourrie* or *drykbot*. The English of this expression is, a feast of drinking about, of which it seems a corruption of language. The drink consisted of pineapples roasted, and casades [casavas] chewed or beaten in mortars; which, after lying some time, ferments, and becomes so strong as to intoxicate when drank in any quantity. We had timely notice given to us of the entertainment. A white family, within five miles of us, told us how the drink was made; I and two others went before the time to the village where the mirth was appointed to be held, and there we saw the whole art of making the drink and also the kind of animals that were to be eaten there. I cannot say the sight of either the drink or the meat were enticing to me. They had some thousands of pineapples roasting, which they squeezed, dirt and all, into a canoe they had there for the purpose. The casava drink was in beef barrels, and other vessels, and looked exactly like hogwash. Men, women, and children were thus employed in roasting the pineapples, and squeezing them with their hands. For food they had many land torpins or tortoises, some dried turtle, and three large alligators alive, and tied fast to the trees. I asked the people what they were going to do with these alligators? and I was told they were to be eaten. I was much surprised at this, and went home not a little disgusted at the preparations. When the day of the feast was come, we took some rum with us, and went to the appointed place, where we found a great assemblage of these people, who received us very kindly. The mirth had begun before we came; and they were dancing with music: and the musical instruments were nearly the same as those of any other sable people; but, as I thought, much less melodious than any other nation I ever knew. They had many curious gestures in dancing, and a variety of motions and postures of their bodies, which to me were in no wise attracting. The males danced by themselves, and the females also by themselves, as with us. The Doctor showed his people the example, by immediately joining the women's party, though not by their choice. On perceiving the women disgusted, he joined the males. At night there were great illuminations, by setting fire to many pine trees, while the drykbot went round merrily by calabashes or gourds: but the liquor might more justly be called eating than drinking. One Owden, the oldest father in the vicinity, was dressed in a strange and terrifying form. Around his body were skins adorned with different kinds of feathers, and he had on his head a very large and high headpiece, in the form of a grenadier's cap, with prickles like a porcupine; and he made a certain noise which resembled the cry of an alligator. Our people skipped amongst them out of complaisance, though some could not drink of their tourrie; but our rum met with customers enough, and was soon gone. The alligators were killed, and some of them roasted. Their manner of roasting is by digging a hole in the earth, and filling it with wood, which they burn to coal, and then they lay sticks across, on which they lay the meat. I had a raw piece of the alligator in my hand: it was very rich: I thought it looked like fresh salmon, and it had a most fragrant smell, but I could not eat any of it. This merrymaking at last ended without the least discord in any person in the company, although it was made up of different nations and complexions.

The rainy season came on here about the latter end of May, which continued till August very heavily; so that the rivers were overflowed, and our provisions then in the ground were washed away. I thought this was in some measure a judgment upon us for working on Sundays, and it hurt my mind very much. I often wished to leave this place, and sail for Europe; for our mode of procedure, and living in this heathenish form, was very irksome to me. The word of God saith, "What doth it avail a man if he gain the whole world and lose his own soul!" This was much and heavily impressed on my mind; and, though I did not know how to speak to the Doctor for my discharge, it was disagreeable for me to stay any longer. But about the middle of June I took courage enough to ask him for it. He was very unwilling at first to grant me my request, but I gave him so many reasons for it, that at last he consented to my going, and gave me the following certificate of my behavior:

> The bearer, Gustavus Vassa, has served me several years with strict honesty, sobriety, and fidelity. I can, therefore, with justice recommend him for these qualifications; and indeed in every respect I consider him as an excellent servant. I do hereby certify that he always behaved well, and that he is perfectly trustworthy.
>
> CHARLES IRVING.
> Miskito Shore, June 15, 1776.

Though I was much attached to the Doctor, I was happy when he consented to my going. I got everything ready for my departure, and hired some Indians, with a large canoe, to carry me off. All my poor countrymen, the slaves, when they heard of my leaving them were very sorry, as I had always treated them with care and affection, and did everything I could do to comfort the poor creatures, and render their condition easy. Having taken leave of my old friends and companions, on the 18th of June, accompanied by the Doctor, I left that spot of the world, and went southward above twenty miles along the river. There I found a sloop, the captain of which told me he was going to Jamaica. Having agreed for my passage with him and one of the owners, who was also on board, named Hughes, the Doctor and I parted, not without shedding tears on both sides. The vessel then sailed along the river till night, when she stopped in a lagoon within the same river. During the night a schooner belonging to the same owners came in, and, as she was in want of hands, Hughes, the owner of the sloop, asked me to go in the schooner as a sailor, and said he would give me wages. I thanked him; but I said I wanted to go to Jamaica. He then immediately changed his tone, and swore, and abused me very much, and asked how I came to be freed! I told him, and said that I came into that vicinity, with Doctor Irving, whom he had seen that day. This account was of no use; he still swore exceedingly at me, and cursed the master for a fool that sold me my freedom, and the Doctor for another in letting me go from him. Then he desired me to go in the schooner, or else I should not go out of the sloop as a freeman. I said this was very hard, and begged to be put on shore again; but he swore that I should not. I said I had been twice amongst the Turks, yet had never seen any such usage with them, and much less could I have expected anything of this kind among the Christians. This incensed him exceedingly; and with a volley of oaths and imprecations he replied, "Christians! damn you, you are one of St. Paul's men; but by G—d, except you have St. Paul's or St. Peter's faith, and walk upon the water to the shore, you shall not go out of the vessel!" which I now learnt was going amongst the Spaniards towards Cartagena, where he swore he would sell me. I simply asked him what right he had to sell me? But, without another word, he made some of his people tie ropes round each of my ankles, and also to each wrist, and another rope round my body, and hoisted me up without letting my feet touch or rest upon anything. Thus I hung, without any crime committed, and without judge or jury, merely because I was a freeman, and could not by the law get any redress from a white person in those parts of the world. I was in great pain from my situation, and cried and begged very hard for some mercy, but all in vain. My tyrant in a rage brought a musket out of the cabin, and loaded it before me and the crew, and swore that he would shoot me if I cried anymore. I had now no alternative; I therefore remained silent, seeing not one white man on board who said a word in my behalf. I hung in that manner from between ten and eleven o'clock at night till about one in the morning; when, finding my cruel abuser fast asleep, I begged some of his slaves to slacken the rope that was round my body, that my feet might rest on something. This they did at the risk of being cruelly abused by their master, who beat some of them severely at first for not tying me when he commanded them. Whilst I remained in this condition, till between five and six o'clock next morning, I trusted and prayed to God to forgive this blasphemer, who cared not what he did, but when he got up out of his sleep in the morning was of the very same temper and disposition as when he left me at night. When they got up the anchor, and the vessel was getting under way, I once more cried and begged to be released; and now, being fortunately in the way of their hoisting the sails, they loosed me. When I was let down, I spoke to one Mr. Cox, a carpenter, whom I knew on board, on the impropriety of this conduct. He also knew the Doctor, and the good opinion he ever had of me. This man then went to the captain, and told him not to carry me away in that manner; that I was the Doctor's steward, who regarded me very highly, and would resent this usage when he should come to know it. On which he desired a young man to put me ashore in a small canoe I brought with me. This sound gladdened my heart and I got hastily into the canoe, and set off whilst my tyrant was down in the cabin; but he soon spied me out, when I was not above thirty or forty yards from the vessel, and running upon the deck with a loaded musket in his hand, he presented it at me, and swore heavily and dreadfully that he would shoot me that instant, if I did not come back on board. As I knew the wretch would have done as he said, without hesitation, I put back to the vessel again; but, as the good Lord would have it, just as I was alongside, he was abusing the captain for letting me go from the vessel; which the captain returned, and both of them soon got into a very great heat. The young man that was with me, now got out of the canoe; the vessel was sailing on fast with a smooth sea; and I then thought it was neck or nothing, so at that instant I set off again, for my life, in the canoe, towards the shore; and fortunately the confusion was so great amongst them on board, that I got out of the reach of the musket shot, unnoticed, while the vessel sailed on with a fair wind a different way; so that they could not overtake me without tacking; but, even before that could be done, I should have been on shore, which I soon reached, with many thanks to God for this unexpected deliverance. I then went and told the other owner, who lived near the shore (with whom I had agreed for my passage), of the usage I had met with. He was very much astonished, and appeared very sorry for it. After treating me with kindness, he gave me some refreshment, and three heads of roasted Indian corn, for a voyage of about eighteen miles south, to look for another vessel. He then directed me to an Indian chief of a district, who was also the Miskito admiral, and had once been at our dwelling; after which I set off with the canoe across a large lagoon alone (for I could not get anyone to assist me), though I was much jaded, and had pains in my bowels, by means of the rope I had hung by the night before. I was therefore at different times unable to manage the canoe, for the paddling was very laborious. However, a little before dark, I got to my destined place, where some of the Indians knew me, and received me kindly. I asked for the admiral; and they conducted me to his dwelling. He was glad to see me, and refreshed me with such things as the place afforded; and I had a hammock to sleep in. They acted towards me more like Christians than those whites I was amongst the last night, though they had been baptized. I told the admiral I wanted to go to the next port to get a vessel to carry me to Jamaica; and requested him to send the canoe back which I then had, for which I was to pay him. He agreed with me, and sent five able Indians with a large canoe to carry me and my things to my intended place, about fifty miles; and we set off the next morning. When we got out of the lagoon, and went along shore, the sea was so high, that the canoe was oftentimes very near being filled with water. We were obliged to go ashore, and drag her across different necks of land; we were also two nights in the swamps, which swarmed with mosquito flies, and they proved troublesome to us. This tiresome journey of land and water ended, however, on the third day, to my great joy; and I got on board of a sloop commanded by one Captain Jenning. She was then partly loaded, and he told me he was expecting daily to sail for Jamaica; and having agreed with me to work my passage, I went to work accordingly. I was not many days on board before we sailed; but, to my sorrow and disappointment, though used to such tricks, we went to the southward along the Miskito shore, instead of steering for Jamaica. I was compelled to assist in cutting a great deal of mahogany wood on the shore as we coasted along it, and load the vessel with it, before she sailed. This fretted me much; but, as I did not know how to help myself among these deceivers, I thought patience was the only remedy I had left, and even that was forced. There was much hard work and little victuals on board, except by good luck we happened to catch turtles. On this coast there was also a particular kind of fish called manatee, which is most excellent eating, and the flesh is more like beef than fish; the scales are as large as a shilling, and the skin thicker than I ever saw that of any other fish. Within the brackish waters along shore there were likewise vast numbers of alligators, which made the fish scarce. I was on board this sloop sixteen days, during which, in our coasting, we came to another place, where there was a smaller sloop called the *Indian Queen*, commanded by one John Baker. He also was an Englishman, and had been a long time along the shore trading for turtle shells and silver, and had got a good quantity of each on board. He wanted some hands very much; and, understanding I was a freeman, and wanted to go to Jamaica, he told me if he could get one or two men more, that he would sail immediately for that island; he also pretended to show me some marks of attention and respect, and promised to give me forty-five shillings sterling a month if I would go with him. I thought this much better than cutting wood for nothing. I therefore told the other captain that I wanted to go to Jamaica in the other vessel; but he would not listen to me; and, seeing me resolved to go in a day or two, he got the vessel under sail, intending to carry me away against my will. This treatment mortified me extremely. I immediately according to the agreement I had made with the captain of the *Indian Queen*, called for her boat, which was lying near us, and it came alongside: and by the means of a North Pole shipmate which I met with in the sloop I was in, I got my things into the boat, and went on board the *Indian*

Queen, July the 10th. A few days after I was there, we got all things
ready and sailed; but again, to my great mortification, this vessel still
went to the south, nearly as far as Cartagena, trading along the coast,
instead of going to Jamaica, as the captain had promised me: and, what
was worst of all, he was a very cruel and bloody-minded man, and was
a horrid blasphemer. Among others, he had a white pilot, one Stoker,
whom he beat often as severely as he did some negroes he had on
board. One night in particular, after he had beaten this man most cruelly, he put him into the boat, and made two negroes row him to a desolate key, or small island; and he loaded two pistols, and swore bitterly
that he would shoot the negroes if they brought Stoker on board again.
There was not the least doubt but that he would do as he said, and the
two poor fellows were obliged to obey the cruel mandate; but, when
the captain was asleep, the two negroes took a blanket, at the risk of
their lives, and carried it to the unfortunate Stoker, which I believe was
the means of saving his life from the annoyance of insects. A great deal
of entreaty was used with the captain the next day, before he would
consent to let Stoker come on board; and when the poor man was
brought on board he was very ill, from his situation during the night,
and he remained so till he was drowned a little time after. As we sailed
southward we came to many uninhabited islands, which were over-
grown with fine large coconut trees. As I was very much in want of provisions, I brought a boatload of the nuts on board, which lasted me and
others for several weeks, and afforded us many a delicious repast in our
scarcity. One day, before this, I could not help observing the providential hand of God, that ever supplies all our wants, though in the ways
and manner we know not. I had been a whole day without food, and
made signals for boats to come off, but in vain. I therefore earnestly
prayed to God for relief in my need; and at the close of the evening I
went off the deck. Just as I laid down I heard a noise on the deck; and,
not knowing what it meant, I went directly on the deck again, when
what should I see but a fine large fish, about seven or eight pounds,
which had jumped aboard! I took it, and admired, with thanks, the
good hand of God; and what I considered as not less extraordinary, the
captain, who was very avaricious, did not attempt to take it from me,
there being only him and I on board; for the rest were all gone ashore
trading. Sometimes the people did not come off for some days: this
used to fret the captain, and then he would vent his fury on me by beating me, or making me feel in other cruel ways. One day especially, in
this wild, wicked, and mad career, after striking me several times with

different things, and once across my mouth, even with a red burning stick out of the fire, he got a barrel of gunpowder on the deck, and swore that he would blow up the vessel. I was then at my wit's end, and earnestly prayed to God to direct me. The head was out of the barrel; and the captain took a lighted stick out of the fire to blow himself and me up, because there was a vessel then in sight coming in, which he supposed was a Spanish *guarda costa,* and he was afraid of falling into their hands. Seeing this, I got an axe, unnoticed by him, and placed myself between him and the powder, having resolved in myself, as soon as he attempted to put the fire in the barrel, to chop him down that instant. I was more than an hour in this situation; during which he struck me often, still keeping the fire in his hand for this wicked purpose. I really should have thought myself justifiable in any other part of the world if I had killed him, and prayed to God, who gave me a mind which rested solely on himself. I prayed for resignation, that his will might be done: and the following two portions of his holy word, which occurred to my mind, buoyed up my hope, and kept me from taking the life of this wicked man. "He hath determined the times before appointed, and set bounds to our habitations." (Acts 17:26) And, "Who is there among you that feareth the Lord, that obeyeth the voice of his servant, that walketh in darkness and hath no light? let him trust in the name of the Lord, and stay upon his God." (Isa. 1:10) And this, by the grace of God, I was enabled to do. I found him a present help in the time of need, and the captain's fury began to subside as the night approached: but I found,

> That he who cannot stem his anger's tide,
> Doth a wild horse without a bridle ride.

The next morning we discovered that the vessel which had caused such a fury in the captain was an English sloop. They soon came to an anchor where we were, and, to my no small surprise, I learned that Doctor Irving was on board of her on his way from the Miskito shore to Jamaica. I was for going immediately to see this old master and friend, but the captain would not suffer me to leave the vessel. I then informed the Doctor, by letter, how I was treated, and begged that he would take me out of the sloop: but he informed me that it was not in his power, as he was a passenger himself; but he sent me some rum and sugar for my own use. I now learned that, after I had left the estate which I managed for this gentleman on the Miskito shore, during which the slaves were well fed and comfortable, a white overseer had supplied my place: this man, through inhumanity and ill-judged avarice, beat and cut the poor slaves most unmercifully; and the consequence was, that everyone got into a large Puriogua canoe, and endeavored to escape; but, not knowing where to go, or how to manage the canoe, they were all drowned; in consequence of which the Doctor's plantation was left uncultivated, and he was now returning to Jamaica to purchase more slaves and stock it again.

On the 14th of October, the *Indian Queen* arrived at Kingston in Jamaica. When we were unloaded I demanded my wages, which amounted to eight pounds five shillings sterling; but Captain Baker refused to give me one farthing, although it was the hardest earned money I ever worked for in my life. I found out Doctor Irving upon this, and acquainted him of the captain's knavery. He did all he could to help me to get my money; and we went to every magistrate in Kingston (and there were nine), but they all refused to do anything for me, and said my oath could not be admitted against a white man. Nor was this all; for Baker threatened that he would beat me severely if he could catch me, for attempting to demand my money; and this he would have done; but I got, by means of Doctor Irving, under the protection of Captain Douglas, of the *Squirrel* man-of-war. I thought this exceeding hard usage; though indeed I found it to be too much the practice there to pay free negro men for their labor in this manner.

One day I went with a free negro tailor, named Joe Diamond, to one Mr. Cochran, who was indebted to him some trifling sum; and the man, not being able to get his money, began to murmur. The other immediately took a horsewhip to pay him with it; but by the help of a good pair of heels, the tailor got off. Such oppressions as these made me seek for a vessel to get off the island as fast as I could: and, by the mercy of God, I found a ship in November bound for England, when I embarked with a convoy, after having taken a last farewell of Doctor Irving. When I left Jamaica he was employed in refining sugars; and some months after my arrival in England I learned, with much sorrow, that this my amiable friend was dead, owing to his having eaten some poisoned fish.

We had many heavy gales of wind in our passage; in the course of which no material accident occurred, except that an American privateer, falling in with the fleet, was captured, and set fire to by his Majesty's ship the *Squirrel*.

On January the seventh, 1777, we arrived at Plymouth. I was happy once more to tread upon English ground; and, after passing some little time at Plymouth and Exeter, among some pious friends, whom I was happy to see, I went to London, with a heart replete with thanks to God for past mercies.

Chapter XII

Different transactions of the Author's life till the present time—His application to the late Bishop of London to be appointed a missionary to Africa—Some account of his share in the conduct of the late expedition to Sierra Leone—Petition to the Queen—His marriage—Conclusion.

SUCH WERE THE VARIOUS SCENES which I was a witness to, and the fortune I experienced until the year 1777. Since that period, my life has been more uniform, and the incidents of it fewer than in any other equal number of years preceding; I therefore hasten to the conclusion of a narrative, which I fear the reader may think already sufficiently tedious.

I had suffered so many impositions in my commercial transactions in different parts of the world, that I became heartily disgusted with the seafaring life, and was determined not to return to it at least for some time. I therefore once more engaged in service shortly after my return, and continued for the most part in this situation until 1784.

Soon after my arrival in London, I saw a remarkable circumstance relative to African complexion, which I thought so extraordinary that I beg leave just to mention it: A white negro woman, that I had formerly seen in London and other parts, had married a white man, by whom she had three boys, and they were every one mulattoes, and yet they had fine light hair. In 1779, I served Governor Macnamara, who had been a considerable time on the coast of Africa. In the time of my service I used to ask frequently other servants to join me in family prayer; but this only excited their mockery. However the Governor understanding that I was of a religious turn, wished to know what religion I was of; I told him I was a protestant of the Church of England, agreeable to the thirty-nine articles of that church; and that whomsoever I found to preach according to that doctrine, those I would hear. A few days after this we had some more discourse on the same subject; when he said he would, if I chose, as he thought I might be of service in converting my countrymen to the Gospel faith, get me sent out as a missionary to Africa. I at first refused going, and told him how I had been served on a like occasion by some white people the last voyage I went to Jamaica, when I attempted, (if it were the will of God) to be the means of converting the Indian prince; and said I supposed they would serve me worse than Alexander the coppersmith did St. Paul, if I should attempt to go among them in Africa. He told me not to fear, for he would apply to the Bishop of London to get me ordained. On these terms I consented to the Governor's proposal to go to Africa, in hope of doing good, if possible, amongst my countrymen; so, in order to have me sent out properly, we immediately wrote the following letters to the late Bishop of London:

To the Right Reverend Father in God, Robert, *Lord Bishop of London,*
The Memorial of Gustavus Vassa,
Showeth,

That your memorialist is a native of Africa, and has a knowledge of the manners and customs of the inhabitants of that country.

That your memorialist has resided in different parts of Europe for twenty-two years last past, and embraced the Christian faith in the year 1759.

That your memorialist is desirous of returning to Africa as a missionary, if encouraged by your Lordship, in hopes of being able to prevail on his countrymen to become Christians; and your memorialist is the more induced to undertake the same from the success that has attended the like undertakings when encouraged by the Portuguese through their different settlements on the coast of Africa, and also by the Dutch: both governments encouraged the blacks, who by their education are qualified to undertake the same, and are found more proper than European clergymen, unacquainted with the language and customs of the country.

Your memorialist's only motive for soliciting the office of a missionary is, that he may be a means, under God, of reforming his countrymen, and persuading them to embrace the Christian religion. Therefore your memorialist humbly prays your Lordship's encouragement and support in the undertaking.

Gustavus Vassa
At Mr. Guthrie's, Tailor,
No. 17, Hedge Lane

My Lord, I have resided near seven years on the coast of Africa, for most part of the time as commanding officer. From the knowledge I have of the country and its inhabitants, I am inclined to think that the within plan will be attended with great success, if countenanced by your Lordship. I beg leave further to represent to your Lordship, that the like attempts, when encouraged by other governments, have met with uncommon success; and at this very time I know a very respectable character, a black priest, at Cape Coast Castle. I know the within-named Gustavus Vassa, and believe him a moral good man. I have the honor to be,

My Lord,
Your Lordship's
humble and obedient servant,
Matt. Macnamara
Grove, 11th March, 1779

This letter was also accompanied by the following from Doctor Wallace, who had resided in Africa for many years, and whose sentiments on the subject of the African mission were the same with Governor Macnamara's:

My Lord,   March 13, 1779
I have resided near five years in Senegambia, on the coast of Africa, and have had the honor of filling very considerable employments in that province. I do approve of the within plan, and think the undertaking very laudable and proper, and that it deserves your Lordship's protection and encouragement, in which case it must be attended with the intended success. I am, my Lord,

Your Lordship's
humble and obedient servant,
Thomas Wallace

With these letters I waited on the bishop, by the Governor's desire, and presented them to his Lordship. He received me with much condescension and politeness; but, from some certain scruples of delicacy, and saying the bishops were not of opinion in sending a new missionary to Africa, he declined to ordain me.

My sole motive for thus dwelling on this transaction, or inserting these papers, is the opinion which gentlemen of sense and education, who are acquainted with Africa, entertain of the probability of converting the inhabitants of it to the faith of Jesus Christ, if the attempt were countenanced by the legislature.

Shortly after this I left the Governor, and served a nobleman in the Dorsetshire militia, with whom I was encamped at Coxheath for some time; but the operations there were too minute and uninteresting to make a detail of.

In the year 1783, I visited eight counties in Wales, from motives of curiosity. While I was in that part of the country, I was led to go down into a coal-pit in Shropshire, but my curiosity nearly cost me my life; for while I was in the pit the coals fell in, and buried one poor man, who was not far from me: upon this I got out as fast as I could, thinking the surface of the earth the safest part of it.

In the spring of 1784, I thought of visiting [the] old ocean again. In consequence of this I embarked as steward on board a fine new ship called the *London,* commanded by Martin Hopkins, and sailed for New York. I admired this city very much; it is large and well-built, and abounds with provisions of all kinds.

Our ship having got laden, we returned to London in January 1785. When she was ready again for another voyage, the captain being an agreeable man, I sailed with him from hence in the spring, March 1785, for Philadelphia. On the 5th of April we took our departure from the land's end, with a pleasant gale; and, about nine o'clock that night the moon shone bright, and the sea was smooth, while our ship was going free by the wind at the rate of about four or five miles an hour. At this time another ship was going nearly as fast as we on the opposite point, meeting us right in the teeth, yet none on board observed either ship until we struck each other forcibly head and head, to the astonishment and consternation of both crews. She did us much damage, but I believe we did her more; for when we passed by each other, which we did very quickly, they called to us to bring to, and hoist out our boats, but we had enough to do to mind ourselves; and in about eight minutes we saw no more of her. We refitted as well as we could the next day, and proceeded on our voyage, and in May arrived at Philadelphia.

I was very glad to see this favorite old town once more; and my pleasure was much increased in seeing the worthy Quakers, freeing and easing the burdens of many of my oppressed African brethren. It rejoiced my heart when one of these friendly people took me to see a free school they had erected for every denomination of black people, whose minds are cultivated here, and forwarded to virtue; and thus they are made useful members of the community. Does not the success of this practice say loudly to the planters, in the language of Scripture—"Go ye, and do likewise"?

In October 1785, I was accompanied by some of the Africans, and presented this address of thanks to the gentlemen called Friends or Quakers, in Whitehart Court, Lombard Street:

Gentlemen,

By reading your book, entitled, *A Caution to Great Britain and her Colonies, concerning the Calamitous State of the enslaved Negroes,* We, part of the poor, oppressed, needy, and much degraded negroes, desire to approach you, with this address of thanks, with our inmost love and warmest acknowledgments; and with the deepest sense of your benevolence, unwearied labor, and kind interposition, towards breaking the yoke of slavery, and to administer a little comfort and ease to thousands and tens of thousands of very grievously afflicted and too heavy burdened negroes.

Gentlemen, could you, by perseverance, at last be enabled, under God, to lighten in any degree the heavy burden of the afflicted, no doubt it would, in some measure, be the possible means, under God, of saving the souls of many of the oppressors; and if so, sure we are that the God, whose eyes are ever upon all his creatures, and always rewards every true act of virtue, and regards the prayers of the oppressed, will give to you and yours those blessings which it is not in our power to express or conceive, but which we, as a part of those captivated, oppressed, and afflicted people, most earnestly wish and pray for.

These gentlemen received us very kindly, with a promise to exert themselves on behalf of the oppressed Africans, and we parted.

While in town, I chanced once to be invited to a Quaker's wedding. The simple and yet expressive mode used at their solemnizations is worthy of note. The following is the true form of it:

Near the close of a meeting for worship, wherein there are frequently seasonable exhortations from some of their ministers, the bride and bridegroom stand up, and, taking each other by the hand in a solemn manner, the man audibly declares to this purpose:

"Friends, in the fear of the Lord, and before this assembly, I take this my friend, M.N. to be my wife; promising, through divine assistance, to be unto her a loving and faithful husband, until it shall please the Lord by death to separate us": and the woman makes the like declaration. Then the man and woman sign their names to the certificate; and as many witnesses as have a mind. I had the honor to subscribe mine to a certificate in Whitehart Court, Lombard Street. This mode I highly recommend.

We returned to London in August, and our ship not going immediately to sea, I shipped as a steward in an American ship called the *Harmony*, Captain John Willett, and left London in March 1786, bound to Philadelphia. Eleven days after sailing, we carried our foremast away. We had a nine weeks passage, which caused our trip not to succeed well, the market for our goods proving bad; and, to make it worse, my commander began to play me the like tricks as others too often practice on free negroes in the West Indies. But, I thank God, I found many friends here, who in some measure prevented him. On my return to London in August, I was very agreeably surprised to find, that the benevolence of government had adopted the plan of some philanthropic individuals, to send the Africans from hence to their native quarter, and that some vessels were then engaged to carry them to Sierra Leone; an act which redounded to the honor of all concerned in its promotion, and filled me with prayers and much rejoicing. There was then in the city a select committee of gentlemen for the black poor, to some of whom I had the honor of being known; and as soon as they heard of my arrival, they sent for me to the committee. When I came there, they informed me of the intention of government; and, as they seemed to think me qualified to superintend part of the undertaking, they asked me to go with the black poor to Africa. I pointed out to them many objections to my going; and particularly I expressed some difficulties on the account of the slave dealers, as I would certainly oppose their traffic in the human species by every means in my power. However, these objections were overruled by the gentlemen of the committee, who prevailed on me to consent to go; and recommended me to the Honorable Commissioners of his Majesty's Navy, as a proper person to act as commissary for government in the intended expedition; and they accordingly appointed me in November 1786 to that office, and gave me sufficient power to act for the government in the capacity of commissary, having received my warrant and the following order:

> *By the principal Officers and Commissioners of his Majesty's Navy.*
> Whereas you are directed, by our warrant of the 4th of last month, to receive into your charge, from Mr. Joseph Irwin, the surplus provisions remaining of what was provided for the voyage, as well as the provisions for the support of the black poor, after the landing at Si-

erra Leone, with the clothing, tools, and all other articles provided at government's expense; and as the provisions were laid in at the rate of two months for the voyage, and for four months after the landing, but the number embarked being so much less than we expected, whereby there may be a considerable surplus of provisions, clothing, etc.; these are, in addition to former orders, to direct and require you to appropriate or dispose of such surplus to the best advantage you can for the benefit of government, keeping and rendering to us a faithful account of what you do herein. And for your guidance in preventing any white persons going, who are not intended to have the indulgence of being carried thither, we send you herewith a list of those recommended by the committee for the black poor, as proper persons to be permitted to embark, and acquaint you that you are not to suffer any others to go who do not produce a certificate from the committee for the black poor, of their having their permission for it. For which this shall be your warrant. Dated at the Navy-Office, January 16, 1787.

To Mr Gustavus Vassa,
Commissary of Provisions and
Stores, for the Black Poor to
Sierra Leone.
J. Hinslow
Geo. Marsh
W. Palmer

I proceeded immediately to the executing of my duty on board the vessels destined for the voyage, where I continued until the March following.

During my continuance in the employment of government I was struck with the flagrant abuses committed by the agent, and endeavored to remedy them, but without effect. One instance, among many which I could produce, may serve as a specimen. Government had ordered to be provided all necessaries (slops, as they are called, included) for 750 persons; however, not being able to muster more than 426, I was ordered to send the superfluous slops, etc. to the King's stores at Portsmouth; but, when I demanded them for that purpose from the agent, it appeared they had never been bought, though paid for by government. But that was not all, government were not the only objects of peculation; these poor people suffered infinitely more; their accommodations were most wretched; many of them wanted beds, and many more clothing and other necessities. For the truth of this, and much more, I do not seek credit from my own assertion. I appeal to the testimony of Captain Thompson, of the *Nautilus*, who convoyed us, to whom I applied in February 1787 for a remedy, when I had remonstrated to the agent in vain, and even brought him to be a witness of the injustice and oppression I complained of. I appeal also to a letter written by these wretched people, so early as the beginning of the preceding January, and published in the morning *Herald*, on the fourth of that month, signed by twenty of their chiefs.

I could not silently suffer government to be thus cheated, and my countrymen plundered and oppressed, and even left destitute of the necessaries for almost their existence. I therefore informed the Commissioners of the Navy of the agent's proceeding: but my dismission was soon after procured by means of a gentleman in the city, whom the agent, conscious of his peculation, had deceived by letters; and who, moreover, empowered the same agent to receive on board, at the government expense, a number of persons as passengers, contrary to the orders I received. By this I suffered a considerable loss in my property: however, the Commissioners were satisfied with my conduct, and wrote to Captain Thompson, expressing their approbation of it.

Thus provided, they proceeded on their voyage; and at last, worn out by treatment, perhaps not the most mild, and washed by sickness, brought on by want of medicine, clothes, bedding, etc. they reached Sierra Leone just at the commencement of the rains. At that season of the year it is impossible to cultivate the lands; their provisions therefore were exhausted before they could derive any benefit from agriculture; and it is not surprising that many, especially the Lascars, whose constitutions are very tender, and who had been cooped up in ships from October to June, and accommodated in the manner I have mentioned, should be so wasted by their confinement as not long to survive it.

Thus ended my part of the long talked of expedition to Sierra Leone; an expedition which, however unfortunate in the event, was humane and politic in its design; nor was its failure owing to government: everything was done on their part; but there was evidently sufficient mismanagement attending the conduct and execution of it to defeat its success.

I should not have been so ample in my account of this transaction, had not the share I bore in it been made the subject of partial animadversion, and even my dismission from my employment thought worthy of being made by some matter of public triumph. The motives which might influence any person to descend to a petty contest with an obscure African, and to seek gratification by his depression, perhaps it is not proper here to inquire into or relate, even if its detection were necessary to my vindication;* but I thank Heaven it is not. I wish to stand by my own integrity, and not to shelter myself under the impropriety of another; and I trust the behavior of the Commissioners of the Navy to me entitles me to make this assertion; for after I had been dismissed, March 24, I drew up a memorial thus:

To the Right Honorable the Lords Commissioners of his Majesty's Treasury.
The Memorial and Petition of Gustavus Vassa, a black man, late Commissary to the Black Poor going to Africa.
Humbly showeth,
That your Lordships' memorialist was, by the Honorable the Commissioners of his Majesty's Navy, on the 4th of December last, appointed to the above employment by warrant from that board;

That he accordingly proceeded to the execution of his duty on board of the *Vernon*, being one of the ships appointed to proceed to Africa with the above poor;

That your memorialist, to his great grief and astonishment, received a letter of dismission from the Honorable Commissioners of the Navy, by your Lordships' orders:

That, conscious of having acted with the most perfect fidelity and the greatest assiduity in discharging the trust reposed in him, he is altogether at a loss to conceive the reasons of your Lordships' having altered the favorable opinion you were pleased to conceive of him, sensible that your Lordships would not proceed to so severe a measure without some apparent good cause; he therefore has every reason to believe that his conduct has been grossly misrepresented to your Lordships, and he is the more confirmed in his opinion, because, by opposing measures of others concerned in the same expedition, which tended to defeat your Lordships' humane intentions, and to put the government to a very considerable additional expense, he created a number of enemies, whose misrepresentations, he has too much reason to believe, laid the foundation of his dismission. Unsupported by friends, and unaided by the advantages of a liberal education, he can only hope for redress from the justice of

*See the *Public Advertiser,* July 14, 1787.

his cause, in addition to the mortification of having been removed from his employment, and the advantage which he reasonably might have expected to have derived therefrom. He has had the misfortune to have sunk a considerable part of his little property in fitting himself out, and in other expenses arising out of his situation, an account of which he here annexes. Your memorialist will not trouble your Lordships with a vindication of any part of his conduct, because he knows not of what crimes he is accused; he, however, earnestly entreats that you will be pleased to direct an inquiry into his behavior during the time he acted in the public service; and, if it be found that his dismission arose from false representations, he is confident that in your Lordships' justice he shall find redress.

Your petitioner therefore humbly prays that your Lordships will take his case into consideration, and that you will be pleased to order payment of the above referred to account, amounting to 32 pounds 4 shillings and also the wages intended, which is most humbly submitted.

London, May 12, 1787.

The above petition was delivered into the hands of their Lordships, who were kind enough, in the space of some few months afterwards, without hearing, to order me 50 pounds sterling—that is 18 pounds wages for the time (upwards of four months) I acted a faithful part in their service.—Certainly the sum is more than a free negro would have had in the western colonies!!!

From that period to the present time my life has passed in an even tenor, and great part of my study and attention has been to assist in the cause of my much injured contrymen.

March the 21st, 1788, I had the honor of presenting the Queen with a petition on behalf of my African brethren, which was received most graciously by her Majesty;*

To the Queen's Most Excellent Majesty.

Madam,

Your Majesty's well known benevolence and humanity embolden me to approach your royal presence, trusting that the obscurity of my situation will not prevent your Majesty from attending to the sufferings for which I plead.

*At the request of some of my most particular friends I take the liberty of inserting it here.

Yet I do not solicit your royal pity for my own distress: my sufferings, although numerous, are in a measure forgotten. I supplicate your Majesty's compassion for millions of my African countrymen, who groan under the lash of tyranny in the West Indies.

The oppression and cruelty exercised to the unhappy negroes there, have at length reached the British legislature, and they are now deliberating on its redress; even several persons of property in slaves in the West Indies have petitioned parliament against its continuance, sensible that it is as impolitic as it is unjust—and what is inhuman must ever be unwise.

Your Majesty's reign has been hitherto distinguished by private acts of benevolence and bounty; surely the more extended the misery is, the greater claim it has to your Majesty's compassion, and the greater must be your Majesty's pleasure in administering to its relief.

I presume, therefore, gracious Queen, to implore your interposition with your royal consort, in favor of the wretched Africans; that, by your Majesty's benevolent influence, a period may now be put to their misery; and that they may be raised from the condition of brutes, to which they are at present degraded, to the rights and situation of men, and be admitted to partake of the blessings of your Majesty's happy government; so shall your Majesty enjoy the heartfelt pleasure of procuring happiness to millions, and be rewarded in the grateful prayers of themselves, and of their posterity.

And may the all-bountiful Creator shower on your Majesty, and the Royal Family, every blessing that this world can afford, and every fullness of joy which divine revelation has promised us in the next.

I am your Majesty's most dutiful and

devoted servant to command,
Gustavus Vassa,
The oppressed Ethiopian
No. 53, Baldwin's Gardens

The negro consolidated act, made by the assembly of Jamaica last year, and the new act of amendment now in agitation there, contain a proof of the existence of those charges that have been made against the planters relative to the treatment of their slaves.

I hope to have the satisfaction of seeing the renovation of liberty and justice, resting on the British government, to vindicate the honor of our common nature. These are concerns which do not perhaps belong to any particular office: but, to speak more seriously, to every man of sentiment, actions like these are the just and sure foundation of future fame; a reversion, though remote, is coveted by some noble minds as a substantial good. It is upon these grounds that I hope and expect the attention of gentlemen in power. These are designs consonant to the elevation of their rank, and the dignity of their stations: they are ends suitable to the nature of a free and generous government; and, connected with views of empire and dominion, suited to the benevolence and solid merit of the legislature. It is a pursuit of substantial greatness. May the time come—at least the speculation to me is pleasing—when the sable people shall gratefully commemorate the auspicious era of extensive freedom. Then shall those persons★ particularly be named with praise and honor, who generously proposed and stood forth in the cause of humanity, liberty, and good policy; and brought to the ear of the legislature designs worthy of royal patronage and adoption. May Heaven make the British senators the dispersers of light, liberty and science, to the uttermost parts of the earth: then will be glory to God in the highest, on earth peace, and goodwill to men,— Glory, honor, peace, etc. to every soul of man that worketh good; to the Britons first, (because to them the gospel is preached), and also to the nations. "Those that honor their Maker have mercy on the poor." "It is righteousness exalteth a nation, but sin is reproach to any people; destruction shall be to the workers of iniquity, and the wicked shall fall by their own wickedness." May the blessings of the Lord be upon the heads of all those who commiserated the cases of the oppressed negroes, and the fear of God prolong their days; and may their expectations be filled with gladness! "The liberal devise liberal things, and by liberal things shall stand." (Isa. 32:8) They can say with pious Job, "Did not I weep for him that was in trouble? Was not my soul grieved for the poor?" (Job 30:25)

As the inhuman traffic of slavery is now taken into the consideration of the British legislature, I doubt not, if a system of commerce was established in Africa, the demand for manufactures will most rapidly augment, as the native inhabitants will insensibly adopt the British fashions, manners, customs, etc. In proportion to the civilization, so will be the consumption of British manufactures.

★Granville Sharp, Esq.; the Reverend Thomas Clarkson; the Reverend James Ramsey; our approved friends, men of virtue, are an honor to their country, ornamental to human nature, happy in themselves, and benefactors to mankind!

The wear and tear of a continent, nearly twice as large as Europe, and rich in vegetable and mineral productions, is much easier conceived than calculated.

A case in point. It cost the Aborigines of Britain little or nothing in clothing, etc. The difference between their forefathers and the present generation, in point of consumption, is literally infinite. The supposition is most obvious. It will be equally immense in Africa.—The same case, namely civilization, will ever have the same effect.

It is trading upon safe grounds. A commercial intercourse with Africa opens an inexhaustible source of wealth to the manufacturing interests of Great Britain, and to all which the slave trade is an objection.

If I am not misinformed, the manufacturing interest is equal, if not superior to the landed interests, as to the value, for reasons which will soon appear. The abolition of slavery, so diabolical, will give a most rapid extension of manufactures, which is totally and diametrically opposite to what some interested people assert.

The manufactures of this country must and will, in the nature and reason of things, have a full and constant employ, by supplying the African markets.

Population, the bowels and surface of Africa, abound in valuable and useful returns; the hidden treasures of centuries will be brought to light and into circulation. Industry, enterprise, and mining, will have their full scope, proportionably as they civilize. In a word, it lays open an endless field of commerce to the British manufactures and merchant adventurer. The manufacturing interest and the general interests are synonymous. The abolition of slavery would be in reality a universal good.

Tortures, murder, and every other imaginable barbarity and iniquity, are practiced upon the poor slaves with impunity. I hope the slave trade will be abolished. I pray it may be an event at hand. The great body of manufacturers, uniting in the cause, will considerably facilitate and expedite it; and, as I have already stated, it is most substantially their interest and advantage, and as such the nation's at large, (except those persons concerned in the manufacturing [of] neck yokes, collars, chains, handcuffs, leg-bolts, drags, thumbscrews, iron muzzles, and coffins; cats, scourges, and other instruments of torture used in the slave trade). In a short time one sentiment alone will prevail, from motives of interest as well as justice and humanity. Europe contains one hundred and twenty millions of inhabitants. Query. How many millions doth Africa contain? Supposing the Africans, collec-

tively and individually, to expend 5 pounds a head in raiment and furniture yearly when civilized, etc., an immensity beyond the reach of
imagination!

This I conceive to be a theory founded upon facts, and therefore an
infallible one. If the blacks were permitted to remain in their own
country, they would double themselves every fifteen years. In proportion to such increase will be the demand for manufactures. Cotton and
indigo grow spontaneously in most parts of Africa; a consideration
this of no small consequence to the manufacturing towns of Great
Britain. It opens a most immense, glorious, and happy prospect—the
clothing, etc. of a continent ten thousand miles in circumference, and
immensely rich in productions of every denomination in return for
manufactures.

Since the first publication of my Narrative, I have been in a great variety of scenes in many parts of Great Britain, Ireland and Scotland, an
account of which might well be added here;* but this would swell the
volume too much. I shall only observe in general, that, in May 1791, I
sailed from Liverpool to Dublin where I was very kindly received, and
from thence to Cork, and then traveled over many counties in Ireland.
I was everywhere exceedingly well treated, by persons of all ranks. I
found the people extremely hospitable, particularly in Belfast, where I
took my passage on board of a vessel for Clyde, on the 29th of January,
and arrived at Greenock on the 30th. Soon after I returned to London,
where I found persons of note from Holland and Germany, who requested of me to go there; and I was glad to hear that an edition of my
Narrative had been printed in both places, also in New York. I remained in London till I heard the debate in the House of Commons on
the slave trade, April the 2d and 3d. I then went to Soham in Cam-
bridgeshire, and was married on the 7th of April to Miss Cullen,
daughter of James and Ann Cullen, late of Ely.†

I have only therefore to request the reader's indulgence, and conclude. I am far from the vanity of thinking there is any merit in this
Narrative; I hope censure will be suspended, when it is considered that
it was written by one who was as unwilling as unable to adorn the

---

*Namely some curious adventures beneath the earth, in a river in Manchester,—and a
most astonishing one under the Peak of Derbyshire—and in September 1792, I went 90
fathoms down St. Anthony's Colliery, at Newcastle, under the river Tyne, some hundreds of yards on Durham side.

†See *Gentleman's Magazine* for April 1792, *Literary and Biographical Magazine and
British Review* for May 1792, and the *Edinburgh Historical Register or Monthly Intelli-
gencer* for April 1792.

plainness of truth by the coloring of imagination. My life and fortune have been extremely checkered, and my adventures various. Even those I have related are considerably abridged. If any incident in this little work should appear uninteresting and trifling to most readers, I can only say, as my excuse for mentioning it, that almost every event in my life made an impression on my mind, and influenced my conduct. I early accustomed myself to look at the hand of God in the minutest occurrence, and to learn from it a lesson of morality and religion; and in this light every circumstance I have related was to me of importance. After all, what makes any event important, unless by its observation we become better and wiser, and learn "to do justly, to love mercy, and to walk humbly before God!" To those who are possessed of this spirit, there is scarcely any book or incident so trifling, that does not afford some profit, while to others the experience of ages seems of no use; and even to pour out to them the treasures of wisdom is throwing the jewels of instruction away.

THE

LIFE,

HISTORY,

AND

UNPARALLELED SUFFERINGS

OF

JOHN JEA,

THE AFRICAN PREACHER.

━━━━

Compiled and Written by HIMSELF.

━━━━

Printed for the Author.

5

———•◦•———

THE LIFE, HISTORY, AND

UNPARALLELED SUFFERINGS OF

JOHN JEA,

THE AFRICAN PREACHER,

COMPILED AND WRITTEN BY HIMSELF

———•◦•———

I, JOHN JEA, the subject of this narrative, was born in the town of Old Callabar, in Africa, in the year 1773. My father's name was Hambleton Robert Jea, my mother's name Margaret Jea; they were of poor, but industrious parents. At two years and a half old, I and my father, mother, brothers, and sisters, were stolen, and conveyed to North America, and sold for slaves; we were then sent to New York, the man who purchased us was very cruel, and used us in a manner, almost too shocking to relate; my master and mistress's names were Oliver and Angelika Triehuen, they had seven children—three sons and four daughters; he gave us a very little food or raiment, scarcely enough to satisfy us in any measure whatever; our food was what is called Indian corn pounded, or bruised and boiled with water, the same way burgo is made, and about a quart of sour buttermilk poured on it; for one person two quarts of this mixture, and about three ounces of dark bread, per day, the bread was darker than that usually allowed to convicts, and greased over with very indifferent hog's lard; at other times when he was better pleased, he would allow us about half-a-pound of beef for a week, and about half-a-gallon of potatoes; but that was very seldom the case, and yet we esteemed ourselves better used than many of our neighbors.

Our labor was extremely hard, being obliged to work in the summer from about two o'clock in the morning, till about ten or eleven o'clock at night, and in the winter from four in the morning, till ten at night. The horses usually rested about five hours in the day, while we were at work; thus did the beasts enjoy greater privileges than we did. We dared not murmur, for if we did we were corrected with a weapon an inch-and-a-half thick, and that without mercy, striking us in the most tender parts, and if we complained of this usage, they then took four large poles, placed them in the ground, tied us up to them, and flogged us in a manner too dreadful to behold; and when taken down, if we offered to lift up our hand or foot against our master or mistress, they used us in a most cruel manner; and often they treated the slaves in such a manner as caused their death, shooting them with a gun, or beating their brains out with some weapon, in order to appease their wrath, and thought no more of it than if they had been brutes: this was the general treatment which slaves experienced. After our master had been treating us in this cruel manner, we were obliged to thank him for the punishment he had been inflicting on us, quoting that Scripture which saith, "Bless the rod, and him that hath appointed it." But, though he was a professor of religion, he forgot *that* passage which saith "God is love, and whoso dwelleth in love dwelleth in God, and God in him." And, again, we are commanded to love our enemies; but it appeared evident that his wretched heart was hardened; which led us to look up unto him as our god, for we did not know him who is able to deliver and save all who call upon him in truth and sincerity. Conscience, that faithful monitor, (which either excuses or accuses) caused us to groan, cry, or sigh, in a manner which cannot be uttered.

We were often led away with the idea that our masters were our gods; and at other times we placed our ideas on the sun, moon, and stars, looking unto them, as if they could save us; at length we found, to our great disappointment, that these were nothing else but the works of the Supreme Being; this caused me to wonder how my master frequently expressed that all his houses, land, cattle, servants, and everything which he possessed was his own; not considering that it was the Lord of Hosts, who has said that the gold and the silver, the earth, and the fullness thereof, belong to him.

Our master told us, that when we died, we should be like the beasts that perish; not informing us of God, heaven, or eternal punishments, and that God hath promised to bring the secrets of every heart into judgement, and to judge every man according to his works.

From the following instances of the judgements of God, I was taught that he is God, and there is none besides him, neither in the heavens above, nor in the earth beneath, nor in the waters under the earth; for he doth with the armies of heaven and the inhabitants of the earth as seemeth him good; and there is none that can stay his hand, nor say unto him, with a prevailing voice, *what dost thou?*

My master was often disappointed in his attempts to increase the produce of his lands; for oftentimes he would command us to carry out more seed into the field to insure a good crop, but when it sprang up and promised to yield plentifully, the Almighty caused the worms to eat it at the root, and destroyed nearly the whole produce; God thus showing him his own inability to preserve the fruits of the earth.

At another time he ordered the trees to be pruned, that they might have brought forth more fruit, to have increased his worldly riches, but God, who doth not as man pleaseth, sent the caterpillar, the canker-worm, and the locust, when the trees bore a promising appearance, and his fond hopes were blasted, by the fruits being all destroyed. Thus was he again disappointed, but still remained ignorant of the hand of God being in these judgements.

Notwithstanding he still went on in his wickedness until another calamity befell him; for when the harvest was full ripe, the corn cut down, and standing in shocks ready to be carried into the barn, it pleased God to send a dreadful storm of thunder and lightning, hail and rain, which compelled them to leave it out, till it rotted on the ground. Often were his cattle destroyed by distempers of various kinds; yet he hearkened not unto the voice of the Lord.

At one time, when his barns and storehouses were filled with all sorts of grain, and he rejoiced in the greatness of his harvest, it pleased the Almighty to send a very dreadful storm of thunder and lightning, which consumed a great part of his property; such scenes as these occurred several times, yet he regarded not the power of the Almighty, nor the strength of his arm; for when we poor slaves were visited by the hand of God, and he took us from time to eternity, he thought no more of our poor souls than if we had had none, but lamented greatly the loss of the body; which caused me very much to wonder at his actions, I being very young, not above eight or nine years of age, and seeing the hand of the Almighty, though I did not at that time know it was his works, in burning up the pastures, in permitting the cattle to die for want of water, and in causing the fruits of the earth to be blighted. At the same time a most violent storm of thunder and lightning was experienced, which, in the space of thirty or forty miles, consumed about thirteen houses, barns, and storehouses, which terrified us poor slaves in a terrible manner, not knowing what these things meant. Even my master and mistress were very much terrified, fearful of being destroyed by the violence of the weather.

About two or three days after this awful scene, a day of fasting, prayer, and thanksgiving, was commanded by General Washington, to pray to Almighty God to withdraw his anger from us; which day was observed by all, but us poor slaves, for we were obliged to fast, but were not exempted from work; our masters thinking us not worthy to go to a place of worship; which surprised me a great deal, being very ignorant, and I asked my parents what all this meant, but they could not tell me, but supposed, from what they had heard them say, they were worshipping their god; then I began to inquire how this could be, having heard my master often say, that all he possessed was his own, and he could do as he pleased with it; which, indeed, was the saying of all those who had slaves. My curiosity being thus raised, I made bold to speak to my master's sons, and asked them the reason they prayed and called upon God, and they told me because of the awful judgements that had happened on the land; then I asked what awful judgements they meant, and they said unto me, have you not seen how the Lord hath destroyed all things from off the face of the earth? and I answered yes; I then asked them who did this, and they told me God; then, said I, ought not God to be feared, seeing that he can build up and he can cast down, he can create and he can destroy, and though we may cultivate our lands and sow our seed, we can never secure the crop without the favor of Him who, is the sovereign disposer of all things? They answered, yes. From this I observed that there were those who feared God when the weather was tempestuous, but feared him not when it was fine.

Seeing them act in such a wicked manner, I was encouraged to go on in my sins, being subject to all manner of iniquity that could be mentioned, not knowing there was a God, for they told us that we poor slaves had no God. As I grew up, my desire to know who their God was increased, but I did not know who to apply to, not being allowed to be taught by anyone whatever, which caused me to watch their actions very closely; and in so doing, I, at one time, perceived that something was going forward which I could not comprehend, at last I found out that they were burying a slave master, who was very rich; they appeared to mourn and lament for his death, as though he had been a good man, and I asked them why they let him die; they said they could not help it, for God killed him: I said unto them, what, could you not have taken him away from God? They said, no, for he killed whomever he pleased. I then said he must be a dreadful God, and was led to fear least he should kill me also; although I had never seen death, but at a distance. But this fear did not last long, for seeing others full of mirth, I became so too.

A short time after this, there were great rejoicings on account of a great victory obtained by the Americans over the poor Indians, who had been so unfortunate as to lose their possessions, and they strove against the Americans, but they overpowered and killed thousands of them, and numbers were taken prisoners, and for this cause they greatly rejoiced. They expressed their joy by the ringing of bells, firing of guns, dancing and singing, while we poor slaves were hard at work. When I was informed of the cause of these rejoicings, I thought, *these* people made a great mourning when *God* killed one man, but they rejoice when *they* kill so many. I was thus taught that though they talked much about their God, they did not regard him as they ought. They had forgotten that sermon of our blessed Savior's on the mount, which you find in St. Matthew's gospel [Matt. 5:43–44]; and I had reason to think their hearts were disobedient, not obeying the truth, though it was read and preached to them; their hearts being carnal, as the Scriptures saith, were at enmity with God, not subject to the law of God, neither indeed could be; for they gave themselves up to the works of the flesh, to fulfill it in the lusts thereof.

My dear reader, consider the great obligations you are under to the Wise Disposer of all events, that you were not born in Africa, and sold for a slave, on whom the most cruel tortures are exercised, but that you were born in Britain, a land of freedom; and above all, be thankful for the opportunities you have of knowing the "true God, and Jesus Christ whom he has sent," and recollect that as you possess much, much will be required; and, unless you improve your advantages, you had better be a slave in any dark part of the world, than a neglecter of the gospel in this highly favored land; recollect also that even here you might be a slave of the most awful description: a slave to your passions, a slave to the world, a slave to sin, a slave to Satan, a slave of hell, and, unless you are made free by Christ, through the means of the gospel, you will remain in captivity, tied and bound in the chains of your sin, till at last you will be bound hand and foot, and cast into outer darkness, there shall be weeping and gnashing of teeth forever.

But, to return to myself, it was evident that our masters did not believe the report God gave of his Son, which the gospel holds forth to us, for if they had they would have instructed us poor slaves; but they did not think us, as have been before observed, worthy their notice. Frequently did they tell us we were made by, and like the devil, and commonly called us *black devils*; not considering what the Scriptures saith in the Song of Solomon, "I am black, but comely. Look not upon me, because I am black, because the sun hath looked upon me; my mother's children were angry with me; they made me keeper of the vineyards; but mine own vineyard have I not kept." This latter sentence was verified in the case of us poor slaves, for our master would make us work, and neglect the concerns of our souls.

From my observations of the conduct and conversation of my master and his sons, I was led to hate those who professed themselves Christians, and to look upon them as devils; which made me neglect my work, and I told them what I thought of their ways. On this they did beat me in a most dreadful manner; but, instead of making me obedient, it made me the more stubborn, not caring whether I lived or died, thinking that after I was dead I should be at rest, and that I should go back again to my native country, Africa (an idea generally entertained by slaves); but when I told them this, they chastised me seven times the more, and kept me short of food. In addition to this punishment, they made me go to a place of worship, while the other slaves enjoyed a rest for an hour or two; I could not bear to be where the word of God was mentioned, for I had seen so much deception in the people that professed to know God, that I could not endure being where there were, nor yet to hear them call upon the name of the Lord; but I was still sent in order to punish me, for when I entered the place I had such malice against God and his people, as showed the depravity of my heart, and verified the Scripture which saith, "That the natural man understandeth not the things which are of God, for they are foolishness unto him; neither doth he know them, because he is not spiritually discerned."

My rage and malice against every person that was religious was so very great that I would have destroyed them all, had it been in my power; my indignation was so increased on my entering the place of worship, that, "the form of my visage was changed," like Nebuchadnezzar's, when he ordered Shadrach, Meshach, and Abednego, to be cast into the fiery furnace. My fury was more particularly kindled against the minister, and I should have killed him, had I not feared the people, it not being in my power to kill him, grieved me very much; and I went home and told my master what the minister had said, and what lies he had told, as I imagined, in hopes that he would send me no more; but he knowing this was a punishment to me, he made me go the more, for it was evident it was not for the good of my soul; this pained me exceedingly, so that I laid the blame to the minister, thinking that it was through his preaching so many lies, as I thought in my foolish opinion, that I was obliged to attend, not knowing that he spoke the truth, and I told the lies. The more I went to hear him preach, the more I wished to lay in wait to take away his life; but, as when the preaching was over, I was forced to return home to my master, and tell him what I had heard, I had no opportunity. At one time, the minister said that God was in the midst of them, which astonished me very much, and I looked all about to see if I could see him, but I could not, and I thought I had as good eyes as anyone; not having any idea that "God is a spirit and they that worship him, must worship him in spirit and in truth" (John 4:24); and only to be seen by a spiritual mind in the exercise of faith.

I was thus sent every Sabbath-day, while the other slaves rested, for while the masters go to worship, the slaves are allowed to rest, but thinking that I deserved punishment I was compelled to go to the chapel; but instead of being benefitted by what I heard, I mocked and persecuted the people of God; and when I went home I told my master of the foolishness of preaching, and that the people were mad, for they cried and beat their hands together. It amazed me very much to think they suffered such a noise in a place which they called *God's house*; on returning home I told my master what I had heard and seen, and what I thought of it, which pleased him very much. My hatred was so much against going to the chapel, that I would rather have received a hundred lashes.

Hearing the minister say that we must pray to God for his presence, I determined when I went away to do the same as I had seen the minister do; so when I got home, I retired into a secret place, and there began folding my hands together, shutting my eyes, and using many words which I had heard the minister say, not knowing whether they were right or wrong; and thinking for my much speaking, God would hear me, like the pharisees of old: little did I think that prayer was the sincerity of the heart, and such only is accepted of God; not being acquainted with his word; but I was obliged still to go and hear the minister, or else I should not have had my daily allowance, which was very small. So after thinking a short time, I consented to go one week more, and endeavor to find out "The Lamb of God, that taketh away the sins of the world," whom the minister pointed out; but all was in vain, for I was so tempted by Satan, that difficulties and troubles, whenever I attempted to pray, attended me. The temptations of the devil were so great, and my repeated attempts to pray so interrupted, that I resolved to go to the minister, and tell him my situation. I therefore went, and told him the state of my mind. He told me it was the works of the devil, to frustrate me in my endeavors to serve the Lord, but bid me go on praying in opposition to him. I thanked him for his kindness in telling me what to do, but believed him not; however, I still continued praying, in order to find out whether there was a God or not, being determined to take the minister's life away, if I could not find God.

Thus I endeavored to pray, but such was my situation, that sometimes I could not utter a word; often when I began to pray, I fell asleep, which grieved me very much; conscience accusing me of neglect in my seeking after God. One day being sent as usual to the chapel, in order to punish me, the minister was preaching about prayer, my attention was immediately fixed on the minister to hear what he had to say on the subject, when he said that if any of us had been praying to God and found no benefit from it, we should pray again and again, and be more earnest, and the Lord would hear our prayers; for, "The effectual fervent prayer of a righteous man availeth much." Not knowing the similarity of experience, I thought the minister was preaching about me, and exposing me to all the people, which so much vexed me, that I could not stay any longer, but left the place of worship, and returned home, crying and weeping all the way.

Having a very strong desire to know God, I often retired into some private place to pray, but did not receive any advantage for a long time, which grieved me very sorely. My own heart still suggested to me that there was no God, being so wicked and sinful; that I have since compared myself with those who were destroyed by the flood. (Gen. 8:21) But I have great reason to bless the Lord, that though my heart was deceitful above all things and desperately wicked, yet he did not destroy me, but that I might by his Spirit be converted to God.

From my being disappointed several times I began to despair of ever finding God, and I made a resolution if I did not find him in one more week, I would seek him no more, and would use all the means in my power to take away the minister's life. By earnest prayer and supplication, before the week expired, I was led to see that I was a sinner; all my sins were brought to mind; and the vengeance of God hanging over my head, ready to crush me to pieces; which filled me with distress and anguish of mind, "The sorrows of death now seemed to compass me, and the pains of hell got hold upon me; I found trouble and sorrow." My sins seemed like great mountains pressing on me, and I thought God would deal with me according to my sins, and punish me for my crimes. I knew not how to pacify the wrath of God, for when I looked round me I saw nothing but danger, for the threatenings of God against rebellious sinners, appeared to my view, some of which you will find in the Ninth and Tenth Psalms; and I had sinned against him with a high hand, and an outstretched arm; and had said in my heart, who is the Lord that I should serve him. But now the Lord showed me my sad state, and that I had spoken against him. I was in great distress and affliction, feeling the truth of what God says in his word, that he will send all the curses upon man for their disobedience; and this caused me to groan and cry in a most dreadful manner. The persecutions and threatenings which I had vowed against religious people, particularly the minister, now came to my mind, and filled me with bitter reflection. Sometimes, my terror of mind was so great, that I thought the earth would open, and swallow me up, as in the case of Korah, Dathan, and Abiram. (Num. 16:31–35)

My master and mistress, seeing my distress, asked me what was the matter; and I told them what a sinner I was, and what I feared on account of it: but they commanded me to go to work, for there was no fear of the earth's opening her mouth, and swallowing me up; that the minister had put the devil in me, and they would beat him out, and then they began beating me in a most dreadful manner, whilst I was in this distress of mind; and to add to my troubles, they would not permit me to attend the chapel, thus altering my punishment, though I felt the burden of my sins almost insupportable. In this state I was forced to go to work, with my flesh torn to pieces by their scourging, having large lumps raised on my back; and my soul was grieved and troubled within me. In this situation I went from one friend to another, crying "What shall I do to be saved?" But they, instead of comforting, ridiculed me, and said I was mad.

In this miserable condition, I went to the minister, whom once I had so much despised, and inquired of *him*, what I must do to be saved; begging of him to read and pray for me, that God's anger might be turned away, and that he might be merciful unto me. After this I used to go to the minister every night, about ten or eleven o'clock, that he might read and pray to me; he told me I must pray for myself; but I said that God would not hear my prayers, because I was so wicked: but he told me to go to God, and tell him what a wicked sinner I was, and beg him to have mercy on me. When I went home, I began calling upon God, but did not dare to look up unto heaven, where his honor dwelleth, being so exceedingly terrified, for I feared that God would send his thunder and lightning to destroy me, because of my sins and wickedness. And in my distress I called upon the Lord, and cried unto my God, which you read of in the Eighteenth Psalm, though I could not believe him to be *my* God, I was so afraid of him.

My distress was so very great, that I could have exclaimed with one of old, that I could not give sleep to my eyes, nor slumber to my eyelids; yea, my bed was watered with my tears: seeing myself hanging over the brink of a burning hell, only by the brittle thread of life. My experiencing such hardships from my master and others led me to cry out, "O

Lord, thou hast made me the off-scouring and the refuse in the midst of all the people; and all mine enemies have opened their mouths against me." My enemies, my master and mistress, my mother, sisters, and brothers, chased me sorely without a cause, and increased my trouble by not permitting me to go to a place of worship; for now I began to see the need of a Savior to save my soul, or else I must have perished forever; and feeling that I was not prepared to die, and appear before the judgement seat of Christ, to give an account of the deeds done in the body. Having been led to see that they were very bad, it caused me to say, "Is it nothing to you all ye that pass by; behold and see if there be any sorrow like unto my sorrow, which is done unto me, wherewith the Lord, hath afflicted me, in the day of his fierce anger; from above he hath sent fire into my bones, and it prevaileth against them. He hath spread a net for my feet; he hath turned me back, he hath made me desolate, and faint all the day. The yoke of my transgressions is bound by his hand, they are wreathed, and come up upon my neck. He hath made my strength to fail; the Lord hath delivereth me into their hands from whom I am not able to rise up. For these things I weep, mine eyes runneth down with water; because the Comforter that should relieve my soul is far from me." (Lament of Jeremiah [Lamentations] 4:12, 13, 14, 16)

In this distress I continued five or six weeks, and found no relief, being derided, persecuted, and tortured in the most cruel manner; everything seemed to be against me; yea, even my victuals seemed like wormwood, and my drink like gall. Thus I bowed my knees and my heart before the Lord, in great distress, begging the Lord to have mercy on my soul, that I might not perish; and in the bitterness of my soul, *"I set my face unto the Lord God, to seek by prayer and supplications, with fastings, and sackcloth, and ashes: And I prayed unto the Lord my God, and made my confession, and said, O Lord, the great and dreadful God, keeping the covenant and mercy to them that love him, and to them that keep his commandments; we have sinned and have committed iniquity, and have done wickedly, and have rebelled, even by departing from thy precepts, and from thy judgements: Neither have we hearkened unto thy servants the prophets, which spake in thy name to our kings, our princes, and our fathers, and to all the people of the land."* (Dan. 9:3, 4, 5, 6)

My troubles were so great, that I had nigh sunk into despair, the world, the flesh, and the devil, pressing on me solely. My enemies increased their persecutions, which led me to cry to the Lord to have mercy on my soul, and deliver me from my cruel enemies. Yea, I cried and mourned like a dove of the valley, upon the tops of the mountains; saying, *"Be merciful unto me, O God: for man would swallow me up; he fighting daily oppresseth me. Mine enemies would swallow me up: for they be many that fight against me, O thou Most High. What time I am afraid, I will trust in thee."* (Ps. 56:1, 2, 3)

But the corruptions of my heart were so held forth to my view, that I exclaimed with David of old, *Psalm* 50, to the eighteenth *verse.*

Such was my desire of being instructed in the way of salvation, that I wept at all times I possibly could, to hear the word of God, and seek instruction for my soul; while my master still continued to flog me, hoping to deter me from going; but all to no purpose, for I was determined, by the grace of God, to seek the Lord with all my heart, and with all my mind, and with all my strength, in spirit and in truth, as you read in the Holy Bible. During five or six weeks of my distress, I did not sleep six hours in each week, neither did I care to eat any victuals, for I had no appetite, and thought myself unworthy of the least blessing that God had bestowed on me; that I exclaimed with the publican of old, *"God be merciful to me a miserable hell-deserving sinner."* And while I was thus crying, and begging God to have mercy on me, and confessing my sins unto him, it pleased God to hear my supplications and cries, and came down in his Spirit's power and blessed my soul, and showed me the clear fountain of living water, which proceeded from the throne of God, as you may read in the Revelations; yea, a fountain of water and blood, which flowed from Emanuel's side, to wash away my sins and iniquities, and he applied it unto my heart, and cleansed it from all iniquities, and said unto me, *"And when I passed by thee, and saw thee polluted in thine own blood, I said unto thee when thou wast in thy blood, Live; yea, I said unto thee when thou wast in thy blood, Live. I have caused thee to multiply as the bud of the field, and thou hast increased and waxen great, and thou art come to excellent ornaments: thy breasts are fashioned, and thine hair is grown, whereas thou wast naked and bare. Now when I passed by thee, and looked upon thee, behold, thy time was the time of love; and I spread my skirt over thee, and covered thy nakedness: yea, I sware [swear] unto thee, and entered into a covenant with thee, saith the Lord God, and thou becamest mine. Then washed I thee with water; yea, I thoroughly washed away thy blood from thee, and I anointed thee with oil. I clothed thee also with broidered work, and shod thee with badgers' skin, and I girded thee about with fine linen, and I covered thee with silk. I decked thee also with ornaments, and I put bracelets upon thy hands, and a chain on thy neck. And I put a jewel on thy forehead, and ear-*

rings in thine ears, and a beautiful crown upon thine head. Thus wast thou decked with gold and silver; and thy raiment was of fine linen, and silk, and broidered work; thou didst eat fine flour, and honey, and oil: and thou wast exceeding beautiful, and thou didst prosper abundantly. And thy renown went forth among the heathen for thy beauty: for it was perfect through my comeliness, which I had put upon thee, saith the Lord God." (Ezek. 16: 6–14)

My dear reader, consider the state I was in, I was nearly naked, and had scarcely food to eat, and when I complained, I was tied up, both hands and feet, or put in chains, and flogged, so that the blood would run from my back to the ground; at one time he broke two of my ribs, by stamping and jumping upon me. Consider what a great deliverance I experienced, being released from the bondage of sin and Satan, and delivered from the misery in which I was in, surely none else but the eternal God could effect so great a change.

I had sinned against God with a high hand and an outstretched arm, and had said in my heart, who is God, or the Almighty, that I should fear him, and what profit is it that we have kept his ordinances, or that we have walked mournfully before the Lord of Hosts, Mal. 3:14. But forever blessed be the Lord God Almighty, who heareth the prayers and supplications of poor unworthy sinful creatures, for when I humbled myself, and walked mournfully before the Lord God Almighty, and kept his ordinances and his commandments, he sent his Spirit into my heart, which convinced me *"Of sin, of righteousness, and of judgement to come."* (John 16:8) This made me confess my sins and my wickedness, with shame and confusion of face; and when I had confessed my sins and my wickedness to God, with grief and sorrow of heart, *"He was faithful and just to forgive me my sins, and to cleanse me from all unrighteousness."* (John 1:13)

I was about fifteen years of age when the Lord was pleased to remove gross darkness, superstition, and idolatry, from my heart, and shined upon me with the glorious reconciliation and light of his countenance, and turned my darkness into day, and created a clean heart within me, and renewed a right spirit within me, and said unto my soul, *"Let there be light, (Gen. 1:3) and there was light."* This *"was the true Light, which lighteth every man that cometh into the* [spiritual] *world."* (John 1:9) He was in my heart, and my heart was made by him a clean, new, and fleshy heart, and the heart of stone he took away, as says the prophet Ezekiel, and he renewed a right spirit within me, and gave me a broken spirit, and a humble and contrite heart, which God wilt not despise. Jesus Christ now revealed himself to me, and appeared as, *"The altogether lovely, and the chiefest among ten thousands,"* as he did to the church of old; and for my sorrow and sadness, he gave me joy and gladness in my heart: he also bound up my broken heart, and strengthened my feeble knees, and lifted up my hanging down hands, and comforted my mourning soul; as says the prophet Isaiah; yea, he also poured out the ointment of his grace, and to my sin-sick soul he made his strength perfect in my weakness; and found his grace sufficient for me, and caused me to exclaim in the language of the Psalmist, in the 103rd Psalm, *"Bless the Lord, O my soul: and all that is within me, bless his holy name, etc."*

This was the language of my heart, day and night, for his goodness and mercy, in delivering me from a wounded conscience, and from a broken spirit, and from all the enemies that rose up against me. Yea, he delivered me from the temptations of the world, the flesh, and the devil; and drew my feet out of the miry clay and horrible pit; hewed me out of the rock of unbelief; and brought me through the waste howling wilderness of sin and iniquity, where my enemies laid in wait to destroy my soul, and watched to take away my life; doing everything to prevent my rest; yea, they hooted, laughed, and scoffed at me; my master beating me to keep me from attending the house of God, but all this did not hinder me, for I blessed and praised his holy name that I was counted worthy to suffer with my blessed Jesus; and in all my sufferings I found the presence of God with me, and the Spirit of the Lord to comfort me. I found the hand of the Lord in everything, for when I was beaten it seemed that the Spirit of the Lord was so great on me, that I did not regard the pain and trouble which I felt. At other times when kept without victuals, in order to punish me, I felt the love of God in me, that I did not regard the food; and all the language of my heart was—

> *Wealth and honor I disdain,*
> *Earthly comforts all are vain;*
> *These can never satisfy,*
> *Give me Christ or else I die.*

At other times when they gave me any refreshment, I acknowledged that it came from the immediate hand of God, and rendered unto him humble and hearty thanks in the best manner I could, as the Spirit gave me utterance, which provoked my master greatly, for his desire was that I should render him thanks, and not God, for he said that he gave me the things, but I said, no, it all came from God, for all was his;

that the Spirit of God taught me so; for I was led, guided, and directed by the Spirit, who taught me all things which are of God, and opened them unto my understanding.

Thus I could join with John in the Revelations, saying, *"Thou art worthy, O Lord, to receive glory, and honor, and power: for thou hast created all things, and for thy pleasure they are and were created."* (Rev. 4:9) For I then viewed all the things upon the earth as coming from God, and I asked my master where the earth came from; from God or man, and who had made it. He answered, that God made it. Then said I unto him, if God made the earth, he made the things on the earth, and the things in the earth, and the waters under the earth. (Exod. 20:4) Yea, and besides this, he made the heaven also, and the things in heaven, and in the firmament of heaven. (Gen. 1) He also made hell for the Devil and his angels; and when I took a survey of all these things, I thought *"I beheld, and I heard the voice of many angels round about the throne and the beasts and the elders: and the number of them was ten thousand times ten thousand, and thousands of thousands; Saying with a loud voice, Worthy is the Lamb that was slain to receive power, and riches, and wisdom, and strength, and honor, and glory, and blessing. And every creature which is in heaven, and on the earth, and under the earth, and such as are in the sea, and all that are in them, heard I saying, Blessing, and honor, and glory, and power, be unto him that sitteth upon the throne, and unto the Lamb forever and ever. And the four beasts said, Amen. And the four and twenty elders fell down and worshipped him that liveth forever and ever."* (Rev. 5:12, to the end)

When I took a view of the smallest insect, it showed me, that none but the Almighty could make them, I therefore asked my master who made the insects. He answered, that they came forth out of the ground, but I said unto him, that if God made the ground, surely he made the insects also; for *"All things were made by him; and without him was not anything made that was made."* (John 1:4) From this passage it is evident that everything which our eyes behold, God made it, and he hath put life into every living, moving, and creeping thing; and that he hath made all the dust of the earth, the sand of the coast of the sea, the rocks and the hills, the forests, the sea, and the fountains of water; yea, everything that can be mentioned.

Seeing then the greatness, power, and goodness, of God, how thankful ought we to be for every mercy and blessing he so richly bestows on us, and what favors we enjoy above many of our fellow creatures; but, on the contrary, how many do we see walking contrary to

God's will and commands; swearing, cursing, and abusing the holy name of God; treating with disdain and contempt the mercies of God; who made all things good for his own glory, and for the good of our souls and bodies; and has left upon record that we should have dominion over all things.

How often do we hear our fellow creatures swear in a most dreadful manner; should the reader be of this class, attend to the words of our Lord and Savior, in that ever-memorable sermon on the mount; *"Ye have heard that it hath been said by them of old time, Thou shalt not forswear thyself, but shall perform unto the Lord thine oaths: But I say unto you, Swear not at all: neither by heaven; for it is God's throne: Nor by the earth; for it is his footstool: neither by Jerusalem; for it is the city of the great King. Neither shalt thou swear by thy head, because thou canst not make one hair white or black: But let your communication be, Yea, yea; Nay, nay: for whatsoever is more than these cometh of evil."* (Matt. 5:33–37) Seeing this to be the case, *"What manner of persons ought ye to be in all holy conversation and godliness."*

The time is drawing nigh when we must all appear at the bar of God, to give an account of the deeds done in the body. *"But, beloved, be not ignorant of this one thing, that one day is with the Lord as a thousand years, and a thousand years as one day. The Lord is not slack concerning his promise, as some men count slackness; but is long-suffering to us-ward, not willing that any should perish, but that all should come to repentance."* (2 Pet. 3:8, 9)

O impenitent sinner! consider the uncertainty of time, and that *"Now is the accepted time, now is the day of salvation."* Consider the many exhortations and admonitions the Scriptures hold out to your view: *"Have I any pleasure at all that the wicked should die? saith the Lord God; and not that he should return from his ways, and live?"* (Ezek. 18:23) *"Who will have all men to be saved, and to come unto the knowledge of the truth."* (1 Tim. 2:4) *"For yourselves know perfectly that the day of the Lord so cometh as a thief in the night."* (1 Thess. 5:2) *"But know this, that if the good man of the house had known in what watch the thief would come, he would have watched, and would not have suffered his house to be broken up. Therefore, be ye also ready: for in such hour as ye think not, the Son of man cometh."* (Matt. 24:43, 44. See Luke 12:39. Rev. 14:15. Rev. 3:3. 2 Pet. 3:10)

My dear reader, though the word of God informs us that it will be in the night, consider that you may not be permitted to live to that night, for you know not when this night will come; and if God should summon thee to appear before his tribunal this day, or this night, how dost thou think to appear before him in thy wickedness? If thou had not been led to Christ for salvation, how awful will the sentence be unto thee, "Depart, ye cursed, into everlasting punishment, prepared for the Devil, and his angels." O! what a dreadful sentence! But should you be holy and righteous what a joyful sound will it be unto you to hear the welcome salutation of "Come, ye blessed of my father, inherit the kingdom prepared for you from the foundation of the world." O! what cheering words!

I would therefore advise you, my dear reader, to endeavor, if you have not, to seek the Lord, to attain this blessing, and to shun that dreadful place of punishment which you have heard of. Consider the multitude of sins which thou hast committed, and remember, that "One leak will sink a ship," and one single sin will sink thy soul into everlasting perdition; or, in plainer terms, into that lake which burneth with fire and brimstone, where the worm dieth not, and the fire is not quenched. (Read the ninth chapter of the Gospel [of] St. Mark. Matt. 16:28; 17:1, 22; 18:1. Luke 11:49. 1 Cor. 12:3. Matt. 10:42; 18:6; 5:29; 18:8. Isa. 66:24. Lev. 2:13. Matt. 5:13)

There are many, it is to be lamented, in our day, that profess religion, but by their life and conduct they betray themselves, and crucify their Lord and Master, by putting him to an open shame; but a true Christian is merciful to all, endeavoring always to do good. But this was not the case with me, for before I knew God, it was always my delight to do evil in persecuting the people of God, and committing all manner of sin and wickedness, to my own shame and confusion; *"Wherefore I give you to understand, that no man speaking by the Spirit of God calleth Jesus accursed: and that no man can say that Jesus is the Lord, but by the Holy Ghost."* (1 Cor. 12:3) *"And whosoever shall give to drink unto one of these little ones a cup of cold water, only in the name of a disciple, verily I say unto you, He shall in no wise lose his reward."* (Matt. 10:42) *"But whoso shall offend one of these little ones which believe in me, it were better for him that a millstone were hanged about his neck, and that he were drowned in the depth of the sea."* (Matt. 18:6) But I did not think while I was persecuting the people of God, that he was able to cast me, both soul and body, into hell, where the worm dieth not, and the fire is not quenched. My dear reader, if you cannot do the followers of Jesus any good, do not injure them; consider what a solemn assertion is made in their behalf.

The least darling lust will prevent thy entering into the heavenly and blessed paradise; *"Wherefore if thy hand or foot offend thee: cut them off, and cast them from thee: it is better for thee to enter into life halt or maimed, rather than having two hands or two feet to be cast into everlasting fire."* (Matt. 18:8) But I thought nothing of this, and was living in the indulgence of my heart, and fulfilling my carnal desires; but blessed and praised be the God of my salvation, for he has turned my darkness into his glorious and marvellous light. May it please the Lord to turn every sinner's heart, as he was pleased to turn mine; and translate them out of the kingdom of Satan into the kingdom of his dear Son; and stop them from going down to the place of eternal punishment.

But, to resume my narrative, when my heart was changed by divine grace, and I became regenerated and born again of the water and of the Spirit, and became as a little child, I began to speak the language of Canaan to my master and mistress, and to my own friends, but it seemed to them as if I was mad, or like one that was mocking them, when I bid them leave off their sins and wickedness, by the aid of God's divine Spirit, and be saved by grace, through faith in the Lord Jesus Christ, and said that they must be regenerated and born again of the water and of the Spirit, or else they could not enter into the kingdom of heaven; showing them the necessity of that important doctrine by the conversation of Jesus Christ with Nicodemus. (John 3) But, though they professed Christianity, they knew nothing of what it meant; which surprised me exceedingly, and I exclaimed, "Are ye Christians, and know not these things?" And when I had thus exclaimed unto them, they thought I had lost my reason; yea, my dear mother and sisters, my master and his family, in particular, thought so of me; thus, *"My foes were those of my own house."*

But being taught and directed by the Spirit of God, I told my master, mistress, my mother, sisters, and brothers, that there was nothing too hard for the Almighty God to do, for he would deliver me from their hands, and from their tyrannical power; for he had begun the work of grace in my heart, and he would not leave it unfinished, for whatsoever grace had begun, glory would end. He gave me to see the first approach of evil; and he gave me power over my besetting sins, to cast them from me, and to despise them as deadly poison. He armed me with the whole armor of divine grace, whereby I quenched all the fiery darts of the wicked, and compelled Satan to retreat; and put him to flight by faithful and fervent prayer.

In addition to these he gave me power over the last enemy, which is death; that is, I could look at it without any fear or dread; though it is the most terrible of all other things. There is nothing in the world that we can imagine, so dreadful and frightful as death. It is possible to escape the edge of the sword—to close the lions' mouths—to quench the fiery darts;—but when death shoots its poisoned arrows—when it opens its infernal pit—and when it sends forth its devouring flames— it is altogether impossible to secure ourselves, to guard ourselves from its merciless fury. There is an infinite number of warlike inventions, by which we defeat the evil designs of the most powerful and dreadful enemies; but there is no stratagem of the most renowned general, no fortification, ever so regular or artificial, no army, every so victorious, that can but for a moment retard the approaches of death; this last enemy, in the twinkling of an eye, flies through the strongest bulwarks, the thickest walls, the most prodigious towers, the highest castles, and the most inaccessible rocks; makes its way through the strongest barricadoes [barricades], passes over trenches, pierces the impenetrable armor, and through the best-tempered breastplates it strikes the proudest hearts, it enters the darkest dungeon, and snatches the prisoners out of the hands of the most trusty and watchful guards. Nature and art can furnish us with nothing able to protect us from death's cruel and insatiable hands. There are none so barbarous, but they are sometimes overcome by the prayers and tears of such as implore their mercy; nay, such as have lost all sense of humanity and goodness, commonly spare in their rage, the weakest age and sex; but unmerciful death hath no more regard to such as are humble, than to those that resist and defy it; it takes no notice of infants' tears and cries, it plucks them from the breasts of their tender-hearted mothers; it stops its ears to the requests of trembling old age, and casts to the ground the grey heads as so many withered oaks. At a battle, when princes and generals of the enemy's are taken prisoners, they are not treated as common soldiers; but unmerciful death treads under feet as audaciously the prince as the subject, the master as the servant, the noble as the vassal, the rich Dives and the begging Lazarus; together it blows out with the same blast, the most glorious luminaries and the most loathsome lamps. It hath no more respect for the crowns of kings, the pope's mitre, and the cardinal's cap, than for the shepherd's crook, or the poor slave's chains; it heaps them all together, and shuts them in the same dungeon. There is no war, though ever so furious and bloody, but it is interrupted with some days, or at least some hours, of cessation or truce; nay, the most inhuman minds are at last tired with bloody conquests; but insatiable death never saith it is enough, at every hour and moment it cuts down multitudes of the human race; the flesh of all the animals that have died since the creation of the world, has not been able to glut this devouring monster. All warfare is doubtful, he that gains the victory today, may soon after be put to flight; he that at present is in a triumphant chariot may become the footstool of his enemy; but death is always victorious, it triumphs with an insufferable insolence over all the kings and nations of the earth; it never returns to its den, but when loaded with spoils, and glutted with blood, the strongest Samson and the most victorious David, who have torn in pieces, and have overcome lions and bears, and have cut off the heads of giants, have at last yielded themselves, and been cut off by death. The great Alexanders and the triumphing Caesars, who have made all the world to tremble before them, and conquered the most part of the habitable earth, could never find anything that might protect them from death's power; when magnificent statues and stately trophies were raised to their honor, death laughed at their vanity, and made sport with their rich marbles, where so many proud titles are engraved, which cover nothing but a little rotten flesh and a few bones, which death has broken and reduced to ashes.

We read in the prophecies of Daniel, that King Nebuchadnezzar saw in a dream a large image of gold, both glorious and terrible: its head was of pure gold, its breasts and arms were of silver, its belly and thighs of brass, its legs of iron, and its feet partly of clay and partly of iron. As the king was beholding it with astonishment, a little stone, cut out of a mountain, without hands, was rolled against the feet of this prodigious image, and broke it all to pieces; not only the clay and iron were broken, but also the gold, the silver, and the brass, all became as the chaff which the wind bloweth to and fro. This great image represented the four universal monarchies of the world, namely, that of Babylon, of the Persians and Medes, of the Greeks, and of the Romans; it represented also the vanity and inconstancy of all things under the sun, for what is the pomp, the glory, the strength, and the dignities of this world, but as smoke driven with the wind, a vapor that soon vanishes away, a shadow that flies from us, or a dream that disappears in an instant. Man, created in the image of God, at his first appearance seems to be very glorious, for a while, and become terrible, but as soon as death strikes at the earthly part, and begins to break his flesh and bones, all the glory, pomp, power, and magnificence of the richest, the most terrible, and victorious monarchs, are changed into loathsome smells, into contemptible dust, and reduced to nothing. *"Vanity of vanities; all is vanity."*

Since, therefore, death is so impartial as to spare none, and its power so great, that none can escape or resist it, it is no wonder if it appears so terrible, and fill[s] with fear, grief and despair, the minds of all mortals who have not settled their faith and assurance on God; for there is no condemned prisoner but trembles when he beholds the scaffold erecting, upon which he is designed to be broken on the wheel, or sees in the fire, irons with which he is to be pinched to death.

In the midst of an impious feast, King Belshazzar saw the fingers of a man's hand, writing these words upon the wall of his palace: *Mene, Mene, Tekel, Upharsin*; which the prophet Daniel thus interpreted: *Mene*; God hath numbered thy kingdom, and finished it. *Tekel*; thou art weighed in the balances, and art found wanting. *Peres; or, Upharsin*; thy kingdom is divided, and given to the Medes and Persians. As soon as this great monarch had cast his eyes upon this miraculous writing, it is said, that his countenance was changed, and his thoughts troubled him, so that the joints of his loins were loosed, and his knees smote one against another. Certainly the proud worldling has a greater cause to be dismayed in the midst of his glory and pleasure, when he may perceive death writing upon every wall of his house, in visible characters, and printing upon his forehead, that God hath numbered his days, and these in which he now breathes, shall be soon followed by an eternal night; that God hath weighed him in the balance of his justice, and found him as light as the wind; and that the Almighty Creator, unto whom vengeance belongs, will soon divest him of all his glory and riches, to clothe therewith his enemies.

What comforts can be found for wretched sinners, who do not only understand their final sentence, but also hear the thundering voice of the great judge of the world, exasperated by their impieties? They now perceive hell prepared to swallow them up, and the fiery chains of that doleful prison ready to embrace them; they may at present feel the hands of the executioner of divine justice, that seize upon them already, and see themselves stretched and tortured in that place where there shall be weeping, and wailing, and gnashing of teeth; they may feel the fierce approaches of that fire and brimstone, which is the second death, for it may be justly said of these wretched varlets, that hell comes to them before they go to it, and that in this life they partly feel the grievous pangs of their future torments: therefore some of them offer violence to themselves, and commit horrid murder upon their own persons, as if they were not afraid to die by a hand wicked enough; the *expectation of death* to them, is more sufferable than *death itself,* and they would rather cast themselves into the bottomless pit of hell, than endure the apprehensions and fears of hell in their guilty consciences; and to be delivered from the flashes of hellfire, they cast themselves in a brutish manner into that unquenchable burning.

But that which is most terrible is, that the horrid and insufferable fears that seize upon the wicked, are not short and transitory; for, as a criminal that knows there is sentence of death pronounced against him, continually thinks upon the torments that are preparing for him; as soon as he hears the doors unlocking, he imagines that some are entering to drag him from his prison to execution; in some sense he desires what he apprehends, and hastens the approach of that which he wishes, but cannot avoid. Thus desperate sinners, that know there is a sentence of eternal death proclaimed against them in the court of the king of kings, and that from this sentence there is no appeal nor escape, must needs be in continual fears, such foresee the fearful image of death that disturbs their quiet, and St. Paul expresses himself, *"Through fear of death were all their lifetime subject to bondage."* (Heb. 2:15) That is, they are like so many wretched slaves, that tremble under the inhuman power of a merciless tyrant.

There are some atheists who talk of death with contempt and scorn, and who make an open profession of braving death, without the least fear; nevertheless, they feel in them some secret thorns with which death often galls them, some fears and apprehensions with which it tortures and disquiets them, when they dream least of it; it is true they for the most part boast of not fearing the approaches of death, and laugh at it when they imagine that it is a distance from them, but these are they who are most apt to tremble at the near approach of the grim countenance of death, and soonest discover their weakness and despair. There are many that seem to laugh at death, while their laughter is only an appearance upon the lips; they are like a child newly born, who seems to smile when it is inwardly tormented in the bowels; or like those that eat of an herb, which causes a pleasant laughter to appear upon the lips of those who partake of it, but into whose noble parts it conveys a mortal poison.

There are some, I confess, that die without any concern, but these are either brutish or senseless persons, much like unto a sleeping drunkard, who may be cast down a precipice, without any knowledge or foresight of the danger; or, they are pleasant mockers, like the foolish criminals who go merrily to the gallows; or, such as are full of rage and fury, who may well be compared to an enraged wild boar, that runs himself into the huntsman's snare. Such monsters of men as these, deserve not to be reckoned among rational and understanding creatures.

From the fear of death it pleased the Lord to deliver me by his blessed Spirit; and gave me the witness of his Spirit to bear witness with my spirit, that I was passed from death unto life, and caused me to love the brethren. At this time I received this full evidence and witness within me, I was about seventeen years of age, then I began to love all men, women, and children, and began to speak boldly in the name of the living God, and to preach as the oracles of God, as the Spirit and love of God constrained me; as the poet says,

> *The Love of God doth constrain,*
> *To seek the wandering souls of men.*

For I beheld them wandering away from God, like lost sheep, which caused me to exhort them to turn unto the shepherd and bishop of their souls, from whom they had so greatly revolted, and to fly from the wrath to come. When they reviled me, I told them of Christ's example: *"Who did no sin, neither was guile found in his mouth: Who, when he was reviled, reviled not again; when he suffered, he threatened not; but committed himself to him that judgeth righteously."* (1 Pet. 2:22, 23) And I endeavored to follow his steps, by exhorting and praying for them to turn from their evil ways, although they were so inveterated against me, and strove to the utmost of their power to make me suffer as an evildoer. But, blessed be God, that I counted it all joy that I was worthy to suffer for the glory of God, and for the good of my soul. For the word of God saith, *"But and if ye suffer for righteousness' sake, happy are ye; and be not afraid of their terror, neither be troubled; But sanctify the Lord God in your heart: and be ready always to give an answer to every man that asketh you a reason of the hope that is in you with meekness and fear: Having a good conscience: that whereas they speak evil of you, as of evildoers, they may be ashamed that falsely accuse your good conversation in Christ. For it is better if the will of God be so, that ye suffer for well doing, than for evildoing."* (1 Pet. 3:14–17)

I was sold to three masters, all of whom spoke ill of me, and said that I should spoil the rest of the slaves, by my talking and preaching. The last master I was sold to, I ran from to the house of God, and was baptized unknown to him; and when the minister made it known to him, he was like a man that had lost his reason, and swore that I should not belong to any society; but the minister informed him it was too late, for the work was already finished, and according to the spiritual law of liberty, I was considered a worthy member of society. My master then beat me most cruelly, and threatened to beat the minister over the head with a cane. He then took me before the magistrates, who examined me, and inquired what I knew about God and the Lord Jesus Christ. Upon this I made a public acknowledgement before the magistrates, that God, for Christ's sake, had pardoned my sins and blotted out all mine iniquities, through our Lord Jesus Christ, whereby he was become my defense and deliverer; and that there is no other name under heaven, given to man, whereby he shall be saved, but only in the name of our Lord Jesus Christ. On hearing this, the magistrates told me I was free from my master, and at liberty to leave him; but my cruel master was very unwilling to part with me, because he was of the world. *"They are of the world: therefore speak they of the world, and the world heareth them."* (1 John 4:5) This was evident, for if my master had been of God he would have instructed me in the Scriptures, as God had given him ability, and according to the oracles of the living God; for we have all one father, and if any man teach[,] let him do it as God gives him ability; so saith the Scriptures. But my master strove to baffle me, and to prevent me from understanding the Scriptures: so he used to tell me that there was a time to every purpose under the sun, to do all manner of work, that slaves were in duty bound to do whatever their masters commanded them, whether it was right or wrong; so that they must be obedient to a hard spiteful master as to a good one. He then took the Bible and showed it to me, and said that the book talked with him. Thus he talked with me endeavoring to convince me that I ought not to leave him, although I had received my full liberty from the magistrates, and was fully determined, by the grace of God, to leave him; yet he strove to the uttermost to prevent me; but thanks be to God, his strivings were all in vain.

My master's sons also endeavored to convince me, by their reading in the behalf of their father; but I could not comprehend their dark sayings, for it surprised me much, how they could take that blessed book into their hands, and to be so superstitious as to want to make me believe that the book did talk with them; so that every opportunity when they were out of the way, I took the book, and held it up to my ears, to try whether the book would talk with me or not, but it proved to be all in vain, for I could not hear it speak one word, which caused me to grieve and lament, that after God had done so much for me as he had, in pardoning my sins, and blotting out my iniquities and transgressions, and making me a new creature, the book would not talk with me; but the Spirit of the Lord brought this passage of Scripture to my mind, where Jesus Christ says, *"Whatsoever ye shall ask the Father in my name, ye shall receive. Ask in faith nothing doubting: for according unto your faith it shall be unto you. For unto him that believeth, all things are possible."* Then I began to ask God in faithful and fervent prayer, as the Spirit of the Lord gave me utterance, begging earnestly of the Lord to give me the knowledge of his word, that I might be enabled to understand it in its pure light, and be able to speak it in the Dutch and English languages, that I might convince my master that he and his sons had not spoken to me as they ought, when I was their slave.

Thus I wrestled with God by faithful and fervent prayer, for five or six weeks, like Jacob of old. (Gen. 32:24; Hos. 12:4) My master and mistress, and all people, laughed me to scorn, for being such a fool, to think that God would hear my prayer and grant unto me my request. But I gave God no rest day nor night, and I was so earnest, that I can truly say, I shed as many tears for this blessing, as I did when I was begging God to grant me the pardon and forgiveness of my sins. During the time I was pouring out my supplications and prayers unto the Lord, my hands were employed, laboring for the bread that perisheth, and my heart within me still famishing for the word of God; as spoken of in the Scriptures, *"There shall be a famine in the land; not a famine of bread, nor of water, but of the word of God."* And thus blessed be the Lord, that he sent a famine into my heart, and caused me to call upon him by his Spirit's assistance, in the time of my trouble.

The Lord heard my groans and cries at the end of six weeks, and sent the blessed angel of the covenant to my heart and soul, to release me from all my distress and troubles, and delivered me from all mine enemies, which were ready to destroy me; thus the Lord was pleased in his infinite mercy, to send an angel, in a vision, in shining raiment, and his countenance shining as the sun, with a large Bible in his hands, and brought it unto me, and said, *"I am come to bless thee, and to grant thee thy request,"* as you read in the Scriptures. Thus my eyes were opened at the end of six weeks, while I was praying, in the place where I slept; although the place was as dark as a dungeon, I awoke, as the Scripture saith, and found it illuminated with the light of the glory of God, and the angel standing by me, with the large book open, which was the

Holy Bible, and said unto me, *"Thou hast desired to read and under-stand this book, and to speak the language of it both in English and in Dutch; I will therefore teach thee, and now read"*; and then he taught me to read the first chapter of the gospel according to St. John; and when I had read the whole chapter, the angel and the book were both gone in the twinkling of an eye, which astonished me very much, for the place was dark immediately; being about four o'clock in the morning in the winter season. After my astonishment had a little subsided, I began to think whether it was a fact that an angel had taught me to read, or only a dream; for I was in such a strait, like Peter was in prison, when the an-gel smote him on the side, and said unto Peter, *"Arise, Peter, and take thy garment, and spread it around thee, and follow me."* And Peter knew not whether it was a dream or not; and when the Angel touched him the second time, Peter arose, took his garment, folded it around him, and followed the angel, and the gates opened unto him of their own ac-cord. So it was with me when the room was darkened again, that I won-dered within myself whether I could read or not, but the Spirit of the Lord convinced me that I could; I then went out of the house to a secret place, and there rendered thanksgivings and praises unto God's holy name, for his goodness in showing me to read his holy word, to under-stand it, and to speak it, both in the English and Dutch languages.

I tarried at a distance from the house, blessing and praising God, until the dawning of the day, and by that time the rest of the slaves were called to their labor; they were all very much surprised to see me there so early in the morning, rejoicing as if I had found a pearl of great price, for they used to see me very sad and grieved on other mornings, but now rejoicing, and they asked me what was the reason of my rejoicing more now than at other times, but I answered I would not tell them. Af-ter I had finished my day's work I went to the minister's house, and told him that I could read, but he doubted greatly of it, and said unto me, "How is it possible that you can read? For when you were a slave your master would not suffer anyone, whatever, to come near you to teach you, nor any of the slaves, to read; and it is not long since you had your liberty, not long enough to learn to read." But I told him, that the Lord had learnt me to read last night. He said it was impossible. I said, "Nothing is impossible with God, for all things are possible with him; but the thing impossible with man is possible with God, for all things are possible with him; but the thing impossible with man is possible with God: for he doth with the host of heaven, and with the inhabi-tants of the earth, as he pleaseth, and there is none that can withstay his hand, nor dare to say what dost thou? And so did the Lord with me as it pleased him, in showing me to read his word, and to speak it, and if you have a large bible, as the Lord showed me last night, I can read it." But he said, "No, it is not possible that you can read." This grieved me greatly, which caused me to cry. His wife then spoke in my behalf, and said unto him, "You have a large bible, fetch it, and let him try and see whether he can read it or not, and you will then be convinced." The minister then brought the bible to me, in order that I should read; and as he opened the bible for me to read, it appeared unto me, that a person said, "That is the place, read it." Which was the first chapter of the gospel of St. John, the same the Lord had taught me to read. So I read to the minister; and he said to me, "You read very well and very distinct"; and asked me who had learnt me. I said that the Lord had learnt me last night. He said that it was impossible; but, if it were so, he should find it out. On saying this he went and got other books, to see whether I could read *them*; I tried, but could not. He then brought a spelling book, to see if I could spell; but he found to his great astonishment, that I could not. This convinced him and his wife that it was the Lord's work, and it was marvellous in their eyes.

This caused them to spread a rumor all over the city of New York, saying, that the Lord had worked great miracles on a poor black man. The people flocked from all parts to know whether it was true or not; and some of them took me before the magistrates, and had me examined concerning the rumor that was spread abroad, to prevent me, if possible, from saying the Lord had taught me to read in one night, in about fifteen minutes; for they were afraid that I should teach the other slaves to call upon the name of the Lord, as I did aforetime, and that they should come to the knowledge of the truth.

The magistrates examined me strictly, to see if I could read, as the report stated; they brought a bible for me to read in, and I read unto them the same chapter the Lord had taught me, as before-mentioned, and they said I read very well and distinct, and asked me who had taught me to read. I still replied, that the Lord had taught me. They said it was impossible; but brought forth spelling and other books, to see if I could read them, or whether I could spell, but they found to their great surprise, that I could not read the other books, neither could I spell a word; then they said, it was the work of the Lord, and a very great miracle indeed; whilst others exclaimed and said that it was not right that I should have my liberty. The magistrates said that it was right and just that I should have my liberty, for they believed that I was of God, for they were persuaded that no man could read in such a manner, unless he was taught of God.

From that hour, in which the Lord taught me to read, until the present, I have not been able to read in any book, nor any reading whatever, but such as contain the word of God.

Through the report of the minister (whose name was the Reverend Peter Lowe, a pastor of the Presbyterian church) and the magistrates, I was permitted to go on in the strength of the Lord, and to proclaim the glad tidings of salvation by Jesus Christ, unto everyone, both great [and] small, saying unto those that were Christians, *"Rejoice with me, for the Lord hath liberated my soul from all my enemies."* I was so overjoyed that I cried out, *"Make a joyful noise unto God, all ye lands: Sing forth the honor of his name: make his praise glorious, etc."* as in the Sixty-sixth Psalm.

I was now enabled, by the assistance of the Holy Spirit, to go from house to house, and from plantation to plantation, warning sinners, in the name of Jesus, to flee from the wrath to come; teaching and admonishing them to turn from their evil course in life; whilst some mocked and others scoffed at me, many said that I was mad, others pointed at me, and said there goes *"the preacher,"* in a mocking and jeering manner. Sometimes after I had been preaching in a house, and was leaving it, some of the people, who were assembled together, without the door, would beat and use me in a very cruel manner, saying, as the Jews of old did to Jesus Christ, when they smote him with the palms of their hands, *"Prophesy unto us it was that smote thee?"*

But, forever blessed be the Lord, he was pleased to give me one soul for my hire, and one seal to my ministry; which caused me to bless the Lord, and ascribe all the honor and glory to his name, for not having let my labors been in vain. This poor soul to whom the Lord was pleased to bless my feeble endeavors, was a poor black slave, the same as I had been; the Lord in infinite mercy, was pleased to liberate his soul from the bondage of sin and Satan, and afterwards from his cruel master.

It was a law of the state of the city of New York, that if any slave could give a satisfactory account of what he knew of the work of the Lord on his soul, he was free from slavery, by the Act of Congress, that was governed by the good people the Quakers, who were made the happy instruments, in the hands of God, of releasing some thousands of us poor black slaves from the galling chains of slavery.

After this poor man had received his liberty from slavery, he joined me in hand and heart, willing *"To follow the Lamb of God whithersoever he goeth.*" His employment while with his master, was sweeping chimneys; but now his master, who was God, had given him his labor to endeavor to sweep the evils out of the hearts of poor slaves. He and I used to go from house to house, and in barns and under hedges, preaching the gospel of Christ, as the Spirit of God gave us utterance; and God added unto our number such as should be saved. In the course of about nineteen months, it pleased the Lord to add to our number about five hundred souls; and when we could not find room enough in the houses, we used to preach out of doors in the fields and woods, which we used to call our large chapel, and there we assembled together on Saturday evenings about eleven o'clock, after the slaves had done their masters' work, and continued until Sunday evening about ten or eleven o'clock. The other black man and myself used to go fourteen miles of a night to preach, and to instruct our poor fellow brethren, and thought ourselves well paid for our trouble in having a congregation together in the name of the Lord.

I knew it was a hard task for the poor slaves to get out, because when I was a slave I had gone fifteen miles to hear preaching, and was obliged to get back before sun rising, to go to my work, and then, if my master knew I had been to hear preaching, he would beat me most unmercifully, so that I encouraged the other poor slaves to seek the Lord, and to be earnest in prayer and supplication, for well I knew that the Lord would hear and deliver them, if they sought him in sincerity and in truth, as the Lord delivered me; for they did not suffer for evildoing, but for doing the will of God. Being under that promise which says, *"But and if ye suffer for righteousness' sake, happy are ye"*: Yea, this was the encouragement that I gave them—*"For as much then as Christ hath suffered for us in the flesh, arm yourselves likewise with the same mind: for he that hath suffered in the flesh hath ceased from sin; That he no longer should live the rest of his time in the flesh to the lusts of men, but to the will of God. For the time past of our life may suffice us to have wrought the will of Gentiles, when we walked in lasciviousness, lusts, excess of wine, revellings, banquetings, and abominable idolatries: Wherein they think it strange that ye run not with them to the same excess of riot, speaking evil of you: Who shall give account to him that is ready to judge the quick and the dead. For this cause was the gospel preached also to them that are dead, that they might be judged according to men in the flesh, but live according to God in the spirit. But the end of all things is at hand: be ye therefore sober, and watch unto prayer."* (1 Pet. 4:1–7)

We informed them that they must cease to do evil, and learn to do well, for the end of all their troubles was near at hand. We told them that they should not desire nor covet the dainties of this world, for it was the deceitfulness of man's evil and wicked heart, which made him desire to partake of those things, which is not for his benefit, but will tend to destroy him; as the lying prophet caused the man of God to be destroyed, enticing him to go back to his house, to eat and drink with him, although the man of God was forbidden to go back, nor to eat bread, nor to drink water, in the place, nor to go back by the way as he came; but the lying prophet persuaded the man of God to return back, for an angel had sent him, and that he was to return back, and to eat and drink, and afterwards he should proceed on his journey. Being over-persuaded by the lying prophet, he returned back, but he lost his life, for not truly believing and keeping the commandments of God, which he had so strictly commanded him. (1 Kings 13)

My dear reader, take care what company you keep, and take care whom you eat and drink with; for many would almost persuade you that they were saints, but by their gluttonous way of living, their hearts are like a knife to your throat. *"When thou sittest to eat with a ruler, consider diligently what is before thee: And put a knife to thy throat, if thou be a man given to appetite. Be not desirous of his dainties: for they are deceitful meat. Labor not to be rich: cease from thine own wisdom. Wilt thou set thine eyes upon that which is not? for riches certainly make themselves wings; they fly away as an eagle toward heaven. Eat thou not the bread of him that hath an evil eye, neither desire thou his dainty meats: For as he thinketh in his heart, so is he: Eat and drink, saith he to thee; but his heart is not with thee. The morsel which thou hast eaten shalt thou vomit up, and lose thy sweet words. Speak not in the ears of a fool: for he will despise the wisdom of thy words. Remove not the old landmark; and enter not into the fields of the fatherless: For their redeemer is mighty; he shall plead their cause with thee."* (Prov. 23:1–12)

We told the poor slaves that God had promised to deliver them that call upon him in time of trouble, out of all their distress; for *"He would be with them in six troubles, and in the seventh he would not forsake them."* We encouraged them to be angry with, and not to commit, sin, as the Scripture saith, *"Be ye angry, and sin not"*; For sin brought all their punishment upon them, whatever they suffered; therefore, I exhorted them to hate sin, and to fly from it as from the face of a serpent; and to remember that our blessed Lord had said, that we should have persecution in the world, but in him we should have peace; for the world hated him and the world knew him not, and therefore they would hate us, because they hated him first; for they knew him not, neither do they know us, because he has chosen us out of the world: therefore our Lord has said, *"It is through many tribulations that you shall enter the kingdom of heaven: for he shall be hated of all men for my name's sake, and they shall cast out your name as evil, and they that kill you will think that they do God service; and they shall say all manner of evil against you falsely, for my sake. Rejoice: and be exceeding glad: for great is your reward in heaven · for persecuted they the prophets and apostles that were before you:"* We encouraged them in the Christian life, and said to them *"Finally, be ye all of one mind, having compassion one of another, love as brethren, be pitiful, be courteous: Not rendering evil for evil, or railing for railing: but contrariwise blessing; knowing that ye are thereunto called, that ye should inherit a blessing. For he that will love life, and see good days, let him refrain his tongue from evil, and his lips that they speak no guile: Let him eschew evil, and do good; let him seek peace, and ensue it. For the eyes of the Lord are over the righteous, and his ears are open unto their prayers: but the face of the Lord is against them that do evil."* (1 Pet. 3:8–12)

Thus we went on preaching in the name of the Lord, and it pleased God to bless our feeble efforts, by adding unto our number such as should be saved.

At this time the Lord was pleased to raise up some white friends, who were benevolent and kind to us, when they saw our simpleness, and that God prospered us in our manner and way of worship; who joined their mites with ours, and purchased a piece of ground, and built upon it a meetinghouse, in the city of New York, for us poor black Africans to worship in, which held about *fifteen hundred people!* They also procured white preachers twice a week to preach, to assist the other black man and myself.

Being thus highly favored, we now had preaching three times on the Sabbath-day, and every night in the week; and the number of them that were added unto the society, was about *nine hundred and fifty souls!*

I continued at this place four years after that, preaching with the other preachers; for we were appointed to preach in rotation. The word of the Lord grew and multiplied exceedingly, for it pleased the Lord, sometimes at one service, to add to our number *fifteen souls!* and, sometimes *more!* At our watch nights and camp meetings, I have known one hundred and fifty, or two hundred, awakened at one time; by which it was evident that the time was like the day of Pentecost; which you have an account of in the second chapter of Acts.

Thus, when we assembled together with one accord, the Lord was pleased to send down his convincing and converting spirit, to convince and convert the congregation, and they were filled with the spirit of prayer, which caused them to groan and cry unto God, begging him to have mercy upon their never-dying souls, to such a degree, that it caused some to say, that the people were drunk, others said they were possessed with devils, many said they were mad, and others laughing, mocking, and scoffing at them; while the people came running in out of the streets and houses to see what was the matter; and many of *them* were convinced of sin, and of righteousness, and of judgement to come; crying out with the jailor of old, *"What shall we do to be saved?"* We still continued speaking as the Spirit gave us utterance.

It was our heart's desire, and prayer to God, that every sinner might be saved; so we went on in the strength of God, by the aid of his Spirit, warning sinners everywhere to repent and believe the gospel, that their souls might be saved through grace, by faith in the Lord Jesus Christ. When the congregation grew numerous, and there were enough preachers besides myself, I was then constrained by the Spirit, and the love of God, to go about four hundred miles from thence, to preach the everlasting gospel to the people there, at a place called Boston, in North America. I continued preaching there about three years and a half, and the Lord crowned my feeble endeavors with great success, and gave me souls for my hire, and seals to my ministry.

After being at Boston three years and a half, I returned to New York, to see my mother, sisters, brothers, and friends, and after arriving there, I thought it necessary to enter into the state of matrimony, and we lived very comfortably together about two years, being of one heart and one mind, both of us belonging to the Methodist society in New York. My wife was of the Indian color. To add to our comfort the Lord was pleased to give us a daughter.

But a circumstance transpired which interrupted our felicity, and made me very unhappy: My wife's mistress had been trying to persuade her not to be so religious, for she would make herself melancholy to be so much at the house of God, and she did not like it; she told her she thought it was no harm to sing songs, and to do as the rest of the people of the world did, and said there was a time for every purpose under the sun: a time to be born, and a time to die; a time to plant, and a time to pluck up that which is planted; a time to kill, and a time to heal; a time to break down, and a time to build up; a time to weep, and a time to laugh; a time to mourn, and a time to dance; a time to cast away stones, and a time to gather stones together; a time to embrace, and a time to refrain from embracing; a time to get, and a time to lose; a time to keep, and a time to cast away; a time to rend, and a time to sew; a time to keep silence, and a time to speak; a time to love, and a time to hate; a time of war, and a time of peace. Thus her mistress spoke, not thinking that these were spiritual times, nor considering that the Scriptures were wrote by inspiration and that they must be understood by the Spirit, *"For what man knoweth the things of a man, save the spirit of man which is in him? even so the things of God knoweth no man, but the Spirit of God. Now we have received, not the spirit of the world, but the spirit which is of God; that we might know the things that are freely given to us of God. Which things also we speak, not in the words which man's wisdom teacheth, but which the Holy Ghost teacheth; comparing spiritual things with spiritual. But the natural man receiveth not the things of the Spirit of God: for they are foolishness unto him: neither can he know of them, because they are spiritually discerned."* (1 Cor. 2:12, 13, 14)

From this it appeared that her mistress did not understand the things which were of God, although she was a professor of religion; for she was continually attempting to persuade her, to turn to the ways of the world, and said that so much religion was not required. By these persuasions, my wife began to listen to the advice of her mistress, and to the temptations of the Devil's cunning arts, and began neither to fear God, nor regard man; and wanted me to turn to the beggarly elements of the world; but I told her I was determined by the grace of God, to live and die for God, so that whether I lived or died I should be the Lord's; begging and beseeching her to turn unto God, with full purpose of heart, that he might have mercy on her poor heart; informing her, that "Thus saith the Lord, turn ye even to me with all your heart, and with fasting, and with weeping, and with mourning; And rend your heart, and not your garments, and turn unto the Lord your God: for he is gracious and merciful, slow to anger, and of great kindness, and repenteth him of the evil. Who knoweth if he will return and repent, and leave a blessing behind him; even a meat offering and a drink offering unto the Lord your God?" (Joel 2:12, 13, 14) But she would not hearken unto me, for she was led away by the advice of her mistress, and temptations of Satan. She now used her poor little innocent and harmless infant very cruel, in order to prevent me from going to the house of God: during my absence from home, she used to try every method in her power to make the poor little babe suffer; her mother always took the child's part, and endeavored as much as possible to hinder her from using it ill, and when I returned home she would acquaint me of my wife's transactions. On account of this she beat her mother in such a manner, that it caused her death, being pregnant at the time, so that she was not able to resist her wicked undertakings. Thus if she had been dealt with according to the law of God, she would have been put to death, for the Scriptures saith, "He that smiteth his father or mother, shall be surely put to death." (Exod. 21:15)

Thus, my wife treated her mother, that she died by her cruel usage. Her mistress on this took her to task, and beat her very much, for using her mother in such a manner, particularly in her situation; and told her that she was become a hardened sinner, desiring her to turn unto the Lord, that he might have mercy upon her, or else she would certainly perish; but she was so hardened in her heart, that she could not bear to hear the name of the Lord mentioned; for she would curse and swear, and break and destroy everything she could get at. It now seemed as if the Devil had taken full possession of her heart, and now her master and mistress persuaded me to intreat her to go to the house of God, but she would not, the more I entreated her, the worse she was, and abused and ill-used me as she did the poor infant.

One day when I was gone to my mother's house, which was about nine miles from home, she was so overpowered by the temptation of the Devil, that she *murdered the poor little infant!* by squeezing it between her hands. When I returned home, I was greatly surprised to see a number of people assembled together at the door of my house; and on inquiring what was the matter, they told me that my wife had killed the child. I said unto her, "What hast thou been doing?" She replied, "I have killed the child, and I mean to kill you, if I possibly can." I then said to her, "My dear wife, what is the reason of your doing this horrid deed? what do you think will become of your never-dying soul?" She said, that she expected to go to eternal misery; and therefore she was determined to do all the mischief she could.

She was taken before the judge, and found guilty of the crime laid to her charge, that murdering of her infant. She acknowledged that she had committed the horrid deed; and therefore suffered according to the law. Before her punishment took place, I frequently visited her, to endeavor to convince her of the state of her soul, and begged her to pray unto God to have mercy upon her soul, and to strengthen her in her dying moments; but her heart was so hardened by sin, that it was all in vain.

This, my dear reader, you must think, was a fiery trial for me to endure; it almost cast me down to the ground, and to make shipwreck of faith and a good conscience: indeed, my state of mind was such, that it caused me to go to a river, several times, in order to make away with myself; thus the old lion would have devoured me; but, thanks be to God, he gave me grace to withstand the temptations of the Devil at last; and enabled me to say, "Blessed be the God and Father of our Lord Jesus Christ, which according to his abundant mercy hath begotten us again unto a lively hope by the resurrection of Jesus Christ from the dead. To an inheritance incorruptible, and undefiled, and that fadeth not away, reserved in heaven for you, Who are kept by the power of God through faith unto salvation ready to be revealed in the last time. Wherein ye greatly rejoice, through now, for a season, if need be, ye are in heaviness through manifold temptations: That the trial of your faith, being much more precious [than] that of gold that perisheth, though it be tried with *fiery trials,* might be found unto praise and honor and glory at the appearing of Jesus Christ." (1 Pet. 1:3–7) Thus the Lord gave me encouragement by his blessed Spirit, saying "Think it not strange concerning the fiery trial which is to try you, as though some strange thing happened unto you: But rejoice, inasmuch as ye are partakers of Christ's sufferings; that, when his glory shall be revealed, ye may be glad also with exceeding joy. If ye be reproached for the name of Christ, happy are ye; for the spirit of glory and of God resteth on you; on their part he is evil spoken of, but on your part he is glorified. But let none of you suffer as a murderer, or as a thief, or as an evildoer, or as a busybody in other men's matters. Yet if any man suffer as a Christian, let him not be ashamed: but let him glorify God on this behalf." (1 Pet. 4:12–16)

The cause of my wife's destroying her child was attributed, by many, to my being so religious, and through religion; but they had forgotten the language of the Scripture which saith, "Can a woman forget her sucking child, that she should not have compassion on the son of her womb? yea, they may forget, yet will I not forget thee." (Isa. 49:15) Thus was this passage exemplified, in my wife forgetting the child of her own womb, but blessed be God, he delivered *me* out of all my distress, and endued me with a double portion of his divine grace, and lifted me up upon my feet again, to travel on to Zion; and gave me strength

> *To bear my cross from day to day,*
> *And learn to watch as well as pray,*
> *And gave me his blessed Union.*

I continued two years after this in New York, preaching the ever-lasting gospel, both to saints and sinners, and the Lord was pleased to bless my weak efforts. After this the love of God constrained me to travel into other parts to preach the gospel, when I again visited Boston, in North America, where I tarried about twelve months, and the Lord blessed my ministry, and owned by labors, to the conversion of many.

From thence I traveled to a place called Salisbury, about forty miles from Boston, where I met with great success; for God, by his Spirit, was pleased to convince and convert *five or six souls of a night!* I tarried at this place between nine and ten months.

After that time, it pleased God to put it into my mind to cross the Atlantic main; and I embarked on board of a ship for that purpose. The name of the ship was the *Superb of Boston,* and the captain's name was Able Stovey, with whom I agreed to sail with for seventeen dollars per month. I was quite unacquainted with the sea, and was very much pleased in going on board the vessel; but the case was soon altered, for the first day I went on board to work, and the captain and the men asked me if I came on board to work. I told them yes. They asked me where my clothes were. I said I had them on my back. They asked me if that was all I had. I told them I thought I had sufficient, for I was not certain of staying longer than one day; for if I did not like it I would not stay out the month; for I thought that a person going to sea, could go one day, and return the next.

After they had told me what to do, which was to clean the coppers, I went and looked all about the ship, but could not find them, not knowing what they were; at last I asked one of the sailors where the coppers were, for the captain had ordered me to clean them, so he showed me where they were. Those which they called coppers, were a couple of black iron things; and they told me I must make them very clean, and that I was to cook the victuals, being cook of the ship. The coppers were very large, for the ship was about four hundred tons burden. I then began to rub the coppers as I was ordered, and the more I rubbed them, the more the rust came off, and the blacker they looked. After two hours after I began cleaning them, the captain asked me if I had cleaned the coppers; I told him I could not get them clean; but he told me I must be sure to clean them well.

During this time the vessel had got under weigh, and was sailing through the river, which was very pleasant, until we got outside of the lighthouse, when the ship began to roll about very much, which greatly terrified me. The captain coming to me, said, "How do you come on?"

I told him that I was tired, and that I wanted to get home. He told me that I should soon get home; and asked me how the sailors' suppers got on. I said, "I cannot get these black things clean; they are certainly not copper." The captain said, "Never mind, let them alone, and have another trial tomorrow." But I said within myself, "You shall not catch me here tomorrow, if I can get on shore." The captain seeing how I was, bade me go below, for the men had some cold beef for supper, and that I should rest myself. When I was going below, I looked at the man at the helm with an evil eye, thinking he made the ship to go on one side on purpose to frighten me the more; but before I got down to the hold I fell down, by the vessel rolling, and all the men sung out, "Hollo, there is a horse down": and they laughing at me so, made me the more afraid and terrified, and after I had got down into the hold, I was afraid the ship would fall, and I strove to keep her up by pushing, and holding fast by different parts of the ship, and when the waves came dashing against the sides of the ship, I thought they were sea lions, and was afraid they would beat a hole through the ship's side, and would come in and devour me; when daylight appeared, I was very much tired and fatigued, for I had been holding and trying to keep the ship upright all the night; in the morning I asked the sailors why they did not keep the ship upright, and one of the men said, pointing to another, "That is the man that makes the ship go on one side." This they said in their scoffing way, to deride me. Having been about eight or ten days at sea, I found out what it was, in some measure. The weather was very boisterous, the sea running very high, and thundering and lightning very much; the reason of which was, I believe, because they so ill-used and abused me, and swore they would throw me overboard, or beat me so that I should jump overboard. When they saw me praying to God, they called me by way of derision, a Jonah, because I prayed to God to calm the tempestuous weather. On the contrary, they were making game of the works of the Lord, and said that the old man had fine fireworks, for it gave them light to go up on the yards to furl the sails; but to their great terror, after they had furled the sails, it pleased the Lord to send his lightning and thunder directly, which killed two men on the spot. One of them was burnt like a cinder, his clothes were totally consumed, not so much as a bit of a handkerchief nor anything else being left. His name was George Begann, about thirty-six years of age. The other's name was James Cash, about twenty-five years of age: his body was entirely burnt up, not a single bit of it was to be seen, nothing but the cinders of his clothes, one of his shoes, his knife, his gold ring, and his key.

Seven more were wounded, some in their backs, and others in

different parts of their bodies: and appeared to be dead for about ten or fifteen minutes.

At the time this dreadful carnage happened, I was standing about seven or eight feet from them; my eyesight was taken from me for four or five minutes, but my soul gave glory to God for what was done. When I recovered my sight I saw the captain standing in the cabin gangway, and the cabin boy and three passengers behind them, lamenting greatly, ringing their hands, and plucking their hair; the captain crying out—"O! my men, we are all lost!" I then took the boldness to speak unto him, and said, "Why do you cry and lament? You see that your ship is not hurt, and that the Lord has been pleased to spare your life; and what the Lord has done is right."

A short time after we had survived this awful scene, the captain exclaimed, "O! my men, my men, the ship is on fire!" On hearing this, the men that were able to move, were roused to take off the hatches, to see where the fire was. But, blessed be God, the ship was not on fire, for it was part of the men's clothes who were consumed, which had got down into the hold, and was burning, which caused a very great smoke; for the sailors stood round the mainmast (excepting four who were at the helm) which was the most materially injured; that part of the cargo which was near the mainmast, consisting of tobacco and staves for casks, was nearly all consumed, but the ship sustained no damage whatever.

The captain and ship's crew were very much terrified when they saw the power of God in killing and wounding the men, and destroying the cargo; which judgements were sent on them, *"Because they rebelled against the words of God, and contemned the counsel of the Most High: Therefore he brought down their heart with labor; they fell down, and there was none to help. Then they cried unto the Lord in their trouble, and he saved them out of their distresses. He brought them out of darkness and the shadow of death, and brake their hands in sunder. Oh that men would praise the Lord for his goodness, and for his wonderful works to the children of men!"* (Ps. 107:11–15)

Should the reader of this be like those, against whom the judgements of God were so remarkably displayed, for their sins and rebellion against him, particularly in making sport with his awful warnings, let me intreat of him to consider the cases above recorded; and let him ask himself, "Am I able to stand before the power of that God who *'Is greatly to be feared'*; whose arm is mighty, and whose hand is strong; and who is called *'The God of the Whole Earth'*?"

We had not been more than a fortnight at sea, after the first deliverance from the thunder and lightning, when we were visited by most dreadful whirlwinds and hurricanes, which dismasted the ship, and made her almost a wreck. We were forty-two days in the Gulf of Mexico, without receiving any assistance whatever; during three weeks of which we had not any dry clothes to put on, not one of us, and we were obliged to eat our victuals raw, for the weather was so very boisterous, that we could not light a fire; we were also put on short allowance, both of victuals and water, for we did not know how long it would be before we should meet with any deliverance. The quantity of provisions and water we were allowed was—half a pound of raw beef or pork, a biscuit and a half, and half a pint of water, for four and twenty hours. During this dreadful tempest, the snow and rain descended rapidly, which we caught, and put into casks, and of this we were only allowed the same quantity as of the good water.

My dear reader, consider what great distress we must have been in at this time, when the ship was tossed and rolled about in such a dreadful manner, and expecting every moment that the ship would be staved in pieces, by the furiousness of the raging sea. Yea, this also terrified me, as well as the rest of the men, when it first began, and I entreated the Lord God Almighty to have mercy on us, that we might once more, by his grace and by the aid of his Spirit, arrive at our desired port; for our hearts were faint within us, and our spirits within us were famishing, that it caused every man on board to be earnestly inclined to call upon the Lord for deliverance; for they now believed that the Lord had sent this distress upon them, that they might earnestly desire the word of God, for the Scriptures saith, *"Behold, the days come, saith the Lord God, that I will send a famine in the land, not a famine of bread, nor a thirst for water, but of hearing the words of the Lord: And they shall wander from sea to sea, and from the north even to the east, they shall run to and fro to seek the word of the Lord, and shall not find it. In that day shall the fair virgins and young men faint for thirst."* (Amos 8:11–13) Thus [were] our hearts faint within us, and we sought for the words of God's promise, unto us wretched miserable sinners, that *"In the time of trouble he would deliver us"*; and I have every reason to believe that the Lord did hear our feeble breathings, for we perished not, but at the end of forty-two days, we saw a sail making towards us, and afterwards another, which both came to our assistance.

Thus, blessed be God, our feeble breathings were heard, when we cried unto God with a sincere heart, he delivered us out of this distress, for these two vessels supplied us with provisions and water, and spars, whereby we were able to make jury-masts, so that we were enabled to gain the state of Merelian [Maryland], in Virginia, which is not far from Baltimore, there we remained until our ship was repaired, and after that, we set sail for England, our destined port being London. When we arrived at the Downs, we were commanded to go to Amsterdam, in Holland; we tarried there about three weeks for further orders, and then we were ordered to go to Liverpool, in England.

When we arrived at Liverpool, I inquired for the people that were followers of the Lord Jesus Christ, seeing that the place was large and populous, I believed in my heart, that God had a people there, and I began to tell the people there of the goodness of God towards me on the sea, and to the ship's company; declaring of his wonderful works on the sea, and rendering God humble and hearty thanks for our safe arrival in port. The love of God constrained me to preach to the people at Liverpool, as I had done to those in North America.

Thus, dear reader, I have informed you, how God had brought me safe into Liverpool, and did not destroy me when I was on the sea, but brought me safe into Liverpool, to preach the everlasting gospel; although I was very ill of a pleurisy, which was occasioned by the ill-treatment I had received on board of ship, for they used to flog, beat, and kick me about, the same as if I had been a dog; they also rubbed grease and dirt over my face and eyes; oftentimes they swore they would beat me till they made me jump overboard, but I never did; and sometimes they would call me a Jonah. This was the treatment I experienced from the officers and men of the ship, until it pleased the Lord to send the thunder and lightning, and the whirlwinds and hurricanes, which was the cause of softening their hearts a little, seeing the Lord pouring down his anger, and destroying some of the men by which they began to be terrified and alarmed, and I had peace even until I came to Liverpool.

While I was at Liverpool I told the people what the Lord had done for me on the seas, and how he had delivered me from the hands of my enemies, and by the grace of God I gave them to understand, that these officers and men were not sinners above all the people in the world; but, unless *they* repented, that they should all likewise perish; as the Scripture saith: *"And Jesus answering said unto them, Suppose ye that these Galileans were sinners above all the Galileans, because they suffered such things? I tell you, nay: but except ye repent, ye shall all likewise perish. Or those eighteen, upon whom the tower in Siloam fell, and slew them, think ye that they were sinners above all men that dwelt in Jerusalem? I tell you, nay: but except ye repent, ye shall all likewise perish."* (Luke 13:2–5)

Thus I preached unto the people in Liverpool, faith, repentance, and remission of sin by Jesus Christ, and the glad tidings of salvation. By these means the people inclined their ears, and believed the report which I gave concerning the Lord Jesus Christ, our blessed Savior, for many were alarmed by the Spirit of God, turned from the evil of their ways, repented, and were converted to God; *"For as much as I saw that my labor was not in vain in the Lord"*; for the Almighty blessed and owned my feeble endeavors; although I was very ill and desired to go to the Infirmary, but the good friends that God had raised up unto me, Christian brethren and sisters, would not suffer me to go, but kept me still with them, in order that I should recover my health.

During the time I stayed with them, I still continued preaching and exhorting them in the name of Jesus; so that the report of my preaching and exhorting spread all through Liverpool, and in the country. I had not preached more than a month at Liverpool, before they sent for me into the country, then

> *The love of God did me constrain,*
> *To seek the wandering souls of men;*
> *With cries, intreaties, tears, to save,*
> *To snatch them from the burning blaze.*
>
> *For this let man revile my name*
> *No cross I shun, I fear no shame;*
> *All hail reproach and welcome shame*
> *Only thy terrors Lord restrain.*
>
> *My life, my blood, I here present*
> *If for the truth they may be spent*
> *Fulfil thy sovereign counsel Lord,*
> *Thy will be done, thy name ador'd.*
>
> *Welcome thy strength, I God of Pow'r*
> *Then let winds blow or thunders roar*
> *Thy faithful witness will I be*
> *They're fixed, I can do all through thee.*

This was the language of my heart, while I paused upon the words which the people had spoken unto me, about my going into the country; for I was not rightly settled in my mind, whether I should stay in Liverpool, go to America, or go into the country; but I saw that the Lord had hitherto blessed and owned my feeble endeavors, and the love of Christ constraining me, I determined to go into the country.

The first place I arrived at was Baudley Mores, about fourteen miles from Liverpool, where I met with Mr. Christopher Hooper, who had traveled in the time of Mr. Wesley. I also met with Mr. Cooper, a Methodist preacher. These were the first brothers in Christ that gave me liberty to preach in the country. Here much good was done in the name of the holy child Jesus, for many were convinced and converted to God, whenever there was preaching.

At Baudley Mores, I was sent for to go to Manchester, and great success attended my preaching there. While at Manchester, I was sent for from Lancashire to preach, and there the Lord gave me many seals to my ministry, and souls for my hire. In this place I was blessed by the Spirit of God, to preach in every chapel and preaching house that was in the place, except it was the Church of England, and there was no place that was sufficient to hold the congregation.

During my stay at Lancashire, I was sent for to go into Yorkshire, and when I arrived there, I preached there also, and had greater success than at any place I ever had preached in before; for I was permitted to preach in every place of worship, in the Methodist, Baptist, Calvinist, Presbyterian, and every other place, excepting the Church of England; and the Spirit of the Lord filled my heart, and the glory of God filled my soul, and the Lord was pleased to send his blessed Spirit with his word, to convince and convert the people, for sinners were convinced and converted to God, transgressors were taught the way of the Lord, believing children of God were edified, and God was glorified. Some nights I think there were *fourteen* or *fifteen souls converted!* sometimes more and sometimes less. Thus the Lord blessed and prospered my ways, even until I got to Sunderland, and there I preached, and had great success. The Lord owning and blessing my ministry in this manner, caused great hatred to spring up among the brethren, so that they desired the people not to follow me, for they said that they could not get a congregation to preach unto, worth speaking of. This was the case with one of the preachers with whom I traveled; while the other was my friend, and desired me to continue preaching in the name of the Lord. His name was Mr. John Booth, about forty years of age. The other's name, who was my enemy, was Mr. Chittle; he was of rich parents, and for the sake of his father he was offended with me: for I and his father preached together in one meetinghouse, his father first, and I afterwards. His father being an old man he did not preach very often, only on particular occasions; for this reason he was to preach the same evening as I did, for he wished to convince the people that they should not follow after a man, but after Christ. He compared me to poor Lazarus; because wherever I went to preach the meetinghouses could not hold the people, but wherever the other preachers went to preach, they had plenty of room, having scarcely any congregation; which caused him to preach on this part of the gospel: *"Now a certain man was sick, named Lazarus, of Bethany, the town of Mary and her sister Martha. (It was that Mary which appointed the Lord with ointment, and wiped his feet with her hair, whose brother Lazarus was sick.) Therefore his sisters sent unto him, saying, Lord, behold, he whom thou lovest is sick. When Jesus heard that, he said, This sickness is not unto death, but for the glory of God, that the Son of God might be glorified thereby. Now Jesus loved Martha, and her sister, and Lazarus. When he had heard therefore that he was sick, he abode two days still in the same place where he was. Then after that saith he to his disciples, Let us go into Judea again. His disciples said unto him, Master, the Jews of late sought to stone thee; and goest thou thither again? Jesus answered, Are there not twelve hours in the day? If any man walk in the day he stumbleth not, because he seeth the light of this world. But if a man walk in the night, he stumbleth, because there is no light in him. These things said he: and after that he saith unto them, Our friend Lazarus sleepeth; but I go that I may awake him out of sleep;* that is to say, that he would raise him from the dead." (John 11:1–11) *"Then when Jesus came, he found that he had lain in the grave four days already. Now Bethany was nigh unto Jerusalem, about fifteen furlongs off: And many of the Jews came to Martha and Mary, to comfort them concerning their brother. Then Martha, as soon as she heard that Jesus was coming, went and met him: but Mary sat still in the house. Then said Martha unto Jesus, Lord, if thou hadst been here, my brother had not died. But I know, that even now, whatsoever thou wilt ask of God, God will give it thee. Jesus saith unto her, Thy brother shall rise again. Martha saith unto him, I know that he shall rise again in the resurrection at the last day. Jesus said unto her, I am the resurrection, and the life: he that believeth in me, though he were dead, yet shall he live."* (17–25) Now Jesus would convince them, that whosoever believeth in him should never die, for they seemed to be doubtful of his words, although he had said unto them that he was the resurrection and the life, yet it seemed to be a doubtful matter for them to believe, for *"When Mary was come where Jesus was, and saw him, she fell down at his feet, saying unto him, Lord, if thou hadst been here, my brother had not died."* (32) Which showed that they believed Jesus was able to keep him alive while living, but not to raise him when stinking in the grave; for they said unto him, *by this time he stinketh.*

"*When Jesus therefore saw her weeping, and the Jews also weeping which came with her, he groaned in the spirit, and was troubled.*" (33) Now we have reason to believe that Jesus was concerned because of their unbelief which caused him to groan in the spirit, and be troubled. "*And said, Where have ye laid him? They said unto him, Lord, come and see. Jesus wept.*" (34, 35) It is evident that he wept because they could not yet believe; as he wept over Jerusalem for their sin and unbelief, and had told them he would save them, but they would not be saved. This showed that he loved them, as he did Lazarus, and all other sinners; and as he raised Lazarus from the grave, so he would raise every sinner from the grave of sin and wickedness, if they would but hearken and listen to the calls, invitations, and preaching of the everlasting gospel, and by his blessed Spirit convince and convert them to God. For "*God is love.*" This the Jews acknowledged, and said, "*Behold how he loved him! And some of them said, Could not this man, which opened the eyes of the blind, have caused that even this man should not have died? Jesus therefore again groaning in himself cometh to the grave. It was a cave, and a stone lay upon it. Jesus said, Take ye away the stone. Martha, the sister of him that was dead, saith unto him, Lord, by this time he stinketh: for he hath been dead four days. Jesus saith unto her, Said I not unto thee, that if thou wouldest believe, thou shouldest see the glory of God? Then they took away the stone from the place where the dead was laid. And Jesus lifted up his eyes, and said, Father, I thank thee that thou hast heard me. And I knew that thou hearest me always: but because of the people which stand by I said it, that they may believe that thou hast sent me. And when he thus had spoken, he cried with a loud voice, Lazarus, come forth. And he that was dead came forth, bound hand and foot with grave clothes: and his face was bound about with a napkin. Jesus saith unto them, Loose him, and let him go. Then many of the Jews which came to Mary, and had seen the things which Jesus did, believed on him. But some of them went their ways to the Pharisees, and told them what things Jesus had done.*" (36–46) Now at this time the Jews' passover was near at hand, so that they were in full expectation that Jesus would come to the feast, they might have an opportunity of laying hands upon him, to destroy him. "Much people of the Jews therefore knew that he was there: and they came not for Jesus' sake only, but that they might see Lazarus also, whom he had raised from the dead. But the chief priests consulted that they might put Lazarus also to death; Because that by reason of him many of the Jews went away, and believed on Jesus." (Luke 12:9, 10, 11)

Thus did this preacher, who I took to be my friend, but was my enemy, for he strove to kill me, as the Scripture saith, "He that hateth his brother without a cause is a murderer." (1 John 3:15) And whosoever hateth his brother whom he seeth daily, how can he say that he loves God. "We love him because he first loved us. If a man say, I love God, and hateth his brother, he is a liar: for he that loveth not his brother whom he hath seen, how can he love God whom he hath not seen? And this commandment have we from him, That he who loveth God love his brother also." (1 John 4:19, 20, 21) It was evident that he hated me without a cause, therefore as the Scriptures inform us, he was a murderer, "And ye know that no murderer hath eternal life abiding in him."

Had he been led by the Spirit of God he would not have hated me. "Now the works of the flesh are manifest, which are these; adultery, fornication, uncleanness, lasciviousness, idolatry, witchcraft, hatred, variance, emulations, wrath, strife, seditions, envyings, murders, drunkenness, revellings, and suchlike: of the which I tell you before, as I have also told you in time past, that they which do such things shall not inherit the kingdom of God. But the fruit of the Spirit is love, joy, peace, long-suffering, gentleness, goodness, faith, meekness, temperance: against such there is no law." (Gal. 4:18–24) Now it is evident, that if he had walked in the Spirit, and lived in the Spirit, he would not have desired vain glory, or envied others: for he and his father strove to the uttermost to prevent my usefulness, and hinder me from spreading the gospel of Jesus Christ; for his father was to preach against me, as has been before mentioned, in order that the people should not go to hear me preach. During which time I was sitting in the pulpit behind him, for I was to preach after him. He then began to explain who Lazarus was, and said that he was a poor man, a porter, of no reputation, and making out that scarcely any notice was taken of him, because he was a poor stinking man. He then exclaimed to the people, that they were all running after a poor dead Lazarus, and that they did not come to see Jesus; and told the people that they might as well throw their bibles and books away, as to be always running after a poor dead man, nothing but a poor wounded Lazarus.

Thus he preached to the people, and told them he was sorry to say, that they had been running to see and hear a poor dead Lazarus, that was risen from the dead, and that they were not then come to see Jesus, but Lazarus. This was his discourse to the congregation, and then he closed the subject; and said, "Our friend, our black brother, will speak a few words unto you."

I then stood up and addressed the congregation, saying, "Men and brethren, I shall not take a text, but only make a few remarks, by God's assistance, on what our brother has spoken unto you concerning poor Lazarus." I then stated unto them the particulars of that transaction, which has been noticed. I then said unto the congregation, "Spiritually speaking, who is this Lazarus? Yea," said I, "every sinner is as Lazarus; for we were all born in sin, and brought forth in iniquity, dead in trespasses and sins, laying in the grave of sin and wickedness, and stinking in the nostrils of the Almighty God."

My dear reader, are you laying in the grave of sin and wickedness? For many have been laying in that state ten, twenty, thirty, yea, and some fifty years, stinking in the nostrils of the Almighty God; and indeed, so are all sinners, who sin against God, and disbelieve his blessed word; it therefore becomes you to inquire and examine whether you have been raised from this awful state or not.

The Jews did not only come to see Lazarus, because of the miracle which was wrought by Jesus Christ on him, but that they might be enabled to lay hands upon him, and kill him, even as they wanted to kill Jesus Christ; for, they said, if they let him alone, his life and conduct, wherever he went, would show that he was that dead stinking Lazarus, whom Jesus had raised from the grave. So it is with everyone, whether they be men or women, that confesses Jesus Christ before man on earth, being an evident proof that they are rise[n] from the grave of sin and wickedness by the resurrection of the Lord Jesus Christ from the dead, even as Jesus Christ himself confesseth.

I told them, our brother that had preached against me, had not always been a preacher, but was once like other men, for he was born in sin, and brought forth in iniquity, and going astray from the womb, telling lies, and was laying in the grave of sin and wickedness, and stinking in the nostrils of the Almighty. But God, in his infinite goodness and mercy, was pleased to send his only begotten Son into the world, to save all such as should not perish, who lay in the grave of sin and wickedness: Jesus Christ being troubled in the spirit for poor sinners, wept over him as he did over Jerusalem, and rolled the stone of unbelief from his heart, and cried with a loud voice, and said unto him, "Awake, thou that sleepest, and arise from the dead, and Christ shall give thee light." Thus the grave of sin and wickedness opened, and the dead sinner arose from it, by the Spirit of God, bound with the grave clothes of lust, and his face bound up with a napkin of speechlessness, but God said unto the Spirit, loose him and let him go.

Thus I said God had done to our brother that preached against me, and that he had opened his grave in which he had once lain stinking in the nostrils of God; and that Jesus had risen him from the grave, and had loosened him by his Spirit, to let him go to the gospel feast, to show himself unto all men, that he was the stinking sinner Christ had risen by his Spirit, to preach the gospel to every creature.

On hearing this the congregation clapt their hands and shouted.

These pretended friends, the father and son, were now more inveterated against me than ever, because I followed the commission of our blessed Lord and Savior Jesus Christ. They wrote many letters against me, and sent them abroad in every direction, to prevent my preaching the gospel of Christ: but, blessed be God, they were not able to prevent me, for the Lord prospered me and blessed my undertakings, which caused a great division amongst the people, and some of them wished me to tarry with them, but I thought it best to go away, and not stay to hurt any of their feelings; because God hath commanded us to live in peace one with another, and hath pronounced his blessing upon them, saying, "Blessed are the peacemakers, for they shall be called the children of God." (Matt. 5:9)

I did not tarry at Sunderland above three or four months after this, but took a journey to Liverpool; and from thence I went to New York, where I stayed about nine months, preaching, and visiting my relations, and my brothers and sisters in Christ. During the time I was at New York, I had the happiness to know that my mother and elder brother were converted to God, but they were afraid to apply to the magistrates for their liberty. I daily exhorted them to hold on until the end, and at last they should receive the crown that fadeth not away. While I was with my brethren and sisters in Christ, the Lord blessed and owned my feeble endeavors, and crowned them with the success of his Spirit.

I was now well acquainted with traveling, both by sea and land, so that I knew what it was to suffer and do well: for you must think that I suffered very much by traveling to and fro; but I counted it all joy that I was worthy to suffer for the glory of God; for our trials and tribulations which are but for a moment, are not worthy to be compared with the glory that shall be given us hereafter. For I did not suffer as an evildoer, nor as a busybody in other men's matter[s], nor as a murderer.

After staying at home about nine or ten months, I was constrained to travel abroad again; so I took shipping at New York for Boston. When I arrived there, I began preaching the everlasting gospel, and found the Lord blessed and owned my feeble endeavors. But I was not contented to stay here above three or four months, being still constrained to go farther, to see how the people lived in the other parts of the world, and to preach the gospel unto them. I accordingly embarked at Boston for Amsterdam, in Holland; and there I preached the gospel for one year, which was the whole time I stayed there; and I preached the gospel unto them, in their own language; and the Lord crowned my feeble endeavors, and blessed them by his Spirit.

From Amsterdam I went to Rotterdam, and tarried about two months and a half, preaching the gospel, and I thank God that my labors were not in vain, for I saw some of the fruit of my labor, and the people treated me very kindly.

From thence I took shipping, and went to Helder, about a hundred miles from Hamburg, and stayed there about two months; here I also found prosperity.

At Helder I embarked for Boston, in North America, and arrived there in safety. I continued two years and a half at Boston preaching the word of life, which was crowned with abundant success and prosperity, many of the people there being convinced, and converted to God.

After that I was constrained by the love of God to take another journey abroad, and I went from Boston to New Orleans, and remained there three months, striving by all possible means, with God's assistance, to do good, but all was in vain, for the people were like those of Sodom and Gomorrah, for it appeared that they neither feared God, nor regarded man. Sunday was their greatest holiday; for they were singing, dancing, playing at billiards, cards, and dice, and every evil thing that could be mentioned, was committed on the Sabbath-day. There were very few persons that had any religion whatever, only here and there one that was a little more serious, which grieved me so much, that I could not content myself to stay at New Orleans any longer, because of the unbelief of the people. Jesus himself declares that when he went into a certain place, he did not many mighty works there, because of their unbelief; and he departed and went into another country. He also gave commission to his disciples that whatsoever country or house they went into, they should say, "Peace be unto this house." And the son of peace was in the house, their peace would abide them; but if not, their peace would return to them again. And, whatsoever house would not receive them, they should shake off the dust of their feet, as a testimony against the people. And thus it was with me, for I did not abide at New Orleans; but by the assistance of God, I took a ship, and sailed for Liverpool, and we had a pleasant voyage thither. But, on the passage, one evening, the captain had forgotten to order his officers to take in a single reef in the topsails of the ship, as had been done every night, though the weather was ever so fine; so the captain asked me, as I was going upon deck, to tell the mate to go down into the cabin. I accordingly told the mate, and he went down to the captain, who asked him if he had ordered the sailors to take in a single reef into the topsails, as usual. The mate told him no, for as the weather appeared so fine, he thought it not necessary. But the captain said it did not signify how fine the weather was, he desired it might be done, for he did not know what the weather might be before the morning. This was about the dusk of the evening, when the sailors were in their beds; the mate therefore called them to turn out, to take in a single reef in the topsails; the sailors grumbled very much, and said there was not wind enough to carry the ship two knots an hour, but they were obliged to do it, whether they liked it or not, which made some of them curse and swear bitterly. Particularly one young man, about nineteen or twenty years of age, for he wished that the vessel might sink, that we might all go to hell together. I could not then help speaking unto him, and asked him if he were not ashamed to talk in such a manner, and what he thought would become of himself. He said unto me, "I do not want any of your preaching, for I am willing to go to hell for my part." One of the sailors said unto him in a jesting manner, "Why, then, you do not care if *we* all go to hell." The young man said no, for he was willing to go. He put on his jacket, and went upon deck, in order to go up on the main topsail yardarm, and was the first there; but no sooner had he got on the yardarm, than he was struck with the dart of death, and fell into the water without a groan or a struggle, and sunk as if he had been a stone, not having enough time to say, The Lord have mercy upon me; for we were all eyewitnesses of it, and could not say any otherwise, but that he had his desire fulfilled.

I engaged myself at New Orleans as steward and cook of this ship, in order to get to Liverpool: and I thanked the Lord that we all arrived in safety at Liverpool, except the young man above-mentioned.

When I arrived at Liverpool, I could not forget God's promises to his people if they were obedient, that he would send blessings upon them, that there should not be room enough to receive them; as the Scriptures saith, "Bring ye all the tithes into the storehouse, that there may be meat in mine house, and prove me now herewith, said the Lord of hosts, If I will not open you the windows of heaven, and pour you out a blessing, that there shall not be room enough to receive it. And I will rebuke the devourer for your sakes, and he shall not destroy the fruits of your ground: neither shall your vine cast her fruit before the time in the field, saith the Lord of hosts. And all nations shall call you blessed." (Mal. 3:10, 11, 12)

But, on the contrary, if they were disobedient, God hath said,

But if ye will not hearken unto me, and will not do all these commandments; And if ye shall despise my statutes, or if your soul abhor my judgements, so that ye break my covenant; I also will do this unto you; I will even appoint over you terror, consumption, and the burning ague, that shall consume the eyes, and cause sorrow of heart: and ye shall sow your seed in vain, for your enemies shall eat it. And I will set my face against you, and ye shall be slain before your enemies: they that hate you shall reign over you; and ye shall flee when none persueth you. And if ye will not yet for all this hearken unto me, then I will punish you seven times more for your sins. And I will break the pride of your power; and I will make your heaven as iron, and your earth as brass; And your strength shall be spent in vain: for your land shall not yield her increase, neither shall the trees of the land yield their fruits. And if ye walk contrary unto me, and will not hearken unto me; I will bring seven times more plagues upon you, according to your sins. I will also send wild beasts among you, which shall rob you of your children, and destroy your cattle, and make you few in number; and your highways shall be desolate. And if ye will not be reformed by me by these things, but will walk contrary unto me; Then will I also walk contrary unto you, and will punish you yet seven times for your sins. And I will bring a sword upon you, that shall avenge the quarrel of my covenant: and when ye are gathered together within your cities, I will send the pestilence among you; and ye shall be delivered into the hand of your enemy. And when I have broken the staff of your bread, ten women shall bake your bread in one oven, and they shall deliver you your bread again by weight: and ye shall eat, and not be satisfied. And if ye will not for all this

hearken unto me, but walk contrary unto me; Then I will walk contrary unto you also in fury; and I, even I, will chastise you seven
times for your sins. And ye shall eat the flesh of your sons, and the
flesh of your daughters shall ye eat. And I will destroy your high
places, and cut down your images, and cast your carcasses upon the
carcasses of your idols, and my soul shall abhor you. And I will make
your cities waste, and bring your sanctuaries unto desolation, and I
will not smell the savor of your sweet odors. And I will bring the land
into desolation: and your enemies which dwell therein shall be astonished at it. And I will scatter you among the heathen, and will
draw out a sword after you: and your land shall be desolate, and your
cities waste. Then shall the land enjoy her sabbaths as long as it lieth
desolate, and ye be in your enemies land; even then shall the land
rest, and enjoy her sabbaths. As long as it lieth desolate it shall rest;
because it did not rest in your sabbaths, when ye dwelt upon it. And
upon them that are left alive of you I will send a faintness into their
hearts in the land of their enemies; and the sound of a shaken leaf
shall chase them; and they shall fall when none persueth. And they
shall fall one upon another, as it were before a sword, when none persueth: and ye shall have no power to stand before your enemies. And
ye shall perish among the heathen, and the lands of your enemies
shall eat you up. And they that are left of you shall pine away in their
iniquity in your enemies' lands; and also in the iniquities of their fathers shall they pine away with them. If they shall confess their iniquity, and the iniquity of their fathers, with their trespass which they
trespassed against me, and that also they have walked contrary unto
me; And that I have also walked contrary unto them, and have
brought them into the land of their enemies; if then their uncircumcised hearts be humbled, and they then accept of the punishment of
their iniquity: Then will I remember my covenant with Jacob, and
also my covenant with Isaac, and also my covenant with Abraham
will I remember; and I will remember the land. The land also shall be
left of them, and enjoy her sabbaths, while she lieth desolate without
them: and they shall accept of the punishment of their iniquity: because, even because they despised my judgements, and because
their soul abhorred my statutes. And yet for all that, when they be in
the land of their enemies, I will not cast them away, neither will I abhor them, to destroy them utterly, and to break my covenant with
them: for I am the Lord their God. But I will for their sakes remem-

ber the covenant of their ancestors, whom I brought forth out of the land of Egypt in the sight of the heathen, that I might be their God: I am the Lord. (Lev. 26:14–45)

Dear reader, how well would it be for us, and all mankind, to confess unto God our sins and our wickedness, and return and repent of our iniquities, that God may have mercy upon us, and forgive us our sins, and cleanse us from all unrighteousness; that we might not be cut off from the land of the living; as that young man was on board of the ship in which I went to Liverpool. That was for our example, that we should not follow his wicked ways, either by life or conversation, but that we should repent and believe the gospel, that our souls might be saved through the grace of our Lord Jesus Christ, and by faith in his precious blood; that we might be holy in all conversation, while we are tabernacling in this vale of tears, and that our speech might be seasoned with divine grace.

This is the way I spoke to the people when I arrived at Liverpool, and they gladly received me as a brother in Christ, and believed the exhortation which I gave them.

During my stay at Liverpool, they provided me a place to preach in, which was in Byram Street. I was as plain with them as God was pleased to give me ability, by his blessed Spirit, preaching the everlasting gospel of our Lord and Savior Jesus Christ; for "I would not have them to be ignorant, how that all our fathers were under the cloud, and all passed through the sea; And were all baptized unto Moses in the cloud and in the sea; And did all eat the same spiritual meat; And did all drink the same spiritual drink: for they drank of that spiritual Rock that followed them: and that Rock was Christ. But with many of them God was not well pleased: for they were overthrown in the wilderness. Now these things were our examples, to the intent we should not lust after evil things, as they also lusted. Neither be ye idolaters, as were some of them; as it is written, The people sat down to eat and drink, and rose up to play. Neither let us commit fornication, as some of them committed, and fell in one day three and twenty thousand. Neither let us tempt Christ, as some of them also tempted, and were destroyed of serpents. Neither murmur ye, as some of them also murmured, and were destroyed of the destroyer. Now all these things happened unto them for ensamples: and they are written for our admonition, upon whom the ends of the world are come. Wherefore let him that thinketh he standeth take heed lest he fall. There hath no temptation taken you but such as is common to man: but God is faithful, who will not suffer you to be tempted above that ye are able; but will with the temptation also make a way to escape, that ye may be able to bear it. Wherefore, my dearly beloved, flee from idolatry. I speak as to wise men; judge ye what I say." (1 Cor. 10:1–15)

Thus I endeavored, by the grace of God, to show the people, that most men and women were baptized in different churches and in different manners, under a great cloud of witnesses; and have passed through seas of troubles and difficulties; and did not eat of that spiritual bread of life, which is the word of God; and did all drink of that spiritual drink, the waters which cometh from the throne of God. But with many of *them* God was not well pleased; but overthrew them in this world: for some of them were mockers, scoffers, drunkards, whoremongers, idolaters, swearers, backbiting their neighbors, and some their own brothers and sisters, yea even their fathers and mothers. But to speak plain, and be candid with you, I would ask, if it is not so nowaday, amongst us? You hear the husband abusing his wife for seeming to take a little of this spiritual drink, which is *faith in the blood of our blessed Redeemer.* On the other hand, you will see the woman mocking and scoffing at her husband, if he appears rather inclined to be baptized in the blood of the Savior, to be purged from dead works, and from sin and wickedness.

My dear reader might be one of these characters, but I hope not, for unless you repent and become baptized in Jesus' favor, and be, by him, washed and cleansed from dead works, which is sin and wickedness, before another day appears to your eyes, you might be cut down as cumberers of God's holy ground, and be added unto the number of the three and twenty thousand, who fell in one day for their sins and abominations. But if you should be baptized with the baptism of Christ, by his Spirit resting and abiding in the altar of your heart, it will convince you that no other baptism will avail you anything, but the blood of Jesus Christ, which cleanseth from all sin.

My young friends, I would intreat of you, by the grace of God, to examine yourselves, and search the bottom of your heart, to know if you are one of those rebellious children. Dost thou love thy father and mother? or dost thou curse and hate them? If thou curse and hate them, consider thou art cursing and hating thy maker; for before thou wast made, God made thy parents; and, did he not make thee? Yea, he did, for he is the maker of us all; and there is nothing made, but what was made by the immediate hand of God; and as he is able to make alive, is he not also able to kill? Yea, my dear reader, consider but for a moment, that if the Lord was able to kill three and twenty thousand in one day, he will not be one moment in taking thy life. For, in the twinkling of an eye, the breath which we now breathe, is taken from us; and, if we are not baptized with the Holy Ghost and with fire, we cannot enter the kingdom of God.

Perhaps some of you may be inquiring what you should do; I would answer you in the words of our Savior, where it is said, *"And the people asked him, saying, What shall we do then? He answereth and saith unto them, He that hath two coats, let him impart to him that hath none; and he that hath meat, let him do likewise. Then came also publicans to be baptized, and said unto him, Master, what shall we do? And he said unto them, Exact no more than that which is appointed you. And the soldiers likewise demanded of him, saying, And what shall we do? And he said unto them, Do violence to no man, neither accuse any falsely; and be content with your wages."* (Luke 3:10–14)

It pleased God to sen[d] the Spirit of his Son into my heart, to bear witness with my spirit that I was a child of God, and that he had chosen me out of the world; therefore the world hated me, because I was not of the world; but they who were of God loved me, because that God had loved them first, and had shed abroad in their hearts the love of his Son, that they should love one another, even as God hath given us commandment. Thus did the people of Liverpool, for they showed me great kindness beyond measure, by God's assisting of them by his blessed Spirit: he that had two coats gave me one, and he that had meat did the same; and God crowned my feeble endeavors with great success, and gave me many seals to my ministry, and souls for my hire.

On taking my farewell of the people at Liverpool, after I had been there about five months, preaching the everlasting gospel, and ministering the ordinances of our blessed Lord and Savior, which was the third time I had been to Liverpool, I said unto them, "Now, my dear and beloved friends in Christ, I am about to leave you in body, but I hope not in spirit; for I trust we shall see each other (who are followers of Christ) and that we shall meet in heaven around his throne: where parting shall be no more, where all trials and troubles shall have an end, where sorrow and sighing shall flee away, where the tears shall be forever wiped from our eyes, where our wearied souls shall be at rest, where the wicked shall cease troubling us, and where our souls shall re-joice with joy unspeakable and full of glory, and join with all the host of heaven, in singing the song of Moses and the Lamb, hallelujahs, and praises unto God forever and ever."

I then embarked at Liverpool for Newberry Port, in North Amer-ica, and, thank God, we arrived in safety. I did not tarry at Newberry Port because I had some business to transact at Boston; where I arrived in safety, and settled my affairs, by God's assistance. I also met with many brothers and sisters in Christ, who were glad for my arrival. I stayed at Boston about three months, preaching the gospel of our blessed Jesus, and him crucified; and blessed and praised be God, my labors were not in vain, for many were alarmed and awaked out of their sleep of carnal security, turned from the evil of their ways, and walked in Christ the good old way to eternal joy, many souls were edified, and God glorified.

It appeared that God had greater work for me to do, and to go through many trials and tribulations, for it is through them that we are to enter the kingdom of God. After I had been at Boston three months and a half, I was constrained by the Spirit of God, to take a journey into a foreign country; so I took my leave from the people at Boston, who were sorry to part with me, so we parted with each other in body, but not in mind; and sung the following hymn:

> *We part in body, not in mind;*
>   *Our minds continue one;*
> *And each to each in Jesus join'd,*
>   *We hand in hand go on.*
>
> *Subsists as in us all one soul,*
>   *No power can make us twain;*
> *And mountains rise and oceans roll,*
>   *To sever us in vain.*
>
> *Present we still in spirit are,*
>   *And intimately nigh;*
> *While on the wings of faith and prayer,*
>   *We each to other fly.*
>
> *In Jesus Christ together we*
>   *In heavenly places sit:*
> *Cloth'd with the sun, we smile to see*
>   *The moon beneath our feet.*

Our life is hid with Christ in God:
　　Our life shall soon appear,
And shed his glory all abroad,
　　In all his members here.

The heavenly treasure now we have
　　In a vile house of clay:
But he shall to the utmost save,
　　And keep us to that day.

Our souls are in his mighty hand,
　　And he shall keep them still;
And you and I shall surely stand
　　With him on Sion's hill!

Him eye to eye we there shall see;
　　Our face like his shall shine:
O what a glorious company,
　　When saints and angels join!

O what a joyful meeting there!
　　In robes of white array'd,
Psalms in our hands we all shall bear
　　And crowns upon our head.

Then let us lawfully contend,
　　And fight our passage through;
Bear in our faithful minds the end,
　　And keep the prize in view.

Then let us hasten to the day,
　　When all shall be brought home!
Come, O Redeemer, come away!
　　O Jesus, quickly come!

God of all consolation, take
　　Thy glory of thy grace!
Thy gifts to thee we render back,
　　In ceaseless songs of praise.

Thro' thee we now together came,
　　In singleness of heart;
We met, O Jesus, in thy name,
　　And in thy name we part.

By the assistance of God, I took ship at Boston for Venneliea, in the East Indies; not to please myself, but for the glory of God, and the good of souls; as the Scriptures saith, *"Let no man seek his own, but every man another's wealth. Whatsoever is sold in the shambles, that eat, asking no question for conscience sake: For the earth is the Lord's and the fullness thereof. If any of them that believe not bid you to a feast, and ye be disposed to go; whatsoever is set before you, eat, asking no question for conscience sake. But if any man say unto you, This is offered in sacrifice unto idols, eat not for his sake that showed it, and for conscience sake: for the earth is the Lord's, and the fullness thereof: Conscience, I say, not thine own, but of the other: for why is my liberty judged of another man's conscience? For if I by grace be a partaker, why am I evil spoken of for that which I give thanks? Whether therefore ye eat, or drink, or whatsoever ye do, do all to the glory of God. Give none offense, neither to the Jews, nor to the Gentiles, nor to the church of God: Even as I please all men in all things, not seeking mine own profit, but the profit of many, that they may be saved."* (1 Cor. 10:24, to the end)

This was my motive in going to the East Indies, that whatsoever I did, to do it for the honor and glory of God; not to seek mine own interest, but the interest of my Lord and Master Jesus Christ; not for the honor and riches of this world, but the riches and honors of that which is to come: I say, not for the riches of this world, which fadeth away; neither for the glory of man; not for golden treasure; but my motive and great concern was for the sake of my Lord and Master, who went about doing good, in order to save poor wicked and sinful creatures.

We had a good passage to Venneliea, but were not permitted to land, although the ship remained there a fortnight. We then received orders to sail to Buenos Aires, where we arrived all safe and well, excepting me, for I was ill a fortnight with pains in my legs. We laid at Buenos Aires about eight months, but I had not the pleasure of preaching the gospel there, on account of the war between the Spaniards and the English; it was the period that General Achmet took Montevideo, and General Whitelock came to assist him with his army. So I continued preaching on board of our own ship, by God's assistance.

During the time we laid there, one of the sailors, a young man about eighteen or nineteen years of age, having considerable property on board of the ship, which he wanted to smuggle on shore, (which indeed was the traffic of the whole ship's crew, both officers and men) was boasting of his money, and that he would go on shore, and get intoxicated, and when we got to our destined port, he would visit every place of riot and vice. So I said unto him, "You had better think about a dying hour; for though you are young you must die, and you do not know how soon; for there is nothing more certain than death, and nothing more uncertain than life." But he said, that he did not want any of my preaching, and that he should live till we arrived at our destined port, and enjoy his pleasure; but to his great surprise he never lived to see it, for that same day he went to go on shore, and from our ship he went alongside of another, when he fell out of the boat, and sunk immediately, not having time to say one word; the whole of the ship's company being eyewitnesses of it. That ship's name was the *Arrow of Boston, in North America*; and the ship to which he and I belonged, was the *Prince of Boston, in North America*. We remained at Buenos Aires eight months, and when all the vessels that were there, were ordered to the different ports to which they belonged: we accordingly made for Boston, where we all safely arrived, except the young man who was drowned.

I had engaged myself on board of the above ship, as cook, for seventeen Spanish dollars per month, in order that I should not be burdensome to the church of God; and this was the way I acted whenever I traveled; for, as St. Paul saith, *"I would rather labor with my hands than be burdensome to the church."*

When we arrived at Boston I was involved in trouble by the captain wanting to wrong me out of my wages, for he entered a lawsuit against me in order to cast me into prison; but thank God it was not in his power, for *"There is no condemnation to them which are in Christ Jesus, who walk not after the flesh, but after the Spirit"*; and this the captain found to his sorrow, for God, by his blessed Spirit, delivered me out of his hands and from the power of the law; the captain and mates having to pay all costs and charges of the court, for injuring my character, which amounted to two thousand dollars for the captain; eight hundred for the chief mate; and eight hundred for the second mate. The amount of which, a man, whom I took for my friend, received for me, and went away with, and I never saw him anymore, which distressed me greatly.

The remainder of my troubles and distresses during my stay in the West Indies, in the different islands, and also in the State of Virginia and Baltimore, where I was put in prison, and they strove to make me a slave, (for it was a slave country) were very severe; but God delivered me by his grace, for he has promised to be with us in six troubles, and

in the seventh he will not leave us nor forsake us; and that there shall be
nothing to harm or hurt us, if we are followers of that which is good. By
these promises I was encouraged not to repine at the losses and crosses
I had met with.

I stayed at Boston about four months, and preached the gospel there
with great success, by the aid and assistance of God's Spirit. After that
time I had a desire to go to Ireland to preach the gospel; so I parted with
the dear people at Boston in body, but not in mind, our minds continuing one, for it grieved them a great deal that I would go from them, but I
was constrained by the Spirit of God, although I had not forgotten the
troubles and difficulties that God had brought me through; for I was
ready to join with the poet, and say,

> *Come all ye weary travelers,*
> *   And let us join and sing,*
> *The everlasting praises*
> *   Of Jesus Christ our King;*
> *We've had a tedious journey,*
> *   And tiresome, it is true;*
> *But see how many dangers*
> *   The Lord has brought us through.*
>
> *At first when Jesus found us,*
> *   He call'd us unto him,*
> *And pointed out the dangers*
> *   Of falling into sin;*
> *The world, the flesh, and Satan,*
> *   Will prove to us a snare,*
> *Except we do reject them,*
> *   By faith and humble prayer.*
>
> *But by our disobedience,*
> *   With sorrow we confess,*
> *We long have had to wander*
> *   In a dark wilderness;*
> *Where we might soon have fainted,*
> *   In that enchanted ground*
> *But now and then a cluster*
> *   Of pleasant grapes we found.*
>
> *The pleasant road to Canaan*
> *   Brings life, and joy, and peace,*

Revives our drooping spirits,
    And faith and love increase.
We own our Lord and Master,
    And run at his command,
And hasten on our journey
    Unto the promis'd land.

In faith, in hope, in patience,
    We now are going on,
The pleasant road to Canaan,
    Where Jesus Christ is gone:
In peace and consolation,
    We're going to rejoice,
And Jesus and his people
    Shall ever be our choice.

Sinners! why stand ye idle,
    While we do march along?
Has conscience never told you
    That you are going wrong?
Down the broad road to ruin,
    To hear an endless curse;—
Forsake your ways of sinning,
    And go along with us.

But if you do refuse us,
    We'll bid you now farewell,
We're on the road to Canaan,
    And you the way to hell;
We're sorry thus to leave you,
    And rather you would go;
Come, try a bleeding Savior,
    And feel salvation flow.

Oh! sinners be alarmed,
    To see your dismal state;
Repent and be converted,
    Before it is too late;
Turn to the Lord by praying,
    And daily search his word,
And never rest contented
    Until you find the Lord.

Now to the King immortal
Be everlasting praise,
For in his holy service,
We mean to spend our days;
Till we arrive at Canaan,
That heav'nly world above,
With celestial praises,
Sing his redeeming love.

Farewell to sin and sorrow,
I bid you all adieu;
And you my friends prove faithful,
And on your ways pursue:
And if you meet with troubles,
And trials in your way;
Then cast your care on Jesus,
And do not forget to pray.

He never will upbraid you,
Tho' often you request;
Will give you grace to conquer
And take you home to rest.

I therefore embarked at Boston for Ireland, and arrived safe at Limerick, where the brethren and sisters in Christ gladly received me. The prosperity of the work of the Lord in this place, was a memorial, like unto the day of Pentecost; for God showered down righteousness into the hearts of the people in copious showers, so that many of the people thought that miracles were wrought, by the weak instrumentality of my preaching the everlasting gospel. By this means the fame of my preaching spread through the country, even from Limerick to Cork. I preached in Limerick and in the country villages round, and by the Spirit of God, many people were convinced and converted. I also preached to the regiment, at the request of the commanding officer and the mayor of Limerick. The mayor was so kind as to go with me to protect me from the Romans [Catholics]; for they were very much inveterated against me, and said they would have my life. And when the mayor did not go with me, a guard of soldiers was sent. By the command of the mayor and the commanding officer, five of the Roman priests were brought before them, and ordered to give a reason why they were so malicious against me. They could only say, that I would not believe their doctrine, neither would they believe mine; and one of the head priests said, that I was going to hell. The mayor and commanding officer then said, that they would defy any person in Limerick to dispute my doctrine. Then three of the priests said unto them, "We cannot deny or dispute his doctrine." They then went out full of rage and fury, and determined [to] lay in wait for my life. After this I had greater success than ever, although running greater hazard of losing my life, but I said,

> *I am not ashamed to own my Lord,*
>   *Nor to defend his cause;*
> *Maintain the honor of his word,*
>   *The glory of his cross.*
>
> *Jesus, my God, I know his name,*
>   *His name is all my trust;*
> *Nor will he put my soul to shame,*
>   *Nor let my hope be lost.*
>
> *Firm as his throne his promise stands,*
>   *And he can well secure,*
> *What I have committed to his hands,*
>   *Till the decisive hour.*

Thus I spoke in the name of Jesus. After having preached a month, three Protestant ministers came to visit me, and to discourse on the doctrines of election and reprobation, at the house of Mr. Wawy, not far from the customhouse, in Limerick, where I was staying. They came three days following, with their bibles, and as many as fifteen people with them, to hear them discourse with me on the subject. They asked me what my opinion was of election and reprobation. I told them what my opinion was, that every person might be elected by the grace of God, through the Spirit of the Lord: for *"By grace are ye saved; and that not of yourselves, for it is the gift of God."* And that my opinion of reprobation was, that they who believed not, should be damned; (Mark 16:16) They then said unto me, "Do you not know that God hath a chosen and peculiar people, whom he hath foreknown, elected, and predestinated? and that they are his peculiar people and his royal priesthood?" I answered, "Yes; I have heard and read it." Then said they, "Do not you recollect that God hath made some vessels to honor, and some to dishonor; some to be saved, and some to be damned? and that we were all in the hands of God as clay in the hands of the potter?"

I then said unto them, "I perceive that you are of a cavilling principle, but I will not argue or cavil on the principles of religion; for where argument and strife is there is confusion and every evil work, which is not of God, but the devil; for as the Scriptures saith, *"Who is a wise man, and endued with knowledge? Let him show out of a good conversation, his works with meekness of wisdom. But if ye have bitter envying and strife in your hearts; glory not, and lie not against the truth. This wisdom descendeth not from above, but is earthly, sensual, devilish: for where envying and strife is there is confusion and every evil work. But the wisdom that is from above, is first pure, then peaceable, gentle, and easy to be intreated; full of mercy and good fruits; without partiality and without hypocrisy; and the fruit of righteousness is sown in peace of them that make peace."* Therefore I said unto them "I will not argue with you at all; will you make out God to be the author of sin and wickedness, as you are yourselves? Do you not recollect that God made all things, made them good, and blessed them? and that God made man after his own lovely image and likeness, crowned him with honor and glory, made him but a little lower than the angels, gave him power over the whole creation, and over everything that liveth, creepeth, and groweth on the face of the earth, and the earth and the fullness thereof? And how is it you say, that there is a certain number to be saved, and a certain number to be lost? Are you so ignorant that you do not know your own bibles? to know what God saith in the first chapter of Genesis, from the twenty-sixth verse to the end? *"And God said, Let us make man in our image, after our likeness: and let them have dominion over the fish of the sea, and over the fowl of the air, and over the cattle, and over all the earth, and over every creeping thing that creepeth upon the earth. So God created man in his own image, in the image of God created he him; male and female created he them. And God blessed them, and God said unto them, Be fruitful, and multiply, and replenish the earth, and subdue it: and have dominion over the fish of the sea, and over the fowl of the air, and over every living thing that moveth upon the earth. And God said, Behold, I have given you every herb bearing seed, which is upon the face of all the earth, and every tree, in the which is the fruit of a tree yielding seed; to you it shall be for meat. And to every beast of the earth, and to every fowl of the air, and to everything that creepeth upon the earth, wherein there is life, I have given green herb for meat: and it was so. And God saw everything that he had made, and, behold, it was very good. And the evening and the morning were the sixth day."*

But should any of my readers be ready to say, How then is man deprived of this great happiness? I answer, By believing the Devil rather than God; for which he was driven out of Paradise: For God had given man a strict charge, and made a covenant with him, that if he broke this covenant by eating of the forbidden fruit, he should lose the happiness of his soul. But, *"The serpent said unto the woman, Ye shall not surely die: For God doth know that in the day ye eat thereof, then your eyes shall be opened, and ye shall be as gods, knowing good and evil. And when the woman saw that the tree was good for food, and that it was pleasant to the eyes, and a tree to be desired to make one wise, she took of the fruit thereof, and did eat; and gave also unto her husband with her, and he did eat."* (Gen. 3:4, 5, 6) Hereby they disobeyed God, and lost the happiness of their souls, which was their life: for they had no more union and communication with God, being driven out of paradise.

This was the case with the man of God that disobeyed God by eating and drinking in the place where God had forbidden him.

This was also the case with the Jews, who were the chosen and elect people of God; for he hath declared because of their unbelief, they should not enter into his rest, although it was appointed for them from the foundation of the world; as the Scriptures saith, "Let us therefore fear, lest, a promise being left us of entering into his rest, any of you should seem to come short of it. For unto us was the gospel preached, as well as unto them: but the word preached did not profit them, not being mixed with faith in them that heard it. For we which have believed do enter into rest, as he said, as I have sworn in my wrath, if they shall enter into my rest: although the works were finished from the foundation of the world. For he spake in a certain place of the seventh day on this wise, And God did rest the seventh day from all his works. And in this place again, If they shall enter into my rest. Seeing therefore it remaineth that some must enter therein, and they to whom it was first preached entered not in because of unbelief. Let us labor therefore to enter into that rest, lest any man may fail after the same example of unbelief." (Heb. 4:1–6, 11) By which it is evident, if we believe we shall enter in, and if we believe not we shall not enter into that rest which remaineth for the people of God.

This was likewise the case with the Israelites, whom the Lord saved and brought safe out of the land of Egypt, but afterwards destroyed them that believed not; as the Scriptures saith, "I will therefore put you in remembrance, though ye once knew this, how that the Lord, having saved the people out of the land of Egypt, afterward destroyed them that believed not. And the angels which kept not their first estate, but left their own habitation, he hath reserved in everlasting chains under darkness unto the judgement of the great day. Even as Sodom and Gomorrah, and the cities about them in like manner, giving themselves over to fornication, and going after strange flesh, are set forth for an example, suffering the vengeance of eternal fire. Likewise also these filthy dreamers defile the flesh, despise dominion, and speak evil of dignities. Yet Michael the archangel, when contending with the devil he disputed about the body of Moses, durst [dared] not bring against him a railing accusation, but said, The Lord rebuke thee. But these speak evil of those things which they know not: but what they know naturally, as brute beasts, in those things they corrupt themselves." (Jude 5–10)

Thus I spoke unto the ministers, and said, "May the Lord change your hearts, your minds, and your thoughts; and give you a better understanding of his blessed word." Now they were contending with me three days, at the end of which time they were convinced by the word of God, and his Holy Spirit, that they were wrong and I was right. They then gave me the right-hand of fellowship, we joined in prayer with each other, shook hands, and parted in love and friendship. I remained two years in Ireland, preaching the gospel, until the year 1805; when I was constrained by the love of God to leave these beloved people, who were very sorry to part with me.

Before my departure from Ireland, I took to me a partner in life, who is still alive and with me. Her name is Mary Jea, a native of Ireland. This was my third time of marriage. My second wife died a natural death, while I was at Holland; she was a Malteese woman; and her name was Charity Jea. My first wife's name was Elizabeth Jea, of whom mention has been made before. I have had several children, none of whom are alive, but I hope they are all in heaven, where I expect to see them, by the grace of God, and spend an endless day of praise around his dazzling throne, where parting shall be no more forever.

I and my wife accordingly took ship at the Cove Cork for St. John's in Halifax; but after we were on board, we found we were obliged to come to England, to take convoy from Portsmouth. When we arrived at Portsmouth, my wife was taken ill; and the friends in Christ thought it necessary that she should remain until her health was restored, and then to follow me, or else for me to return for her. But to our sad disappointment we set sail from Portsmouth in the evening with a breeze of wind, which lasted till near the morning, when about eight or nine o'clock we were becalmed; and as we were laying to becalmed off Torbay, about five or six miles from the land of Torbay, and striving to get up with the convoy, we were taken by a French privateer, who carried us into Paimpol in France. Our vessel was the brig *Iscet of Liverpool*, Henry Patterson, Master.

After we landed at Paimpol, we were marched to Cambrai, which was seven hundred miles from Paimpol. After a long march we arrived safe at Cambrai, after many severe troubles and trials. Here I remained five years in the prison at that place; and was constrained by the love of God to preach to the people there, the unsearchable riches of Jesus Christ, and God was pleased to crown my feeble endeavors with great success; and, in eighteen months, the Lord was pleased to add to my number two hundred souls; the number of the people in the prison was about three thousand: and I had liberty from the commissary general of the Depot, to preach to all of them.

After I had been there eighteen months, orders came from the minister of Paris, that all who were called Americans, were to go away; we were accordingly marched away to Brest, seven hundred miles from Cambrai; and all the dear prisoners in the depot were very sorry to part with me, the same as if I had been their own father; but I was forced to go. This was the Lord's doings and it was marvellous in our eyes. I told them that God had promised me in his word that he would deliver me from all my enemies, both temporal and spiritual, by his blessed Spirit; but they would not believe me, until they saw me going away; they then were exceedingly sorrowful, and made a subscription for me, which amounted to about nine crowns. On the morning before I went away, I preached my farewell sermon, which was from the 2 Corinthians 13:11. "Finally, brethren, farewell. Be perfect, be of good comfort, be of one mind, live in peace, and the God of love and peace shall be with you." We arrived safe at Brest, thanks be to God, but we had great trials and difficulties on our march thither, being obliged to walk without shoes, and having no more provisions than what we could buy by our scanty allowance, which was a half-penny per mile; and when our feet were so sore that we could not march, we were not allowed anything. Some of us had no clothes to cover our nakedness; and our lodgings at nights were in barns and cow-houses, and we were obliged to lay down the same as beasts, and indeed not so comfortable, for we were not allowed straw nor anything else to lay on.

As soon as we arrived at Brest we were sent on board of a French corvette, under American colors, to go and fight against the English, but twenty, out of two hundred that were sent on board, would not enlist under the banner of the tyrants of this world; for far be it from *me* ever to fight against Old England, unless it be with the sword of the gospel, under the captain of our salvation, Jesus Christ. Those of us who would not fight against the English, were sent on board of a French man-of-war, that they should punish us, but they would not, but sent us to Morlaix, about thirty miles from Brest, where they put us in prison, and kept us upon bread and water for a fortnight, then all the rest consented to go back on board of the corvette, rather than to be sent again to the depot, for we were to be sent back loaded with chains, and under joint arms. I was the only one that stood out; and I told them I was determined not to fight against anyone and that I would rather suffer anything than do it. They said they would send me back to Cambrai, and they would keep me upon bread and water, until the wars were over. I said I was willing to suffer anything, rather than fight. They then took me before the council and the head minister of the Americans, to examine me. They asked me which I liked to do, to go back to the ship, or to be marched to Cambrai. I told them they might send me on board of the vessel, if they liked; but if they did I was determined not to do any work, for I would rather suffer anything than fight or kill anyone. They then consulted together what they should do with me; and made up their minds to turn me out of the prison. The head minister then asked me what I was at, that I would not fight for my country. I told him that I was not an American, but that I was a poor black African, *a preacher of the gospel.* He said, "Cannot you go on board, and preach the gospel there?"—"No, Sir," said I, "it is a floating hell, and therefore I cannot preach there." Then said the council, "We will cool your negro temper, and will not suffer any of your insolence in our office." So they turned me out of their office; and said that I had liberty to go anywhere in the town, but not out of the town; that they would not give me any work, provisions, or lodgings, but that I should provide it myself. Thus was I left upon the mercy of God, but was enabled to cast my care and dependance on the Lord Jesus; for he has promised to deliver those who call upon him in the time of trouble; and I did call upon him in the time of my trouble and distress, and he delivered me.

I was two days without food, walking about without any home, and I went into the hospitals, gaols, and open streets, preaching the gospel unto every creature, as Christ hath commanded us.

Thus I went about preaching the gospel of our Lord and Savior Jesus Christ. Often, at the conclusion of my sermons, many of the nobility and gentry came to me, and said, "We are much edified by your preaching; when do you preach again?" I told them, in the mornings at nine o'clock, and in the afternoons at three, by God's assistance. Thus I did both Sundays and other days, when the weather would permit, during the time I was at Morlaix.

It pleased God to raise up a friend unto me on the second day of my distress, after I was turned out of Morlaix prison into the streets, by order of the American counselor Mr. Dyeott, and Mr. Veal the American minister of France. The French commissary-general gave me liberty to preach everywhere God would permit me; so I went on in the name of the Lord, preaching and exhorting the people to put their trust in the Lord, and serve him truly with fear, reverence, and godly sincerity. This dear friend, whom God was pleased to raise up unto me, was so alarmed by my preaching, that he was constrained by the love of God to come and speak unto me, and asked me where I lived. I told him nowhere. He asked me if I had any place to stay at. I told him no; for I had been turned out of prison two days, and was not suffered to work, and was not allowed to go farther than the bounds of the town; that I might humble myself to the order of the American counselor, to go on board of the corvette, to fight against the English. Thus they strove to punish me; but it was utterly in vain, for this friend took me to his house and family; his family consisted of a wife and four children; who received me into their house as an angel of God, and gave me food, raiment, and lodging, for fourteen months, and charged me nothing for it, but said, that the Lord would repay them sevenfold for what they had done. Thus they gladly received me into their house, as Lot did the angels. (Gen. 19)

But Mr. Dyeott, the American counselor, told the people that received me into their house, that they should turn me out of doors, in order that I should go on board of the corvette, to fight against England; and if they would not order me out of their house, they should not have any satisfaction for what they were doing for me; for they were preventing me from going on board the corvette. Thus he endeavored to lay every obstacle in my way, by trying to prevent those people from doing for me; but the dear man and woman said, that if no person satisfied them for their doings, God would, and as for me I should not perish, for as long as they had a mouthful of victuals, I should have part of it, and such as they had I should be welcome to, the same as their own children. Some said that I was imposing on these people, for Mr. Tangey had only one shilling and three pence per day, which he earned by hard labor, and said it would be far better for me to go on board of the corvette, for thereby I should be enabled to obtain a great sum of prize money. But I told them, as I had Mr. Dyeott, that I would not go on board if they would give me a guinea for every breath I drew, and that I would sooner starve and die first, than I would go on board; and that if they carried me on board in irons I would lay there and die before I would do the least work. I had been on board four weeks before, laying upon the bare deck, without bed or blankets; and I counted it a floating hell, for the evil language of the officers and sailors, continually cursing and swearing; and my humble supplications and petitions were unto God that he would deliver me from this vessel; and God did deliver me.

Some persons said unto those of the house where I was staying, that they were wrong in keeping me, but they would not hearken unto them, and kept me, until peace was proclaimed between France and Great Britain, and all the soldiers were out of France. I then made application to Mr. Dyeott for a passport to England, but he denied me, and said that he would keep me in France until he could send me to America, for he said that I was an American, that I lied in saying I was married in England, and that I was no African. I told him with a broken heart, and crying, that I was an African, and that I was married in England. But he contradicted me three times. When I told the people where I lived, they said that he was rich, and that it was impossible for me to get clear, and asked me if I thought I should. I told them yes, for all things were possible with God, and to him that believed all things were possible, and according to our faith it should be unto us; and my faith was such, that I believed God would deliver me.

A captain of an English ship-of-war, laying at Morlaix, advised me to go to the French commissary, to get a passport to England, and that if I succeeded, he would take me in his ship. Accordingly I went to the French commissary, who sent me to the mayor, and I asked him if his honor would have the goodness to grant me a passport to England, to see my wife. The mayor answered and said unto me; "You must go to Mr. Dyeott, the American counselor, to get a passport." I said unto him, "Sir, it is no use; I have been to him three times, and he pushed me out of doors, and would not suffer me to speak to him." Then the mayor said, "Stop a moment, and I will send a letter to him"; he then wrote a letter, and gave it to me, saying, "Take this to Mr. Dyeott." I accordingly carried the letter to Mr. Dyeott, who opened the letter and read it; after he had so done, he said unto me, "Had you the impudence to go to the mayor?" I said, "Yes, sir, for I was compelled to do it." He then took me by the shoulders, and pushed me out of doors, and said that he would keep me as long as he possibly could. I then returned to the house where I lived, crying and mourning, and my spirit within me was troubled; and the people asked me what made me cry. I told them that I had been to the counselor, and he would not let me go, and said that he would keep me as long as he could. They said it was what they expected. I said that God had told me to call upon him in the time of trouble, and he would deliver me. So I passed that night in fasting and prayer unto God, and wrestled with him as Jacob did with the angel; and blessed be God, I *did* prevail. I went to the mayor in the morning, and asked him if Mr. Dyeott had said anything to him concerning me. He said no; and asked me what Mr. Dyeott said unto me. I said that he would not give me anything, for he would not suffer me to work, or to go to England; but said he would keep me perishing in France, until he could send me to America. The mayor said, "Stop awhile, and I will send a gentleman with you to Mr. Dyeott." The gentleman accordingly went with me to him, and asked him what he meant to do with me. He said that he meant to keep me, and send me to America, for I was an American. The gentleman then said, "You must not keep this poor black man in this manner; you have kept him already fourteen months without food or employment; and if he be an American, why do you not give him American support?" He said, "Because he will not go on board the vessel I have provided for him." At that moment the mayor came in, and said, "What do you mean to do with this man?" He said, "I mean to keep him in France until I can send him to America." The mayor said, "You cannot keep him in this manner, you must give him a passport to England." But he said he would not. The mayor said if he would not, he would; and told me to come with him to his office: I went with him, and he gave me a passport to embark at St. Malo on board of any vessel that was going to England.

As I was going to St. Malo I met with an English captain, whose brig was laying at Morlaix, and he said that he was going to Guernsey, in three hours time; and as he had heard me preach at Morlaix, he would give me my passage for nothing.

Then I told the dear people at the house where I had lived, who were exceedingly glad, and thankful to God for my deliverance. I also was thankful to God our blessed Lord and Savior Jesus Christ, that brotherly love had continued.

I arrived safe at Guernsey, and brotherly love did not withdraw itself from me there, for the brethren in Christ gladly received me, and gave me the right-hand of fellowship, treated me as a brother, and gave me liberty to preach in the different chapels; and I can say with truth, there was no chapel large enough to hold the congregations. I remained there fifteen days, and during that time there were many souls convinced and converted to God. After that I departed from them in the Guernsey packet, for Southampton, and they furnished me with everything convenient for me; and thank God, I arrived there in safety, and was cordially received by the brethren, who gave me the use of their chapels to preach in, and much good was done during my stay. They kindly furnished me with everything that was necessary. But I did not stay there any more than four days, because I wanted to come to Portsmouth. I arrived safe at Portsmouth, and found my wife well, which I bless God for; I was gladly received by the brethren in Christ, and preached for several of them; and I can say with truth, that all those who have received me in the name of Christ, are brethren unto me, and I pray that the Lord will bless them, and give them all a happy admittance into his kingdom, there to sing the song of Moses and the Lamb, forever and ever.

My dear reader, I would now inform you, that I have stated this in the best manner I am able, for I cannot write, therefore it is not so correct as if I [had] been able to have written it myself; not being able to notice the time and date when I left several places, in my travels from time to time, as many do when they are traveling; nor would I allow alterations to be made by the person whom I employed to print this narrative.

Now, dear reader, I trust by the grace of God, that the small house in Hawk Street, which the Lord hath been pleased to open unto me, for the public worship of his great and glorious name, will be filled with converts, and that my feeble labors will be crowned with abundant success.

A Hymn

Come, O thou Traveler unknown,
Whom still I hold, but cannot see!
My company before is gone,
And I am left alone with thee:
With thee all night I mean to stay,
And wrestle till the break of day.

I need not tell thee who I am;
My misery and sin declare:

Thyself hast call'd me by my name;
Look on thy hands, and read it there:
But who, I ask of thee, who art thou?
Tell me thy Name, and tell me now.

Lo vain thou strugglest to get free,
I never will unloose my hold,
Art thou the Man who died for me?
The secret of thy love unfold:
Wrestling I will not let thee go,
Till I thy Name, thy Nature know.

Wilt thou not yet to me reveal
Thy new, unutterable Name?
Tell me, I still beseech thee, tell;
To know it now, resolv'd I am;
Wrestling I will not let thee go,
Till I thy Name, thy Nature know.

What though my shrinking flesh complain,
And murmur to contend so long?
I rise superior to my pain:
When I am weak, then I am strong:
And when my all of strength shall fail,
I shall with the God-man prevail.